THE PHILOSOPHICAL LIFE

ALSO BY JAMES MILLER

Flowers in the Dustbin: The Rise of Rock and Roll, 1947–1977

The Passion of Michel Foucault

Democracy Is in the Streets: From Port Huron to the Siege of Chicago

Rousseau: Dreamer of Democracy

History and Human Existence: From Marx to Merleau-Ponty

THE PHILOSOPHICAL LIFE

TWELVE GREAT THINKERS AND

THE SEARCH FOR WISDOM:

FROM SOCRATES TO

NIETZSCHE

JAMES MILLER

ONEWORLD

A Oneworld Book

First Published in Great Britain and the Commonwealth by
Oneworld Publications 2012

Copyright © James Miller, 2011

Originally published in the United States of America as *Examined Lives*
by Farrar, Straus and Giroux

The moral right of James Miller to be identified as the
Author of this work has been asserted by him in accordance with the
Copyright, Designs, and Patents Act 1988

ISBN: 978-1-85168-859-3

Cover design by Richard Green
Printed and bound in Denmark by Nørhaven

Oneworld Publications
185 Banbury Road
Oxford OX2 7AR
England

Learn more about Oneworld. Join our mailing list to

find out about our latest titles and special offers at:

www.oneworld-publications.com

FOR RUTH

CONTENTS

THE PHILOSOPHICAL LIFE

PREFACE

Of all those who start out on philosophy—not those who take it up for
the sake of getting educated when they are young and then
drop it, but those who linger in it for a longer time—most
become quite queer, not to say completely vicious; while the
ones who seem perfectly decent . . . become useless.
—PLATO, *Republic* (487c–d)

O nce upon a time, philosophers were figures of wonder. They were sometimes objects of derision and the butt of jokes, but they were more often a source of shared inspiration, offering, through words and deeds, models of wisdom, patterns of conduct and, for those who took them seriously, examples to be emulated. Stories about the great philosophers long played a formative role in the culture of the West. For Roman writers such as Cicero, Seneca, and Marcus Aurelius, one way to measure spiritual progress was to compare one's conduct with that of Socrates, whom they all considered a paragon of perfect virtue. Sixteen hundred years later, John Stuart Mill (1806–1873) similarly learned classical Greek at a tender age in order to read the *Lives of the Eminent Philosophers*, as retold by Diogenes Laertius, a Greek follower of Epicurus who is thought to have lived in the third century A.D.

Today, by contrast, most highly educated people, even professional philosophers, know nothing about either Diogenes Laertius or the vast majority of the ancient philosophers whose lives he recounted. In many schools in many countries, the classical curriculum has been largely abandoned. Modern textbooks generally scant the lives of philosophers, reinforcing the contemporary perception that philosophy is best understood as a purely technical discipline, revolving around specialized issues in semantics and logic.

The typical modern philosopher—the Kant of the *Critique of Pure Reason* (1781), say, or the John Rawls of *A Theory of Justice* (1971)—is largely identified with his books. It is generally assumed that "philosophy" refers to "the study of the most general and abstract features of the world and the categories with which we think: mind, matter, reason, proof, truth etc.," to quote the definition offered by the outstanding recent *Oxford Dictionary of Philosophy*. In the modern university, where both Kant and Rawls practiced their calling, aspiring philosophers are routinely taught, among other things, that the value of a theory should be evaluated independently of anything we may know about the person holding that theory.

Such a principled disregard of any evidence about philosophers' lives is a characteristically modern prejudice. For most Greek and Roman thinkers from Plato to Augustine, theorizing was but one way of living life philosophically. To Socrates and the countless classical philosophers who tried to follow in his footsteps, the primary point was not to prove a certain set of statements (even when the ability to define terms and analyze arguments was a constitutive component of a school's teaching), but rather to explore "the kind of person, the sort of self" that one could become as a result of taking the quest for wisdom seriously.

Or, as Socrates puts it in the pages of Xenophon's *Memorabilia*, "If I don't reveal my views in a formal account, I do so by my conduct. Don't you think that actions are more reliable evidence than words?"

In ancient Greece and Rome, it was widely assumed that the life of a philosopher would exemplify a specific code of conduct and form of life. As a result, biographical details were routinely cited in appraisals of a philosophy's value. That Socrates faced death with dignity, for example, was widely regarded as an argument in favor of his declared views on the conduct of life.

The transition from ancient to modern modes of living life philosophically was neither sudden nor abrupt. Writing a generation after Montaigne, Descartes (1596–1650) could still imagine commissioning a kind of mythic biography of himself, whereas, fewer than two hundred years later, Rousseau (1712–1778) can only imagine composing an autobiography that is abjectly honest as well as verifiably true in its most damning particulars. It should come as no surprise, then, that so many modern philosophers, though still inspired by an older ideal of philosophy as a way of life, have sought refuge, like Kant, in impersonal modes of theorizing and teaching.

This sort of academic philosophizing notoriously left Friedrich Nietzsche cold. "I for one prefer reading Diogenes Laertius," he wrote in 1874. "The only critique of a philosophy that is possible and that proves something, namely trying to see whether one can live in accordance with it, has never been taught at universities; all that has ever been taught is a critique of words by means of other words."

A century later, Michel Foucault (1926–1984) expressed a similar view. In the winter of 1984, several months before his death, Foucault devoted his last series of lectures at the Collège de France to the topic of parrhesia, or frank speech, in classical antiquity. Contemplating, as Nietzsche had a century before, possible antecedents for his own peculiar approach to truthfulness, Foucault examined the life of Socrates and, using evidence gathered by Diogenes Laertius, the far odder life of Diogenes of Sinope (d. c. 320 B.C.), the archetypal Cynic, who was storied in antiquity for living in a tub, carrying a lit lamp in broad daylight, and telling anybody who asked that "I am looking for a man."

Foucault of course knew that the lore surrounding a philosopher like Diogenes was no longer taken seriously. But he, like Nietzsche, decried what he called our modern "negligence" of what he called the "problem" of the philosophical life. This problem, he speculated, had become eclipsed for two reasons: first, because religious institutions, above all Christian monasticism, had absorbed, or (in his words) "confiscated" the "theme of the practice of the true life." And, second, "because the relationship to truth can now be made valid and manifest only in the form of scientific knowledge."

The twelve biographical sketches of selected philosophers from Socrates to Nietzsche that follow are meant to explore these issues by writing, as Foucault suggested, a "history starting from the problem of the philosophical life." Instead of recounting one life in detail, I recount a number of lives in brief. Anecdotes and human incident flesh out the philosopher under discussion. Distinctive theories and doctrines are summarized concisely, even though their nuances and complexities often puzzle philosophers to this day. And following the example of such ancient biographers as Plutarch in his *Lives of the Noble Greeks and Romans*, I am highly selective, in an effort to sum up the crux of a character. My aim throughout is to convey the arc of a life rather than a collection of doctrines and moral maxims.

Modern standards of evidence are acknowledged—I am a historian by training, and facts matter to me. But for the ancient philosophers especially, the myths must be acknowledged, too, for such legends long formed a constitutive part of the Western philosophical tradition. That the lives of many ancient philosophers have beggared belief is a cultural fact in its own right: It helps to explain the enduring fascination—and sometimes the resentment—aroused by spiritual athletes whose feats (like those of the early Christian saints) have so often seemed beyond credibility.

This history begins with Socrates and Plato, for it was Plato in his Socratic dialogues who first gave currency to the word *philosophy*. In the century after the death of Socrates, a distinct, identifiable group of "philosophers" flourished for the first time. Monuments to their memory—busts, statues—were erected in Athens and elsewhere in the Greek-speaking world. For the purposes of this study, I generally picked figures who sought to follow in Socrates' footsteps by struggling to measure up to his declared ambition "to live the life of a philosopher, to examine myself and others."

For Socrates, as for many (though not all) of those who tried to measure up to his example, this ambition has in some way revolved around an effort to answer to the gnomic injunction, *Know thyself*. (Aristotle, for one, assumed that this injunction was a key motive for Socrates' lifework.)

Of course, what, precisely, the Delphic injunction means—and what it prescribes—is hardly self-evident, as we learn in Plato: "I am still unable," confides Socrates in the *Phaedrus*, "to know myself; and it really seems to me ridiculous to look into other things before I have understood that."

Moreover, self-examination, even in antiquity, is only one strand in the story of philosophy. From the start—in Plato, and again in Augustine—the problem of the philosophical life evolves in a complicated relationship between what we today would call "science" and "religion"—between mathematical logic and mystical revelation in the case of Plato, between an open-ended quest for wisdom and the transmission of a small number of fixed dogmas in the case of Augustine.

The series of biographies that follows is not comprehensive. It omits Epicurus and Zeno, Spinoza and Hume, and such twentieth-century philosophers as Wittgenstein, Heidegger, Sartre, and Foucault. But I believe the twelve ancients and moderns I selected are broadly representative.

While I include some figures rarely taken seriously by most contemporary philosophers—Diogenes, Montaigne, and Emerson, for example—I also include several canonic figures, notably Aristotle, Descartes, and Kant, whose life's work helped lead philosophy away from its classical emphasis on exemplary conduct toward a stress on rigorous inquiry, and whose biographies therefore raise larger questions about the relation of philosophy as a way of life to the mainstream discipline of philosophy as it currently exists in academic institutions around the world.

Taken as a whole, these twelve sketches raise many more questions than they can possibly answer:

- If, like Plato, we define philosophy as a quest for wisdom that may prove unending, then what is the search for wisdom really good for?

- What is the relation of reason to faith, of philosophy to religion, and how does the search for wisdom relate to the most exacting forms of rigorous inquiry and "science"?

- Is philosophy best pursued in private or in public? What are its implications, if any, for statecraft, for diplomacy, for the conduct of a citizen in a democratic society?

- Above all, what is the "self" that so many of these philosophers have sought to know, and how has our conception of the self changed in the course of history, in part as a result of how successive philosophers have embarked on their quests? Indeed, is self-knowledge even feasible—and, if so, to what degree? Despite years of painful self- examination, Nietzsche famously declared that "we are necessarily strangers to ourselves, we have to misunderstand ourselves."

• If we seek, shall we find?

Here, then, are brief lives of a handful of philosophers, ancient and modern: Socrates and Plato, Diogenes and Aristotle, Seneca and Augustine, Montaigne and Descartes, Rousseau and Kant, Emerson and Nietzsche. They are all men, because philosophy before the twentieth century was overwhelmingly a vocation reserved for men: a large fact, which has limited the kinds of lives—stubbornly independent, often unattached, sometimes solitary and sexless—that philosophers have tended to lead. Within these common limits, however, there has been considerable variation. Some philosophers were influential figures in their day, while others were marginal; some were revered, while others provoked scandal and public outrage.

Despite such differences, each of these men prized the pursuit of wisdom. Each one struggled to live his life according to a deliberately chosen set of precepts and beliefs, discerned in part through a practice of self-examination, and expressed in both word and deed. The life of each one can therefore teach us something about the quest for self-knowledge and its limits. And as a whole, they can tell us a great deal about how the nature of philosophy—and the nature of philosophy as a way of life—has changed over time.

SOCRATES

Socrates in profile, a graphite drawing, c. 1820, by the British poet, printmaker, and mystagogue William Blake (1757–1827). "I was Socrates," Blake remarked near the end of his life. "I must have had conversations with him. So I had with Jesus Christ. I have an obscure recollection of having been with both of them." (Yale Center for British Art, Paul Mellon Collection, USA/The Bridgeman Art Library International)

I n the middle of the fifth century B.C., the city-state of Athens was at the zenith of its power and influence. After leading an alliance of Greek city-states to victory over the Persian Empire in battles at Marathon (490 B.C.), Salamis (480), and Plataea (479), the city consolidated a democratic regime. It peacefully extended political power to all citizens—native-born male residents—and created a model of the enlightened rule of law. At the same time, it established a far-flung hegemony over a variety of maritime colonies and vassal Greek city-states. Prospering from the trade and tribute provided by its empire, the city amassed the eastern Mediterranean's most feared military machine, a lavishly equipped navy, backed up by cavalry and infantry. The de facto leader of the Greek-speaking world, Athens led the Hellenes in education as well, attracting teachers from throughout the region.

Its people "believed themselves to be a priestly nation to whom, at a time of universal famine, Apollo had entrusted the mission of taking vows on behalf of all the Greeks and barbarians," wrote Jacob Burckhardt, the great Swiss historian. "Attica was traditionally credited with the inventions of civilization to an extent positively insulting to all other nations and the rest of the Greeks. According to this tradition, it was the Athenians who first taught the human race how to sow crops and use spring water; not only were they first to grow olives and figs, but they invented law and justice."

And they in fact invented "philosophy."

Socrates, the first man to be renowned as a philosopher, was born in Athens around 469 B.C. Although he grew up in a golden age in a great city, the ancient sources agree that there was nothing glittering about his pedigree or upbringing. He was the son of Sophroniscus, a stonemason, and of Phaenarete, a midwife. A citizen of Athens by birth, he belonged to the district of Alopece. The externals of his life were nondescript—his family, they say, was neither rich nor poor.

But his inner experience was extraordinary. Socrates heard a voice inaudible to anyone else. In some situations, the voice ordered him to halt what he was doing and to change his course of conduct. According to Plato, our primary source for almost everything we think we know about the first philosopher, Socrates considered the voice to be uniquely his own, as if it were directed to him alone from a supernatural sort of tutelary spirit. A source of wonder and disquiet, the voice set Socrates apart. From the time he was a child, he felt isolated and different—an individual in a collective that prized its sense of community, vividly expressed in its web of customary rituals and traditional religious beliefs, and crowned by a set of political institutions that embodied the novel ideal of democracy, a new form of collective self-rule.

Every Athenian citizen was expected to fight for the fatherland. The waging of war was an almost constant concern in these years, as Athens struggled to maintain its regional supremacy over its only real rival in the Greek world, the fortified land power of Sparta. Though never rich, Socrates had sufficient wealth to outfit himself with armor and serve as a foot soldier, or hoplite, in the city's citizen army. In 432, Socrates participated in the siege of Potidaea, where he demonstrated an almost superhuman stamina—one of the few salient traits recorded in virtually every ancient story told about him.

In these years, Athens was politically divided. On the one side stood proponents of extending political rights and obligations to every citizen, no matter how poor. This party of avowed democrats was headed by Pericles (c. 495–429), the city's elected commander in chief, who was the unchallenged leader of Athens in the 440s and 430s, and an orator who used his formidable gifts to frame a rationale for the self-government of the city by its ordinary citizens. In response, some wealthier Athenians fought, as the rich often do, to exercise unconstrained power; they denigrated the intelligence of the Athenian common man, and in some cases they commended the authoritarian institutions characteristic of other Greek city-states, such as Sparta.

Where Socrates stood in these epochal debates over democracy is not known—an odd fact, given that Athens expected its citizens to participate actively in the political life of the polis. As a young man, some say, he frequented the circles around Pericles, who was no friend of tyranny. There is sketchy evidence that his wife, Xanthippe, whom he married around 420, may have been an aristocrat. There are also stories, all of them unreliable, about a younger half brother who may have been one of the archons, or rulers, of Athens in the period after the fall of the Thirty Tyrants in 403 B.C.

According to Diogenes Laertius, "he was so orderly in his way of life that on several occasions when pestilence broke out in Athens [in 430, at the start of the Peloponnesian War] he was the only man to escape infection"—an exaggeration, obviously, though a vast number of citizens did perish, and it was the plague that cost Pericles his life. In any case, Socrates prided himself on living plainly and "used to say that he most enjoyed the food which was least in need of condiment, and the drink which made him feel the least hankering for some other drink; and that he was nearest to the gods when he had the fewest wants."

Sometime after assuming the duties of adult citizenship, Socrates began to behave strangely. Ignoring custom, he refused to follow in his father's footsteps as a stonemason. Instead of learning how to earn a living by carving rock, Socrates became preoccupied with learning how to live the best life conceivable. He expressed astonishment that "the sculptors of marble statues should take pains to make the block of marble into a perfect likeness of man, and should take no pains about themselves lest they turn out mere blocks, not men."

The ancient authorities do not agree on precisely why or when Socrates took up his strange new calling. The association of the word *philosophy* with Socrates and his way of life was largely the work of one man, Plato, who was the most famous of his followers. A conjunction of the Greek word *philo* ("lover") and *sophos* ("wisdom"), *philosophos*, or philosopher, as Plato defined the term, described a man who yearned for wisdom, a seeker of truth—a man like Socrates, whom Plato sharply distinguished from other sages, or Sophists. (According to Plato, who was not impartial, Sophists were neither truly wise nor were they sincere seekers of truth—they were charlatans, skilled mainly in devious forms of debate. Before Plato, by contrast, Sophists were widely admired as experts and wise men—the legendary Attic lawgiver Solon was a Sophist, in this original honorific sense, and so was Thales of Miletus, another one of the so-called Seven Sages.)

When Socrates was coming of age, Athens was teeming with teachers from throughout the Greek-speaking world. The city's most influential democratic leader, Pericles, championed the new learning and is said to have consorted with some of the era's most prominent professors of wisdom, including Anaxagoras. A theorist of nature, Anaxagoras discoursed for a fee, specializing in presenting theories about the organizing principles of the cosmos. He shocked some Athenians by his bold claim that the sun was a large, incandescent stone. Other teachers, like the orator Gorgias (c. 485–380 B.C.), made money by showing students how to shape the opinion of the citizenry through artful speech when the demos met each month in the open-air assembly that was the hallmark of the Athenian democracy.

According to Plato, it was Socrates' dissatisfaction with teachers like Anaxagoras and Gorgias that led him to go his own way and to raise questions independently about the best way to live. But Aristotle claimed that Socrates was primarily inspired by the motto inscribed on the Temple of Apollo at Delphi, "Know thyself."

Perhaps the most famous of the maxims associated with the temple at Delphi ("Nothing too much" is another), the injunction to "Know thyself" first appears in Greek literature in the fifth century, most notably in Aeschylus's play *Prometheus Bound*. In defiance of the wishes of Zeus, Prometheus has stolen fire from the gods and given it to mankind; though he is punished for this presumptuous act, Prometheus remains stubbornly defiant, which provokes the god of the sea, Oceanus, to admonish him to "know yourself, and make compliant your youthful ways"—by obeying the will of Zeus. In other words, know your limits.

Whatever motivated Socrates—and however he may have interpreted the

Delphic maxim to "Know thyself"—he evidently began to elaborate in practice a new mode of inquiry. It was remarkable for its public, and implicitly egalitarian, style. Spurning the more formal settings preferred by other professors of wisdom, who generally held court in households wealthy enough to host a lecture, Socrates strolled through the city. He visited the marketplace when it was crowded with shoppers, talking with anyone who was interested, young or old, rich or poor. When bystanders gathered, they were invited to join in the ongoing argument he was holding, with himself and with others, over the best conceivable way to live.

At some point after Socrates had embarked on this eccentric new career, Chaerephon, a friend since youth and a loyal supporter of the democracy, journeyed to the Temple of Apollo, where cities as well as individuals throughout this period frequently went to receive divine guidance on rules of purity and questions of religious observance, and sometimes about law. At Delphi, according to Plato, Chaerephon consulted (as one normally did) the Pythia, the priestess through whom the god Apollo spoke.

There were two ways to consult the Delphic oracle. A written response required the sacrifice of an animal. But a simple yes or no cost nothing. Whether the answer was yes or no was determined by lot: it depended on whether the Pythia randomly plucked from an urn a bean that was white or one that was black. Since Chaerephon was probably too poor to offer an animal for sacrifice, it is likely that he popped a simple question, and that the Pythia plucked a bean to produce a response.

Was anyone wiser than Socrates?

No.

According to Plato in his *Apology*, Socrates reacted to news of this oracle as any pious Greek would. The god never lied. But Socrates did not regard himself as wise. So what could the oracle mean?

From this point forward, the life of Socrates became a consecrated quest—an epic inquiry, meant to unriddle a message from a god. His search for wisdom became an obsession. According to Plato, he ceased "to engage in public affairs to any extent"—a noteworthy decision, given the prevailing belief, most memorably expressed by Pericles, that abstention from public affairs rendered a citizen "useless."

The longer that Socrates struggled to know himself, the more puzzled he became. What, for example, was the meaning of his inner voice? Was there any rhyme or reason behind the audible interdictions he experienced as irresistible? Did Socrates in fact embody a good way of life? And, if so, how could he possibly have acquired the ability to be so good?

Whether or not his way of life was useful to the city—and on this point his friends and enemies disagreed—Socrates was storied for the abstracted states that overtook him. "He sometimes stops and stands wherever he happens to be," reports a friend in Plato's *Symposium*. Later in the same dialogue, Plato depicts another friend recalling an even more striking episode that occurred when both men served together on the campaign to Potidaea:

> One time at dawn he began to think something over and stood in the same spot considering it, and when he found no solution, he didn't leave but stood there inquiring. It got to be midday, and people became aware of it, wondering at it among themselves, saying Socrates had stood there since dawn thinking about something. Finally some of the Ionians, when evening came, after they'd eaten—it was then summer—carried their bedding out to sleep in the cool air and to watch to see if he'd also stand there all night. He stood until dawn came and the sun rose; then he offered a prayer to the sun, and left.

Famously aloof, Socrates could also be, in Plato's metaphor, a "gadfly"—a chronic source of irritation. Serenely self-assured, perhaps because he was blessed by a divine sense of mission, he was also ostentatiously self-doubting, professing repeatedly his own lack of wisdom. To critics, his avowed humility seemed obnoxious, even disingenuous: Was not Socrates like those Athenian aristocrats who struck a Spartan pose of austere self-restraint, in order to show their superiority to the ordinary run of vulgar men?

This was perhaps the most disturbing aspect of Socrates' character. The more strenuously he tried to prove the god right, by exposing the ignorance of supposed experts while protesting his own lack of knowledge, the more admirable he seemed to followers like Chaerephon, who worshipped him as if he were the wisest man alive.

Abjuring the material trappings of his class, he became notorious for his disdain of worldly goods. "Often when he looked at the multitude of wares exposed for sale, he would say to himself, 'How many things I can do without!'" He took care to exercise regularly, but his appearance was shabby. He expressed no interest in seeing the world at large, leaving the city only to fulfill his military obligations. He learned what he could by questioning the beliefs held by other residents of Athens, scrutinizing their beliefs rather than pondering the heavens or poring over books: "They relate that Euripides gave him the treatise of Heraclitus and asked his opinion upon it, and that his reply was 'The part I understand is excellent, and so too is, I dare say, the part I do not understand; but it needs a Delian diver to get to the bottom of it.'"

Still hoping to learn how to live the best life conceivable, Socrates, according to Plato, began to query anyone with a reputation in any field for knowledge. Craftsmen knew a thing or two about their crafts and were even able to train their children to follow in their footsteps. But most craftsmen had nothing coherent to say about justice, piety, or courage—the kinds of virtues that Socrates, like most Athenians, supposed were crucial to living a good life. As Socrates kept searching, a conviction took shape: craftsmen had no more wisdom than Socrates himself, and neither did poets, politicians, orators, or the other famous teachers he queried.

In fact, all these people seemed even *more* ignorant than Socrates. Unlike him, most of them were complacent, not disquieted; vainglorious, not humble; and arrogantly unaware, unless irritated by the gadfly, of just how limited their knowledge really was.

A primary obstacle to true wisdom was false confidence. And so Socrates now set out to destroy such confidence, not by writing books (he evidently wrote nothing) and not by establishing a formal school (for he did no such thing), but rather through his unrelenting interrogation of himself and others, no matter their rank or status.

Such behavior did not make Socrates popular. "Frequently owing to his vehemence in argument, men set upon him with their fists and tore his hair out; . . . for the most part he was despised and laughed at, yet bore all this abuse patiently."

At the same time, his fearless habit of cross-examining powerful men in public won him a growing circle of followers—and helped turn him into one of the most recognizable figures in the Athens of his day. In busts erected shortly after his death—Socrates was the first Greek sage to be so honored—he appears as a balding older man with a big belly, bug eyes, and thick, protuberant lips. According to Plato, his friends compared him with Silenus—an ugly and aging satyr traditionally associated with uncanny wisdom. Centuries later, retailing the lore surrounding the physical ugliness of the philosopher, Nietzsche gleefully recounted how the physiognomist Zopyrus was said to have sized him up: "A foreigner who knew about faces once passed through Athens and told Socrates to his face that he was a *monstrum* . . . And Socrates merely answered, 'You know me, sir!'"

Anecdotes like this began to circulate about Socrates, and Diogenes Laertius recounts a number of emblematic episodes, for example: One day a young man came to Socrates with an apology, saying, "'I am a poor man and have nothing else to give, but offer you myself,' and he answered, 'Nay, do you not see that you are offering me the greatest gift of all?'" Socrates was walking on a narrow street in central Athens when he first met Xenophon, who would become, along with Plato, his most influential follower. Barring the way with his walking stick, Socrates asked the young man "where every kind of food was sold. Upon receiving a reply, he put another question, 'And where do men become good and honorable?' Xenophon was dumbfounded. 'Then follow me,' said Socrates, 'and learn.'"

There is an even more revealing story in an essay by Plutarch (c. A.D. 46–119):

> Aristippus, when he met Ischomachus at Olympia, asked him by what manner of conversation Socrates succeeded in so affecting the young men. And when Aristippus had gleaned a few odd seeds and samples of Socrates' talk, he was so moved that he suffered a physical collapse and became quite pale and thin. Finally he sailed for Athens and slaked his burning thirst with draughts from the fountainhead, and engaged in a study of the man and his words and his philosophy, of which the end and aim was to come to recognize one's vices and so rid oneself of them.

By 423, Socrates was sufficiently renowned to be caricatured by one of the most celebrated playwrights in Athens, Aristophanes, in his comedy *The Clouds*. With poetic license, the playwright condensed the features of a variety of contemporary professors of wisdom into the character he called Socrates.

Though Socrates in fact organized no school, Aristophanes portrayed him as the guru in charge of a cloistered think tank. In the play, a dishonest farmer named Strepsiades sends his son Phidippides to learn from "the high priest of subtlest poppycock," hoping that he will acquire enough rhetorical tricks to help the father evade his creditors. When the son emerges from the care of Socrates and turns his gift for gab against his father, Strepsiades burns down the school.

Onstage, Socrates first appears in a basket, gazing skyward, and treating his earthbound interlocutors as an Olympian god might treat a manifestly lower form of life—with sovereign disdain. He is a purveyor of holy secrets, hair-splitting arguments, and a peculiar sort of contemplative introspection that does not, on the face of it, promise practical results. Modesty is not one of his salient traits, and he comports himself strangely: "You strut around like a grand gander, roll your eyes, go barefoot, endure all, and hold such high opinions." He peppers his pupils with pointed questions, meant to probe and test their personal character. When his school goes up in smoke, it seems like rough justice for a prattler and a parasite.

In 423, when *The Clouds* was first produced, Athens and its allies were entering the eighth year of the Peloponnesian War (431–404) with Sparta and its allies. That year, Socrates apparently saw action again as a foot soldier, this time in an expedition to Delium, where the Athenian army suffered a signal defeat. Socrates is said to have acted with exemplary courage in the retreat, helping to keep the enemy's cavalry at bay.

The defeat at Delium, coming on the heels of the plague that had devastated the city in the first years of the war, broke Athenian morale. Doubts about the city's military strategy and tactics boiled over in the assemblies of the people (which were regularly scheduled public meetings led by elected generals and dominated by popular orators of variable talent and uncertain integrity).

Though Plato says that Socrates disclaimed any ability to teach, just as he evidently refused to accept fees from prospective students, wealthy young men flocked to his side. They offered him friendship and patronage, hoping that he, like other prominent teachers, might help them win public influence and exercise political power. With their support, he was free to pursue his calling without material concerns.

A cross section of the Athenian elite, his best-known companions fell into different political camps. Among his disciples were Nicias and Laches, generals loyal to the democracy, but also Charmides and Critias, pro-Spartan oligarchs. But the most famous disciple of all was Alcibiades—a man too cunning to be categorized politically.

The ancient authorities stress Alcibiades' sheer beauty as a young man. He was descended from a family sufficiently rich to equip a trireme, a warship powered by a team of rowers and the mainstay of the city's imperial fleet. After the death of his father, it is said that Pericles himself became one of his guardians. "Soon a large number of high-born men began to gather around him and follow him around." A career in politics beckoned: he was, after all, the kind of aristocrat tailor-made for the role of a democratic leader (or demagogue)—dashing and handsome, clever, and quick on his feet.

Socrates knew Alcibiades from at least the time of their campaign together at Potidaea, when Alcibiades would have been eighteen years old and Socrates about forty. By the standards of the day, this made the boy a normal object of the older man's erotic interest. (There is no Greek or Latin word that corresponds to the modern term *homosexuality*, and erotic relations were judged according to the age, social status, gender, and active or passive role of the participants.) According to Plutarch (who credits the account of Plato), "The fact that Socrates was in love with him strongly suggests that the boy was endowed with a natural aptitude for virtue."

The philosopher now faced a daunting, and perhaps impossible, challenge: to convert his most prominent potential disciple from his lust for power to a love of wisdom.

His ally in this venture proved to be Alcibiades' desire for Socrates. To the astonishment of others, the beautiful boy couldn't get enough of the ugly old man. Yet when Socrates did sleep with him, Alcibiades was disappointed by his master's superhuman self-restraint: "When I arose after having slept with

Socrates, it was nothing more than if I'd slept with my father or an elder brother."

This passage from the *Symposium* remains the classic image of Platonic love, a form of unsatisfied carnal desire that Socrates characteristically tried to harness and redirect toward spiritual objects, according to Plato and several other contemporary sources. How Socrates set about trying to effect this transformation is the subject of the *Alcibiades*, a Socratic dialogue by an unknown ancient author that was included in the Platonic corpus and was widely read as an introduction to Platonic thought until the nineteenth century.

Like most of the other extant Socratic dialogues by Plato, the *Alcibiades* consists mainly of a series of short questions and answers that begins when Socrates raises a doubt—in this case, about the ability of the younger man to realize his naked ambition: "You want your reputation and your influence to saturate all mankind."

Socrates in the dialogue proceeds to question Alcibiades about the specific know-how that might enable him to realize his stated goal. Is he really sure that he is "better" than other men? How does he understand his superiority? Does he behave more justly than others? Is he wiser?

As their conversation proceeds, the cocky young man becomes more and more confused: "I must be in some absolutely bizarre condition! When you ask me questions, first I think one thing, and then I think something else."

If Alcibiades is this confused, how can he presume to have his influence "saturate all mankind"? "Don't you realize that the errors in our conduct are caused by this kind of ignorance, of thinking that we know when we don't know?" When Alcibiades resists the implications of this line of reasoning, Socrates asks him to "trust in me, and in the Delphic inscription 'know thyself.'"

Still suspicious, Alcibiades asks Socrates what, precisely, he must know about himself. "The command that we should know ourselves means that we should know our souls."

What follows is so abstract and woodenly didactic that most modern scholars doubt that Plato himself could have written it (never mind whether Socrates could have ever really said any such thing). The crux of the philosopher's quest, according to this text, is to attain true knowledge of *psyche*, a

Greek word usually translated into English as "soul" (and also a Greek root of the English word *psychology*). In Homer, *psyche* is what leaves the body on death—perhaps it is breath, perhaps life itself. In the *Alcibiades*, Socrates goes farther, asserting that *psyche* is immaterial and immortal—and that the soul of a man is like a god within. What Alcibiades needs to prosper is what Socrates already exemplifies: because he has come to know his true soul, he is now able to lead a life of perfect justice, moderation, and reasoned inquiry.

Toward the close of the *Alcibiades*, Socrates vows to his prize pupil that "I will never forsake you now, never"—but then adds, ominously, "unless the Athenian people make you corrupt and ugly." And the last lines of the dialogue foreshadow the real fates of Alcibiades and of his teacher: "I should like to believe that you will persevere, but I'm afraid—not because I distrust your nature, but because I know how powerful the city is—I'm afraid it might get the better of both me and you."

As Plutarch tells the rest of the story, Socrates at first shamed Alcibiades into compliance. "'He crouched down in fear, like a defeated cock, with wing aslant,' and he believed that Socrates' mission really was a way of carrying out the gods' wishes by looking after young men and keeping them free from corruption. He began to despise himself and admire Socrates; he began to value Socrates' kindness and feel humble because of his goodness." Infatuated with philosophy, he became "cruel and intractable to the rest of his lovers," including Anytus, the son of Anthemion (who many years later would charge Socrates with impiety and corrupting the youth).

The battle for Alcibiades' soul now began in earnest.

In Plutarch's account in his *Lives of the Noble Greeks and Romans*, Socrates bravely persevered "against all the odds and despite the number and importance of his rivals." But as time passed, Alcibiades wavered in his devotion to philosophy. Sometimes, he would give Socrates the slip, acting "like a runaway slave," in order to slake his thirst for pleasure. Yet "time and again," according to Plutarch, "Socrates took him back in a state of complete promiscuity and presumptuousness, and by force of argument would pull him together and teach him humility and restraint, by showing him how great his flaws were and how far he was from virtue."

But Socrates was finally no match for the prospect of glory held out to Alcibiades by his political consultants: "it was by pandering to his ambitious longing for recognition that his corrupters set him prematurely on the road to high endeavor." And in Plutarch's cautionary version of the story, Alcibiades, by breaking free of Socrates and his influence, becomes the perfect antiphilosopher—a paragon of unprincipled viciousness: cruel, deceitful, prepared to say whatever he thinks his audience wants to hear and to feign whatever character he reckons will win popular approval. "He could change more abruptly than a chameleon."

With a student like this, it is no wonder that Plato sometimes depicts Socrates expressing skepticism about his ability to teach anybody anything. And although the accounts in both Plato and Plutarch put the blame for the vices of Alcibiades squarely on the institutions of the Athenian democracy and on the young man's unruly will to power, one has to wonder about the judgment of Socrates, who first courted, and then failed to convert, an apparently promising pupil to the quest for true wisdom.

In the years that followed, Alcibiades entered politics with a vengeance. Exploiting his extensive network of highly placed friends, and also his talent for flattery, he rose rapidly to become one of the city's most powerful leaders. Meanwhile, the war with Sparta dragged on inconclusively. (It was in these same years that Aristophanes poked fun at Socrates on stage.) Elected commander of the Athenian forces in 419 (the same position from which Pericles had effectively governed Athens), Alcibiades skillfully sowed chaos throughout the Peloponnese. He was a shrewd military strategist, and his physical courage further enhanced his reputation and influence.

He was eyed warily by "the notable men of Athens," who (writes Plutarch) "combined feelings of abhorrence and disgust with fear of his haughty and lawless attitude, which struck them as tyrannical in its excessiveness." But the common people were impressed by "the donations he made, the choruses he financed, the superlative extravaganzas he put on for the city, the fame of his ancestors, his eloquence, his physical good looks and fitness, and his experience and prowess in war."

In 415, knowing that the Athenians had long coveted control of Sicily, Alcibiades overcame the qualms of his rivals and persuaded the Athenian assembly to send out a large fleet to conquer the island. What happened next, as witnessed by Thucydides and recounted by Plutarch, remains unrivaled in the annals of ruthless realpolitik.

After he set sail with the Athenian fleet for Sicily, Alcibiades was summoned back to Athens in order to stand trial for impiety—opponents alleged that he and his supporters had mutilated the city's herms, sacred statues of Hermes, which were supposed to protect Athens and its residents. Defying the city's summons, Alcibiades instead defected to Sparta, where he betrayed the Athenian strategy in Sicily. Understandably unable to convince his Spartan hosts of his trustworthiness, and learning that they were planning to condemn him to death, he fled to Persia in 412. He worked from afar to broker support for an oligarchic revolution in Athens, which promised to serve both Persian and his own political interests. Unable to provoke an oligarchic revolution in Athens from a distance, he offered his services to the Athenian fleet in Samos. Desperate for military leadership, the sailors elected him to be their commander, and after leading the fleet to victory in 410, he was allowed to return to Athens, where he was cleared of the old charges of impiety, though of course doubts ran deep about his loyalty. After he was unfairly blamed for a series of Athenian military setbacks, Alcibiades fled again, to Asia Minor, where he died in 404 after his enemies in Sparta and Athens arranged to have him assassinated by a Persian satrap.

By then, the Athenians had surrendered to Sparta, and the Thirty Tyrants had come to power. Led by Critias, a former ally of Alcibiades, another prominent companion of Socrates, and a longtime champion of Spartan-style political institutions, the Thirty quickly moved to abolish democracy and to kill a number of citizens the group regarded as political enemies.

According to Xenophon, Socrates tried to stay out of the fray, telling friends that it was "extraordinary that a man appointed as a political leader who was making the citizens fewer and worse than they were before was not ashamed and did not consider himself a bad political leader." The Thirty subsequently forbade Socrates from speaking in public. They nevertheless tried to implicate him in the policies of the regime, by asking his help in seizing a citizen who had been condemned to death. According to Plato, Socrates refused.

Although Socrates survived the reign of terror that followed, perhaps because of his friendship with Critias, his companions suffered mixed fortunes.

Charmides, for one, joined the Thirty. But Chaerephon, who had consulted the Delphic oracle years before, was forced into exile for his democratic sympathies. Late in 404, a civil war erupted in Athens. In the spring of 403, Critias died in a skirmish. Six months later, the democracy was restored, a political amnesty was decreed, and the stage was set for the last act in Socrates' life.

In 399 B.C., a poet named Meletus, supported by two other citizens, Lycon and Anytus (the lover whom Alcibiades had jilted while infatuated with philosophy), posted an indictment. It charged that "Socrates does injustice by not believing in the gods in whom the city believes and by introducing other new divinities. He also does injustice by corrupting the youth. The penalty demanded is death."

Despite the amnesty, feelings ran deep against citizens with Spartan sympathies. Everyone knew that Socrates had been associated with Alcibiades and Critias. And anyone who recalled the character he inspired in *The Clouds* might well conclude that he was a heretic, if not a traitor. His radically different way of life threatened a society that was still largely organized around ritual religious observances.

Two accounts of the subsequent trial survive, one by Xenophon, the other by Plato. Though professional orators often prepared texts for clients, Plato and Xenophon agree that Socrates improvised his own speech on the spot. They also agree that he was defiant and sometimes spoke in an "arrogant tone."

The charge of impiety—and such accusations were routinely brought against one's political enemies in the Athens of the day—Socrates rebutted by reference to the oracle at Delphi. He explained how his way of life grew out of his earnest effort to take the message of the god seriously: "What does the god mean? What is his riddle? I am very conscious that I am not wise at all; what then does he mean by saying that I am the wisest? For surely he does not lie; it is not legitimate for him to do so." As Socrates sees it, his quest for wisdom proves his pious regard for the commands of Apollo.

The next charge, that he had introduced new divinities, was harder to dispute. Socrates had to concede that he had commerce with a unique kind of tutelary spirit, which he called his daimon: "This began when I was a child. It is a voice, and whenever it speaks it turns me away from something I am about to do, but it never encourages me to do anything." Most Greeks supposed that every human being was haunted by a specific daimon, an immaterial and normally mute figure of one's unique fate (and happy was the man with a good daimon—hence the Greek word for happiness, *eudaimonia*). By referring in his defense to his inner voice as a daimon, Socrates tried to deflect the charge that he worshipped a new—and literally self-serving—god.

When he came to answer the charge of corrupting the young—and one cannot help but think of Alcibiades and Critias—Socrates dropped his mild manner and turned on his principal accuser, the poet Meletus. Xenophon reports a series of taunts: "Do you know anyone who is less a slave to bodily desires than I am? Do you know anyone more free? . . . Could you plausibly regard anyone as more upright? . . . Mustn't it be reasonable to describe me as wise, seeing that, ever since I began to understand speech, I have never stopped investigating and learning any good thing I could?"

The implication amounts to a counterindictment. By obeying the command of the god at Delphi and living a philosophical life utterly different from the conventional forms of life followed by Meletus or Anytus, or any of the assembled jurors—or, implicitly, any of his disgraced former companions, including Alcibiades and Critias—it is he, Socrates, who has become a paragon of perfect virtue. Those who have charged him with injustice are themselves unjust. It is they who should stand trial.

Under the Athenian democracy, the jury at a trial consisted of a large panel of citizens; in the case of Socrates, there were probably 501 in all (odd numbers were used to avoid a tie in voting). The accusers and the accused spoke in turn. When the speeches were over, jurors delivered a verdict by voting with stones.

By a slim margin, the jury found Socrates guilty.

It was Athenian custom that a defendant found guilty was asked to propose a penalty that he considered just. According to Plato, the arrogance of Socrates now reached a sublime pitch. Rejecting any penalty at all, he suggested instead that Athens should house and feed him at public expense. He wished to be duly honored for being what he defiantly still claimed to be—the best of men.

Understandably exasperated by such insolent behavior, the jury voted, this time by a larger margin, to condemn the philosopher to death.

Socrates was escorted to a jail. As the appointed day for his execution drew near, his closest surviving companions rallied round him—Phaedo, Aeschines, Antisthenes, Apollodorus, Crito, Critoboulos, Plato. Although some of them had offered to help him escape—going into exile for a period of time was a common Athenian practice, which often led to rehabilitation and a return to the city—Socrates adamantly refused to consider this customary expedient. He insisted instead on fulfilling the letter of the Athenian law by accepting the jury's death penalty, arguing (according to Plato's account) that anyone ought to obey the laws of his country, and "endure in silence whatever it instructs you to endure."

In his last days, some say Socrates wrote poems in an effort to record some of his dreams. Plato reports that he maintained a preternatural calm, in part by conversing to the very end about the nature of the soul, his conviction that it was immortal, and his views on how best to care for it. Xenophon and Plato both express astonishment at his composure. He seemed to welcome death.

Socrates' martyrdom became the crowning event of his life in the eyes of those companions who watched Socrates drink the hemlock. His serenity in the face of death seemed to confirm the perfection of his goodness: he was a man completely at peace with himself in his final hours. And in the months and years that followed, an informal group of admirers worked hard to keep his memory alive.

Some of these professed Socratics took to wearing shabby garb and gabbing in public. They made a fetish out of cross-examining compatriots and doubting their beliefs about how best to live. As one contemporary witness sneered, some of them "aped the manners of Sparta, let their hair grow long, went hungry, refused to wash, 'Socratized,' and carried walking sticks."

Other disciples—Plato above all—spurned the master's example by turning to the written word. In his Socratic dialogues, the largest extant body of such literature, Plato inaugurated two major traditions that survive to the present day.

One tradition is that of systematic theorizing, which Plato linked to the figure of Socrates and the practice of "philosophy." Within this discipline, as it has evolved since, the claims of reason, advanced through detached analysis and logical arguments, are commonly regarded as paramount, while a wary eye is cast on poetic invention and the workings of the unchecked imagination: images are made strictly subordinate to clearly defined ideas.

The other tradition is that of the exemplary biography—a selective, often creatively embellished recounting of an archetypal life, conveyed through images, anecdotes, and aphorisms, meant to serve as an inspiration or warning. In a letter long attributed to Plato, readers are reminded that his Socratic dialogues represent neither Plato's personal views nor the views that Socrates himself may actually have held, nor do they represent accurately the life of a real person, but rather "a Socrates idealized and made new." A venerable but often neglected genre of writing, exemplary biography conveys the ideal through the imaginary, in order to dramatize a notable character. In the case of Plato's Socrates, readers behold an idealized image of a life worth imitating—the mythic life of someone unswervingly committed to just action and right reasoning.

Plato was an unrivaled master of both impersonal theorizing and exemplary biography. But he was not alone. After the death of Socrates, a number of his other companions and disciples—Antisthenes, Phaedo, Aristippus, Aeschines, and Xenophon, among others—recounted various of the master's sayings, as well as anecdotes and episodes from the life of Socrates, elaborating a new genre, the *Sokratikoi logoi* (or "Socratic conversations"), as Aristotle called it. Although only works by Plato and Xenophon survive intact, fragments of works by other authors depict the first philosopher in a handful of stock situations: at a dinner party, giving advice to Alcibiades, demonstrating his erotic self-mastery, debating the best way to live, defending himself at his trial, and preparing to die.

The Socratic conversations mark one of the first important experiments with biography in the West. Yet while the dialogues of Plato present a beguiling picture of a living intellect in argumentative action, the genre itself, as Aristotle observed, was a species of poetry—a form of dramatic fiction, not a chronicle of attested incidents. In effect, the life of Socrates was transformed into a myth—and this became the norm for all the biographies of the philosophers of the ancient world until the rise of modern philological scholarship and the creation of documentary archives in the Renaissance and after made such mythologizing infinitely more difficult. (Montaigne is arguably the first modern "philosopher," since he understands that the exemplary lives of antiquity invite skeptical scrutiny, if only because his own earnest efforts to imitate them suggest that these ways of life may in fact be impossible to emulate.)

In any case, the first Socratics depicted their hero inconsistently. He is a different character in the different writings of different authors. The "Socrates" of Xenophon is wise and good, but he is also something of a bully and a blowhard. The "Socrates" of Plato is more modest, and also more inquisitive, wondering almost obsessively about the reasons why one might prefer one way of life over another, one code of conduct rather than some other. Still, his approach to inquiry varies dramatically from one Platonic dialogue to another. In some of Plato's conversations, "Socrates" presses for clear definitions without defending any positive doctrine at all. In still others (including, famously, the *Republic*), he seems at some points to assert confidently various sweeping propositions about reality, human nature, and political justice (even though the dramatic context leaves it unclear whether Plato, or "Socrates," really feels any such confidence, or rather is feigning certainty in order to placate impatient interlocutors).

After undertaking a comparative study of the surviving Socratic conversations by Plato and all the others, one modern scholar felt able to enumerate only a handful of characteristics exemplified by the "Socrates" depicted by more than one Socratic author. Among the common characteristics were moral toughness and physical stamina, a love for theorizing—the ability to produce reasons for what one believes, an interest in distinguishing knowledge and opinion, and an appreciation for eros and impassioned friendship as motive forces in a shared quest for wisdom.

Unfortunately, the authors of the Socratic conversations disagree about almost everything else concerning Socrates.

The "Socrates" of Antisthenes is hostile to pleasure, while in the fragments of Aristippus, he is indulgent. The "Socrates" of Eucleides thinks that there are many different names for one thing, while in the pages of Antisthenes, he asserts that there is only one logos for one thing. The "Socrates" of Plato routinely uses parallel cases to clarify his views, while the character in Eucleides criticizes the use of analogies. There is some irony in the fact that such wildly conflicting evidence has turned modern scholarship about the first philosopher into "a paradise of inconclusive guesswork."

Under these circumstances, to search for the "historical Socrates" in Plato would be like looking for the historical Napoleon in Tolstoy's *War and Peace*. Still, if one is going to try—and it is impressive how many modern scholars have been unable to resist—there is no better place to start than Plato's *Apology*.

This is perhaps the first of Plato's Socratic conversations, and it is certainly the only one constrained by the need to dramatize an event witnessed by more than five hundred other people. And whether or not it is an accurate representation of what really happened in some sense scarcely matters: Plato's *Apology* is the most beguiling, and influential, of the Socratic myths we possess.

The Socrates of Plato's *Apology* is a *philosophos* in the purest possible sense: lacking wisdom, he is a seeker, in quest of self-knowledge. Once he has learned of Apollo's answer to Chaerephon's question, he feels compelled to assay its meaning. He is humbled by the recognition that he lacks knowledge about "the greatest things"—how to live well, how to be happy, what death holds in store. Truly ignorant, he has no specific propositions to present. Yet because he knows that he does not know, he paradoxically is—just as Apollo had proclaimed—the wisest of Athenians. And even though he has no systematic doctrines to communicate, no dogmas to teach, he *has* lived a good life, conducted by relentlessly examining himself and others. Skeptical of the convictions commonly held by his fellow citizens, he will steer clear of public affairs. Instead, within a circle of like-minded friends, he will endeavor "to care for himself" properly. And skeptical though he may be about his own understanding of the greatest things, he will consistently refuse to do anything that he has found reason to regard as unjust or wrong—even if he is tempted to avenge the unjust act of another, as custom would dictate.

His enemies suspected Socrates of speaking with *eirôneia*, or "irony" in its original, primarily pejorative sense of deliberate deceit. But the Socrates of Plato's *Apology* is emphatically no ironist: "Throughout my life, in any public activity I may have engaged in, I am the same man as I am in private life." He is the opposite of a chameleon like Alcibiades: he refuses to flatter the jury, he will not don masks or lie about his beliefs. "From me you will hear the whole truth, though not, by Zeus, gentlemen, expressed in embroidered and stylized phrases." If he has "neglected what occupies most people: wealth, household affairs, the position of general or public orator or other offices," that is because "I thought myself too honest to survive." He consistently says only what he thinks to be true, and does only what he believes to be right—demonstrating his convictions "not in words but in action."

Here, as in other texts by other Socratic writers, we are encouraged to appraise the character of Socrates by judging his integrity—and this requires judging how his life harmonizes, or fails to harmonize, with his declared convictions. Like its classical cognate, the English word *integrity* has a range of connotations, from wholeness and completeness to soundness and freedom from defect. In certain contexts, the word has a physical bearing, as when an engineer speaks of a sound physical structure as having integrity; in still other contexts, the word in English more simply evokes moral goodness.

The Socrates of Plato's *Apology* has integrity in all these senses. He is physically sound and morally unblemished, and he is consistently able to harmonize his actions with the beliefs he provisionally holds after rationally examining them. On trial, he represents himself not just as a model of moral perfection but also as a paragon of rational unity.

This aspect of Socrates' character is important, for it helps to distinguish Socrates from other models of moral perfection. In his landmark study *The Great Philosophers*, Karl Jaspers began with four "paradigmatic individuals": Socrates, Buddha, Confucius, and Jesus. The lives of all four exemplified moral teachings that could later be codified and expressed in rational systems of belief, in this way offering a spur to different traditions of philosophical reflection. But only Socrates taught that "there is no greater evil one can suffer than to hate reasonable discourse." And only Socrates demanded of his followers that they jettison traditional certainties and strive toward a rational unity of word and deed.

To achieve such a goal implicitly requires that one gain an accurate understanding of oneself; that one self-consciously uphold a set of beliefs about the best way to live that is consistent and reasonable, and also that one's conduct comport with these beliefs. Meeting all these requirements is especially tough for anyone committed, as Socrates is in the *Apology*, to a way of life based on a continuing examination of one's core beliefs.

After all, to be prepared constantly to question what one thinks, one must be ready to speak frankly about one's beliefs, and be ready, under examination, to revise them. Because the beliefs at issue concern the conduct of one's life, one must, if one revises one's core beliefs, be willing as well to change how one lives. To be able, in addition, to resist doing anything that one believes (however provisionally) wrong or unjust requires a degree of self-control—an unwavering attention to one's habits of thought and patterns of behavior— that is difficult, if not impossible, to maintain consistently. If he would organize and integrate his impulses and impressions, habits and beliefs into a consistent form of life, the philosopher must improve his ability to reason consistently and to act resolutely, in part by purging his soul of unwelcome bodily passions and appetites that he judges unhealthy.

Yet despite his professed ignorance, and despite his inconclusive efforts to become wise, the Socrates of Plato's *Apology* nevertheless personifies the most sublime sort of conviction: he is prepared to die rather than renounce his beliefs. Serene in his willingness to sacrifice himself, he will give up living in order to prove his unswerving commitment to his transcendental project, his unending search for wisdom.

From the sheer number of Socratic conversations that were published posthumously, we can be sure that Socrates was an impressive, even awe-inspiring moral figure. But we will never know whether Socrates, as he actually existed, was as consistently good as the character depicted in the *Apology*. The ascetic hero of Plato's dialogue has nevertheless subsequently chastened countless readers, inspiring them to try harder, to aim higher—and, by choosing to emulate Socrates, to take pains to embody philosophy as the best conceivable form of life, even if that entails a willingness to die for one's convictions.

Can one live in accordance with this idealized character? Or is the image of the first philosopher in Plato's *Apology* too good to be true?

This is not a merely theoretical question; one will never know unless one tries. And we are enjoined to *try* (as Alcibiades did not)—even if our efforts fail, and even if, by really trying, we prove only that the rational unity that the Socrates of Plato's *Apology* embodies is, in practice, not feasible for us.

Such, in effect, is the peculiar challenge posed by Plato's image of the first philosopher—a vaulting and possibly self-defeating ambition ratified, more than two millennia later, by Friedrich Nietzsche: "I know of no better aim of life than that of perishing *animae magnae prodigus*, in pursuit of the great and the impossible."

PLATO

Marble bust of Plato, artist unknown, a Roman copy of a Greek original. Ancient Athenians commemorated Plato with public monuments and annually celebrated his birth in verse, singing, "On this day the gods gave Plato to mankind." (Vatican Museums and Galleries, Vatican City, Italy/Alinari/The Bridgeman Art Library International)

One man all but single-handedly invented the images and the ideals that define the way of life that we still call "philosophy." Plato accomplished this feat primarily through writing a series of dialogues, many of them dramatizing the life of Socrates and the paradox of his characteristic venture. The life of the philosopher, as Plato represents it, starts with a systematic contravention of received opinions (what Cicero called *paradoxa*, his Latin rendering of the Greek cognate). The resulting uncertainty provokes an arduous and sometimes fruitless quest, in conversation with others, to secure more reliable knowledge—about justice, about laws, about the soul, about the cosmos, about the nature of knowledge itself. Plato's artistry turned this recondite vocation into a new kind of epic adventure, which he conveyed to posterity in a series of texts that have been ardently read and carefully analyzed, more or less continuously, ever since their first transcription in the fourth century B.C.

Plato was born in Athens around 424 and died there almost eighty years later. Unlike his literary alter ego, Socrates, Plato was born into one of the city's first families. His father was descended from the Athenian chief magistrate Aristocles, and his mother was, they say, descended from Solon, the great Athenian lawgiver.

One night, according to the earliest sources on Plato's life, the handsome young Ariston tried to force himself on Perictione, who would not yield. Ariston regained his self-control and Perictione preserved her honor. Later that night, when alone, Perictione was visited in a dream by the god Apollo, who was said in this way to have sired the sage Pythagoras. Nine months later, the virgin gave birth to a boy. "He was originally called Aristocles after his paternal grandfather, but his name was later changed to Plato, either because of his broad chest or because of the breadth of his forehead [the Greek *platus* means "broad" or "wide"], or (the true reason) because of the 'broad,' i.e., expansive character of his style."

In traditional accounts, this miracle was said to have occurred on the same day that Apollo had been born and Pericles died—a coincidence that linked the newborn child to the gods of Olympus and the greatest statesman of Athens in its golden age. As a life of Plato written sometime around the second half of the sixth century A.D. sums up the traditional biographical evidence, "Plato was a divine man, an Apollonian man. That he was divine appears from his own words and from certain dreams concerning him: from his own words, because he called himself a 'fellow servant of the swans.'"

In the same biography, the author reports that Plato's mother shortly afterward took her newborn son "to Mount Hymettus, where she wanted to sacrifice [him] to Apollo god of herds and to the Nymphs. In the meantime she laid him down there, to find, on her return, that he had his mouth full of honey: bees had come and done this, as an omen that the words flowing from his mouth would be, as the poet has it, 'sweeter than honey.'"

He was raised on a strict regimen—"the food on which he was brought up was not animal, but vegetarian." As a child, he was "so modest and orderly that he was never seen to laugh outright."

He trained in gymnastics and is said to have wrestled in the Isthmian Games, one of the Greek world's four major venues for athletic competition. He learned to write in the school of Dionysius, an Athenian orator who had led a pan-Hellenic expedition under Athenian leadership to colonize Thurii on the Italian peninsula in 443 B.C. He painted and wrote poetry and also developed a taste for the theater.

Plato, like key members of his extended family, was fascinated by the teachers and teachings that constituted the so-called Attic Enlightenment of the fifth century B.C. According to Diogenes Laertius, the young man was first drawn to the texts of Heraclitus of Ephesus (c. 540–480 B.C.), whose style was oracular: "You cannot step into the same river twice; for fresh waters are ever flowing in upon you." "Time is a child playing checkers; the kingly power is a child's." "Man's *daimon* is his fate." "I have inquired for myself." The obscurity of such aphorisms earned Heraclitus the epithet "Dark."

But given his family ties, it was only a matter of time before Plato met Socrates, the teacher idolized by his uncle, Charmides, and one of his mother's cousins, Critias. "It is stated that Socrates in a dream once saw a swan on his knees that all at once put forth plumage and flew away, after uttering a loud sweet note. And the next day Plato was introduced as a pupil, and thereupon he recognized in him the swan of his dreams."

The day that Socrates met the swan of his dreams, according to Diogenes Laertius, was a day when Plato was planning to enter a theatrical work into a playwriting competition. Preparing to enter the theater where the contest was to be held, he saw Socrates arguing, as he characteristically did, over what, precisely, he and his interlocutors did and didn't know. Plato stopped and listened. He didn't leave. Overwhelmed by what he was seeing and hearing, he decided to burn his play, saying, " 'Come hither, O fire-god, Plato now has need of thee.' " From then on, he was the pupil of Socrates, consumed by the "yearning for divine wisdom" that Plato was evidently the first man to define as philosophy.

In his *Seventh Letter*, the most informative of the letters traditionally attributed to Plato, and arguably the earliest surviving autobiography in the West, Plato recounts his discovery of philosophy and also describes the other consuming passion of his early years—politics. "When I was a young man," he writes, "I had the same ambition as many others: I thought of entering public life as soon as I came of age." In this regard, Plato could not have been more different in his youthful goals from Socrates, who was trying to remain above the political fray.

These were dire years for Athens. The ongoing Peloponnesian War had divided the citizens of Athens as well as the larger Greek world. After a series of military victories, Sparta had established a garrison at Deceleia, within sight of the Athenian Acropolis, and every citizen was asked to be on guard.

His family's nobility and wealth meant that Plato probably belonged to the class of horsemen who were expected to stable a horse and serve in the cavalry. This was the unit of the citizen army responsible for repelling Spartan raiding parties from Deceleia. At Arginusae in 406, and again at Aegospotami in 405, Athens mustered forces to fight the city's last, desperate battles before the Spartans laid siege to the city, establishing a blockade and creating a famine that left many residents dead.

The city's surrender to Sparta in 404 cleared the way for the brief reign of the Thirty Tyrants. Under the peace terms imposed by the Spartans, three thousand wealthy Athenians were asked to choose thirty men to run the government and write new laws in conformity with an "ancestral constitution" that was presumed to be oligarchical rather than democratic. Among the leaders of the Thirty were Critias and Charmides, who were both sympathetic to Sparta and its authoritarian political constitution.

In his *Seventh Letter*, Plato describes in retrospect how "certain happenings in public affairs favored me, as follows. The constitution we then had"—a democracy—

> being anathema to many [such as Critias and Charmides] was overthrown. A new
> government was set up consisting of fifty-one men, two groups—one of eleven and
> another of ten—to police the market-place and perform other necessary duties in
> the city and the [port of] Piraeus respectively, and above them thirty other officers
> with absolute power. Some of these men happened to be relatives and acquain-
> tances of mine, and they invited me to join them at once in what seemed to be a
> proper undertaking . . . I thought they were going to lead the city out of the unjust
> life she had been living and establish her in the path of justice.

He was soon disabused of such hopes. A reign of terror followed, as the most radical of the oligarchs, led by Critias, struggled to purge the regime of moderates and also to rid the city of democrats. A large number of citizens were murdered. When a group of citizens took up arms in revolt, the Thirty invited Spartan forces to garrison the Acropolis—a fatal misstep that made the junta seem unpatriotic. In May 403, in a climactic showdown between the rebels and the regime at Piraeus, the democrats defeated the oligarchs and killed Critias. Six months later, with the tacit support of Sparta, democracy—and stability—was restored in Athens.

In his epistolary account of these events, Plato does not say anything explicit about the terror or civil war, referring instead to "impious deeds." He stresses his relative youthfulness, as if to excuse his initial enthusiasm. He says that he quickly came to see that "the preceding constitution had been a precious thing." Above all, Plato expresses outrage that the junta tried to implicate Socrates in its actions. "I was appalled and drew back from that reign of injustice," he writes—omitting any mention of the bloodshed.

After this youthful flirtation with tyranny, Plato says that he still "felt the desire, though this time less strongly, to take part in public and political affairs." After the defeat of Critias, the restored democracy declared an amnesty for crimes committed during the civil war. But in 399, five years after the Thirty's reign of terror, Plato was forced to witness what he regarded as an even worse kind of injustice, when a democratic jury condemned his philosophical hero, Socrates, to death.

As a result, Plato went into a kind of inner exile. Despite his ongoing interest in politics, and still hoping to form a better political regime, Plato "refrained from action, waiting for the right time," taking the measure of current events in Athens based on two radical conclusions: (1) "All existing states are badly governed and the condition of their laws practically incurable, without some miraculous remedy and the assistance of fortune"; and (2) "The ills of the human race would never end until either those who are sincerely and truly lovers of wisdom come into political power, or the rulers of our cities, by the grace of God, learn true philosophy."

A short time later, perhaps in 397, Plato left Athens. As the great German scholar Paul Friedländer put it, "he set out in quest of the best state, and on this quest he discovered the world of Forms."

His first stop was Megara, a city not far from Attica, on the isthmus with the Peloponnese. Megara was home to the sage Eucleides, a friend of Socrates and proponent of the theories of Parmenides (b. c. 515 B.C.). Like Socrates, Eucleides conducted his arguments dialectically, by asking a series of questions. Like Parmenides, Eucleides also maintained that "all is one," and that the multiplicity of existing things, their changing forms and motion, are but an appearance of a single eternal reality ("being")—a thesis that Plato would grapple with in later dialogues, including the *Parmenides*, the *Sophist*, and the *Thaetatus* (in which Eucleides himself appears).

The ancient biographers represent Plato as a latter-day Odysseus. Continuing his journey, he sailed to Cyrene, the largest Greek colony in Africa, to study with the mathematician Theodorus; to Egypt, to learn about geometry and to study with "those who interpreted the will of Gods"; to Phoenicia, to meet with Persians and learn about the teachings of Zoroaster; and finally to Mount Etna on Sicily, in "order to view the craters."

In the *Seventh Letter*, the author fails to mention any journeys to Cyrene, to Egypt, or to Phoenicia—but he does recount in detail the time he spent in "Magna Graecia," visiting some of the colonies established by the Greeks along the coastline of southern Italy. The colony of Croton in these years was home to one of the oldest and most mysterious of the ancient Greek wisdom sects, a closed community founded by Pythagoras. Active in the second half of the sixth century B.C., Pythagoras and his followers asserted that what really exists is numbers, and that all natural phenomena are amenable to mathematical explanations. Members were bound together not just by adherence to the primacy of numbers and a handful of other key doctrines—the immortality of the soul, the reincarnation of souls in all kinds of animals, the eternal recurrence of the same—but also by elaborate religious rituals and a shared dietary regimen (some say they were strict vegetarians). Despite forming an exclusive community, the Pythagoreans had by 510 gained control of Croton's government. Contemporary observers commonly credited the city's military success in the years that followed to the austere code of conduct enforced by the sect.

Some aspects of the Pythagorean ethos reinforced lessons that Plato had already learned from Socrates, for example, the advice recorded in "The Golden Verses of Pythagoras": "Let reason, the gift divine, be your highest guide." In the same text, the Pythagoreans admonish the initiate to examine himself at the end of each day by asking, "Wherein have I erred? What have I done? What duty have I neglected"—a spiritual exercise consistent with the Socratic quest for self-knowledge. (In his dialogue *Phaedrus*, Plato shows

Socrates similarly preoccupied with interrogating himself about the nature of his soul, asking, for example, "Do I participate in the divine? Or am I a more savage sort of beast?")

Other aspects of the Pythagorean way of life would likely have been unfamiliar to Plato. The fellowship was well known for its practice of ritual sacrifices in sanctuaries, and also its strict burial rites. Before becoming a full-fledged member, an initiate had to put his property in common and spend several years listening in silence to the sayings of a master, who was veiled by a curtain, at communal "hearings." After five years, if he passed a test, the initiate could become an "esoteric"—a member of the inner circle, who could finally meet the master.

Though the content of the Pythagorean teaching was supposed to be secret, classical sources have preserved some characteristic sayings, one of them especially prized by Plato: "Friends have all things in common." But other extant Pythagorean sayings and maxims are more gnomic: Do not eat beans. Go not beyond the balance. Do not pick up crumbs that fall from the table. The most just thing is to sacrifice, the wisest is number. Do not eat white roosters. The thunder is to frighten those in Tartarus. Do not eat sacred fish. The sea is the tears of Cronus. Do not break the bread, for bread brings friends together. The most beautiful figures are the circle and the sphere. Place not the candle against the wall. Threaten not the stars.

The group's cultic way of life naturally aroused the suspicion of outsiders, particularly when the Pythagoreans in political power pursued aristocratic policies in a number of southern Italian cities. During the fifth century, the sect's meeting places were attacked and burned down, leading some adepts to flee for safety to Greece itself. Despite the pogroms, the Pythagoreans remained politically prominent in several cities in southern Italy, including Tarentum, which Plato visited sometime around 388 B.C.

There he may have met Philolaus (c. 460–380 B.C.), the first Pythagorean to write a book. And he certainly met Archytas (fl. c. 400–350 B.C.), a key figure in the history of Pythagoreanism who also played an active role in the politics of Magna Graecia in these years.

Archytas, according to Diogenes Laertius, "was the first to bring mechanics to a system by applying mathematical principles." Besides being an outstanding scientist, Archytas rose to political power in Tarentum. Elected general of the city seven times, he for many years played a leading role in the affairs of southern Italy and Sicily.

The image of Archytas differs sharply from that of Socrates. Archytas neither professed ignorance nor eschewed involvement in politics. No itinerant teacher, he turned a closed community of disciples into a base of intellectual and political power—and it seems likely that Plato's political and theoretical views now took on a Pythagorean hue.

In some of his later dialogues, Plato has Socrates espouse such characteristically Pythagorean doctrines as reincarnation, metempsychosis, the immateriality and immortality of the soul, and the communism practiced by philosophical friends. For Plato's fictional Socrates in the *Republic*, as for Archytas, the study of mathematics becomes a key element in philosophical training, turning the mind away from the visible realm of change toward the invisible realm of unchanging Forms. Through such mathematical training, a soul might come to know the Form (or Idea—the Greek word is *eidos*) of justice—and so become able to rule with justice.

After spending some time in Tarentum, Plato sailed to Sicily, to visit the city of Syracuse, then under the control of Dionysius (fl. 406–367 B.C.), a sovereign who brooked no limits on his political power. Perhaps the ablest military strategist of his age, and certainly one of the bravest of Greek generals, Dionysius governed an empire that included much of Sicily and parts of southern Italy. From his political base in Syracuse, and in frequent alliance with Sparta, Dionysius had launched a series of expeditions in an effort to wrest control of western Sicily from Carthage, a powerful Phoenician colony located on the coast of modern-day Tunisia. Syracuse had prospered under the tyranny of Dionysius, and the influence of Syracuse on the Greek-speaking world in this period was rivaled only by that of Athens and Sparta to the east.

In one of his letters, Plato recounts his dismay at the luxury and license he discovered in Syracuse, where men were "gorging themselves twice a day and never sleeping alone at night." He also recounts his first encounter with Dion (c. 408–353 B.C.)—a young man whose fate would become intertwined with Plato's own.

Dion was heir to one of the biggest fortunes in the Greek-speaking world;

his family was one of the wealthiest in Sicily. Though he was only twenty years old, he was friendly with the ruler of Syracuse, Dionysius, who had married Dion's sister Aristomache, and who prized her brother's intelligence. It is likely that Dion had also proved his military mettle by serving under Dionysius in several of his campaigns against Carthage. In addition, some of the ancient sources imply that he had already developed ties to the Pythagorean brotherhood.

Meeting Plato changed Dion's life. According to the account given in the *Seventh Letter*, Plato "imparted to him my ideas of what was best for man, and urged him to put them into practice ... Dion was in all things quick to learn, especially in the matters upon which I talked with him; and he listened with a zeal and attentiveness I had never encountered in any young man, and he resolved to spend the rest of his life differently from most Italians and Sicilians, since he had come to love virtue more than pleasure and luxury."

With the enthusiasm of a fresh convert, Dion rashly talked Dionysius into meeting Plato as well. Plutarch recounts how "the general theme of the conversation was human virtue. Here Plato took the line that of all mankind the tyrant possessed the smallest share of this quality, and then turning to the subject of justice, he maintained that the life of the just is happy, while the life of the unjust is full of misery."

Thus provoked, Dionysius lost his temper. "You talk like a dotard," he said.

"And you like a tyrant," retorted Plato.

So why had Plato come to Sicily?

To find a man of virtue, replied Plato.

Well, then, said the tyrant: Your quest has been futile.

One legend has it that Dionysius put Plato under arrest—and then sold him into slavery. The ancient sources differ on what happened next. Some say it was only a personal appeal from Archytas of Tarentum that secured Plato's freedom. Others say that Plato was rescued when Anniceris, a disciple of the Socratic philosopher Aristippus, agreed to buy his freedom.

However, contradictory tales about Dionysius, Dion, and Plato are also preserved in the Hellenistic sources. For example, according to Diogenes Laertius, Dionysius donated a substantial sum of money to Plato, which enabled him to purchase three rare Pythagorean books—a story recorded in an essay (now lost) by an author named Onetor, on the theme "Whether a wise man will make money." Elsewhere, Diogenes Laertius reports that Dion, too, in these years shared part of his own substantial fortune with Plato, who used it to purchase the grounds of the Academy. These anecdotes concern a philosophical school that eschewed material possessions as illusory goods and denounced the love of money as a cardinal vice. And they suggest that Plato, unlike his master Socrates, had to worry about being perceived as inconsistent.

Plato was back in Athens by 387, his wandering years evidently over. Shortly afterward, he established a school and began to lecture at the Academy, a public sanctuary and gymnasium. He bought a small estate nearby, where he could teach small classes in private.

By the time Plato opened the Academy, several other avowed Socratics, including Eucleides of Megara, Aristippus of Cyrene, and, most important, Isocrates of Athens, had also established schools where masters and pupils could converse and live the philosophical life together. Isocrates was celebrated as a speechwriter and charged his students a fee for learning the arts of oratory. Like Euclid and Aristippus, Isocrates also tried to institutionalize the Socratic practice of endless cross-examination. In the case of all these schools, prospective adepts needed to have sufficient free time and material resources if they were to devote themselves wholeheartedly to a life of research and study.

From the start, Plato's Academy was something different. Emulating the example of Socrates, Plato refused to charge students a fee, asking instead for voluntary donations. (If Dion or other rich trustees in fact supported the Academy financially, they may also have endowed it with sufficient resources to allow even poor students to study for nothing.) Some ancient sources indicate that the school admitted a few women as students, which would be in keeping with the radically egalitarian approach to the teaching of women Plato describes in a famous passage in the *Republic*. Though the Academy was neither a secret nor a closed society, it was, like the Pythagorean schools, a fellowship—a community of friends, in practice holding "all things in common"—and sharing, above all, a love for wisdom.

The *Seventh Letter* describes in some detail how the Academy evaluated a prospective student. The "true lover of wisdom" will have a "divine quality that makes him akin to wisdom and worthy of pursuing it." Native intelligence does not suffice: The aspiring student must, in addition, conduct him or herself appropriately. "Whatever his occupation may be, above everything and always he holds fast to philosophy and to the daily discipline that best makes him apt at learning and remembering, and capable of reasoning soberly with himself."

Apart from Plato, who was the school's leader, or scholarch, members of the Academy apparently fell into one of two categories: masters or pupils. Among the masters were Eudoxus, Helikon, Theatatus, and other eminent mathematicians and astronomers. Since modern scholars have confirmed that the Academy was a birthplace of mathematical axiomatics, it is possible that the course of study resembled the curriculum prescribed for the rulers of Plato's *Republic*: arithmetic, plane geometry, solid geometry, astronomy, and harmonics.

Students expecting to get a few easy tips on how to win friends and influence people were bound to be disappointed. According to Aristoxenus, a later follower of Aristotle,

> That is what happened, as Aristotle always used to tell the story, to most of the audience at Plato's lecture "On the Good." They all arrived, you see, supposing that they would get out of it some of the things which men have considered good: wealth, for example, or health, or power—in short, some remarkable source of happiness. But when the account proved to be about mathematics, numbers, geometry, astronomy, and—finally—about oneness as the good, it seemed to them, I guess, to be something completely unfathomable. The upshot was that some expressed contempt for the whole business, others severe criticism.

As Plato explains in the *Republic*, the study of mathematics helped to purify the soul of its attachments to the visible world, by mastering an abstract and immaterial representation of key aspects of reality that could be conceptualized independently of the ever-changing flux of sentient experience. By mastering such a mode of pure inquiry, the soul was elevated and oriented to seek properly abstract and immaterial truths about such matters as justice and the good. The capstone of the curriculum was dialectics—the art of using reason in concert with others, testing one's convictions through sustained argument, in a joint effort to arrive at knowledge of the truth, a conception of the world that is to the largest possible extent independent of the local perspectives or idiosyncrasies of inquirers. According to Plato, the acquisition of such knowledge required a longing to know the Form, or type, of a thing (the Latin translation of the Greek word *eidos* is *species*). Recounting the ascent toward true knowledge in the *Republic*, Plato describes how the summit is reached with the now famous image of a philosopher escaping from a shadowy cave to behold the sun, and the correlative revelation that justice exists independently of its instantiation in any particular soul or city.

Still, the meaning of this image is ambiguous, since Plato's Socrates explicitly says he has only opinions, not knowledge, about such things. And in a later passage referring to the image of the cave, he has his fictional Socrates insist that "there is some such thing to see"—but "whether it is really so or not" cannot be demonstrated through reasoned argument alone.

The conditions necessary for securing real knowledge about such matters, according to Plato in the *Seventh Letter*, are daunting—and perhaps impossible to fulfill: "First, the name [of something]; second, the definition; third, the image; knowledge comes fourth, and in the fifth place we must put the object itself, the knowable and truly real being." The revelation of "truly real being" turns out to be an especially arduous matter: it can appear only after a community of friends has tested the souls of each member through sustained dialogue between masters and pupils. Those who would see real being must first demonstrate, in the way they live their lives as well as the spirit in which they argue, a good nature. "Only when all of these things—names, definitions, and visual and other perceptions—have been rubbed against one another and tested, pupil and teacher asking and answering questions in good will and without envy—only then, when reason and knowledge are at the very extremity of human effort, can they illuminate the nature of any object."

According to the *Seventh Letter*, the kind of illumination that Plato aimed at could not be adequately expressed in language. Beyond the dialectic of conceptual thought, there was a sort of revelation that could be achieved only through a turning, or conversion, of the soul: "There is no writing of mine about these matters, nor will there ever be one. For this knowledge is not something that can be put into words like other sciences; but after long-continued intercourse between teacher and pupil, in joint pursuit of the subject, suddenly, like light flashing forth when a fire is kindled, it is born in the soul and straightaway nourishes itself."

The climax of Plato's curriculum may have been such a moment of vision—his texts have deeply influenced a number of later mystics—but most of a student's time was spent learning how to define things, often in front of an audience of curious bystanders. In a fragment that survives from a contemporary comedy by Epicrates, we are given a glimpse at life inside the Academy:

> At the Panathenaea I saw of group of boys in the gymnasia of the Academy. And there I heard strange and indescribable things. They were defining and dividing up the world of nature, and were distinguishing the habits of animals and the natures of trees and the species of vegetables. And there in the middle of them they had a pumpkin and were inquiring of what species it was . . . At first they all stood silent and bent over it for some time considering. Then suddenly, while they were still bending over it and examining it, one of the boys said that it was a round vegetable, and another said it was grass, and another that it was a tree. On hearing this a Sicilian doctor who was there exploded with wrath . . . But Plato, who was there, told them very kindly, without being in the least disturbed, to try again from the beginning to define its species. And they went on with their definitions.

The Academy's curriculum was not, in any case, an end in itself. Dialectical inquiry was one means to become as perfectly good as possible. And this goal Plato did not teach only in theory, but (like Socrates) in practice as well, through his own living example. Contemporary accounts suggest that Plato's senior associates upheld a Socratic dress code, austerely garbed in cloak and carrying a cane. They talked and moved with a certain solemnity, sometimes mimicking the slight stoop of Plato's posture, or the arched eyebrows and frown of the master lost in meditation.

Still, and above all, they argued over ideas—for Plato welcomed the open-ended pursuit of wisdom with philosophical friends. Aristotle, the most famous product of Plato's school, recalled witnessing sharp disagreements between Plato and some of his most prominent research associates. In this respect, the Academy was a radically different kind of community from the Pythagorean fellowships, simply because Plato upheld in practice the Socratic maxim that "there is no greater evil one can suffer than to hate reasonable discourse."

Besides presenting himself in this way as an example for his associates to emulate, Plato produced a number of written works in these years, almost all depicting exemplary philosophical conversations. These texts evidently formed part of the curriculum, since Plato seems to have made a practice of reading his dialogues aloud to friends and followers. Scrolls were also deposited and preserved in the Academy's library. According to the canon of Plato's works established sometime in the first century A.D. by Thrasyllus, an astrologer and Platonist who lived in Alexandria, the body of Plato's writing consisted of the thirteen letters and thirty-five dialogues. Of the works in this canon, the majority—twenty in all—are *Sokratikoi logoi*, dramatic dialogues built around the character of Plato's most important hero.

In none of his writings, apart from the letters, does Plato speak in his own voice or advance any opinions as his own. In some of the dialogues, the characters, including Socrates above all, present and vehemently defend specific views on ethics, the nature of reality, and the character of genuine knowledge. But in most dialogues, a close reading suggests that no conclusive results have been reached. Such subtleties in the corpus of the Platonic texts led ancient readers to sharply disagree about whether Plato meant primarily to provoke a global skepticism, or rather to transmit a few authoritative doctrines (for example, about the reality of the Forms, the immortality of soul, and the ideal political regime of the philosopher-king). They also disagreed about whether the best life resulted from the endless search for wisdom or from acting in accord with acknowledged truths.

Plato's written works apparently reached a relatively wide audience, even in Plato's own lifetime. In a fragment that has survived from one of his lost dialogues, Aristotle describes a farmer from Corinth who has read Plato's dialogue *Gorgias*. Overwhelmed, the farmer "at once gave up his farm and his vines, mortgaged his soul to Plato, and sowed and planted Plato's views there."

Gorgias is a good example of Plato's literary style—and also of the political interests that are never far from the center of his concerns. Although scholars cannot agree on precise dates for the composition of different dialogues, it is not unlikely that the *Gorgias* was written shortly after Plato's trip to southern Italy and the founding of the Academy.

Like every other dialogue, the *Gorgias* has a dramatic unity of its own, even when treating themes, arguments, and ideas that are elaborated in more detail in other dialogues. It revolves around the fictional representation of five more or less historical characters: Socrates; Chaerephon, the disciple who asked the Delphic oracle whether anyone was wiser than Socrates; Callicles of Acharnae, an aristocratic young man depicted as an associate of oligarchs and a demagogue willing to advance his career by flattering a demos he holds in contempt; Polus of Acragas (b. c. 440), a Sicilian expert on rhetoric; and Gorgias of Leontini (c. 485–c. 380), also from Sicily, the most influential orator of his generation (he visited Athens in 427, supposedly took Diogenes the Cynic as a student, and is said to have lived past the age of one hundred).

In some of his dialogues, Plato takes care to establish a dramatic date, but not in the *Gorgias*. The setting is equally vague, though the Athenian context is not. We are reminded that Athens is a democracy ostensibly ruled by the people in the Assembly, and that orators like Gorgias claim to be able to help aristocrats like Callicles to acquire political power by perfecting their ability to persuade the people gathered in the regular meetings of the demos. We are also reminded of the fate that awaits Socrates at the hands of this regime. "In this city," Plato has Socrates say, "anything can happen to anybody."

Gorgias has just finished a public display of rhetorical prowess, a series of speeches improvised in response to questions from an audience, when Socrates and Chaerephon arrive. A conversation unfolds in front of a crowd that at one point bursts into applause. We, as readers, join the crowd of spectators. We are implicitly asked to judge a competition over how best to appraise the soundness of ideas.

At issue are a series of specific questions: Must an orator know the difference between right and wrong, the just and the unjust? Is it better to do wrong, or to suffer it? Is it better to wield power and enjoy pleasures without restraint, or to live a life regulated and restrained by an understanding of

what is right and just? What must we know about a human being to understand "who he is"? What must a man know if he is to be good, just, and successful in his life?

In the course of the conversation, Socrates cross-examines Gorgias, Polus,
and Callicles, whose vehement defense of immoralism greatly impressed
Nietzsche many centuries later.

What we witness is not simply a competition in words. By questioning
Gorgias, Pollus, and Callicles, Socrates puts the character of each orator to the
test. The spectator is invited to judge who that person *is*, by seeing if that person's conduct consistently follows from his professed beliefs. Under questioning, Gorgias, Pollus, and Callicles are forced to contradict themselves.

The life and beliefs of the three orators depicted in the *Gorgias* don't hang
together, an existential incoherence that is even more important than any
inconsistency in their professed opinions. Socrates by contrast appears here
as he does in the *Apology*, a model of integrity: "I think it is better for my lyre
to be out of tune, . . . and better for most men to disagree and contradict me,
than that I, but one man, should be in contradiction and out of tune with myself."

Because of his commitment to hold only reasonable beliefs, a true lover of
wisdom like Socrates will best be able to rule himself consistently. And because his life and beliefs will hang together, he will also be especially suited to
help his city, by ruling justly over others: "I think that I am one of the few
Athenians, and I say few in order that I may not say only, who undertakes to
practice the true art of politics."

Gorgias is one of Plato's greatest works, and also one of the longest. The
only longer dialogues, the *Republic* and the *Laws*, are, like the *Gorgias*, cen-
trally preoccupied with politics. Even in the years he spent teaching and writing in Athens, puzzling over the incorporeal nature of the soul and the
proper way to grasp the Forms, the fate of the Greek polis remained an obsession with Plato: "He gave everyone the impression of greater concern for civic
matters," according to one ancient *Life of Plato* ascribed to Olympiodoros.

In the *Republic*, Plato implies that the soul should be understood by analogy with the city. Justice in a city depends on the form of its regime, and so it
is with each soul. In the best city, he hypothesizes that the best men—those who

know, the philosopher-kings who have become acquainted with the world of Forms—will rule over the soldiers and laborers who make up the rest of the population. Similarly, in the best soul, its best element—reason—will regulate its passions and bodily needs. Furthermore, Plato implies, the best soul is most likely to flourish in the best city, where the rule of the best men will reinforce the best element in the soul of each citizen. Like a wise monarch, the best soul will be clear, consistent, courageous, and unswerving in its dedication to the good. It will strive to know clearly its true bent, its special talents, its mettle—and therefore to acknowledge how it properly ought to fit into the political order of things.

In a democracy, by contrast, according to Plato, passions and bodily needs run riot. In such circumstances, and to ensure their own survival, the lovers of wisdom must create a community of their own—a group of philosophers not unlike the one Plato had assembled at the Academy. By living a cloistered life of contemplation and learning, a circle of friends might search for wisdom together, guided by the philosopher's own example: If Plato's students "could not govern a city, he wanted them at least to be able to govern their own selves."

Plato himself remained largely disengaged from the political life of his native city, as if participating directly in the freest and most open society of his day were beneath the dignity of a true philosopher. In 366, according to Diogenes Laertius, Plato did come to the defense of Chabrias, an Athenian general who had been hauled before the Assembly after losing a battle to Theban forces at Oropus. "On this occasion, as he was going up to the Acropolis along with Chabrias, Crobylus the informer met him and said, 'What, are you come to speak for the defense? Don't you know that the hemlock of Socrates awaits you?' To this Plato replied, 'As I faced dangers when serving in the cause of my country, so I will face them now in the cause of duty for my friend.'"

Despite Plato's limited direct participation in the public affairs of Athens, the Platonic Academy, like the Pythagorean fellowships it was modeled on, came to exercise a great deal of indirect political influence throughout the whole of the Greek-speaking world. Through the circulation of written works like the *Gorgias*, Plato became renowned as a statesman, possessing expert knowledge of how to rule a city justly, and was in some demand as a lawgiver.

Invitations to draft new laws came in to the Academy from Cyrene in Africa, Megalopolis and Elis in the Peloponnese, Atarneus and Assos in Asia Minor, and Macedonia to the north of Greece. In response, Plato sent various associates: Aristonymos, Phormion, Euphraios, Koriskos, and Erastos. In some cases, Plato's disciples are said to have encouraged tyrants to introduce a milder and more lawful regime; in others, Plato urged his disciples to supplement their "knowledge of the Forms" by learning the art of exercising power from a tyrant. In the case of Macedonia, it is said that Plato's emissary urged the king to "study geometry and philosophize."

In Athens, the most politically prominent of Plato's pupils was Phocion (402–318), who had entered the Academy as a young man, become a protégé of the general Chabrias, and continued his studies under Plato's disciple Xenocrates.

A picture of stiff rectitude, Phocion was according to Plutarch a marvel of controlled emotion: "hardly any Athenian ever saw him laugh or shed tears." Like Socrates, he was indifferent to the elements, wearing neither cloak nor sandals when he was on active duty "unless the cold was unendurably bitter . . . After a while his soldiers used to make a joke of this habit and say that when Phocion put on his cloak it was the sign of a hard winter." An able and courageous officer, he was a cautious, sometimes pusillanimous politician. Faced with the rising power of Macedonia under Philip and Alexander, he negotiated with Philip, acquiesced in Macedonian demands for the surrender of specific Athenians, and finally allowed a Macedonian garrison to control access to the port of Piraeus.

Though the demos in the Assembly elected him commander in chief a record number of times, forty-five, Phocion was hostile to democracy, regarding it an inferior form of government. In 322, he initiated a change to the constitution of Athens that limited the franchise to wealthier citizens. The upper class called him "the Good." But when democracy was briefly restored in Athens in 318, the people exacted a bloody revenge. They hauled Phocion in a cart through a jeering mob in the Assembly, which condemned him to drink the hemlock and then ordered that his corpse be cast out beyond the city limits.

Still, the fate of Phocion pales beside that of Plato's most notorious protégé—Dion of Syracuse, who was unrivaled in his ruthless devotion to what he took to be Plato's political ideals.

After Plato's visit to Syracuse in 387 B.C., Dion had married one of the daughters of Dionysius, the city's king, making Dion simultaneously the tyrant's brother-in-law and son-in-law. At the behest of Dionysius, he served as Syracuse's admiral, and it is likely that he served as well as the city's ambassador to Sparta, which conferred upon him the rare honor of citizenship. For more than two decades, he loyally served his political master, Dionysius.

In these years, Dion was also a frequent visitor to Athens and proud of the fact that "he had spent a long time in the Academy studying how to overcome anger, envy and the spirit of rivalry." He had likely imbibed the counterintuitive idea, expressed in the *Gorgias*, that the philosopher alone was the true statesman. And like Phocion, he certainly practiced philosophy as a way of life: ostentatiously upright, he abstained from the ordinary vices of his class. His behavior annoyed his rivals—but so long as Dion had the ear of Dionysius, there was nothing his enemies in Syracuse could do about it.

Then, in 367 B.C., after a reign of nearly forty years that had left Syracuse powerful and prosperous, Dionysius died. Power fell to his son, Dionysius the Younger. The young man, barely twenty, naturally turned for help to his father's most trusted counselors, and to Dion above all.

This was the moment that Dion, under Plato's tutelage, had been waiting for. He wrote to Plato at once, urging him to set sail to Sicily in order to train the new ruler of Syracuse.

"What better opportunity can we expect," wrote Dion, "than the situation which Providence has presented us with?"

As Plato recalls in the *Seventh Letter*, his old friend and disciple also "mentioned the empire in Italy and Sicily, his own power in it, the youth of Dionysius, and the eager interest he was showing in philosophy and culture; Dion's nephews and other relatives, he said, could be easily persuaded to accept the life and doctrine that I have always taught, and would be a very strong additional influence upon Dionysius; so that now, if ever, might we confidently hope to accomplish that union, in the same persons, of philosophers and rulers of great cities."

In the *Republic*, Plato imagines the possibility of a city ruled by "philosopher-kings." But he also imagines that a true philosopher, being happiest when contemplating the Forms, will have to be *compelled* to rule over others and forced to descend into the "cave" of human affairs—a treacherous realm where the semblance of good and evil, the just and the unjust, shadowbox for supremacy. In the event, however, Plato didn't need forcing (though he does halfheartedly suggest that Dion "compelled me, in a way").

In the *Seventh Letter*, Plato confides that he felt ashamed at the prospect of shirking this extraordinary opportunity, "lest I appear to myself as a pure theorist, unwilling to touch any practical task." But what decisively "tipped the scales," he explains, was "the thought that if anyone ever was to attempt to realize these principles of law and government, now was the time to try, since it was only necessary to win over a single man and I should have accomplished all the good I dreamed of." The stakes could not have been higher: "If in [Dionysius's] empire there had been brought about a real union of philosophy and power, it would have been an illustrious example to both Greeks and barbarians."

So off to Syracuse sailed Plato.

He arrived to find a court teeming with intrigue. Rivals distrusted the motives of Dion and were jealous of his power over the impressionable young monarch. In an effort to curb Dion's influence at court, his enemies recalled from exile a seasoned soldier and politician named Philistus. A faction dedicated to preserving the powers and prerogatives of the tyranny accused Dion of plotting to seize power under cover of instituting a new and milder mixed constitution.

Plato started to work as he always did: he made the young man study geometry. For a while, the palace entourage followed suit, filling the air with dust kicked up by countless sycophants tracing geometrical figures on the dirt floor.

Meanwhile, the prospect of watching a distracted man-child fritter away the assets of an empire on the study of geometry provoked Philistus into action. Winning his young sovereign's ear, this courtier raised doubts about Dion's true intentions, implying that Dion was using Plato as a means to manipulate and control Dionysius the Younger. And when an indiscreet letter from Dion to the city's longtime enemies in Carthage was intercepted, Dion's fate was sealed. Accused of treason, Dion was banished from Syracuse. Dionysius the Younger's only concession was to permit him to keep his assets and real estate, which ensured Dion a comfortable exile.

The young tyrant meanwhile retained Plato as his tutor. He put him under surveillance but also showered him with flattery.

In a scene of instruction that recalls the encounter between Socrates and Alcibiades, the battle for the ruler's soul now began in earnest. Plato persevered with his customary pedagogical methods, not only teaching the young man mathematics but also trying to persuade him of his ignorance. Philistus and his allies urged Dionysius the Younger to treat Plato's unrelenting cross-examination as an insult to the powerful ruler of a great empire.

Because he wished to be seen as a lover of wisdom, Dionysius the Younger seems to have kept up his studies—but only fitfully. He refused to live his life in the disciplined manner prescribed by Plato. Still, Plato kept trying to convert the tyrant, "hoping that [Dionysius] might somehow come to desire the philosophical life."

The great teacher had little choice, since Dionysius the Younger wouldn't allow Plato to leave. It was only after some months had passed—and Plato had reached an agreement with the tyrant that he would return to Syracuse if asked, so long as Dion was permitted to return as well—that Dionysius the Younger agreed to let Plato sail back to Athens.

There are four letters addressed to Dionysius the Younger that Thrasyllus included in the Platonic corpus, and in all of them the issue of money looms large. In one letter, the author refuses a gift of gold from Dionysius ("the offer of it did you a great dishonor"). In a second letter, the author worries out loud that people may think that he has acted "for the sake of money." In still another letter, the author gives a detailed accounting of how he plans to use some money that Dionysius has given him—to build a tomb for his mother, when she died, and to provide wedding dowries for the four daughters of his nieces.

In one of the letters, Plato pleads with Dionysius the Younger to keep an eye on the judgment of posterity. "It is a law of nature," the author avers, "that wisdom and great power go together; they exert a mutual attraction and are forever seeking to be united." Imagine, he goes on, if subsequent generations were to mention Dionysius the Younger and Plato in the same breath as Pericles and Anaxagoras, Croesus and Solon—legendary examples of the marriage of power and wisdom. "I say all this to show you that when we are dead, men will still talk about us, and we must have a care for their opinions." Even if this and all the other letters to Dionysius the Younger are forgeries (as they probably are), the fact that they are preserved in the canon suggests that latter-day Platonists felt the need to explain—and perhaps excuse—the nature of Plato's relationship with the tyrant.

Sometime around 362 B.C., Dionysius the Younger asked Plato to honor his promise that he would, if asked, return to Syracuse.

Dion was still in exile. Yet, according to the author of the *Seventh Letter*, Plato's old friend "persistently urged me not to disobey the summons," implicitly because Dion had hopes that Plato would persuade the tyrant to recall him from exile. Plato was now sixty-five years old and not eager to face the rigors of travel. But he was, he says, still hoping to help Dion, and he was also irritated that Dionysius was telling others that "he had mastered all my thought."

While he was trying to decide how to respond, news came from Sicily. Dionysius the Younger had sent a trireme to ease Plato's journey. On it he had also sent a delegation of Pythagoreans bearing a letter from his old friend, Archytas of Tarentum. Archytas and the other Pythagoreans agreed that Dionysius the Younger was making splendid progress in his studies. And Dionysius himself promised in yet another letter, hand-delivered to Plato, that "all the issues that concern Dion" would be resolved, if only the philosopher returned to Syracuse.

By his own account, Plato temporized. Still unconvinced, he received more letters from friends in the Pythagorean brotherhood at Tarentum, imploring him to return to Syracuse. "Besides, I thought, it is not an unusual thing that a young man of native intelligence who has overheard some talk of lofty matters should be seized by a love for an ideal of life." The prospect of marrying power and knowledge remained as tantalizing as ever.

Despite misgivings, Plato at last agreed to return to Sicily. He arrived to learn that Dionysius had lied.

Instead of trying to bring Dion's exile to an end, the tyrant ordered that the city seize his assets. And he was no more eager than before to submit to the philosopher's austere curriculum of study.

At this point in the *Seventh Letter*, the author launches into a long digression. This is the famous place where Plato (if he is in fact the author) adverts to his "unwritten" doctrines and complains that Dionysius was an unworthy student, unable to comprehend the ineffable essence of his teaching about the Forms, and therefore tempted to spread misinformation about Plato's true teaching.

Once again, Dionysius slapped Plato under house arrest. Seeing that Plato was angered by his seizure of Dion's assets, Dionysius offered to give Plato power of attorney over them. The tyrant also promised that he would deposit Dion's money in the Peloponnesus or at Athens, and follow Plato's advice to let Dion "enjoy the revenues from it, but be without power to dispose of the principal without your consent."

Why Plato would believe anything Dionysius now said is a mystery. But he was in such a desperate state that even a knowledge of the Forms would have been of no practical use. The author of the *Seventh Letter* protests that he wanted to do whatever he could do to protect Dion and his interests: "I told Dionysius . . . that I had decided to remain" (as if he had any real choice in the matter). Plato also insisted that he and Dionysius write a joint letter to Dion "explaining the agreement we have just made" (as if the tyrant's words had any meaning).

Whether Dion ever received such a letter is unclear. In the event—and predictably—Dionysius the Younger violated his agreement. Without telling Plato, he sold all of Dion's real estate.

Meanwhile Plato, though his friend had been betrayed, and despite being under virtual house arrest, pretended in public that nothing was amiss. "Before all Sicily" he and Dionysius "professed to be friends." No wonder Plato worried what people might think: by the author's own account in the *Seventh Letter*, he was behaving hypocritically.

After some months and more misadventures, Plato finally managed to free himself from the tyrant's clutches and escape through the embassies of Archytas and his allies in Tarentum. Sailing from Syracuse to the Peloponnesus in the spring of 360, Plato hastily arranged to confer with Dion at

Olympia. Since the quadrennial games were then being held, it was a very visible summit meeting between two men long linked in the public eye.

Dion was marshaling an army to liberate Syracuse. He invited Plato to join his forces. But on this occasion, the philosopher balked. In the *Seventh Letter*, he explains that Dionysius had after all spared his life; he also expresses his principled opposition to political violence and acts of vengeance (though such scruples had not prevented his previous trips to Syracuse). In addition, he casts himself as an improbably neutral bystander, as if he had hoped to be able to serve both Dion and Dionysius as an honest broker, restraining the worst impulses of each.

If such was his hope, he failed utterly to fulfill it.

In 357, after marching an army from western Sicily to Syracuse, Dion seized the city and had himself elected general plenipotentiary. He immediately fell afoul of a populist rival, Heraclides, who forced Dion and his troops to retreat to the city of Leontini. Then, in 355, after more intrigues and more promises of restoring the city to freedom, Dion and his army were called back to Syracuse in order to expel forces loyal to Dionysius the Younger. In triumph, Dion brooked no opposition, breaking his promises much like the tyrant he had driven from office. Fearful of popular opinion and hoping to consolidate a Platonic regime ruled over by high-minded souls such as himself, he declared himself king and ordered that Heraclides be murdered. (As the Victorian scholar George Grote summed up the situation, "He fancied himself competent to treat the Syracusans as a tame and passive herd; to carve out for them just as much liberty as he thought right, and to require them to be satisfied with it.")

In 353, after little more than a year of exercising dictatorial powers, Dion was assassinated. His clumsy attempt to establish a Platonic republic had helped to plunge his city into an orgy of bloodshed that would not abate for years.

In the *Seventh Letter*, which is one of two in the corpus addressed to the friends and relatives of Dion, the author takes pains to quell any suspicion that Plato may have betrayed his old friend's trust in his dealings with Dionysius the Younger. He also refuses to take any responsibility whatsoever for the behavior of either tyrant, complaining instead that "they did not listen to me;

and in failing to heed my attempts at reconciliation, they are themselves responsible for all the misfortunes that have come over them."

Such special pleading makes it hard to avoid applying to Plato himself the
judgment that Callicles expresses in the *Gorgias*: "Philosophers in fact are inexperienced in the laws of their city, inexperienced in the language to be used
in business contracts, public and private, inexperienced in human pleasures
and desires, utterly inexperienced, in a word, in human character. So when
they come to action, public or private, they make fools of themselves."

Understandably chastened by his experience, Plato speaks in the *Seventh
Letter* of his "disgust" at his "Sicilian 'adventure.'" Yet Plato in principle supposed that his vision of the Forms, the yearning for knowledge that had oriented his failed quest to realize the best state in practice, remained unaffected
by this failure, unsullied by the inevitable vicissitudes of experience. His adventure in Syracuse cannot, in the terms set by his own theory, refute the vision of perfect justice represented in some of the most vivid passages in his
dialogues. Indeed, an unbending faith in the power of his guiding vision may
account for Plato's otherwise astonishing claim, in his last text, the *Laws*, that
the "ideal starting point" for creating a city of just laws is . . . a tyranny!

In the grip of his idées fixes, the convinced idealist has difficulty learning
from experience.

An overweening faith in the ideal may account, too, for the stubborn
pride that Plato seems to have shared with some of his disciples. Both Dion
and Phocion certainly seem to have been puffed up by their philosophical
training and self-interrogation, filled with an unwarranted confidence in the
righteousness of their person and their political program. In practice, it
proved all too easy for the Platonic analogy between soul and society to be
taken literally—"I embody the good; l'état, c'est moi."

Plato was not unaware of this problem—one sign of the ongoing self-
examination that informs all his written work. In the *Laws*, Plato warns against
the temptation of "self-love," which is perhaps an inevitable by-product of the
effort to master oneself by honoring—and identifying with—what is best in
oneself.

Yet understood properly, the quest for self-knowledge and self-mastery is
endless. Our ignorance—not least of ourselves—is boundless. The man who

deludes himself into thinking that he has achieved real knowledge of the true, the just, and the good is liable to be a very poor judge of what is really true, just, and good, since the Forms exist independently of any earthly embodiment, and perhaps beyond any mortal comprehension.

It is worth recalling, too, that the *Seventh Letter* contains what may well be the first frankly confessional passage in Western literature. In the context of explaining his decision to return to the court of Dionysius the Younger for a second time, Plato writes, "I must tell the truth, and put up with it if anyone, after hearing what happened, despises my philosophy." It is a humbling moment in what otherwise seems a self-confident apologia.

A life of cloistered contemplation left Plato largely removed from politics in his later years. He evidently devoted most of his intellectual energy to theorizing about the nature of the Forms. But his unflagging commitment to ongoing inquiry in a community of like-minded souls helped him to create one of Athens's most enduring public institutions—the Academy, which survived for three hundred years, until 87 B.C., when its members fled during the sack of the city by the Roman general Sulla.

Besides the Academy, the best reflection of Plato's philosophy is his written work: his poetic representation, sometimes comic, sometimes tragic, of the dialectic in action. Through these dialogues, readers are drawn into the drama of a life devoted to the questioning of oneself and of others, in introspection and through cross-examination. For what Plato admired, above all, was the way of life exemplified in the words and deeds that the author attributes not to himself but quite often to Socrates: an austere model of rational unity and moral integrity—an artfully crafted image of a better self.

Plato died in 347. Shortly before his death, it is said that he "had a dream of himself as a swan, darting from tree to tree and causing great trouble to the fowlers, who were unable to catch him. When Simmias the Socratic heard this dream, he explained that all men would endeavor to grasp Plato's meaning, none however would succeed, but each would interpret him according to his own views, whether in a metaphysical or a physical or any other sense."

Plato's body was laid to rest in the Academy, the place where he had spent the later years of his mortal life in seclusion and study, pondering the immortality of the soul, practicing a way of life so purely contemplative and careless of bodily concerns that he had died, so the gossips said, from an untreated infestation of lice.

According to Diogenes Laertius, "his wish always was to leave a memorial of himself behind, either in the hearts of his friends or in his books." This wish was granted. Athens honored Plato's memory with busts, while his disciples preserved a set of dialogues and letters they regarded as authentic. Faithfully transmitted over the course of more than two millennia, the corpus of these Platonic texts became his last will and testament: to the practical goodness of Socrates, and to a certain vision of the soul, purified by its contemplation of the Forms of the Good and the Just, and inspired to act by the Promethean possibility that such a rarefied philosophy, in conjunction with the wise exercise of unfettered political power, might finally end "troubles," not only "for our states," but also "for the whole human race."

A beatified ideal, the classical sources suggest. For as one of the biographers from late antiquity concluded, one can

infer the divinity of his nature from what happened after his death. A woman went to consult the oracle whether she ought to rank Plato's monument with the images of the gods, and the godhead gave her this answer: "You would do well to honor Plato, the teacher of a divine wisdom. Your reward will be the favor of the blessed gods, among whom that man is reckoned." Another oracle was given that two children would be born, Asclepius, son of Apollo, and Plato, son of Aristo, one of whom would be a healer of bodies, the other of souls. And when the city of Athens celebrates his birthday, they sing this song:

"On this day the gods gave Plato to mankind."

DIOGÉNES

A nude study of Diogenes with his lamp ("I am looking for a man"), oil on canvas, prepared for the Salon of 1873 by the French painter Jules Bastien-Lepage (1848–1884). A "Socrates gone mad," Diogenes was a popular motif in later literature and art. (Musée Marmottan, Paris, France/ Giraudon/The Bridgeman Art Library International)

Of the first followers of Socrates, the most controversial, and certainly the most striking, was Diogenes the Cynic—a man, they say, who wandered the streets, carrying a lit lamp in broad daylight, "looking for a man." Among the ancient Greeks, Romans, and Arabs, he was storied for his eccentric behavior, his feats of self-mortification, and his fearless exercise of freedom. In word and deed he took the life of the philosopher to an extreme—in order, he said, to follow "the example of the trainers of choruses: for they set the note a little high, to ensure that the rest should hit the right note."

Though little of what we know about Socrates is certain, we know even less about Diogenes. The whole of his life and work is a tissue of legends, an improbable palimpsest of anecdotes and maxims, many cryptic, repeated and embellished by subsequent philosophers and satirists, some sympathetic, others hostile.

Some say he died, aged eighty or ninety, on the same day that Alexander the Great died, June 13, 323 B.C.—an apt but improbable coincidence that would place his birth in the Greek city of Sinope between 412 and 403 B.C. His father, Hicesias, was prominent in Sinope's civic affairs: the master of the town mint, he was the man in charge of issuing, and guaranteeing the value of, the city's coinage. And so Diogenes was born into a life of relative privilege.

According to the ancient biographers, his conversion to philosophy started with a scandal. In those days, the city-state of Sinope was a bustling seaport on the southern coast of the Euxine (the ancient Greek name for the Black Sea). An entrepôt situated at a crossroads between Crimea to the north and Upper Mesopotamia to the south, and populated in part by settlers sent from Athens by Pericles, Sinope was a regional center of Greek culture. Its coins were the currency of choice for regional trade—and its prosperity made the city a target of Persia's imperial ambitions.

One ancient historian, Diocles, reports that Diogenes was forced into exile with his father after Hicesias was accused of corrupting the city's coinage. But Eubulides, a contemporary of Aristotle, claims that it was Diogenes himself who worked at the mint and damaged the coinage, and was thus forced to flee. Still another source reports that both men were convicted, and that Hicesias died in prison, while Diogenes managed to escape.

In the twentieth century, scholars were able to confirm that a man named Hicesias had in fact been the master of the mint of Sinope for some period of time after 362 B.C., and also that the city's currency in these years was being widely counterfeited. Experts in ancient numismatics identified a large cache of counterfeit coins purporting to be from Sinope that had been deliberately defaced by a large chisel, presumably in order to render them worthless as legal tender. They also discovered some genuine coins from Sinope that had been similarly defaced. Some modern historians thus speculate that political rivals (possibly pro-Persian) seized upon problems with the city's coinage in order to drive Hicesias from office.

In any case, Diogenes lost his home, his citizenship, and all his material possessions. Some claim that, fleeing from Sinope, he journeyed to Delphi, to visit the sanctuary of Apollo and consult the Pythia. What, he asked, could he do to restore his good reputation?

"Deface the currency," she replied.

Diogenes reacted to his oracle as piously as Socrates had a generation earlier. Apollo never lied. But since it is possible that Diogenes (or his father) had just been accused of defacing Sinope's currency—a criminal act that may have provoked his flight—what could the oracle possibly mean?

In search of enlightenment, Diogenes journeyed on to Athens. Perhaps an inchoate conviction was starting to take shape; perhaps his misfortune marked the start of a calling now consecrated by the gods. Exiled for "defacing the currency" of his native city, perhaps he should now try to "deface the currency" of society, by somehow forcing counterfeit moral values out of circulation. According to the biographical account of Diogenes Laertius, "He really defaced the currency, giving to matters of convention nothing of the weight that he granted to matters that accord with nature, and asserting that the manner of life he lived was the same as that of Heracles when he preferred freedom to everything."

Turning necessity into a virtue—one of the characteristic traits that commended him to later Stoics—Diogenes began to assert pride in his status as a stateless exile, defiantly proclaiming himself a "citizen of the world," or *cosmopolitan* (a word he may well have coined). Settling for a while in Athens, he turned for guidance first to Gorgias, the famous orator, who may have helped him refine a flair for repartee and aphoristic utterance. The followers of Socrates were also flourishing, and Diogenes in time met many of them: Plato, of course, but also Aristippus, Aeschines, Eucleides of Megara, and—above all—Antisthenes, whom he chose as his master.

Of all the Socratics, Antisthenes had perhaps the strongest will and the keenest commitment to living a life of radical freedom. "Virtue," Antisthenes declared, "is a matter of acts, not of discourses or learning." Unlike other Socratics, he spurned teaching. When he was asked what he found useful about philosophy, he answered, "the ability to converse with myself." Inspired by his example, Diogenes began to shadow him. Once, when Antisthenes brandished his staff to keep him at bay, Diogenes said, "Strike, for you will find no wood hard enough to keep me away from you, so long as I think you've something to say." From then on, Diogenes emulated Antisthenes' acerbic wit and exacting way of life.

One night shortly after Diogenes had pledged himself to philosophy, the Athenians were noisily celebrating a holiday with public banquets and drunken revelry while Diogenes was trying to fall asleep in a corner. As Plutarch recounts the episode, the stranger from Sinope "fell into some very disturbing and disheartening reflections," comparing the pains he was taking to live simply with the tempting pleasures he could hear the other Athenians enjoying. "A moment later, however, a mouse, it is said, crept up and busied itself with the crumbs of his bread, whereupon he once more recovered his spirits, and said to himself as though rebuking himself for cowardice, 'What are you saying, Diogenes? Your leavings make a feast for this creature, but as for you, a man of birth and breeding, just because you cannot be getting drunk over there, reclining on soft and flowery couches, do you bewail and lament your lot?'" If a mouse could be satisfied with so little, he thought, why not a man?

Diogenes was not young when these events took place—he was at least thirty years old, perhaps older. But accustomed though he may once have been to living a life of luxury, Diogenes now took Socratic ideals to a new pitch of ascetic purity.

A vagabond by choice, he traveled light, carrying only a knapsack and a folded cloak that he could use to sleep in. Unlike Socrates, he had no wife, and any family seems to have been left behind in Sinope. A nomad unbound by domestic cares or any bonds of strong fellow feeling, he moved from place to place, staying most often in either Athens or Corinth, where he lived not in a house but in a clay wine jar as large as a tub. In order to inure himself to hardship, he rolled in hot sand in the summer and embraced statues covered in snow in the winter. He tried to live as naturally as possible. After watching a boy drink water from the hollow of his hand, he took out the cup he had been carrying in his knapsack and broke it, exclaiming, "Fool that I am, to have been carrying superfluous baggage all this time!"

His appearance was disheveled, his insignia was his staff, and they called him "the Dog" (*kuon* in Greek, or "cynic" in English). Once, when he was asked why he was called the Dog, he replied that "I fawn on those who give me anything, I yelp at those who refuse, and I set my teeth in rascals." Lacking any other source of income, he lived off alms. The beggars who copied his way of life were called doglike, or "cynics." They were moralizing buskers, street people who survived on the indulgence of others, serious clowns supported by members of a social order they had chosen to mock in word and deed.

The number of Diogenes' written works—indeed, whether he wrote anything at all—was disputed in antiquity. One author attributed thirteen dialogues to him, including a *Republic*, a *Pordalos* (with a title derived from the Greek word for "fart"), and seven tragedies, including an *Oedipus* that may, like many of these works, have been a parody (since Diogenes is shown elsewhere suggesting that Oedipus was an arrogant ignoramus who should simply have legalized incest in Thebes).

According to Philodemus (c. 110–35 B.C.), Diogenes broached a number of impious ideas in these written works. Arguing that nothing is good, beautiful, or just by nature, he defended such practices as cannibalism; incest; promiscuity, even with slaves; and the killing of one's father. Philodemus argued that the content of this corpus was so scandalous that the works themselves had been deliberately suppressed and summaries often bowdlerized, especially by respectable Stoics who wished to count Diogenes, along with Socrates, as a forerunner and role model.

As a result, Diogenes became a creature of conflicting legends, and as the debate over his virtues and vices grew, his myth began to spread. He became a favorite figure for satirists, and also for Greek and Roman artists, and a number of representations survive, in marble, bronze, and terra-cotta, in wall paintings and figurines, on mosaics and coins and medallions. The sheer wealth of such material makes it clear that his example, however mythic, exerted a broad influence.

Most of the ancient accounts agree that Diogenes, unlike Socrates, did not seek out orators and Sophists in order to question their beliefs. Unlike Plato, he did not organize a group of philosophical friends to give public lectures or groom disciples in private, nor did he evince the slightest interest in public affairs or political power. Instead, he was a solitary man who kept largely to himself, other than venturing out on rare occasions to visit the great athletic venues and to join the crowds from the Greek-speaking world that flocked to the Olympian, Pythian, Nemean, and Isthmian games. "For it was his custom at the great assemblies to make a study of the pursuits and ambitions of men, of their reasons for being abroad, and of the things on which they prided themselves." When curious bystanders gathered around him, he made a spectacle of himself with fearless speech and shameless antics, promising that "all who should follow his treatment would be relieved of folly, wickedness, and intemperance."

Valuing freedom above everything, he exemplified a life of primitive independence, shorn of needless wants and material possessions. At the same time and perhaps with the same goal in mind, Diogenes routinely flouted what he took to be unnecessary rules and customs. In both of these ways, the Dog offered a model of conduct to a series of subsequent philosophers, from Zeno in ancient Greece to Jean-Jacques Rousseau in eighteenth-century France.

His behavior could seem gratuitously repulsive. He thought masturbating in public was a perfectly natural thing to do: "It was his habit to do everything in public, the works of Demeter and Aphrodite alike. He used to produce such arguments as this. 'If taking breakfast is nothing out of place, then it is nothing out of place in the marketplace. But taking breakfast is nothing out of place, therefore it is nothing out of place to take breakfast in the marketplace.' Behaving indecently in public, he wished 'it were as easy to banish hunger by rubbing the belly.'"

When some people in his audience at the games kept "throwing all the bones to him as they would have done to a dog," he "played a dog's trick and drenched them." On another visit to the Isthmian Games, Diogenes discoursed on virtue and how to struggle against the temptations of pleasure. As he spoke, a large crowd gathered. When he finished his discourse, he "ceased speaking and, squatting on the ground, performed an indecent act." Outraged that he would shit in public, the crowd called him crazy, quickly dispersed, and left him undisturbed.

Once, when an admirer brought Diogenes into a magnificent house and "warned him not to spit," the Dog "cleared his throat" and "discharged the phlegm into the man's face." He could not, he said, find "a meaner receptacle."

Diogenes was seized by pirates during a voyage to Aegina—an ordeal he endured with admirable poise, according to Philo of Alexandria (c. 20 B.C.--A.D. 50).

When he was taken prisoner . . . , and when they fed him very sparingly, and scarcely gave him even necessary food, he was not weighed down by the circumstances which surrounded him, and did not fear the inhumanity of the masters into whose power he had fallen, but said, "that it was a most absurd thing for pigs or sheep, when they are going to be sold, to be carefully provided with abundant food, so as to be rendered fat and fleshy; but for the most excellent of all animals, man, to be reduced to a skeleton by bad food and continual scarcity, and so to be rendered of less value than before." And then, when he had obtained sufficient food, and when he was about to be sold with the rest of the captives, he sat down first, and breakfasted with great cheerfulness and courage, giving some of his breakfast to his neighbors. And seeing one of them not merely sorrowful, but in a state of extreme despondency, he said, "Will you not give up being miserable? Take what you can get."

When the pirates put him up for sale as a slave in Crete, the auctioneer asked him what he was good for. Diogenes replied, " 'ruling over men.' And then he at once, with his natural indifference and serenity, turned to facetious discourse," turning the auction into a farce.

In his *Discourses*, the Stoic philosopher Epictetus (c. A.D. 55–c. 135) depicts Diogenes as the truest kind of king, since he exercises perfect sovereignty over himself. The Cynic's life he presents as a rebuke and a challenge: "in all that pertains to yourself, you must change completely from your present practices, and must cease to blame God or man; you must utterly wipe out desire, and must turn your aversion toward the things which lie within the province of the moral purpose, and these only; you must feel no anger, no rage, no envy, no pity."

Diogenes was not only self-controlled, self-sufficient, and shameless in his life, but also fearless in his speech—as witness his conversations with Alexander the Great.

Legend has it that their paths crossed in the autumn of 336 B.C. At the time, Diogenes was at least seventy years old, and Alexander was twenty. A few months before, Alexander's father, King Philip of Macedonia, had been assassinated, and Alexander had assumed his throne. Shortly afterward, the Macedonian army escorted the young king to Corinth, where Alexander, succeeding his father as the leader (or hegemon) of the League of Corinth, convened a congress of Greek city-states. Ignoring objections from an Athenian delegation led by the orator Demosthenes, the congress ratified Alexander's call for an allied crusade against the Persians. After the congress was over, according to Plutarch, "many statesmen and philosophers came to [Alexander] with their congratulations." But a famous one was missing: allergic as he was to flattery, Diogenes was nowhere to be seen.

Minding his own business, and paying no attention at all to the visiting young potentate, Diogenes was staying in a suburb of the city, parked in his trademark tub. His curiosity piqued, Alexander decided to make a special trip to meet at firsthand the old man who had refused to pay him obeisance.

When the king and his entourage arrived, Diogenes was basking in the sun, wearing only a loincloth. "When he saw so many people approaching him, Diogenes raised himself a little on his elbow and fixed his gaze upon Alexander. The king greeted him and inquired whether he could do anything for him. 'Yes,' replied the philosopher. 'Stand aside. You're keeping the sun off me.'"

His audience with Diogenes over, Alexander retreated, and his entourage began to joke about the Cynic. "You may say what you like," remarked the king, "but if I were not Alexander, I would be Diogenes."

As a modern biographer of Alexander remarks, "This shows shrewd percipience. Both men shared (and surely recognized in each other) the same quality of stubborn and alienated intransigence. But whereas Diogenes had withdrawn from the world, Alexander was bent on subjugating it: they represented the active and passive forms of the identical phenomenon. It is not surprising, in the circumstances, that their encounter should have been so abrasive"—or the subject of so much subsequent lore.

According to anecdotes preserved in the Arab tradition, the two men struck up some kind of continuing relationship. "Alexander [once] came to visit him while he was asleep and kicked him with his foot and then said to him, 'Get up, I have just conquered your city.'

"Diogenes replied, 'Conquering cities is not to be held against kings, but kicking is how donkeys act.'"

On another occasion, a messenger from Alexander invited Diogenes to come see the king, but the philosopher refused, instructing the messenger to tell the king, "That which prevents you from coming to us is that which prevents us from coming to you."

The messenger imagined the king's response: "So what prevents me and what prevents you?"

"You are too powerful to need me—and I am too self-sufficient to need you."

If Alexander functions as a political foil for Diogenes in the literature, then Plato is his philosophical nemesis. They say he considered Plato's lectures a waste of time and ridiculed the dialectical form of teaching, which demanded that students carefully define key terms. Once, when "Plato had defined Man as an animal, biped and featherless, and was applauded, Diogenes plucked a fowl and brought it into the lecture-room with the words, 'Here is Plato's man.' In consequence of which there was added to the definition, 'having broad nails.'"

Another time Plato was conversing about the Forms and using the nouns *tablehood* and *cuphood*. "'Table and cup I see,'" said Diogenes, "'but your tablehood and cuphood, Plato, I nowhere see.'"

Once, Plato saw Diogenes washing a head of lettuce and said to him, "Had you paid court to Dionysius"—the Sicilian tyrant Plato supposedly tried, more than once, to tutor and advise—"you wouldn't now be washing lettuces." Replied Diogenes: "If you had washed lettuces, you wouldn't have paid court to Dionysius."

The implication is clear: It is Diogenes, and not Plato, who represents the life of the philosopher in its purest form. Unlike the Cynic, Plato is seduced by his cleverness, is vainglorious in his pursuit of superfluous scientific knowledge, and is beholden to rich and powerful friends. In other words, Plato lacks integrity, and it is Diogenes who is truly following in the footsteps of Socrates.

While Diogenes regarded Plato as a hypocrite, Plato saw Diogenes as "a Socrates gone mad"—and by Plato's standards, he certainly was. In some ways, the Cynic resembles not Socrates but the figure of Callicles, whom Plato portrays as an amoral egoist in his dialogue about Diogenes' first teacher, *Gorgias*. Diogenes, like Plato's Callicles, declares that he shall do all things according to nature, no matter how shameful they seem. A proponent of freedom in all things, the amoralist is silenced not by the force of dialectical argument—which he, like Diogenes, scorns as so much quibbling—but rather by the sense of shame Socrates finally elicits when he dares Callicles to condone the practices of a boy who takes the active role in a homosexual affair with an older man. The freethinking orator hasn't flinched at the prospect of cruelty or murder—but he can't help but flinch at this idea: "Aren't you ashamed, Socrates, to lead the argument into a topic like this?" Even for the proponent of freedom in all things, as Plato represents him, it seems that some acts are simply beyond the pale—whether by nature or by convention scarcely seems to matter.

It is not at all clear whether Diogenes would have been susceptible to being shamed in this manner. The anecdotal evidence is contradictory. On the one hand, the Cynic is shown exploiting the rhetoric of shame himself in a series of maxims preserved by the Greek historians: "Seeing a young man behaving effeminately, Diogenes said, 'Are you not ashamed . . . that your own intention about yourself should be worse than nature's: for nature made you a man, but you are forcing yourself to play the woman.' Observing a fool tuning a psaltery, 'Are you not ashamed,' said he, 'to give this wood concordant sounds, while you fail to harmonize your soul with your life?' To one who protested that he was ill adapted for the study of philosophy, he said, 'Why then do you live, if you do not care to live well?'"

This somewhat priggish mode of admonition—a stock feature of later Stoicism—stands in stark contrast, even contradiction, with the unbridled shamelessness that Diogenes elsewhere seems to champion. When we hear of him masturbating in public, and defending such practices as incest and cannibalism, we have to wonder what, if anything, this philosopher took to be viscerally repugnant, or unnatural, or evil.

If we are meant to take his most disturbing quips and stunts seriously—and who is to say?—then Diogenes represents the most radical challenge imaginable to common norms of decency, even as he leaves us wondering just how he regulated so successfully his own simple life. He embodies a radical ideal, a naked existence, unencumbered by possessions, unburdened by any ties of kinship or love or fellow feeling, unawed by taboos, unintimidated by the threat of eternal punishment, and thus free to be perfectly independent, a sovereign beholden to no other.

The Roman sage Cicero found this prospect appalling, "for it is the enemy of considerate behavior, and nothing correct or honest can exist without that." Augustine of Hippo, though clearly fascinated, also recoiled, struggling to explain why the Cynic's life fell short.

For Augustine had to concede that Diogenes was a spiritual avatar, a man like the desert saints, someone who lived his corporeal life at the highest possible pitch of self-abnegation in quest of a transcendent ideal. Doubtless Diogenes exemplified one kind of perfect asceticism. But he also had made a habit of transgressing the limits of common decency. And writing in *The City of God* about the supposed Cynic practice of sometimes masturbating in public, Augustine, like some Stoics in the centuries before, had to wonder whether Diogenes had in fact done any such thing.

"I am inclined to think," writes Augustine,

> that even Diogenes himself, and the others about whom this story is told, merely went through the motions . . . before the eyes of men who had no means of knowing what was really going on under the philosopher's cloak. I doubt whether the pleasure of that act could have been successfully achieved with spectators crowding round . . . Even now we see that there are still cynic philosophers about . . . However, none of them dares to act like Diogenes. If any of them were to venture to do so, they would be overwhelmed, if not with a hail of stones, at any rate with a shower of spittle from the disgusted public. Human nature then is, without any doubt, ashamed about lust, and rightfully ashamed.

For Augustine, as for Plato in the *Gorgias*, it all comes back to shame, and lust, and shame at lust, as if sexual desire was the most dangerous and disruptive of animal appetites, and something a man must at all costs learn to restrain and suppress.

But for most ordinary Greeks, the moral of the story seems to have been rather more ambiguous. In Corinth and Athens, long before Christ was born, they had turned Diogenes into an object of adoration, taking in stride the Cynic's uncommon indecency, his ostentatious refusal to conform—as if sexual desire nakedly fulfilled was a perfectly fine emblem of a life lived freely. The people showered the Cynic with love, not stones or spittle. Once, when a boy shattered his clay tub, leaving the sage without a shelter, the Athenians, furious at the wrong done, gave the boy a good flogging and then presented Diogenes with a new tub.

The philosopher's popularity is paradoxical. Unlike Socrates, Diogenes was never brought to trial, and unlike Aristotle, he was never forced to flee Athens in fear. He wasn't perceived as any sort of threat, perhaps because most people didn't take him seriously. Instead, he was feted as a merry prankster, as if he were a harmless clown or a holy fool.

He lived in peace to a ripe old age. In one account, Diogenes is said to have died after eating a raw octopus. In another, he died from a bite sustained while trying to divide an octopus among dogs. According to still another account, he simply held his breath—and so perished through an act of pure will.

In Sinope and Corinth and Athens, the citizens raised statues to his memory. "Even bronze grows old with time," read the epitaph inscribed at Sinope, "but your fame, Diogenes, not all Eternity shall take away. For you alone did point out to mortals the lessons of self-sufficiency, and the path for the best and easiest life."

Long after his death, the stories told about Diogenes exercised an influence in their own right, as an episode from the life of Dio Chrysostom demonstrates. Having acquired a reputation as a good man and an orator of an ascetic cynical bent, Dio was invited to deliver a series of four speeches before the Roman emperor Trajan. In the fourth of his speeches, Dio represented Diogenes at some length discoursing with Alexander the Great, in order to show Trajan that a life of perfect self-control alone equips a man to rule rightly over others. It is an edifying instance of life imitating art. Diogenes may never have actually met Alexander the Great—but Dio Chrysostom was in fact a friend and confidant of Trajan, a ruler widely hailed for his wisdom, restraint, and regard for justice.

And so the legend of Diogenes lived on. Despite, or because of, its comic flavor, improbable details, and frisson of scandal, the myth has never lost its potential to provoke and even to transform the conduct of anyone willing to take it seriously—from Dio Chrysostom to Michel Foucault, nearly two thousand years later.

ARISTOTLE

Aristotle instructing Alexander the Great, artist unknown, illumination on vellum, in Ibn Bakhtishu, *Manafi al-Hayawan* (Uses of Animals), Persia, thirteenth century. A famous physician and one of the leading Islamic zoologists of the eighth century, Ibn Bakhtishu was also an authority on the works of Aristotle. (British Library, London,

I t is a curious fact about the reputation of Aristotle—who from late antiquity to the early Renaissance was widely revered as "the Master of those
who know," "the limit and paragon of human intelligence," or, simply,
"*the* philosopher" (*Ille Philosophus*)—that, in the first two centuries after his
death, surprisingly few philosophers treated him as a worthwhile interlocutor.

The problem seems to have been his alleged character and conduct. To a
near contemporary like the philosopher Epicurus, Aristotle was neither "an
ideal of human excellence" nor an exemplary researcher "untroubled by passion, and undimmed by any great moral defects"—to quote two modern
authorities—but rather a wily political operator and pedant who was unworthy of being associated with philosophy as a way of life. In Athens and elsewhere throughout the Greek-speaking world, in the first centuries after
Aristotle's death in 322 B.C., doubts about his character and conduct ran deep.
They were persistent, and they were widespread. Indeed, such doubts help to
explain the virtually complete neglect, otherwise puzzling, of his written
work until the first century B.C., when scholars belatedly established the corpus of texts upon which Aristotle's posthumous fame came to rest.

Apart from an apparently genuine will and a few fragments from pur-
ported letters, Aristotle's extant texts shed little light on his life. All of his

originally published works, including a number of early dialogues, have disappeared, aside from a few excerpts quoted by later writers. The reliable biographical evidence is so sparse that one is almost tempted to leave the topic where the German philosopher Martin Heidegger did in a famous 1924 lecture course on Aristotle: "The man was born, he worked, and then died."

The classical Aristotelian corpus has traditionally been regarded as a creation of Andronicus of Rhodes, a scholar who organized what survived of Aristotle's writings into more or less coherent accounts of topics by excerpting passages from a large number of manuscripts and rough drafts, probably including lecture notes. The resulting text fills two thousand modern printed pages, roughly twice the size of the surviving Platonic corpus. The range of this material is encyclopedic, with more than forty independently organized texts on (among other topics) metaphysics, theology, physics, astronomy, meteorology, zoology, botany, psychology, ethics, politics, rhetoric, and poetics.

A flesh-and-blood personality cannot be discerned in these treatises, which are artless in style, often opaque, and relentlessly impersonal. As the eighteenth-century English poet Thomas Gray quipped, reading Aristotle "is like eating dried hay."

This did not stop Andronicus himself from doing for Aristotle what any proper ancient editor would for do anyone who claimed to be a true philosopher: he evidently prefaced his edition with an edifying biography, taking care to reprint the text of Aristotle's will. Though the biography by Andronicus has disappeared, subsequent editors of the Aristotelian corpus followed his example, and modern scholars have been able to trace a variety of idealized medieval accounts of Aristotle's life to a common idealizing source, a partisan biography that appeared around A.D. 500 as a preface to the standard edition of Aristotle that was used in the Aristotelian school of Athens at that time.

Aristotle was born in the Greek city of Stagira, probably in 384 B.C. A self-governing city of no special importance, Stagira had been colonized by settlers from Ionia and was allied for much of the fifth century with Athens. The ancient authorities agree that Aristotle's pedigree was distinguished: his mother, Phaestis, possessed considerable wealth and descended from the first colonists, while his father, Nicomachus, was an accomplished doctor who belonged to the priestly family guild of the Asclepiadae, an ancient order that controlled the sacred secrets of healing, which were passed from father to son. Among the Asclepiad arts was training in physical observation and the dissection of bodies—skills that Aristotle may have learned from his father.

Stagira lay near the frontier with Macedonia, an ancient inland kingdom composed of barbaric tribes in the north and Greek-speaking towns in the south, which bordered on the northernmost coast of ancient Greece. Aristotle's father had served for some time as a doctor and confidant to King Amyntas III of Macedonia (r. 393–370/369), a Greek-speaking monarch who had solidified control of the region's uplands and plains, laying the basis for his successor Philip II (r. 360–336) to extend the kingdom toward the coast. But Aristotle's father and mother both died while he was young, and some sources report that he was subsequently raised in Stagira by an uncle, Proxenus, who had originally been a citizen of Atarneus in Asia Minor.

If the medieval biographical tradition tended to glorify Aristotle, other, earlier accounts tended to be libelous. Some ancient biographers declared that Aristotle was a "debauchee and a glutton," and that he "sold drugs." Others said that the pursuit of political power at first interested him more than the pursuit of knowledge, and that he excused his interest in power on the grounds that "one who lacks experience of current events in politics finds everything unfriendly to him" and that "he was disgusted with most of the contemporary politicians who were consistently involved in party strife." Still other early sources claim that after a wasted youth, he was forced to return to Stagira in order to take over his father's medical practice (and presumably his pharmacy), arriving in Athens when he was some thirty years old and turning to philosophy only after he had failed to make a living either as a politician or a doctor.

But a dramatically different tale is told by Hermippus of Smyrna (fl. c. 200 B.C.), whose biography is the first favorably disposed account of Aristotle to survive (if only in fragments). According to Hermippus, Aristotle traveled to Delphi and (like Socrates and Diogenes before him) followed the advice of the oracle there by journeying to Athens at the age of seventeen in order to become a philosopher.

According to Hermippus, Aristotle first followed Plato. Other hagiographies from late antiquity have him being initiated into the search for wisdom by Socrates himself—a chronological impossibility, perhaps explained by confusing the man martyred in 399 with one of his disciples who was still alive and active in fourth-century Athens, Isocrates (436–338 B.C.).

The school of Isocrates was rivaled at that time only by Plato's Academy. The two men had both been companions of Socrates, and had both declared "philosophy" to be their chosen way of life, making the cultivation of a good character the shared goal of their search for wisdom. An implicit debate unfolds in their written works over how best to exemplify, and teach, what both authors call "philosophy." Where Plato favored a curriculum built around mathematics, geometry, and dialectics, Isocrates trained his students to "speak well and think right," in part by studying rhetoric, in part by emulating the master's own upright conduct.

This much seems clear: if Aristotle reached Athens around 367, as Hermippus claims, then he cannot at that time have been instructed in any continuous way by Plato, who was preoccupied in these years with the instauration of Dionysius the Younger as the philosopher-king of Syracuse.

As an immigrant, Aristotle by law became a metic, or resident alien, of Athens. He was never a citizen. As a result, he could neither participate in the city's political life nor own property within the city limits.

Virtually all the anecdotal and circumstantial evidence suggests that Aristotle was independently wealthy. Thanks to his family estate, he was able to buy an unlimited number of papyrus-roll manuscripts, amassing one of the first and finest large private libraries in the Greek-speaking world.

It is likely that by the time Aristotle became active in the Academy, Plato had completed his Sicilian adventures. In the aftermath of this fiasco, and perhaps in response, Plato had modified the picture of the philosophical life he had presented in his earlier dialogues. In place of the defiant martyr at the center of Plato's early account of the *Apology* of Socrates, there emerged in later works like the *Thaetatus* a new fictional image of Socrates as a kind of mathematical recluse, methodologically self-conscious and committed to a new and relatively austere conception of theorizing as the best possible life.

Although Aristotle may have been inspired in part to join Plato's Academy by the intensely ethical way of life dramatized in a number of Plato's *Sokratikoi logi*, it was not just an ethical enterprise that Aristotle was joining by the time the two men finally met face-to-face. A cloistered community of scholars bound by friendship, the Academy was primarily committed to conducting research in mathematics, astronomy, medicine, and the logical relations between different ideas and concepts.

Although he was expected to master this research agenda like any other aspiring philosopher, Aristotle stood apart from his other colleagues for a variety of reasons from the start. In a society where writing and reading were not widespread habits, Aristotle was an avid bibliophile. In a school where mathematical research was prized, he was critical of the Pythagorean assumption that all that really exists is numbers. And in a community where rhetoric was frequently derided, he displayed a scholarly interest in the arts of persuasion.

According to a number of the ancient sources, Plato nicknamed Aristotle "*nous*" (Greek for "mind") and sometimes called him "the Reader," alluding to his insatiable appetite for books. Some suggest that the nicknames were meant affectionately. But others imply that they were belittling, an indication that Plato thought Aristotle somewhat facile, an indiscriminate reader who devoured too many books for his own good.

In the fragments that survive from his earliest dialogues, Aristotle faithfully conveys the Platonic view that only a philosopher fixed on eternal truths could promulgate laws that were just and good: "To the philosopher alone among craftsmen belong laws that are stable and actions that are right and noble. For he alone lives by looking at nature and the divine. Like a good helmsman, he moors his life to what is eternal and unchanging, drops his anchor there, and lives his own master." (It is interesting that in the nautical analogy deployed by Aristotle, the philosopher has found a safe harbor—not unlike Plato at the Academy, after he had completed his sorties to Syracuse.)

Aristotle was Plato's associate at the Academy for roughly two decades. The ancient sources say that he gave public lectures at the Academy in these years on rhetoric, which he evaluated more positively than Plato but less generously than Isocrates.

Whereas most of his mentors and colleagues in the Academy specialized in a single field, such as astronomy or study of the Forms, Aristotle was a polymath. He wanted to appropriate everything that had been thought prior to him and to use it as material to build a new and all-encompassing system of thought, the construction of which became one focal point of his life.

The other great goal of his philosophical life, which became evident only as time passed, was to improve on Plato's efforts in practice to join power and knowledge, in part by moderating the radical idealism of his mentor's political philosophy with a crafty sense of realism. Aristotle's appreciation of rhetoric was one aspect of this project—but even more important was an appreciation, evident in his political theory, for the particulars at issue in any actual exercise of political power that is effective (a form of pragmatism that Aristotle associated with the capital virtue he called *phronesis*, a Greek word variably translated into English as "prudence," "common sense," "political judgment," or sometimes simply "wisdom").

Given his talents and the scope of his philosophical interests, it is not surprising that Aristotle rose to a position of prominence within Plato's Academy. Even though he was a resident alien, he may even have entertained the hope of becoming his master's successor. But on Plato's death in 347, it was not Aristotle but Plato's nephew Speusippus who became the school's new scholarch.

Either shortly before or shortly afterward, Aristotle set sail with Xenocrates (396/95–314/313 B.C.), an equally prominent companion of Plato. The two men were headed for Mysia in Asia Minor, where they had been invited to offer philosophical aid and comfort to Hermias, who exercised absolute authority over the Greek coastal city of Atarneus (where Aristotle's uncle Proxenus had been born).

Some ancient historians say that Hermias was once a slave; others, that he was a eunuch. A man of lowly origin, he supposedly once worked as a money changer for a local bank. At some point, he entered into the service of Eubulus, the tyrant of Atarneus, and fought vigorously to repel recurrent Persian attacks. Some sources also claim that Hermias traveled to Athens to spend time at the Academy, perhaps hearing Plato lecture and becoming friendly with Aristotle.

Upon the death of Eubulus, Hermias became his undisputed successor (just how or when is unclear). In the years that followed, Hermias added territory to his kingdom, building a small Greek-speaking empire along the Asiatic coast. Inspired by Platonic political ideals, he fancied turning himself into something like a philosopher-king and entered into correspondence with Plato himself.

In a letter that Plato supposedly addressed to Hermias and two of Plato's own former students, Erastus and Corsicus, he urged the three men to pool their talents. The tyrant, he pointed out, had money and arms to spare, while his former students were amply endowed with the "noble love of ideas." Hermias sought wisdom, while Erastus and Corsicus needed political experience if they were ever to learn the dark arts of "self-defense against the base and wicked." By knitting themselves tightly together "into a single bond of friendship," advised Plato, the three men conjointly could "practice philosophy," each to the fullest possible extent.

This philosophical triumvirate expanded with the arrival of Xenocrates and Aristotle. According to Didymus, the Alexandrian author of a commentary on Demosthenes' fourth *Philippic* that has been preserved on papyrus fragments, Hermias "made friends of Coriscus and Erastus and Aristotle and Xenocrates . . . He listened to them . . . he gave them gifts . . . he actually changed the tyranny into a milder rule; therefore he also came to rule over all the neighboring country as far as Assos, and then, being exceedingly pleased with the said philosophers, he allotted them the city of Assos. He accepted Aristotle most of all of them, and was very intimate with him." (If true, this account would mean that Aristotle and his Platonic philosophical colleagues succeeded in creating a relatively durable alliance with Hermias, in stark contrast to Plato, who had spectacularly failed to win the confidence of Dionysius the Younger.)

All this occurred against a backdrop of mounting political unrest throughout the Greek-speaking world. The proximate cause was the fall of Olynthus, by far the largest and most important self-governing Hellenic center in Chalcidice, and a city long coveted by Philip of Macedonia, who had relentlessly extended the frontiers of his empire in the years since Aristotle had left the region.

Alarmed by Philip's ongoing military campaign in Chalcidice, the citizens of Olynthus had turned for help to the citizens of Athens. Although Demosthenes, the city's most influential orator, tried to rally support for the Olynthian cause, Athens sent only token military aid. After a lengthy siege,

Olynthus surrendered to Philip in 347.

As was his custom—the king had behaved in the same way when he conquered Aristotle's hometown Stagira in 350—Philip was merciless in victory, leveling the city and selling its inhabitants into slavery. Before his campaign in Chalcidice was over, he had annihilated a total of thirty-two Greek-speaking city-states.

Atrocities on this scale had not befallen the Greek world since the invasion by the Persians in the previous century. When other Greeks learned of Philip's massacres, there was an outpouring of anger. In Athens, Demosthenes desperately tried to rally support for an alliance against Macedonia; he rightly sensed that the survival of the independent Greek city-states was at risk, for Macedonia was now the dominant political power in the Greek-speaking world.

Meanwhile, Aristotle carried on his research undisturbed, under the protection of his patron and philosophical friend, the tyrant Hermias. At some point he married a girl close to the court at Atarneus. Critics claimed that he had foolishly fallen in love "with a concubine of Hermias, and married her with his consent, and in an excess of delight sacrificed to a weak woman." But other sources explain that the woman Aristotle married was Pythias, the niece and adoptive daughter of Hermias, who blessed the union in hopes of binding the philosopher more closely to himself by ties of kinship as well as of friendship.

Sometime around 345, another one of Aristotle's former colleagues at the Academy, Theophrastus (372–287 B.C.), convinced him to leave the court of Hermias and join a new philosophical colony located in Mytilene, on the island of Lesbos, just off the coast of Asia Minor. To judge from the number of fauna native to the northern Aegean mentioned in his several treatises on animals, Aristotle continued to conduct a great deal of research into zoology at Mytilene, as he had done at Assos.

Less than three years later, Aristotle and his wife and daughter moved again—this time to Macedonia. The ancient biographers say that King Philip had invited Aristotle to tutor his son Alexander, then thirteen years old. At the time, of course, neither Aristotle nor Alexander loomed large in human affairs. Still, for anyone preoccupied by the union of knowledge and power—as

Aristotle obviously was—this was an extraordinary opportunity, though it also carried certain risks.

Never before had a philosopher been invited by a king to mold the character of a young man being groomed to govern the most powerful kingdom of its day. And never before had a philosopher of Greek ancestry been asked to put himself in the service of an alien empire. As the modern German scholar Werner Jaeger justly remarked, "That [Aristotle] undertook the work is more significant of his character than all of his political theories."

For centuries, the most widely read version of the encounter between Aristotle and Alexander was that of Plutarch in his *Parallel Lives*:

> Now, Philip could see that although Alexander was stubborn when it came to resisting compulsion, he was easily led by reasoned argument to the proper course of action, so he not only tried for his own part to use persuasion rather than order him about, but also, because he did not entirely trust the teachers of . . . the usual curriculum to take care of him and educate him well (since education was, in his opinion, a matter of considerable importance and, as Sophocles puts it, "a job for bridles a-plenty and rudders too"), he sent for the most famous and learned of the philosophers, Aristotle.

Most modern scholars doubt that Aristotle was yet that famous. But Philip would presumably have known that Aristotle's father had been a doctor and confidant to his own father. And if he needed an additional reference, he could have turned to Hermias, who had coincidentally struck up a secret partnership with Philip, offering Macedonia an important and powerful ally in Asia Minor, in return for the promise of military aid if Persia attacked Atarneus.

With the blessings of Hermias and a liberal wage from Philip, Aristotle took up the challenge of making a good king out of a headstrong young man, by bridling him with reasoned argument. Plutarch asserts that "Alexander not only received from Aristotle his ethical and political doctrines, but also took in his more profound, secret teachings, which Aristotle's successors used to call the 'oral' and 'esoteric' teachings and did not offer to the public."

In return, according to Plutarch, Philip promised to let Aristotle rebuild and resettle Stagira. At the same time, "Philip gave Aristotle and Alexander, as a place of resort where they could go and study, the sanctuary of the Nymphs at Mieza, where even now people point out the stone seats and shady walks Aristotle used to frequent."

Shortly after Aristotle had started to tutor Alexander, disaster struck his old friend Hermias. In 341, the Persians lured Hermias to a parley under false pretenses. Placed under arrest, the Greek ruler was questioned under torture about his treaty with the Macedonians. His resolute silence earned him a crucifixion. According to the legend, his last wish was that his colleagues be told that "I have done nothing weak or unworthy of philosophy." Aristotle in turn commemorated his philosophical friend in an impassioned panegyric:

> Virtue, greatly striven for by mankind,
> noblest quarry in life,
> for your form, maiden,
> to die is an enviable fate in Greece . . .

Elsewhere in Greece, however, the news about Hermias produced a very different reaction. In Athens, Demosthenes had revealed, and then denounced, the secret alliance between the king of Macedonia and the tyrant of Atarneus. Macedonia was viewed with growing alarm as a barbaric usurper of traditional Greek liberties; the death of her most prominent Greek ally in Asia Minor was cause for celebration. And Aristotle from afar had to know that, by remaining in Macedonia and openly praising Hermias, he had more or less completely mortgaged his future in the Greek-speaking world to the fate of his imperial patrons.

Aristotle in these months supposedly composed several dialogues meant for the edification of Alexander, including one on monarchy and another on colonies. Plutarch claims that Alexander inherited a love for books from his new tutor and cites as evidence a story told by Onesicritus, a court historian who chronicled the king's later campaigns in Asia: "He regarded and referred to the *Iliad* as a handbook on warfare, and carried about with him Aristotle's recension of the text, which he . . . always kept under his pillow along with a dagger." For many years, according to Plutarch, Alexander thus "admired Aristotle and felt just as much affection for him as for his father, as he himself used to say, on the grounds that while his father gave him life, Aristotle gave him the gift of putting that life to good use."

In 340, before Philip left Macedonia for a campaign against Byzantium, he named sixteen-year-old Alexander regent of Macedonia, to govern in the king's absence. No longer needed as a tutor, Aristotle supposedly repaired to Chalcidice, where, according to some ancient sources, he supervised the rebuilding and resettlement of Stagira, for which he also drafted a new constitution.

One thing is clear: for the rest of Aristotle's life, wherever he went, he remained in close contact with Macedonian patrons. In one ancient biography, we read that Aristotle "was so valued by Philip and [his wife] Olympias that they set up a statue of him with themselves; and the philosopher, being such a considerable part of the kingdom, through his philosophy used his power as an instrument for benefaction, doing good both to individuals and to entire cities and to all men at one and the same time. For the benefits he bestowed on individuals are revealed in the letters which he wrote on various subjects to the royal couple."

In these years, Aristotle also developed an even closer friendship with Antipater, one of Philip's most trusted associates, who had taken a personal interest in Alexander's education. Antipater served as Macedonia's ambassador to Athens in 346 and 338, and after Alexander succeeded Philip as king, he came to function as an imperial viceroy for Europe. Aristotle's ties to Antipater strengthened as time went by, and they apparently corresponded regularly (though no one can be certain if the letters that survive are genuine). That they were indeed close friends is confirmed by the particulars of Aristotle's will, which names Antipater as his executor.

Philip was relentless in his efforts to widen the scope of the Macedonian empire. By besieging Byzantium (where present-day Istanbul is situated), he aimed to gain control of the Bosphorus and the Hellespont. Since Athens fed its population with grain shipped through the waters connecting the Euxene (the present-day Black Sea) to the Aegean, Philip's actions posed a direct threat to the city. Athens responded by dispatching a military force to Byzantium, which helped that city break Philip's siege.

Turning his attention back to the Greek mainland, Philip next marched south. In 338, with Alexander at his side, Philip's forces defeated the combined armies of Thebes and Athens at Chaeronea. Moderating his previous scorched-earth policy, Philip merely garrisoned Thebes and demanded that Athens capitulate by affirming formally the king's leadership of what he now characterized as a pan-Hellenic campaign against Darius of Persia. A congress of Greek city-states was duly convened in Corinth, to create the so-called League of Corinth and to put the military forces of various city-states at the king's disposal.

Two years later, the king was dead, killed by one of his bodyguards—and Alexander became the new king. He was twenty years old.

Sensing a chance to throw off the Macedonian yoke, Athens and Thebes rose in revolt. Alexander and his soldiers marched promptly to Thebes, where they crushed the army defending the city, then raped women, looted property, and razed every building, selling most of the former residents into slavery—a savage reminder of the sort of rough justice meted out to the empire's enemies.

When news of this catastrophe reached Athens, the city promptly capitulated—and Alexander, in a display of sovereign mercy as capricious as the slaughter that preceded it, showed clemency. Shortly afterward, almost all the other Greek city-states duly reconvened in Corinth, in order to swear fealty to Alexander.

In 335, under the tacit protection of Alexander and Antipater, Aristotle returned in triumph to Athens, which was still the cultural capital of the Greek-speaking world. He promptly organized a new school of his own. Since the time of Pericles, the city had been host to a variety of schools run by Sophists and philosophically minded orators like Isocrates. But Aristotle chose to create a new community of philosophical friends, not unlike Plato's Academy, and to compete directly with his former friend Xenocrates, who had become scholarch of the Academy after the death of Speusippus. Perhaps as a result, rumors began to spread about Aristotle's "vanity and prodigious ingratitude" toward Plato, and toward the school that had nurtured his philosophical interests for two decades.

Because Aristotle's new school was located in a gymnasium attached to the temple of Lycian Apollo, it became known as the Lyceum. And because the site included a *peripatos*, a colonnaded garden "where he would walk up and down philosophizing with students until it was time for a rub-down," his followers were called Peripatetics.

Aristotle became the school's formal scholarch, "first among equals." But as had been true at the Academy, there was no requirement that members of Aristotle's community slavishly parrot his own theoretical views. Some associates like Theophrastus were old friends and senior scholars who taught and conducted independent research; others were younger men who came to study at their side. It was an institution open to the public, though of course most auditors were gentlemen of means, who didn't need to work for a living. Aristotle began to number important men among his pupils, though the great majority of the school's known members were, like Aristotle himself, resident aliens, not Athenians.

Just how the school paid for its ambitious program of instruction and research is unclear. The Lyceum, like the Academy under Plato, did not take tuition from students. As a foreigner, Aristotle could not legally own property in Athens, so his school had only a tenuous title to its grounds. But since Aristotle himself was wealthier than ever, he may have been able to defray personally some of the expenses. Pliny the Elder (A.D. 23–79) claimed that Alexander gave Aristotle a large cash gift to build his library and also put "thousands of men" at his disposal to gather information about flora and fauna. This may be a wild exaggeration. But under the circumstances, there can be little doubt that the Lyceum depended on Macedonian support, both financial and political. (In pointed contrast, Xenocrates refused gifts to the Academy from the Macedonians, in protest of what he, like many Athenians, regarded as an illegitimate occupation.)

Aristotle had amassed a vast personal library of books, maps, and scholarly documents, and he put this archive at the disposal of his colleagues and students. This archive became a model for the famous ancient library at Alexandria (supposedly first organized a few decades later by one of Aristotle's students, Demetrius of Phaleron). Scholars at the Lyceum began to collate and catalog material from the archive in order to publish sets of related documents (for example, a collection of the constitutions of different Greek city-states)—the first time information like this had been systematically compiled and organized.

Aristotle's scholarly manuscripts and lecture notes were also archived, and those that survived form the basis of the Aristotelian corpus as we know it today. The sheer range of the topics discussed in this corpus suggests that Aristotle was a paragon of disciplined inquiry, with an apparently insatiable appetite for information about the phenomenal world, in addition to his ongoing curiosity about rhetoric and the proper criteria for evaluating competing arguments. By now, he had evolved an independent approach to many of the questions that had puzzled Plato and Socrates. Aristotle was the first to establish logic as a field of inquiry in its own right. He was the first to classify and categorize flora and fauna in an organized way, and one of the first to produce causal explanations for a variety of physical phenomena. Unlike Plato, he refused to entertain the theory that reality ultimately consisted of immaterial Forms. Instead, he chose to examine perceptible things and natural bodies—plants, animals, human beings, cities, the sun, the stars—in an effort to acquire concrete knowledge about the particulars of what really exists. This reality he believed to be blessed by the gods: "All things have by nature something divine in them," he said; and also, "God and nature create nothing that does not fulfill a purpose."

Instruction in empirical research as well as in logic played a large role in the curriculum. It is said that Aristotle lectured at night to the Lyceum's students, and in the morning to a large public. Where Plato had prized debate and "dialectic," Aristotle (or his ancient editors) preferred to present the results of his school's inquiries in the form of systematic summaries. Unlike Plato's dialogues, which are open to multiple readings that often yield inconclusive results, Aristotle's treatises generally consist of authoritative statements that reflect apparently expert knowledge about things that actually exist. As the twentieth-century political philosopher Leo Strauss put it, Aristotle believed that "wisdom and not merely philosophy is available. This . . . [is] *the* difference between Plato and Aristotle."

It seems true that Aristotle thought that we could develop reliable information about a great many matters. Whereas Plato in many contexts implies a need to separate sharply real knowledge, which is of unchanging Forms, from the transient world of sentient experience, Aristotle favors an approach to understanding that, in principle, allows a philosopher to *learn* from experience. This helps to explain the sheer range of Aristotle's research on a vast array of concrete topics and may also help to explain his relative adroitness in practical affairs: unlike Plato, whose intransigent idealism proved self-defeating in Syracuse, Aristotle was a pragmatist whose political experience taught him, among other things, how to build strategic alliances with powerful patrons.

In 330, presumably with the support of the Macedonian authorities who now controlled Delphi, Aristotle was honored with an official inscription. Whatever his enemies might say, he was now a consecrated Greek hero, as renowned as such Athenian contemporaries as Isocrates, Diogenes, and Demosthenes. An ancient bust of Aristotle excavated in Athens in 2007 depicts a man with "an aquiline nose, protruding forehead, floppy hair and minute eyes and mouth."

As happened with Socrates, Plato, and Diogenes, stories began to circulate about the famous philosopher. The ancient sources report that Aristotle spoke with a lisp, that his calves were slender, his eyes small, and "he was conspicuous by his attire, his rings, and the cut of his hair." They say that "when Diogenes offered him dried figs, Aristotle saw that the Cynic had prepared a caustic quip if he did not accept them; so he took them, and said Diogenes had lost his figs, and his joke as well. On another occasion, he took the figs when offered, lifted them aloft . . . , and returned them with an exclamation: 'Great is Diogenes.'" (Anecdotes like this are about the only evidence that Aristotle had a sense of humor.)

During the first years of the Lyceum's existence, Alexander the Great was cutting a triumphant, if bloody, swath across Asia with his army and attended by a small retinue of philosophers, including Callisthenes (c. 360–328 B.C.), Aristotle's nephew and also a graduate of the Lyceum. As Plutarch tells the story, Alexander's worst impulses were bridled for a while by the love for philosophy that Aristotle had been the first to instill. This love Callisthenes valiantly endeavored to reinforce through his personal integrity: exemplifying a kind of rational unity, his way of life was "so orderly, dignified, and self-sufficient" that it annoyed "all the other sophists and flatterers" in the king's entourage.

Unfortunately, as Alexander conquered more kingdoms to add to his growing empire, he grew increasingly capricious and cruel, and also more credulous about various superstitious beliefs at odds with his enlightened upbringing. The ancient sources say that Alexander began to dress and act like an oriental despot and demanded that his subjects prostrate themselves before him and worship him as if he were a god—conduct that Callisthenes had the courage (or recklessness) to tell the king directly that he thought was wrong.

In 330, Alexander successfully quelled a mutiny among some of his troops who had lost confidence in his leadership. But as his army plunged deeper into Asia, the qualms of his soldiers and the king's paranoia grew. Alexander gradually became convinced that Callisthenes was out to get him, and that the philosopher's "haughty" demeanor—or perhaps his continued willingness to criticize the king's increasingly arbitrary behavior—"smacked of the intention to overthrow the monarchy." So Alexander placed Aristotle's nephew under arrest, charging that he was part of a conspiracy to kill the king.

One might anticipate that Aristotle would be upset when he heard about what had happened to his nephew, who after all had tried to live up to the original Socratic model of moral perfection. But according to the classical biographers, Aristotle neither criticized Alexander nor rushed to defend Callisthenes. On the contrary, Plutarch recounts how he criticized his nephew's lack of prudence, or "common sense," and in this context, it is telling that Aristotle's capital virtue of *phronesis* seems synonymous with expedience, as if common sense suggests that Callisthenes should have found some way to acquiesce in his sovereign's erratic and increasingly destructive behavior. (If Socrates were to have exercised "prudence" in this sense, he presumably should have escaped into exile rather than drunk the hemlock.)

Some say that Alexander planned to keep Callisthenes in prison until he was able to bring him back to Greece for a public trial so that Aristotle could witness, and participate in, his protégé's ritual humiliation. But before that could happen, in 327, "Callisthenes died a vastly overweight, louse-ridden man," writes Plutarch, who (like Aristotle in his account) apparently thinks this fate was a just desert for Callisthenes' frank criticism of Alexander's imperious conduct.

Less than four years later, in 323, while planning a voyage by sea around Arabia, Alexander died suddenly. He was thirty-three years old. The cause was probably a fever. But Plutarch also reports a rumor (which he doubts to be true) that "Aristotle put Antipater up to the deed, and that the collection of the poison was entirely Aristotle's doing."

This sort of rumor shows how biography had become a political football in the ancient world. In matters of life and death, calumnies were answered tit for tat. Some scholars speculate that later Aristotelians, hoping to dissociate Aristotle from the most sensational charges of his ancient biographers and the infamous acts of his most famous student, spread the rumor that Aristotle and his best friend in the Macedonian court had ultimately turned on and killed the tyrant. But this seems unlikely, since Aristotle had continued to depend on Alexander and the Macedonian regime for support and protection after the death of his nephew.

In any case, Alexander's death left Aristotle in an exposed position. When news of the king's death reached Athens, it unleashed popular outrage and violent demonstrations against Macedonian rule. Aristotle had made a number of enemies in the city, from his estranged former friends in the Academy to patriotic politicians like Demosthenes, who had never ceased to inveigh against the Macedonian usurper. Aristotle's enemies in Athens lost no time in cobbling together an indictment against him. He was of course suspected of treason, because of his ties to Alexander and Antipater. But the main charge (as usual in ancient Athens) was "impiety." The evidence in support of this accusation included Aristotle's paean to Hermias, and possibly as well a passage in which he is alleged to have said that prayers and sacrifices to the gods were of no use. The problem with his panegyric to Hermias was that Aristotle had lauded the tyrant alongside Heracles, Achilles, and Ajax—an insulting juxtaposition, at least to pious democrats.

According to the ancient biographers, Aristotle's honorific inscription at Delphi was torn down and thrown into a well. (In the twentieth century, archaeologists in fact found fragments of a tablet honoring Aristotle at the bottom of a well in Delphi.) "As for the honor which was voted me at Delphi and of which I have now been stripped," Aristotle wrote Antipater in a fragment of a letter (perhaps authentic) that survives, "I am neither greatly concerned nor greatly unconcerned."

He was, however, concerned for his physical safety. So he took the step that Socrates, in the same circumstances, had defiantly refused to take: exile. Facing a trial by democratic jury, he fled from Athens to Chalcis, a city safely garrisoned by Macedonian troops under the control of Antipater. "I will not allow the Athenians to wrong philosophy twice," he wrote Antipater in another fragment of a letter that survives. Even if this passage is a forgery, it effectively anticipates, and tries to forestall, an unfavorable comparison between Aristotle and Socrates.

In 322, less than a year after he arrived in Chalcis, Aristotle died, probably of natural causes (though early Christian writers spread the rumor that he had been so mortified at his inability to explain the ebb and flow of a river that he hurled himself into its waters, and so drowned).

In his will, Aristotle named Antipater executor of his estate, "in all matters and in perpetuity." To Herpyllis, the common-law wife he took after the death of Pythia, he left a house of her choice, several slaves, a great deal of silverware, and a dowry, should she wish to remarry. He left money to erect two statues—of Zeus and Athena—in Stagira, the city of his birth. He carefully explained how his two teenage children by Pythia were to be cared for, and he provided generously for the well-being of his extended family and friends. As a modern scholar remarks, "Aristotle reveals himself in this testament as having the virtues you would expect of a gentleman of ample property, who recognizes the responsibilities that come with wealth."

Aristotle's disciple Theophrastus became scholarch of the Lyceum, and for several years the Peripatetics maintained their presence in Athens. But in the generation after the death of Theophrastus in 287, the Peripatetics were overshadowed by the schools of Epicurus, Zeno, and Pyrrho, as well as the Academy of Plato and the shameless antics of the Cynics. Copies of Aristotle's published works (with a few exceptions) became hard to come by. His private papers remained unpublished.

That left the field open to Aristotle's critics. The most zealous was perhaps Epicurus, who in 306 founded the Garden, which quickly rivaled the Academy and Lyceum as a school for aspiring philosophers, in part by retailing a "four-part cure" for the worries of human beings ("Don't fear god, don't worry about death; what's good is easy to get, and what's terrible is easy to endure"). Epicurus lashed out at the unseemliness of Aristotle's lavish manner of life and charged that he was a learned "busybody" and "show off"—a useless bookworm. Aristotle in his conduct contradicted key tenets of the Epicurean ethic and made it perversely hard to reach what Epicurus regarded as the true goal of philosophy: a life lived in tranquillity, undisturbed by superfluous luxuries and idle curiosity. As a result, Epicurus charged that Aristotle posed a greater danger to philosophy, properly understood, than "those whose profession it is to train young men for engaging in politics."

Writing from a completely different point of view, Theocritus of Chios (310–250 B.C.), an Athenian from the school of Isocrates, emphatically agreed, composing a bitter epitaph: "To Hermias the eunuch, the slave withal of Eubulus, an empty monument was raised by empty-witted Aristotle, who by constraint of a lawless appetite chose to dwell at the mouth of a muddy stream rather than in the Academy."

And so it happened that the man posterity would come to know as "the philosopher" fell into disrepute among many of Athens's most prominent philosophers. Only with the publication of the corpus established by Andronicus did Aristotle's reputation begin to revive, and even then the revaluation occurred slowly and took many centuries.

Given the vehemence of his critics, though, one has to wonder: Did Aristotle disgrace philosophy as a way of life, as Epicurus alleged? Was he a hypocrite who failed to exemplify in practice his own professed morality?

To the second question, the only appropriate answer is no. Epicurus was characteristically dogmatic in supposing that philosophy could have only one proper goal, attained through only one manner of living. A primary goal of a good life according to Aristotle was not tranquillity but the exercise of reason or intellect, which he regarded as the divine element in the human being. Unlike Epicurus, Aristotle regarded the quest for knowledge as an end in itself and not just a means to attaining existential peace and quiet. Moreover, some of the most salient facts about Aristotle's conduct—his extraordinary industriousness as a scholar, the vast range of his interests, the rigor of his reasoning, his unflagging insistence on clear definitions and logical argument—exemplify what many philosophers today regard as capital virtues.

That Aristotle was no ascetic like Socrates seems obvious from what bio-graphical evidence has survived. But it is also true that he never endorsed such asceticism. At one point, he remarks that "roughly speaking, perhaps," when it comes to the good things of life, "necessities are more desirable, while su-perfluities are better." In analogous fashion, in the *Eudemian Ethics* he writes that "any choice or possession of the natural goods—goods of the body, wealth, friends, or any other goods—which will best produce contemplation . . . is best, and is the finest standard; and any which, either because of deficiency or because of excess, prevents us from cultivating [the mind] and from contem-plating, is bad." In other words, if great wealth, or the patronage of a tyrant, helped to support a life of unfettered empirical inquiry and quiet reflection, then it might justly be judged a good thing, and not an evil.

At first glance, then, there seems no glaring contradiction between the conduct advocated in Aristotle's ethical theories and the life that he appears to have lived. The situation with his political theories, however, is more compli-cated.

In his treatise *Politics*, Aristotle rejects Plato's argument for philosopher-kings in favor of what superficially appears to be a more measured and realis-tic evaluation of different forms of government. The ideal scale of association, Aristotle holds in one passage, is an independent city the size of a Greek polis: as one modern translator has rendered one of Aristotle's most famous asser-tions, "Man is by nature an animal intended to live in a *polis*." Elsewhere in his treatise on politics, Aristotle suggests that the best practicable form of polis is a so-called polity, a constitutional government composed of mixed elements, both oligarchic and democratic, enabling ordinary citizens, through periodic voting, to elect a government composed only of wealthy gentlemen.

But in reality, the Greek city-states in Aristotle's day were pawns of the Macedonian monarchy. And Aristotle in practice ignored his avowed prefer-ence for a compact polis with a mixed constitution, allying himself instead with an imperial monarchy of unprecedented scale and aggressive brutality. This was moreover a choice Aristotle made in full knowledge of the regime's cruel character: after all, a few years before he moved to Macedonia, Philip had razed the city of his birth and sold its inhabitants into slavery.

When deeds and words conflict, Aristotle teaches in his *Ethics*, it is the deeds and not the words that are dispositive: "Hence we ought to examine what has been said by applying to it what we do and how we live; and if what has been said harmonizes with what we do, we should accept it, but if it conflicts, we [should] account it [mere] words." By this criterion, most of what Aristotle says about the best possible polis in the *Politics* is mere words.

When Aristotle moved back to Athens in 335, the quid pro quo seems to have been simple: the Lyceum would serve as a cultural monument to the edifying aims of the colonial occupier, and Aristotle would in turn be enabled to pursue a very ambitious program of empirical and theoretical research.

For many years afterward, Aristotle lived a peaceful life at the Lyceum while Alexander marched from victory to victory in the East. But at least one modern scholar has speculated that he did not die a happy man, alone as he was in exile, far from his circle of friends and community of scholars.

It was bad luck that Alexander's death left Aristotle vulnerable to his enemies in Athens, and it was even worse luck that Aristotle fell ill and died when he did. At the time, his most powerful ally, Antipater, was preoccupied in Macedonia with a messy struggle over the dynastic succession, and in Greece itself with the need to put down yet another Athenian-led revolt against Macedonian rule. If he had lived awhile longer, Aristotle might have been able, with the help of Antipater, to return triumphantly to Athens and resume his teaching at the Lyceum under Antipater's protection.

In any case, if Aristotle had any second thoughts about the choices he had made en route to his unfortunate exile, we will never know. It is probably true, as a sympathetic modern biographer has remarked, that "the absolutely objective way in which Aristotle presented himself to the outside world was already based on a conscious separation of personal from externalized activities." Still, it is striking that we have no evidence whatsoever that Aristotle, like Plato in his *Seventh Letter*, ever offered an introspective account in which he tried to explain the key moral and political decisions that helped determine the course of his life.

Instead, Aristotle implicitly externalized the rational unity that Socrates had sought to realize through a harmony between conduct and core beliefs.

He differed sharply from Diogenes in that his central public achievement was not the way he conducted his life but the systematic and dispassionate fashion in which he aimed to understand empirical reality, by describing in his public lectures and writings a visible world that he represented as an awe-inspiring rational unity.

This distinctively naturalistic vision is perhaps most beautifully expressed in a passage from an early work:

> Suppose there were men who had always lived underground, in good and well-lighted dwellings, adorned with statues and pictures, and furnished with everything in which those who are thought happy abound. Suppose, however, that they have never gone above ground, but had learned by report and hearsay that there was a divine spirit and power. Suppose that then, at some time, the jaws of the earth opened, and they were able to escape and make their way from those hidden realms into those regions that we inhabit. When they suddenly saw earth and seas and skies, when they learned the grandeur of clouds and the power of winds, when they saw the sun and realized not only its grandeur and beauty but also its power, by which it fills the sky with light and makes the day; when, again, night darkened the lands and they saw the whole sky picked out and adorned with stars, and the varying light of the moon as it waxes and wanes, and the risings and settings of all these bodies, and their courses settled and immutable to all eternity; when they saw those things, most certainly would they have judged both that there are gods, and that these great works are the works of gods.

This is a beguiling vision of divine order—it is easy to understand why Cicero quoted these words—and passages like this facilitated the rediscovery of Aristotle's work and the rehabilitation of his reputation in later centuries.

A key turning point came when the pagan philosopher Porphyry (c. A.D. 232–c. 304) produced a philosophical system that reconciled and synthesized what he took to be the core moral and metaphysical teachings of Plato and Aristotle. By the Middle Ages, the sovereign authority of Plato and Aristotle over the thinking of Jewish, Christian, and Muslim theologians, scientists, and poets was rivaled only by the final authority of God's word in the Torah, Bible, and Koran. Treated as an indispensable and encyclopedic supplement to sacred scripture and Plato's dialogues, Aristotle's corpus was for many centuries carefully examined by those seeking authoritative information about natural and social phenomena, and also authoritative answers to classical philosophical questions.

One result was scholasticism, in which the quest for wisdom was replaced by a close reading of Aristotle's consecrated texts and the composition of detailed, often lifeless commentaries on them.

But another, and even more consequential, result was the creation of a lasting link between philosophy and science (*episteme*). When Aristotle in the *Posterior Analytics* says that one knows (*epistatai*) a thing unconditionally when one knows the appropriate explanation of it, and knows that the thing cannot be otherwise, he represents scientific knowledge as the fruit of an analytic inquiry into a natural world composed of empirical facts, and he implies—*pace* Plato— that the acquisition of such knowledge requires neither a conversion of the soul in practice, nor a crowning moment of divine revelation.

"All men by nature desire to know," declares the first sentence of Aristotle's *Metaphysics*. "In everything natural there is something marvelous," we read in his treatise on *Parts of Animals*.

In Aristotle's voracious desire to comprehend the particulars of the visible world, especially as expressed in the most beautiful of his surviving texts, there is, indeed, something marvelous. But in his overmastering passion for scientific knowledge, as in his expedient alliances with tyrants, there also seems something Faustian.

Aristotle himself insisted that it is sometimes "difficult to know whether one knows or not." But in the matter of his life and character, it is not that hard.

"As with most ancient personalities," observes one scholar, "we know just enough about Aristotle's to realize that we cannot really know anything about it." Given the conflicting scraps of evidence that survive, we will never be sure if Aristotle in fact embodied "an ideal of human excellence"—or, instead, as his earliest detractors insinuated through the anecdotes they chose to preserve, something else entirely.

SENECA

The Death of Seneca, 1633, oil on canvas, by Claude Vignon (1593–1670), a French painter influenced by Caravaggio. Condemned to death by Nero in 65, the philosopher has voluntarily sliced open his veins—his retinue includes a scribe who is poised to record his every dying thought. (Louvre, Paris, France/Peter Willi/The Bridgeman Art Library International)

W hat is personal integrity? How can one cultivate and maintain a consistently good will? These were pressing questions for Lucius Annaeus Seneca, the most important of the pagan philosophers to write, and to think, in Latin. Yet Seneca's personal inconsistencies are so well documented that his foremost modern biographer simply takes his hypocrisy for granted, in order to analyze the extent of the gulf between his words—as a moralist, a dramatist, and a philosopher—and his deeds, especially in his years as the principal adviser to the Roman emperor Nero (A.D.3 7–68).

Some contradictions seem obvious. In many passages in his writing, Seneca praises poverty, but he amassed great wealth. He championed a life of contemplation but spent many years as Nero's most powerful adviser. His most personal texts depict their author as a man of apparent humility and highlight the common experience of common men as a precious source of philosophic insight, but more public declamations, including an essay on clemency he dedicated to Nero, reveal a master of rhetoric superbly skilled in making a lawless sovereign seem like a perfectly fine embodiment of the common good.

It is no wonder that students of his life and work should sharply disagree about their merits. The most painstaking of the Roman historians, Tacitus, was not unsympathetic to Seneca's aims as Nero's most powerful minister. In the fourth century, a legend arose that Seneca had met and corresponded with Paul—the spurious letters survive—and he was one of the few pagan thinkers that the theorists of early Christianity regarded as pertinent to their own quest for wisdom, as attested by Jerome. Modern historians, working with much more substantial evidence than the patristic fathers had available, have argued at length that Seneca was "the conscience of an empire," a man whose moral integrity for long stayed the hand of Nero and spared Rome from even greater atrocities.

But from the start, Seneca had enemies—and they had their doubts about his true character. In 58, Publius Sullius Rufus, a venal administrator under Nero's predecessor, the emperor Claudius, taunted Seneca in public: "By what wisdom, by which precepts of the philosophers had he procured three hundred million sesterces"—an extraordinary sum of money—"within a four-year period of royal friendship?" The Roman historian Dio Cassius concurred, saying that "though he censured the extravagance of others, he had five hundred tables of citrus wood with legs of ivory, all identically alike, and he served banquets on them." (This accusation is improbable but amusing, since, if true, it would unmask a famous Stoic as a gourmandizing showman, with a taste for lavish spectacle.)

Though the sources for Seneca's life are far more abundant than those for the lives of Socrates, Plato, Diogenes, or Aristotle, the evidence is uneven. The externals of his political career are recounted by three different Roman historians: Tacitus, Dio Cassius, and Suetonius. Still, we know much less about how Seneca behaved in public—as an orator, a senator, a tutor to Nero, the emperor's principal policy maker for several years—than we know about his inner life. That is because the historical sources, vivid though some of them are, are greatly outnumbered by the many eloquent texts by Seneca himself, describing in even more vivid detail his quest to become a perfectly wise man.

And there is a further paradox. Though the written texts sometimes take the outward form of letters written to a friend, these letters cannot be regarded as straightforwardly autobiographical: they are also hortatory, highly stylized, and written as admonitions to oneself, even when they are ostensibly reports of events in the author's life that are addressed to others.

Thus, in a series of 124 *Moral Letters* he wrote at the end of his life, Seneca presents an idealized account of a moral odyssey, in order to compose his thoughts for at least three audiences: for himself; for Lucilius, his explicit addressee and philosophical friend; and for posterity.

Though various personal details imply that the odyssey is the author's own, a reader must keep in mind the idealizing and fictive aspects of biography and autobiography in the ancient world, and also keep in view Seneca's two parallel lives: the one external, lived in the public eye; the other internal, called to judgment every day before the court of his conscience.

The externals of the author's life rarely enter into the written exhortations to himself, perhaps because one of the primary aims of the *Moral Letters* is to enable the author to purge himself of concern for such externals, in order to cultivate a feeling of inward freedom, serenely independent of the vagaries of fate, indifferent to the waxing and waning of public renown, political power, private property—external goods a wise man should be able to have, or have not, at will.

"Never have I trusted Fortune, even when she seemed to be offering peace; the blessings she most fondly bestowed upon me—money, office, and influence—I stored all of them in a place from which she could take them back without disturbing me. Between them and me, I have kept a wide space."

Money, office, and influence were things that Lucius Annaeus Seneca had been raised to appreciate. He was born around 1 B.C. in Corduba, in Hispania, at the time the largest province of the Roman Empire. The second of three children of colonial settlers who had emigrated from Italy, Seneca grew up speaking Latin. His father, Lucius Annaeus Seneca the Elder, was a man of letters and a gentleman wealthy enough to belong to the "equestrian order" of Roman citizens, a rank that entitled a man to participate in the administration of the empire. Despite his fame as a writer and repeated sojourns in Rome, the elder Seneca, thwarted in his ambition to become a Roman senator, devoted himself to preparing his two oldest sons for a career in politics, bringing them at an early age to Rome to be trained in declamation and debate. It was in this context—as a young man being groomed to enter politics, not unlike Plato before he met Socrates—that Seneca first came into contact with philosophy in general, and Stocism specifically.

By this time, during the reigns of Augustus (31 B.C.–A.D. 14) and Tiberius (A.D. 14–37), philosophers were not hard to find in Rome. The prominence of philosophy in the city's public life dates to the middle of the second century B.C., roughly the same time that the cities of the Greek peninsula, including Athens, became Roman protectorates. In 155 B.C., Athens had sent an embassy of philosophers to Rome, to argue, successfully, for the remission of a fine that the Romans had imposed on their city. "These men argue so well that they could gain anything they ask for," remarked Cato the Elder, who persuaded his fellow senators to settle the matter of the fine, "so that these men may return to their schools and lecture to the sons of Greece, while the youth of Rome give ear to their laws and magistrates, as in the past."

In the first centuries after Plato's founding of the Academy, Athens remained the primary place to study philosophy as a way of life. In addition to the informal training on offer from Cynics hoping to follow in the footsteps of Diogenes, four major schools flourished in the city, associated with various locales and exemplary figures: besides Plato's school and that of Aristotle (resurrected once his treatises became widely known in the first century B.C.), there was the garden where Epicurus established the first avowedly materialist sect of philosophers—and the stoa (or porch) where Zeno of Citium (c. 334–262 B.C.) first organized the philosophical tendency known as Stoicism.

Zeno had started out in philosophy by conducting an ascetic life modeled on those of Socrates, Diogenes, and Crates, an avowed Cynic and Zeno's first teacher. Like Socrates, Zeno preached a stern ethic of integrity and aimed in practice to present a perfect example of consistently good conduct, in this way offering others an existential "pattern for imitation in perfect consistency with his teaching." Like Plato, Zeno wrote books, including one on political institutions; like Aristotle, he promoted a beguiling vision of divine order, arguing that the visible world of nature offered evidence of a cosmos that was providentially organized and governed by intelligible laws, which offered a pattern for both just political institutions and the proper conduct of life.

In the centuries that followed, under the leadership of Chrysippus of Soli (c. 280–207 B.C.) and Panaetius of Rhodes (185–109 B.C.), Stoicism evolved into a comprehensive system of philosophy. For example, Stoics taught that an individual's perceptions could be considered reliable only if they met certain conditions, including clarity, probability, and agreement with the perceptions of others. Stoic cosmology depicted a deterministic universe that ran through repeating but predetermined cycles (a notion that was doubtless one inspiration for Nietzsche's similar concept of "eternal recurrence"). Because Stoics adhered to a set of characteristic doctrines, they became particularly bitter opponents of the Academy throughout the Hellenistic period, when Plato's old school was associated not with upholding a positive theory of the Forms but rather with thoroughgoing skepticism.

Although students of the stoa were expected to uphold core teachings and master the rudiments of the school's distinctive logic, which concerned the structure of language as well as the validity of various types of reasoning, the crux of Stoicism remained firmly practical, as one might expect from a school descended from Socrates and Diogenes. As one modern scholar puts it, the intellectual energies of most prominent Stoics were focused on elaborating "a systematic plan of life that would, ideally, assure purposefulness, serenity, dignity, and social utility at every waking moment, irrespective of external circumstances." The goal of a good life was to attain tranquillity, or peace of mind, which the Stoics regarded as synonymous with true happiness. Reaching this goal required understanding and reconciling oneself to the divine (and inevitable) order of the universe, and also training oneself through spiritual as well as physical exercises to become inured to physical pain and indifferent to a host of potentially overpowering and disquieting emotions, such as anger, lust, jealousy, grief, and—above all—the fear of death. Committed adherents characteristically wore a short coat made of coarse cloth (the so-called philosopher's cloak) and slept on a hard bed—an austerity that even wealthy Stoics were enjoined to practice from time to time.

For two centuries, roughly from 155 B.C. until A.D. 65, the training of a proper Roman gentleman climaxed with a study of philosophy. Cicero (106–43 B.C.) was only one of many aspiring Roman noblemen who journeyed to Athens in the first century B.C. to complete his training to enter public life by visiting the city's famous philosophical schools. In Seneca's day, by contrast, Greece was no longer the center of the philosophical world—and Seneca, despite being bilingual like any other cultured Roman nobleman, himself never made the pilgrimage to Athens. By then, some of the city's traditional schools had been closed, and Greek-speaking philosophers had migrated throughout the empire.

This philosophical diaspora changed the nature of philosophy as it had been practiced in Athens. Gone were the small circles of friends gathered around a spiritual master, a living scholarch whose way of life carried on the example of the founding master. The tendency of some Academic and Peripatetic philosophers to value the contemplative life above all others was reinforced by the rise of scattered communities of aspiring philosophers who, in the absence of a living scholarch, dedicated themselves to what later generations would call "scholasticism"—the close reading of consecrated texts and the composition of detailed commentaries on these texts as the heart of philosophical practice.

This theoretical and bookish trend in philosophy had to contend with the pragmatic cast of Rome's political culture, which scorned abstract idealism and stressed civic duties. Cynics and many Epicureans and Stoics also stoutly resisted scholasticism. One result was the rise among Roman philosophers of a lively debate over the relative merits of a life of service to the res publica versus a life of leisure (*otium* in Latin) primarily devoted to philosophizing. Another result was the rise of a distinctively Roman version of Stoicism, which managed to fuse, albeit in an unstable admixture, a contemplative cosmology with a strict code of personal conduct, as well as a renewed fascination with the idea, first broached by Plato, of somehow producing a philosopher-king—not a surprising development, given the evolution of Roman political institutions in Seneca's day.

These were troubled years for the Roman Empire. Edward Gibbon remarked on the "peculiar misery of the Roman people under the tyrants" and avowed that no people had suffered as much as the Romans under their emperors Tiberius, Caligula, Claudius, and Nero. All these emperors were the objects of cult worship: Caligula was a madman, Nero, an infantile sadist, and none of them proved able to resist purging their enemies through means fair and foul. "Fortune will totter back and forth between them," Seneca wrote in his greatest play, the tragedy of *Thyestes*, speaking of ancient Greece but in terms that perfectly evoked the Julio-Claudian dynasty: "power follows misery and misery power, and waves of disaster batter the kingdom." The consolidation of arbitrary power in the person of the Roman emperor in these decades certainly helps to explain the renewed appeal of the Platonic idea of training a philosopher-king, whose good character might restrain his sovereign will.

But at first, Seneca was far more interested in the search for wisdom than in the pursuit of political power. One of Seneca's first important teachers, the Stoic Attalus (fl. A.D. 14–37), a Greek-speaking philosopher from Alexandria, stressed the value of cultivating few wants and endorsed the paradox (familiar since Diogenes the Cynic) that the wise man, even if he lacks political power or material wealth, was nevertheless a true king. "When I used to hear Attalus denouncing sin, error, and the evils of life," Seneca recalled years later, "I often felt sorry for mankind and regarded Attalus as a noble and majestic being—above our mortal heights . . . Whenever he castigated our pleasure-seeking lives, and extolled personal purity, moderation in diet, and a mind free from unnecessary, not to speak of unlawful, pleasures, the desire came upon me to limit my food and drink . . . And later, when I returned to the duties of a citizen, I did indeed keep a few of these good resolutions."

At the same time, Seneca was reading the works of Quintus Sextius, who a century before had become the first Roman to found a school of philosophy: "My God, what strength and spirit one finds in him! This is not the case with all philosophers . . . They ordain, dispute, quibble"—wooden pedants, unable to inspire or convert a soul to a better way of life. Revering Sextius as a model of virtue—he would later claim that he was at heart a Stoic—Seneca adopted his master's daily routine of introspective self-examination: "Sextius had this habit, and when the day was over and he had retired to his nightly rest, he would put these questions to his soul: 'What bad habit have you cured today? What fault have you resisted? In what respect are you better?' . . . And how delightful the sleep that follows this survey—how tranquil it is, how deep and untroubled, when the soul has either praised or admonished itself."

Seneca finally came under the spell of the foremost living follower of Sextius, Papirius Fabianus, a Roman teacher who seems to have been even more vehemently committed to the Socratic and Stoic ideal of integrity: "the man communicated a disposition, not mere words, that spoke to the soul, and not just the ears." No armchair philosopher, Fabianus was, Seneca writes elsewhere, a philosopher in the "true and ancient" sense, a man who despised dialectical debating tricks, preferring to teach by example, showing students in practice how he had mastered his passions.

By following in the footsteps of Fabianus and Sextius as well as of Attalus, while simultaneously mastering rhetoric, Seneca became a characteristically Roman sort of philosophical pragmatist, skilled in both introspection and oratory. "Philosophy is both contemplative and active," he declares in one of his *Moral Letters*. He treats every form of experience, properly examined, as a potential source of wisdom.

Around A.D. 25, Seneca departed for Egypt, where he continued his study of philosophy and also investigated a growing range of natural phenomena, from comets to the annual flooding of the Nile, both among the topics analyzed in his one surviving treatise, *Naturales Quaestiones*. It is not clear whether he was away for a few months, or a few years. But by 31, he was back in Rome, and by around 35 or 36, he had entered the Senate and embarked on a belated political career. He may have delayed an entry into politics out of a supervening interest in the pursuit of wisdom and the study of nature, or he may have waited until his rhetorical talents had ripened. He took an innovative approach to composing orations in Latin, refining a style that was distinctively terse and condensed—and of great appeal to the public.

By 39, Seneca had become perhaps the most famous orator in the empire. Legend has it that the emperor Gaius, better known to posterity as Caligula, grew jealous of Seneca's reputation. After hearing an especially eloquent speech to the Senate that year, the emperor ordered his execution, only to be talked out of the idea by a "female associate," who argued that since Seneca suffered from consumption, he would be dead soon in any case.

Seneca did suffer from poor health. "His body was ugly, weak, and subject to many kinds of illnesses," writes his Renaissance biographer Giannozzo Manetti, "and he was an invalid, though he tolerated his ailments with a steady spirit." And after Caligula spared his life, it seems that Seneca dramatically lowered his public profile: in one of the letters to Lucilius, evoking the swift passage of time, he remarks that it "was but a moment ago" that "I began to plead in public, that I lost the desire, that I lost the ability."

Two years later, Caligula was dead—and Seneca's political career was abruptly aborted. The new emperor, Claudius, accused Seneca of committing immoral acts with Caligula's sister Julia Lavilla, a charge evidently concocted at the behest of the new emperor's wife at the time, Valeria Messalina, who feared that Seneca's silver tongue posed a threat to her husband and her own ambitions. (Besides being Seneca's alleged paramour, Julia Lavilla was rumored to have slept not only with Caligula himself but also with the emperor's favorite catamites. But since Roman politicians often used accusations and rumors of moral turpitude as a means to vanquish enemies, one cannot assume that the twenty-four-year-old Julia had ever done any such things.) Declared guilty, Seneca was again spared the death penalty in a show of mercy by the new emperor and exiled to the island of Corsica.

For the next eight years, Seneca lived a life of not quite spartan leisure, with a financial allowance and a library at his disposal. (Like Aristotle, he was a bibliophile who read avidly.) Though confined to the island, he was free to resume his pursuit of wisdom in peace and quiet, and he was also at liberty to write.

Although there is no agreed-upon chronology of Seneca's writings, it seems that five of his so-called *Dialogi*, which are in fact moral essays, date from this period: three related essays on anger, which Seneca considers the worst of passions, because it is so hard to control; a consoling essay dedicated to his mother, Helvia, which includes several passages that implicitly align Seneca with the Senate opposition to imperial tyranny; and a thinly veiled plea for a pardon, disguised as yet another consoling essay, this one addressed to Polybius, a minister in the court of Claudius.

In 48, Seneca's nemesis, Valeria Messalina, was summarily executed after it was revealed that she had committed bigamy with Gaius Silius, with whom she had plotted to depose the emperor. A year later, Claudius married his niece Agrippina—another sister of Caligula's—a woman of equally large lusts, especially for power. And the emperor now recalled Seneca, apparently at the behest of Agrippina.

Why would Claudius suddenly change his mind about Seneca? In his *Annals*, Tacitus gives three reasons apart from the death of Messalina: Agrippina wanted to curry favor with the public by rescuing from oblivion a well-known man of letters; she wanted to have Seneca train Domitus, her headstrong son from a prior marriage, and the future emperor Nero; and she apparently hoped to enlist Seneca as an ally who might help her advance her own political ambitions.

This explanation implies that Seneca had developed a reputation not just as an orator and writer but also as an adroit political operative. But apart from tutoring Nero, what Seneca actually *did* over the next five years is unknown. There is no hard evidence that he aided and abetted Agrippina in various bloody schemes—and no evidence that he did not. Agrippina supposedly regarded philosophical studies as a complete waste of time and banned them from Nero's curriculum. And Seneca is said to have "hid the works of the early rhetoricians" from Nero, "intending to be admired himself as long as possible." (If these stories are true, it would mean that Seneca did not train Nero in the two subjects, rhetoric and philosophy, that he was perhaps most suited to teach.)

Some scholars speculate that Seneca composed most of his plays in these years. Eight tragedies survive—the only extant tragedies in Latin, which reflects the relative unimportance of this form of drama within Rome's political culture. The staging of new tragedies was not a defining civic event in Rome, as it had been in classical Athens. Instead, plays were either declaimed or staged privately, in the villas and palaces of the rich and powerful. Some modern scholars thus suggest that Seneca's plays were originally meant, in part, to edify young Nero and other spectators from the imperial court.

As a group, the plays stand in stark contrast to Seneca's moral essays. In general, Seneca does not stage virtue, nor does he portray Stoic heroes. Of course, what characters say in a play need not reflect a playwright's personal views, but the views expressed by many of Seneca's dramatic characters pose a sufficient challenge to the Stoic views he expressed elsewhere that modern accounts of his philosophy often avoid them altogether.

Rehearsing sagas from Greek mythology previously recounted by Greek poets and playwrights, Seneca in his tragedies dramatizes a world gone mad, in which the central obsession is the acquisition of arbitrary power. Although a chorus interrupts the action to issue episodic moral exhortations to tame destructive passions, the principal characters are unbridled in their sound and fury, as if the collapse of reason is inevitable, and we in the audience must bear witness to the inevitable result—a chaotic world of infinite cruelty.

The young Nero was an aspiring singer and actor who had a passion for poetry and drama, as well as for chariot races, gladiatorial contests, and lavish parties. Perhaps Seneca hoped that his plays might capture the young man's imagination and so supplement his moral instruction, though one can only wonder what an artistically inclined young man like Nero might take to be the moral of Seneca's gory dramas.

It is true that his tyrants invariably come to grief. Anger unleashed leads to misery, as one would predict from reading Seneca's moral essays. To that extent, the plays can be understood as cautionary tales, meant to warn an omnipotent sovereign of the wretchedness suffered by those who would exercise power unlimited by either law or conscience.

But in a tragedy like *Thyestes*, there is an odd imbalance between the tepid and sometimes incoherent moralizing of the chorus and the stunning acts of cruelty on display. When the king wreaks vengeance on his nasty brother Thyestes by feeding him the organs and entrails of his children, evil has rarely seemed so radical—or so entertaining.

Claudius's rule, at first mild, devolved into a reign of terror as fearful as that of Caligula, or Tiberius before him, as suspected enemies were tried behind closed doors or simply murdered. Agrippina meanwhile convinced Claudius, who had a young son, Britannicus, by his marriage to Messalina, to adopt Domitius as his own, and then persuaded Claudius to give Octavia, his daughter by Messalina, in marriage to Domitius. The wedding, held in 52 or 53, strengthened the claim that Domitius, rather than Britannicus, should succeed Claudius as emperor.

In these years, Seneca secured his reputation as Rome's most famous living writer of verse and prose. His moral essays advising readers how to search for wisdom and attain tranquillity were widely distributed and widely read, and his tragedies were well known. "Finally, Rome had a thinker of a scope to rival those of Greece," remarks one modern historian. "Sometimes, to soothe the Roman inferiority complex, Seneca would drop a xenophobic phrase, granting that the Greeks were not perfect, and could even be childish, so laying claim to intellectual independence from the founders of his own sect," Zeno and Chrysippus.

In October 54, someone slipped Claudius poisonous mushrooms—the work of Agrippina, rumor had it. She lost no time in having the seventeen-year-old Nero swiftly named the new emperor, amid general relief that a reign of terror was ending and a renewed hope that the young man would prove wiser than his unlamented predecessor.

Seneca rose along with his pedagogical protégé, becoming one of the three most powerful people in the Roman Empire. As an officially appointed *amicus principis*, or "friend of the emperor," Seneca functioned as a confidant, speechwriter, and in-house intellectual rolled into one. At first, he worked closely with Nero's other key *amicus*, Burrus, the prefect in charge of the Praetorian Guard, the emperor's personal unit of armed bodyguards. Together, Seneca and Burrus for the next several years promulgated the emperor's policies, and—perhaps more important—protected his public image. According to Tacitus, Seneca had a penchant for straight talk and a dislike of sycophancy, which meant that Nero "more often experienced free speaking from Seneca than servitude." No one knows if Nero actually listened, but for the first few years of his reign, it is certainly true that Nero implemented relatively prudent public policies.

The growing influence of Seneca and Burrus over Nero displeased Agrippina. Angling to find another base of power, she shifted her allegiance to Britannicus and started to promote him as of "true and worthy stock," a direct descendant of the Claudian line, unlike Nero—and therefore a more legitimate emperor (as well as someone she might be more able to manipulate). Aware of Agrippina's plans for Britannicus, and evidently unable to keep his anger and fear in check according to sound Stoic precepts, Nero secretly had aides slip poison to Britannicus at a public banquet held in 55.

Tacitus reports that Nero impassively witnessed the boy's death rattle, remarking that there was no cause for alarm, that it was probably just an epileptic seizure. The murder at a stroke dispatched his chief rival and foiled Agrippina's ambitions.

Seneca and Burrus carried on as if nothing had happened: "to begin a reign with the murder of a potential rival had become a dynastic tradition." And a few months later, neither Seneca nor his Roman readers evidently thought it odd that he dedicated an essay on mercy to the emperor Nero.

This was not a new theme for Seneca. It was highly desirable that the emperor appear clement, and Seneca had already composed several speeches for Nero to deliver before the Senate, promising a policy of mercy, to distinguish the new emperor from his predecessor. The speeches helped Seneca, too, to "testify to the honorableness of his precepts (or for vaunting his talent)," as Tacitus acidly remarks.

Seneca's essay begins with the image of a mirror—a familiar rhetorical device, since (as Seneca writes elsewhere) "mirrors were invented in order that man may know himself, destined to attain many benefits from this: first, knowledge of himself; next, in certain directions, wisdom." His essay on clemency will, like a mirror that flatters, display the sovereign in an edifying light by describing how a good ruler wisely uses his unrestricted powers (a trope that inspired the "Mirror for Princes" genre of Renaissance court literature).

The good ruler is "chosen to serve on earth as vicar of the gods," an absolute arbiter of life and death, with all things at his disposal—and, yet, he shall also become a paragon of monumental self-restraint, "sparing to the utmost of even the meanest blood." "It is the rarest praise," writes Seneca, "hitherto denied to all other princes, that you have coveted for yourself—innocence of wrong."

Coming in the wake of Nero's infamous murder of his younger half brother, this fawning admonition is a breathtaking blend of realpolitik and moral exhortation—a plea that the young sovereign persist in a public policy of mercy, precisely because of his discretionary authority: "In a position of unlimited power this is in the truest sense self-control and all-embracing love of the human race even as of oneself."

Throughout the essay, Seneca implicitly endorses a form of rule without accountability, addressing his remarks to a *Rex*, or King—a taboo idea in Rome ever since the Republic had made monarchy, never mind tyranny, suspect in theory. In effect, Seneca was dangling the prospect that Nero might become a "true" king, an exemplar of philosophical self-restraint, bound not by laws but rather by his own manifest goodness.

According to Tacitus, Seneca and Burrus did for a while block "the general trend toward slaughter" during Nero's reign. The second of Rome's "five good emperors," Trajan (53–117), is even said to have argued that no Roman princeps had ever matched the "five good years" of Nero.

But Seneca's service to the emperor left him open to the charge of hypocrisy, an opening seized by Publius Sullius Rufus, a defendant accused of venality under Claudius. Taking the stand in his trial, Sullius rounded on the *amicus principis*, accusing him of dangerous liaisons with *both* of Caligula's sisters—not just Julia Lavilla but also Agrippina herself. And one by one he enumerated the apparent contradictions between Seneca's words and his conduct, starting with the most unforgivable of all: "For while denouncing tyranny, he was making himself the teacher of a tyrant."

In response to Sullius's attack on his reputation, Seneca likely composed a veiled apologia, in the form of the essay *De Vita Beata* (The Happy Life). In composing this response, certain facts had to be conceded in advance: In return for his services to the emperor, Seneca had been rewarded liberally with estates, lands, villas. Because he was a principal friend of the emperor, he was also in a position to extend loans to various imperial subjects, including the chiefs of Great Britain, recently brought under Roman rule. He worked assiduously at "increasing his mighty wealth," as Tacitus writes, loaning money at interest and investing in land, amassing one of the greatest fortunes of his age.

Implicitly acknowledging these facts, Seneca's rejoinder was disarming: "I am not wise nor . . . shall I ever be. Require me not to be equal to the best, but better than the worst. I am satisfied if every day I reduce my vices and reprove my errors."

Moreover, what the moralist says in his essays "is not said of myself—I am sunk deep in vice of every kind—but said for someone who may actually achieve something great."

Apparently unable to defend straightforwardly the integrity of his own words and deeds, Seneca tries to shift the terms of the argument. It is too easy, he suggests, to "taunt Plato because he sought for money, Aristotle because he accepted it," and easier still to "bring up Alcibiades as a reproach." It would be foolish, Seneca implies, to blame Socrates or any of the other great philosophers—never mind Seneca himself—for honestly trying to transform Alcibiades, Dionysius the Younger, and Alexander the Great into good rulers. Critics who carped about the shortcomings of the great philosophers when they attempted to bridle absolute sovereigns would do better to examine their own consciences and to heed the advice of the author, "who, looking from a height, foresees the storms" that threaten to turn the souls who populate imperial Rome upside down, "whirled and spun about as if some hurricane had seized them." In other words, if a philosopher has access to a powerful ruler, it is better to try taming him, and fail, than never to try restraining him at all.

Seneca certainly had his hands full. Despite the death of Britannicus, Agrippina remained so intent on trying to exercise power over her son that "in the middle of the day, at a time when Nero was warm with wine and with banqueting, she quite often offered herself to him in his drunken state, smartly made up and prepared for incest."

Struggling to prevent the emperor from turning himself into a hopelessly compromised and "perverted prince" who could no longer command the loyalty of his troops, Seneca, according to Tacitus, "sought from a female some defense against these womanly allurements," soliciting a concubine to distract Nero from his mother's amorous advances.

Finally, in 59, the twenty-two-year-old sovereign put his foot down. He concluded that the only sure way of ending the unwelcome advances of his mother was, in the words of Tacitus, "to kill her, debating only whether by poison or the sword or some other violence." He planned to set her afloat in a boat booby-trapped to sink. The boat sank, but Agrippina swam to safety—and Nero, in a panic, summoned Burrus and Seneca to solicit their advice about what to do next. There was a long silence, reports Tacitus, and then Seneca joined Nero and Burrus in mulling over how best to finish the botched murder. The emperor in the meantime decided to make it seem as if he had foiled a plot by a lone assailant sent by Agrippina to have *him* assassinated, in order to make it plausible that she would subsequently take her own life upon hearing that her treason had been discovered. He then dispatched a trio of assailants to make sure a sword was sunk into her belly.

As Nero's public relations expert, Seneca was left to put the best possible spin on this new turn of events. In the speech he composed for Nero to deliver to the Senate, the emperor accused Agrippina of many acts of treachery and treason, laying the tyranny of Claudius at her feet and also explaining how he had thwarted her scheme to usurp his legitimate authority. He retailed the story of Agrippina's shipwreck and her subsequent attempt to kill the emperor.

Unfortunately, as Tacitus puts it, "Who could be found so dull as to believe that [the shipwreck] had been a chance occurrence? Or that a shipwrecked woman had sent a single man with a weapon" to kill the emperor? "Therefore it was no longer Nero, whose monstrousness outstripped the complaints of all, but Seneca who was the subject of adverse rumor, because in such a speech he had inscribed a confession"—in effect, he had condoned a matricide.

Nero's "five good years" were now at an end. The emperor continued to affect generosity of character, in 62 going so far as to drum up a phony charge of treason in order to commute the death penalty, in a parody of the moral principles championed by Seneca. In the spring of that year, Seneca's longtime ally, Burrus, died in murky circumstances—some say of ill health, others say of poison slipped into his food on Nero's orders.

The death of Burrus left Seneca dangerously isolated. More vulnerable to public criticism than ever, he had to contend with mounting complaints from some of Nero's companions that the philosopher was still increasing his wealth beyond the limits appropriate to a private person, that he was living in unseemly luxury in villas and estates more suitable to an emperor, and that he was unjustly taking credit for everything brilliant and honorable that the emperor said or did.

It was under these circumstances that Seneca pleaded with Nero to let him retire from public life. It was an extraordinary speech, at least as represented in the pages of Tacitus: "You have surrounded me with immeasurable favor, with money uncountable," the philosopher acknowledges, expressing his gratitude for his good fortune but also expressing a personal anxiety. "Where is that spirit contented with modesty?" Why has he compromised his Stoic ideals?

"I am confronted with only one defense," Seneca continues, "that I was obliged not to defy your gifts"—a real concern for an *amicus principis*, for whom the possession of wealth would be a conventional sign of authority, an expected concomitant of the good fortune enjoyed by truly great men, and hence a kind of duty.

Seneca formally asks Nero to release him from this duty. "Every surplus creates resentment," he points out, and the luxuriousness of his life has become a burden "that hangs over me," filled as it is with too many possessions that "dazzle me by their flash." The philosopher is at risk of being corrupted by the perquisites of his position. Still, Seneca concedes that Nero has absolute power over him, can do with him whatever he wants. So he begs his sovereign for his help and asks him please to "order my estate to be administered by your procurators and accepted as part of your fortune," suggesting that such a gesture will add to the emperor's glory.

Nero is unmoved. He proudly points out that he is no longer susceptible, as he once was, to his old tutor's seductive rhetoric. He disagrees with Seneca's assertion that he has received too much from him, saying that rather the opposite is true: "More has been held by men who are in no way equal to your artistic skills." Above all, he sharply disputes the assertion that allowing Seneca to pursue a more philosophical way of life will enhance his ruler's reputation: "It will be neither your moderation, should you return the money, nor your retirement, should you abandon your princeps, but my greed and the dread of my cruelty that will be on the lips of all; and, however much your self-denial may be praised, it will certainly not be appropriate for a wise man to accept glory from the same circumstances as procures infamy for his friend."

This would not be the last time that Seneca tried to distance himself from the increasingly odious acts of his erstwhile protégé. In 64, after Nero had looted precious objects from temples throughout the empire in order to fill the imperial coffers in the wake of Rome's Great Fire, Seneca, hoping to avoid being associated with the sacrilege, again "pleaded for retirement to the distant countryside and, when that was not granted, fabricated ill health and, as if with a muscular disease, did not leave his bedroom." Once again, Nero refused Seneca's request to retire (though he did accept Seneca's offer of money).

For three years after the death of Burrus, the emperor steadfastly insisted that Seneca maintain the pretense that he was still an *amicus principis*, even if he was out of the public eye and no longer consulted on matters of policy and preferment. Unable to retire in any formal way, Seneca in these months retreated instead to a kind of inner exile, devoting his time to writing a treatise on natural questions and simultaneously reinventing himself by writing the series of

Moral Letters that represent his finest philosophical achievement.

These letters are ostensibly addressed to Lucilius, one of Seneca's oldest friends. A self-made man who had reached the equestrian order, Lucilius had risen to become a procurator in Sicily before retiring from politics around the time Seneca took to feigning illness in order to stay in his study. Younger than Seneca by several years, Lucilius wrote poetry and pursued philosophy in addition to his career in politics; their convergent interests made Lucilius a natural interlocutor once Seneca turned his energy to writing, and he evidently asked Lucilius to work his way through his book *Natural Questions*, and also—perhaps—drafts of some of his *Moral Letters*.

From the start, Seneca meant to publish these letters. A means of redeeming his good name and securing the esteem of posterity, the collected letters represented his last will and philosophical testament. The particulars of his friendship with Lucilius offered him a pretext for staging a conversation with himself in an epistolary epic that is completely one-sided (we never see a single letter from Lucilius himself).

In the earliest letters, Lucilius is still a procurator, and Seneca warns him of the blandishments of public life. His correspondent is depicted as challenging Seneca's own inconsistencies as a Stoic and also trying to decide whether to commit himself to following the Stoic program for achieving peace of mind. In subsequent letters, Seneca becomes more adamant about the corrosive effects of politics on the pursuit of wisdom and the cultivation of a good will—and he praises his friend's eventual decision to retire gradually from politics, in order to take up philosophy as his new way of life.

The remainder of the letters concern what form of philosophy to pursue and how best to pursue it.

Modern scholars have noted the inconsistent persona that Seneca adopts, sometimes lecturing Lucilius in a patronizing manner, at other times presenting himself as an imperfect student just like his addressee. The moral progress ascribed to Lucilius is also improbably rapid. In effect, Seneca seems to describe a number of episodes from his own convoluted quest for wisdom and organize them into an artfully arranged series of essays. Written as if off-the-cuff, and initially concerned with quotidian experiences, the letters gradually rise from the particular to the universal, finally rehearsing core Stoic arguments about the power of reason, the art of self-control, and the strength of the wise man's will.

Along the way, Seneca commends *otium*, or "retirement," a retreat into the peace and quiet appropriate to self-examination, while urging the philosopher to avoid untoward displays of either arrogant censoriousness or ostentatious humility that might provoke the jealousy of his sovereign. At the same time, the letters bristle with scarcely veiled criticism of vices and cultural trends that a contemporary reader would naturally associate with Nero. For example, in one passage, Seneca describes walking past a Neapolitan theater that is jammed with people who want to hear a musical show, on his way to a nearly empty hall where a handful of people are discussing "how to be a good man." (His former student now fancied himself a singer, and Nero had in fact appeared at a Neapolitan theater.) "I am ashamed of mankind," writes Seneca.

Under the pretext, not wholly false, of ill health, he calls himself a "sick man." He had wagered that he could use philosophy in practice to teach his sovereign to curb his impulses to behave badly—but that wager was lost. His king was a tyrant, and this tyrant was a fool. His tutor had been a fool, too. The educator must be educated. The sick soul can, and must, heal itself—by reflecting, day after day, on how to become better, healthier, more upright and firm, more free and just. The free time that Seneca now took for himself, over Nero's objections, was a time to take stock, and the *Moral Letters* are the written record of that self-examination.

As was the custom in those days, Seneca probably dictated his letters to a secretary, and probably published at least some of them while still in the midst of composing the series. "His last years," remarks a modern historian, "were those of a writer fully occupied with writing, of a meditator fully occupied by his interior life, of a subject of Nero knowing that his days were numbered, and of a citizen confronted by a political drama that demanded he take a stand."

Again and again in the course of these letters, Seneca returns to the topic of integrity: "Nature weds us to no vice," he writes in one letter. "She brought us forth whole and free [*integros ac liberos*]." But still struggling, as he is, to purge himself of bad habits based on false opinions about what a good life really involves, Seneca himself is obviously unable to realize what Nature intends: he is not yet free and whole. Unable (yet) to achieve integrity, Seneca tries to understand what his manifold shortcomings might mean.

"Hasten to find me," he writes early in the correspondence, "but hasten to find yourself first. Make progress, and before all else, endeavor to be consistent with yourself. And when you would find out whether you have accomplished anything, consider whether you want [*voles*] the same things today that you wanted [*veils*] yesterday. A shifting of the will [*voluntatis*] indicates that the soul is at sea, blown by the wind." Constancy and resoluteness are hallmarks of integrity in this account: being good hinges on the cultivation of a will sufficiently strong and unwavering to be consistently effective in practice.

"Let this be the kernel of my idea," Seneca writes later in the correspondence: "say what we feel, and feel what we say; harmonize talk with life." That this is easier said than done is proved by Seneca's own daily examination of himself: "I will watch myself continually, a most useful habit, and review each day." A key motive for moral progress is shame at one's inconsistency: "It is a great thing to play the role of man. Only the wise man can; the rest of us slip from one character to another."

Read with an open mind, and as a whole, the *Moral Letters* leave a striking impression: although we scarcely glimpse Seneca as a public figure, we do find a three-dimensional personality, a changeable self, an individual who is recognizably human—all too human—because imperfect, inconstant, in conflict and contradiction with himself, someone, in short, utterly unlike the stick-figure representation of perfect integrity we find on display in Plato's *Apology*.

This is something new. Seneca's representation of inner experience in his *Moral Letters* occupies a pivotal place in the histories of autobiography and self-examination. As Michel Foucault put it, "The task of testing oneself, examining oneself, monitoring oneself in a series of clearly defined exercises, makes the question of truth—the truth concerning what one is, what one does, and what one is capable of doing—central to the formation of the ethical subject." Because a Stoic is aiming for perfect integrity and often falling short, one is constantly reminding oneself of one's failings. The result is an intransigently conflicted self, someone who must struggle to become better—someone worthy of comparison with Socrates.

And that is not all. By choosing to write a serious work of philosophy in

Latin, and by choosing, unlike Cicero, to *think* in Latin, Seneca elaborates a new vocabulary for analyzing this protean self. It is Latin that allows him to link *voluntas* (the noun for "will," "wish," and "inclination") and *voluntarium* (a noun for what is done by free choice) to *volo* (the verb for "willing," "wanting," and "wishing"), and to link all these terms to the philosophic quest for rational unity and moral perfection. Similarly, consistency of character, the cultivation of conduct that hangs together logically, is linked to *constantia*, perseverance (or constancy) in willing one thing, or, to gloss it differently, a resolute adherence to principle no matter the consequences, even death.

For the first time in Western thought, the concept of a *will* that is naturally *free* comes to play a central role in philosophy. In voluntary action, body and soul commingle, and in a good will, bodily impulse becomes subordinated to self-conscious purpose, in order to create (or forestall) physical motion; hence, the will is that part of the human being that one must struggle most mightily to control, by purging the body of irrational impulses, of needless desires, passions, and emotions, so that one becomes able to act, instead, only on reasonable impulses. "Conduct cannot be right unless the will is right, for the will is the source of action"—what we want determines how we conduct ourselves. "The will cannot be right unless the soul is right," for *animus*, the soul, is what animates our being and what becomes manifest in what we want.

A life conducted according to the dictates of reason can be virtuous. And virtue becomes a synonym for a will that is strong, and healthy, and resolutely effective—the good will.

Such a will, according to the *Moral Letters*, ought to be good enough to be applied effectively in any, and every, conceivable circumstance. "So the wise man will develop virtue, if he may, in the midst of wealth, or, if not, in poverty ... Whatever fate hands him, he will do something memorable."

Here is a good example of Seneca applying a general rule of morality in specific circumstances. The particulars of a situation will alter the challenges that a man of virtue will face in his conduct of life: someone who is poor must steel his will to withstand privations serenely; someone who is lucky enough to be rich must develop the strength to resist the temptations of luxury. Whether he is pitiably poor or, like Seneca himself, enviably rich, does not finally matter, for a man with a good, strong will can be virtuous in *any* circumstances. Ergo, being rich is not, in principle, incompatible with philosophy as a way of life. This is how a good casuist proves consistency where others might perceive only a contradiction.

Anyone inclined to find fault with Seneca will probably hear in such passages special pleading or—to use another pejorative term given currency in the twentieth century by Freudian psychoanalysis—a rationalization.

To complicate matters, Seneca frequently confesses that though he praises virtue, and can describe the kind of life a wise man ought to live, he is *not*, like Socrates, a man whose talk harmonizes with his life. By his own account, he doesn't yet hang together; he is still inconsistent in word and deed: "Listen to me as you would if I were talking to myself. I am admitting to you my inmost thoughts and, with you as my guest, I'm taking myself to task." Whereas the reader of Plato's *Apology* may behold Socrates as a model of perfect integrity, the reader of Seneca's *Moral Letters* is invited to evaluate the author's moral character against the backdrop of his conscious struggle to forge a rationally unified self, in part by writing letters that lay out his manifold shortcomings.

But this means, paradoxically, that anyone inclined to credit Seneca is liable to see him as one version of a real philosopher: a man of authentically Socratic *aspirations*, who knows that he does not know, who concedes, over and over again, that he is *imperfectus*—incomplete, unfinished, imperfect.

However one judges the character of Seneca as the author represents himself in his *Moral Letters*, one is liable to be struck by the evenness and serenity of his tone, which suggest that a calm, composed mood had settled over the seeker of wisdom. And while Seneca acknowledges the insurmountable obstacles that fate may sometimes place in a philosopher's path, just as he sometimes acknowledges his frustration at his failure to make more moral progress, as a last resort he takes heart from Socrates and the example he set at the end of his life: "If you like, live. If not, return to where you came from." The ability to take one's life proved the power of the will. Suicide was a guarantee of independence—"dying well" was always an option, if living well proved impossible.

Up to the very end, Seneca had tried to make philosophy compatible with imperial politics—but Nero, having marginalized Seneca, regarded him with growing suspicion. One is reminded of how Alexander the Great eventually turned against Aristotle's nephew and protégé, the philosopher Callisthenes.

Eminent philosophers had won the confidence of both Alexander and Nero while they were still young. But both kings rapidly lost their appetite for philosophy after they had tasted the perquisites of power, and they became suspicious of the moralists still in their midst. Whereas Alexander simply placed Callisthenes under arrest, Nero increasingly treated *all* of Rome's philosophers as potential enemies.

"It is a mistake," Seneca writes in the *Moral Letters*, "to believe that those who have loyally dedicated themselves to philosophy are stubborn and rebellious and defiant towards magistrates or kings or those who administer affairs." Though this missive amounted to an open letter to the emperor, begging him to change his mind, Nero was evidently unconvinced. He had resolved to make Seneca an early victim of his campaign against Rome's philosophers.

According to Tacitus, Nero had first tried to poison Seneca, but the plot was foiled when Seneca refused a drink offered by a visitor in order to adhere to his modest diet of wild fruit and spring water. But then, in 65, Nero got wind of a plot to assassinate him, organized in part by Calpurnius Piso, a popular descendant of the Republican nobility who was relatively unsullied by the court intrigues that had engulfed the Julio-Claudian dynasty from Caligula on. His coconspirators included senators, imperial administrators, officers of the Praetorian Guard, and one of the imperial prefects. The plot fell apart when the conspiracy was revealed. Nero's paranoia, already pronounced, now became florid, and he condemned a great many innocent men to death, Seneca the most prominent among them.

The fullest account of Seneca's final hours appears in the *Annals* of Tacitus. When Nero's emissaries conveyed the charges against him, and asked if the philosopher was intending a voluntary death, he showed "no signs of panic; nothing gloomy had been detected in his language or look." When a soldier refused to let him compose a final testament, Seneca "turned to his friends and testified that, since he was prevented from rendering thanks for their services, he was leaving them the image of his life, which was the only thing—but still the finest thing—he had; if they were mindful of it, men so steadfast in friendship would carry with them the reputation for good qualities." When some of those present started to weep, Seneca reminded them of Stoic precepts and "recalled them to fortitude."

Seneca embraced his wife, Pompeia Paulina, who begged to be allowed to take her life simultaneously, and the philosopher said, " 'In such a brave outcome as this, let equal steadfastness be within reach of us both—but the greater brilliancy in that ending of yours.' After that they sliced their arms with the same blow of the sword."

The philosopher was frail, and the blood seeped slowly from the veins that he had sliced open on his arms, his legs, and the back of his knees. When Nero learned that Paulina, too, was taking her life, he ordered his servants to keep her from dying, worried that it might provoke resentment at his cruelty. While slaves and soldiers bound her wounds and stanched the bleeding, Seneca begged his friends to produce the poison that he had previously prepared, "by which those condemned by the Athenians' public court had their lives extinguished."

He asserted his freedom. He drank hemlock, gave thanks to Jupiter the Liberator, the god of the Stoics, and then asked to be carried to a hot tub.

And there he died, "asphyxiated by the steam," according to Tacitus.

In the years that followed, the practice of philosophy generally, and Stoicism specifically, came under harsh attack at Rome. In 65, Nero exiled the Stoic Musonius Rufus, and in 66 banished Demetrius the Cynic from Rome as well. For the next forty years, philosophy was virtually outlawed in Rome. The ban was lifted only when the emperors Nerva (r. 96–98) and Trajan became friends of the philosopher Dio Chrysostom. This rapprochement laid the basis for a reversal in the fortunes of Stoicism at Rome and the apotheosis of the first and only real philosopher-king in the annals of ancient history, Marcus Aurelius (r. 161–180)—the last of Rome's "five good emperors" and the author of the *Meditations*, the most important expression of Roman Stoicism apart from the *Discourses* of Epictetus (55–135) and the *Moral Letters* of Seneca.

In later centuries, scholars and writers naturally linked Seneca with Socrates, given the obvious similarities in their way of dying. "Both were men most zealous for wisdom, the most extraordinary philosophers of their time," writes Giannozzo Manetti in the paired biographies of Socrates and Seneca that he dedicated to King Alfonso of Aragón. "Both were extremely temperate and just; and both eventually suffered utterly unjust deaths because of the envy and enmity of some extremely powerful men."

Philosophy had produced another martyr—and perhaps its most cunning courtier yet.

AUGUSTINE

The Conversion of St. Augustine (detail), tempera on panel, by Fra Angelico (1387–1455), showing Augustine in 386, shortly after reading Romans 13:14 ("Put on the Lord Jesus Christ, and make no provision for the flesh in its lusts"): "At once, with the last words of this sentence, it was as if a light of relief from all anxiety flooded my heart." (Musée d'Art Thomas Henry, Cherbourg, France/Giraudon/The Bridgeman Art Library International)

T he quest for wisdom can be wayward, and a wise man cannot live by reason alone. These are two of the morals that one might draw from Augustine's own account of the first half of his life in his *Confessions*. He began to write this text in 397, shortly after he had been ordained to lead the Catholic church of Hippo, a coastal city in Numidia (modern Algeria), the North African province where he had grown up. Its narrative portions recount his errant early years and how he successively fell under the sway of Cicero's eloquence, Manichaean Gnosticism, systematic skepticism, and pagan Neoplatonism, as he moved from the margins of the Roman Empire to the centers of power in Rome and Milan.

In the story he tells in the *Confessions*, Augustine was forever trying to find the truth, the one and only way of life that might make a man perfectly happy. But the spiritual odyssey he recounts could have occurred only in a culture that was contentiously pluralistic—containing, as late antiquity did, a host of competing programs for securing happiness that left pilgrims free to pass through contradictory communities of shared belief in search of individual enlightenment and personal transformation.

At the end of his odyssey, Augustine dramatically converts to Christianity, after a sequence of events that fuse a growing faith in the transcendent truth-value of Christian Scripture with the kind of mystic rapture promised by a revelation of the Good, as understood by Plotinus (c. 205–270), a pagan Neoplatonist.

But the synthesis of Christianity and Platonism that Augustine so lyrically depicted in the first of his works to be preserved for posterity proved to be inherently unstable in a world of warring and sometimes mutually exclusive sects, both philosophical and religious.

"There is more than one road to wisdom," Augustine had averred in an early dialogue. But he gradually grew wary of "a lust for experimenting and knowing" and became convinced that a good life was best achieved not through the contingencies of one person's reasoned quest for knowledge but rather in a closed community of shared beliefs that authoritatively united argument and order, reason and faith—and forcibly excluded the alternatives.

As Karl Jaspers remarked, Augustine thought "in questions." But he came to preach conformity. The youthful heretic spent his adult life attacking heresies. The man who did more than any other ancient philosopher to elaborate an understanding of every single human being as an animate creature divinely blessed with both intellect and free will also did more than any other classical philosopher to justify explicitly the use of spiritual and political coercion to curb the intellect and tame the will.

Augustine was a voracious reader and a prolific writer. In the years that followed his baptism in 387, he wrote a large number of philosophical dialogues as a Catholic layman, all of them extant. First as a priest and then after he had been installed as bishop of Hippo in 396, he delivered countless sermons and maintained an extensive correspondence, and much of this material survives (indeed, modern researchers continue to discover new manuscripts of previously unknown sermons). After completing his *Confessions*, Augustine concentrated on writing two long treatises, one on the biblical creation story in Genesis, the other on the Trinity. In later years, he wrote an even longer argument for the superiority of Christianity to pagan philosophy, *The City of God*. In addition, he was repeatedly drawn into sectarian disputes, and he produced a voluminous and frequently vehement stream of anathemas against his doctrinal opponents. All these formal Christian works survive, with specific dates assigned to them by Augustine himself. That the first editor of his works and his first biographer, Possidius, composed a *vita* no longer than one of Plutarch's *Lives* tells us more about the conventions of classical biography—which aimed at an edifying brief epitome—than it does about the surviving documentation, which is more than enough to fill the pages of a typically capacious modern life.

Moreover, we apparently know more about Augustine's inner life than we know about that of any other ancient thinker. Even though his *Confessions* cannot be treated simply as a compendium of reliable facts—since the narrative of his life, like any good classical biography, is meant to be an idealizing narrative, as well as a parable of predestination and an allegory of God's inscrutable grace, replete with biblical analogies—the book nonetheless dramatizes some key moments in the author's life, from childhood until his baptism as a Christian. Despite its poetic embellishments, it remains the first great example of autobiography in the West.

Augustine was born in 354 in Thagaste (modern Souk Ahras), a remote inland town in Numidia. His father, Patricius, owned enough land to become a tax collector and town official. His mother, Monica, was a fiercely observant Catholic, who raised her son in the Christian verities: "When I was still a boy, I had heard about eternal life promised to us through the humility of our Lord God, coming down to our pride, and I was already signed with the sign of the cross."

Two generations before Augustine's birth, in 312, the emperor Constantine had converted to Christianity and proclaimed religious toleration throughout the Roman Empire. In the decades that followed—until the emperor Theodosius decreed that the form of Christianity professed by Pope Damasus and by Peter, bishop of Alexandria, represented the one true faith—pagan temples and various heterodox philosophical schools and religious sects continued to flourish alongside the Christian churches. Still, an education in classical (that is, pagan) literature throughout this period remained the passport to imperial advancement.

His father gave Augustine the best education he could afford, sending him away to school between the ages of twelve and sixteen, grooming him for a career in the civil service. Because the boy's talents were manifest and his father's resources limited, he introduced Augustine to one of Thagaste's grandees, Cornelius Romanianus. In the meantime, the boy spent a year out of school, carousing with friends. He acquired a "concubine"—a young woman from a lower class—and fathered a son, Adeodatus, going on to live in a monogamous long-term relationship with the two of them. In the *Confessions*, he also recounts how he stole a pear from a garden for the sheer pleasure of stealing—an emblematic act meant to recall the forbidden fruit of the Garden of Eden and the original sin of Adam and Eve.

In 371, with financial aid from Romanianus, Augustine went to study rhetoric in Carthage, in those days the second-largest city in the Western Empire. Although Augustine struggled with Greek, he excelled in Latin, and he aspired to become a real writer, someone who "weighed the precise meaning of every word." Augustine was nineteen years old when, in the course of this curriculum, he read a hortatory philosophical work, now lost, by Cicero, the *Hortensius*. Overnight, Augustine became a philosopher in the "true and ancient" sense, struggling to transform his conduct of life in accord with Cicero's revelation: "Suddenly, all empty hope for my career lost its appeal; and I was left with an unbelievable fire in my heart, desiring the deathless qualities of Wisdom."

Cicero himself, like many students trained in Plato's Academy in these years, had concluded that a man in search of wisdom can come to know little, if anything, with certainty; a prudent Skeptic, the wise man will be content to expose the erroneous opinions of others, while trying to find the most plausible beliefs to hold on various topics on a case-by-case basis. Inspired though he was by Cicero's account of the quest for wisdom, Augustine bridled at the Skeptic's willingness to settle for beliefs that were merely plausible. Yearning to find more certain sources of knowledge, the adolescent philosopher turned first to the Bible—and then to the esoteric teachings of Mani.

A self-proclaimed "Apostle of Jesus Christ," Mani was a Gnostic visionary from Mesopotomia. In the four decades after his first prophetic vision in 228, Mani had elaborated a new universal religion on missionary tours from India in the East to Egypt in the West. In 276, Persian authorities, alarmed by the challenge the new religion posed to the country's ruling caste of Zoroastrian priests, condemned Mani as a dangerous heretic and had him crucified.

Fortified in their faith by their master's martyrdom, the Manichaeans survived despite continuing persecution and spread Mani's gospel ever more widely, organizing a vanguard party of the embattled but spiritually pure, consisting of clandestine groups of ascetic adepts, the "Elect," who convened followers, or "Auditors," to lecture on Mani's teachings as well as select books from the New Testament. The world was divided into two opposing realms, Mani taught: one of Good, the other of Evil. By nature an inhabitant of the Kingdom of Light, the soul was trapped in a carnal Kingdom of Darkness. Wisdom required a rational understanding of the causes of Evil, which might lead to a divine illumination of the Good, and also an appreciation for certain exemplars, Jesus Christ above all: "Honor to the Perfect Man, the way of peace whereby thou didst come. We bless thy Light-familiar, Christ, the author of our good. Honor to thy Wisdom that has defeated the Error of the Sects."

In 374, when Augustine at the age of twenty briefly returned from Carthage to Thagaste, he was a missionary of his new faith. His mother was hurt by her son's heresy and banned him from her side, until she was reassured by a vision that he would eventually be restored to the Catholic Church. But inspired by his example, two old friends—Romanianus and Augustine's nephew Alypius—converted to the Gnostic faith.

Shortly afterward, Augustine relocated to Carthage, in order to teach rhetoric. A rising star in the Manichaean firmament, he published his first book (now lost), a Manichaean treatise, *The Beautiful and the Appropriate*, in around 380. He was "enthusiastic for wisdom" and ambitious for worldly advancement, the kind of man the imperial elite still liked to count as a friend— and his intellectual brilliance began to attract the attention of powerful patrons. In 383, he moved first to Rome, and then to Milan with the help of Manichaean friends in high places, landing a plum job as public orator at the court of Valentinian II, who was technically the ruler of Italy and the African areas of the empire. In his new post, Augustine was expected to write and deliver annual panegyrics to Valentinian, and give regular speeches publicizing his court's policies. Named to a chair of rhetoric as well, Augustine could reasonably expect further preferments, perhaps even appointment to a high administrative position.

In these years, the empire was in a constant state of emergency, and Milan, near the empire's troubled northern frontier, had grown in importance as a result. The imperial court, which had moved to Milan in response to the crisis, still ruled over a vast territory, but the emperor's standing armies were forced to defend that territory from escalating attacks, by barbarian war bands to the north, just over the Alps, and by the Persian Imperial army to the east.

Milan's most powerful spiritual leader in these years was Ambrose, the city's Catholic bishop, a wily politician who had previously served as the imperial governor of Liguria. Although the new public orator was preoccupied with his career and managing his growing retinue—which included his common-law wife, his son, his mother, and various slaves and stenographers—Augustine was politic enough to pay the bishop a courtesy call to introduce himself. He also occasionally went to church. In the *Confessions*, he recalls seeing the bishop deliver sermons that praised a radically idealistic outlook that seemed to infuse Christianity with a type of abstract fervor that was then fashionable in Milan: "I noticed, repeatedly, in the sermons of our bishop . . . that when speaking of God, [he said] our thoughts should not dwell on any material reality whatsoever, nor when speaking of the soul, for of all things the soul is nearest to God."

Despite his continuing Manichaean connections and attendance at Catholic church services, Augustine recollects in the *Confessions* that he had drifted away from Gnostic orthodoxy without becoming an orthodox Christian, quietly embracing instead a sort of skeptical detachment—paying lip service to different beliefs in different circumstances, without inwardly accepting any of them as true, on the impeccably Socratic grounds that the moral beliefs that mattered most could never be known with the certainty that one can know that $2 + 2 = 4$.

For an imperial orator especially, such an attitude was understandable, even expedient. But Augustine also recalls in the *Confessions* that he was dissatisfied by his doubts, unhappy to feel uncertain.

He decided to organize a group of philosophical companions, jointly committed to learning how to lead a *beata vita*, or a perfectly happy life. This circle at first involved only old friends from Thagaste, including Monica, his older brother Navigius, the teenaged Adeodatus, his patron Romanianus, Alypius, and Nebridus. His mother meanwhile instructed him to send his common-law wife back to Africa so that she could arrange a more suitable marriage.

In the months that followed, Augustine and his circle met regularly to discuss "the ultimate nature of good and evil" and to study the views of different schools of thought, with Augustine as their preceptor. Increasingly disenchanted by Skepticism, Augustine flirted briefly with a materialist account of the cosmos, purged of all supernatural references to a separate, immaterial, and invisible spiritual realm, "for I was so submerged and blinded that I could not think of the light of moral goodness and of a beauty to be embraced for its own sake—beauty seen not by the eye of the flesh, but only by inward discernment."

Augustine was now thirty-two years old. He was successfully launched on an imperial career, at the center of temporal power in Milan. He attended church services, like many of his other philosophical friends, without being a committed Christian and despite his ongoing interest in pagan forms of philosophy. And he had evidently succeeded in creating a vibrant community of fellow philosophers, who took a shared pleasure in reasoned debate about the best life to live.

Still, Augustine was dissatisfied. Although he had complied with his mother's wishes and had asked the mother of his son to go back to Africa, Augustine reports that he wept at her departure—and that, in her absence, his carnal "sins multiplied." A casual Christian with a troubled conscience, he was still ransacking pagan programs for attaining happiness, still searching for knowledge about things both human and divine, still hoping to find the best way of life, trying to become wise in an intellectual context where no one drew a sharp distinction between religion and philosophy, and where a serious attempt to harmonize pagan moral perfectionism with Holy Scripture was championed by the newest member of his philosophical circle, Mallius Theodorus, a committed Neoplatonist who had retired from a succession of high imperial offices in order to devote himself exclusively to study and contemplation.

On one level, Augustine seems to have moved in a fairly tolerant milieu in which Manichaean, Christian, and philosophical thought worlds coexisted. But Ambrose, for one, sternly discouraged any easy compromise between the "worldly" wisdom of the pagan philosophers and the otherworldly teachings of Christ. And it was under these ambiguous yet charged circumstances that Augustine finally embarked on a serious study of the most important philosophical school of late antiquity, founded by the Neoplatonist Plotinus in Rome during the reign of Gallienus (r. 253–268). With Mallius Theodorus as his guide, Augustine began to read with mounting excitement a recent Latin translation of the school's consecrated writings, the *Enneads* (from the Greek *ennea*, for "nine," since each of the treatise's six books contains nine sections).

"We thought that the flame with which we were burning slowly was really the greatest flame," he writes to his old patron Romanianus a few months later: "But look! When certain books *brimming full* . . . wafted their exotic scents to us, and when a few drops of their precious perfume trickled onto that meager flame, they burst into an unbelievable conflagration—unbelievable, Romanianus, unbelievable, and beyond what perhaps even you believe of me—what more shall I say?—even beyond what I believe of myself!"

A set of manuscripts and lectures transcribed and edited in Greek by one of Plotinus's disciples, Porphyry, the *Enneads* begins with an edifying short biography, also by Porphyry, addressed to readers who might wish to perpetuate the master's way of life.

"Plotinus," the *vita* starts, "seemed ashamed of being in a body." He had been born in Egypt in 204 or 205. The precise date was unknown, since Plotinus scorned any celebration of himself, though in later years he did annually celebrate the birthdays of Socrates and Plato with his community of philosophical friends. Like Augustine, Plotinus grew up in a spiritual culture teeming with rival sects—Stoics, Skeptics, Orphics, Cynics, Gnostics, Christians—and was converted to philosophy in Alexandria at the age of twenty-seven by a Platonist preacher named Ammonius.

After mastering the written corpus of Plato's dialogues and letters, Plotinus went abroad to study various contemplative practices, including the "Persian methods [of seeking wisdom] and the system adopted among the Indians." After several years in the East, he settled in Rome, established his own school, and started to give lectures and train adepts, preaching a radically ascetic renunciation of bodily pleasures and elaborating an original doctrine of his own that combined Platonic, Aristotelian, and Stoic elements, all meant to prepare converts for a life exclusively devoted to contemplation and introspective spiritual exercises.

"Plotinus possessed by birth something more than is accorded to other men," Porphyry declares. Like Socrates, he was possessed by a daimon "of the more divine degree," but unlike Socrates, he elaborated a set of meditative techniques to keep "his own divine spirit unceasingly intent upon that inner presence."

His supernatural feats were legendary: Plotinus could read minds and predict the future, and he famously disdained participation in pagan rituals and Christian ceremonies, saying, "It is for those Beings to come to me, not for me to go to them."

The distinctive goal of Plotinus's school became direct communion with God, an out-of-body experience achieved after a separation, through contemplation, of the divine element within, the immaterial soul, from its all-too-human material embodiment. As a result of his own firsthand experience of the divine, Plotinus became convinced that the Manichaeans were mistaken to depict a cosmos divided in two, in perpetual conflict between Good and Evil. Contemplation instead revealed that the world was One, and that only God—the Good—exists, overflowing into the Forms, which offered divine insights intelligible to adepts, who, by carefully studying the dialectical arguments of Plato and Plotinus, could prepare themselves to behold God in a crowning moment of introspective revelation.

The school's proof text, the *Enneads*, is a mixture of dizzying exegesis, often of passages in Plato relating to understanding the immaterial essence of the divine Forms, and direct exhortations, urging the philosopher to become "filled with God" so that "utterly resting, he has become very rest." The style of the writing varies greatly as well, from the esoteric to the eloquent:

> Go back inside yourself and look: if you do not yet see yourself as beautiful, then do as the sculptor does with a statue he wants to make beautiful; he chisels away one part, and levels off another . . . Like him, remove what is superfluous, straighten what is crooked, clean up what is dark and make it bright, and never stop sculpting your own statue, until the godlike splendor of virtue shines forth to you . . . If you see that this is what you have become, then you have become vision. Be confident in yourself: you have already ascended here and now, and no longer need someone

to show you the way. Open your eyes, and see.

In the *Confessions*, Augustine vividly evokes the impact of reading Plotinus and recounts how, by following his example and turning inward to contemplate the divine within, he beheld God—and momentarily felt as One:

> By the Platonic books, I was admonished to return into myself . . . I entered into
> my innermost citadel . . . I entered and with my soul's eye, such as it was, saw
> above that same eye of my soul the immutable light higher than my mind—not the
> light of every day, obvious to anyone, nor a larger version of the same kind which
> would, as it were, have given out a much brighter light and filled everything with
> its magnitude. It was not that light, but a different thing, utterly different from all
> our kinds of light. It transcended my mind, not in the way that oil floats on water,
> nor as heaven is above earth. It was superior because it made me, and I was inferior
> because I was made by it. The person who knows the truth knows it, and he who
> knows it, knows eternity. Love knows it. Eternal truth and true love and beloved
> eternity: you are my God. To you I sigh day and night. When I first came to know
> you, you raised me up to make me see that what I saw is Being, and that I who saw
> am not yet Being. And you gave a shock to the weakness of my sight by the strong
> radiance of your rays, and I trembled with love and awe. And I found myself far
> from you in the region of dissimilarity, and . . . you cried from far away: "Now, I am
> who I am." I heard in the way one hears within the heart, and all doubt left me.

His moment of vision left Augustine certain that God exists and convinced that the Manichaeans were mistaken: "Whatever things exist are good,
and the evil into whose origins I was inquiring is not a substance." Evil as such
is nonexistent. The apparent wickedness of mankind is to be explained instead by "a perversity of will," a darkening of the soul, when it turns "away
from the highest substance," God—the radiant Being within.

Augustine's elation, however, was transient. His moment of vision passed.
"My God, I was caught up to you by your beauty, and quickly torn away from
you by my weight." He sank back into his old way of life and resumed his customary habits, even though he believed his worldly ambitions and sexual desires to be blameworthy. But the memory of what he had witnessed endured,

along with "a desire for that of which I had the aroma, but which I had not yet the capacity to eat."

Augustine no longer had any doubts about the reality of God. But he still had questions about the relationship between the teachings of Plotinus and the Word of God. It seemed as if God could be comprehended through the Intellect and experienced directly through a set of spiritual exercises that purged the soul of its material trappings. But if so, what room did such exercises leave for the example of Jesus Christ, and what role should the Intellect assign the authority of Holy Scripture? Was it possible to reconcile Neoplatonism and Christianity—or, as Ambrose had preached, was it necessary for Augustine to choose one way of life over the other?

In a state of perplexity about how he might turn his ecstatic moment of vision into something more permanent and sustaining, Augustine "looked back on the religion implanted in us as boys," he wrote to Romanianus shortly afterward. "And so stumbling, hastening, hesitating, I snatched up the Apostle Paul." He read again Paul's letters, especially those addressed to the Romans and the Corinthians, at the suggestion of Simplicianus, a priest in Milan and a Christian Neoplatonist who, like Augustine, was an avid reader of the *Enneads*.

Inspired by Plotinus's vision of creating a "Platonopolis" populated by seekers after God, Truth, and Beauty who would live together under "Plato's laws," and inspired as well by the contemplative life then being led by Mallius Theodorus, Augustine now revived his own dream of retiring from public life in order to form a little community of like-minded souls, jointly committed to undertaking an introspective search for God—not by living under Plato's laws but rather by living through the spirit of Christ, as expressed in faith, hope, and love, and in the liturgy, rituals, and outward patterns of a piously Catholic life.

In the late summer of 386, Augustine resigned his imperial post as public orator and moved with his extended family and old friends and young students to a villa at Cassiciacum, near Como, to the north of Milan, in view of the Alps. There the philosophical community busied themselves with domestic chores, read Virgil together, and talked for hours on end, sometimes in the baths, at other times under a tree in a meadow, ever ready to debate the limits of reason, the nature of the soul, and the quest for wisdom, invariably under the tutelage of Augustine, who functioned as the school's informal scholarch.

Day in and day out, Augustine sought to persuade his companions that there is "one system of really true philosophy," the system elaborated by Plotinus and Plato: "This philosophy is not of this world—the philosophy that our Holy Writ rightly abhors—but the other world, the intelligible world." In this way, he hoped to realize an ideal of "friendship," as Cicero had defined it, by forging an "agreement on human and divine matters with charity and good will." He revered Christ as a morally perfect man of exceptional wisdom, a paragon of Neoplatonism in practice, not different in kind from Plotinus (or Socrates).

The earliest works of Augustine to survive all date from these heady months. Carefully preserved by Augustine himself in his personal library, they consist of four dialogues: the *Answer to Skeptics*, dedicated to Romanianus; *The Happy Life*, dedicated to Mallius Theodorus; *Divine Providence and the Problem of Evil*; and, the most original of them all, his *Soliloquies*—an interior dialogue between the soul of Augustine and the inner voice he calls Reason.

The first three dialogues purport to be more or less verbatim transcripts of actual conversations, written down by a stenographer, whose presence, claims Augustine, was meant to give the conversations a certain air of gravity—even if one assumes that Augustine later revised and edited the dialogues for dramatic effect, much as Seneca had artfully arranged and polished his letters to Lucilius.

Though the four texts show Augustine in the first flush of enthusiasm as a recent convert to a Christian form of Platonism, the texts are striking for their virtually complete lack of scriptural references (quite unlike the incantation of Scripture that accompanies Augustine's account of the same months in the *Confessions* a decade later).

The earliest of these dialogues leave the impression that a wise man can achieve divine union and a blessed life by dint of a "rational choice." From the standpoint of Augustine's later and more orthodox Christian works, this is an actionable heresy, representing a puffed-up conception of the powers of the human being unaided by the grace of God—as Augustine suggests in his description of these events in the *Confessions*, by rebuking the "monstrous pride" of a nameless spiritual companion (perhaps Mallius Theodorus).

Some sense of his exalted state of mind and inner tumult in these crucial months can be gleaned from the most extraordinary of these early works, the conversations with himself that, coining a new word, Augustine called *Soliloquia*—the *Soliloquies*. Here he presents a literally divided self:

"For a long time I had been turning over in my mind many diverse things; for many days I had been diligently searching for myself and my own good, and for what evil should be avoided, when suddenly someone spoke to me. Whether it was I myself or someone else . . . I just do not know"—in any case, he calls his alter ego "Reason."

"Reason" instructs him to "Pray for good health and aid," and "Augustine" complies: "I call upon you, God, truth, in whom and by whom and through whom all true things are true; God, wisdom, in whom and by whom and through whom all the wise are wise; God, true and complete life . . ."

Reason then asks Augustine, "What then do you wish to know?"

Augustine: "I want to know God and the soul." The convert to Christian Platonism yearns for knowledge of things he cannot see.

Reason: "Then begin to search."

As time passes, and the search of this divided soul unfolds, the conversation between Augustine and Reason comes to focus on the nature of the soul, and specifically on the question of whether or not the soul is immortal.

Augustine is made understandably uneasy by the labored quality of some of the arguments advanced by Reason, saying that he is bothered that "we have used such a convoluted path, following some unknown line of reasoning," in a way that seems almost "treacherous."

Reason responds by reminding Augustine that "we cannot despair of finding what we want" in the books he has recently read (perhaps following the convoluted path laid out by Plotinus, who, as Augustine says in another of these early dialogues, has resurrected Plato, the "cleanest and brightest" countenance in philosophy): "Will he who has taught us in his writings of the right manner of life, allow us to be without a knowledge of the nature of that life?"

Reason ends by exhorting Augustine to "believe your reasoning, believe the truth. It cries out that it lives in you, that it is immortal, and that its home cannot be taken from it by any death of the body."

Still, the opening prayer of the *Soliloquies* implies that Reason is impotent without God. "Believe in God," commands Reason to Augustine at one point. "Give yourself over to Him as much as you are able. Do not wish for your own will to be yours and at your own disposal; but proclaim yourself His slave— the slave of a merciful and capable master." Rarely have "Reason" and "God" been so lyrically combined, and confused, in such a way as to leave one bewildered about the power, and limits, of reason alone to put man in touch with God.

Moving beyond the introspective spiritual exercises of Plotinus, Augustine represents himself in the *Confessions* taking a series of symbolic steps. One of the most important was to read a hagiographic life of the famous desert anchorite Anthony (c. 250–356), written by Athanasius (c. 295–373), an important early Christian theologian. Often regarded as a founder of Christian monasticism, Anthony was a paragon of spiritual perfection according to Athanasius—and a perfect model for an aspiring Christian to emulate. As one modern expert on late antiquity, Peter Brown, has shown, "No small part of the work of late antique hagiography was the attempt to bring order to a supernatural world shot through with ambiguity, characterized by uncertainty as to the meaning of so many manifestations of the holy, and, as a result, inhabited by religious entrepreneurs of all faiths." To be inspired by the life of an exemplary Christian was to be reminded that this way of life was a real possibility—a reminder that might well change the way that one judged rival programs for making God manifest.

Shortly after he was done reading about Anthony's blessed life, Augustine, according to the *Confessions*, heard a mysterious voice in a garden, picked up a Bible, and chanced upon a passage from one of Paul's letters to the Romans: "put on the Lord Jesus Christ, and make no provision for the flesh in its lusts." In this manner, Augustine symbolically reverses Adam's exile from Eden by undergoing a crisis in a garden, similar to the agony of Jesus at Gethsemane. "Dying to be alive," he now submits himself to God's commands, placing himself under the authority of Holy Scripture, and feels a renewed commitment to emulate an ascetic way of life exemplified not by the learned Plotinus but rather by an unschooled Christian saint, Anthony of Egypt, who had indeed "put on the Lord Jesus Christ."

Augustine now had before him two dramatically different exemplars, Plotinus on the one hand, and Anthony on the other. Like Augustine, Plotinus was a classically trained man of letters, a close reader of philosophical texts, steeped in the dialectical method of his school, and surrounded by philosophical friends who could help him, through conversation and dialogue, in the effort to divinize the self through a stringent application of the intellect and the power of reason in meditation and spiritual exercises. Though Anthony was a reader, too, he was relatively uncultured and focused exclusively on Holy Scripture. Despite lacking the dialectical expertise and philosophical community of Plotinus, Anthony, too, had divinized himself, more consistently it seemed than the Platonist. By living alone in a cave in the desert, and going without food and sleep for endless days, Anthony had conquered his bodily needs as well as the many different demons the devil had dispatched to tempt and deceive him.

The two ways of life seemed incommensurable: Augustine faced an either-or. Implicitly choosing to emulate Anthony, and to renounce once and for all worldly entanglements, Augustine recounts in the *Confessions* how he chose in 387 to be baptized—a radical step, symbolizing a moment of death and rebirth, the end of one life and the beginning of another.

In the *Confessions*, Augustine recalls that after his baptism he "meditated taking flight to live in solitude"—becoming a hermit like Anthony.

But the contemporary evidence indicates that Augustine in fact did nothing of the kind. "He did not sell all he had, give to the poor, and follow Jesus," as a recent biographer acidly remarks. "He quit his job, went home, and lived very comfortably. Very little really changed, apart from his sleeping arrangements and the venue of his quite ordinary rustication."

After a short period in Ostia and then in Rome, the baptized philosopher decided to return with his philosophical entourage to North Africa and his hometown of Thagaste. There Augustine dedicated himself to philosophy as a Christian way of life, hoping to live a life of perfect goodness in seclusion with his spiritual companions. Instead of the clean break with the past depicted in the *Confessions*, Augustine now embarked on a more difficult and protracted intellectual transformation that slowly unfolded over a span of several years.

At first, he eschewed as a matter of principle any direct involvement in public affairs. His primary link to the outside world became his writing, and he produced a stream of letters and texts meant to bring to life "the voice of Christ, and the teaching of Plato and of Plotinus." But as time passed, the weight of his writing slowly shifted, as *De Vera Religione* of 389 indicates: "In the inward man dwells truth," he writes there, repeating a truism of Plotinus. But, he adds, "if you find that you are by nature mutable, transcend yourself. But when you transcend yourself, remember that *you are transcending your reasoning soul.*" Augustine began to urge his circle to reject anything in Neoplatonism that contradicted the teachings of the Catholic Church. Abandoning the assumption that Jesus was a paragon of moral perfection no different in kind from Plotinus or Socrates, Augustine now affirms the doctrine of incarnation and teaches that Jesus was God made flesh and that He embodied the Word of God.

By 391, when Augustine and his friends moved from Thagaste to the seacoast city of Hippo, fifty miles to the north, the slow process through which Augustine was becoming a devout Christian, rather than a Christian Neoplatonist, was almost complete. He thought about founding a monastery with the formal blessing of church authorities. Instead, as Possidius recounts, Augustine found himself more or less forced into becoming a priest.

In those days, church officials were drafted on the spot by the acclaim of a congregation, and one could not in conscience resist a congregation's call. As a layman, Augustine had steered clear of attending churches where he knew there was a vacancy, for fear his philosophical retirement might be jeopardized. But according to Possidius, his reputation had preceded him, and one day while in church at Hippo, it caught up with him: "Catholics were by now aware of the holy Augustine's teaching and way of life and they seized hold of him—he was standing in the congregation quite unconcerned and with no idea of what was going to happen to him."

Like the philosopher who has seen the sun of perfect justice in Plato's parable of the cave in the *Republic*, only to be forced afterward to bring a semblance of justice back to those in the shadows, Augustine now had to forgo his life of Christian contemplation and descend into the murky world of church politics: "And while they were demanding this with eager shouts," writes Possidius, "he was weeping copiously."

The new priest was authorized to establish a monastery in the garden of the church at Hippo. From then on, Augustine was an increasingly public figure, exercising ever more ecclesiastical authority, his rhetorical prowess helping to secure his position as an influential Christian thinker.

In 392, he challenged the city's resident Manichaean preacher to a public debate and rebutted his arguments so forcefully that the poor man was forced to flee, and the Gnostic heresy went into decline among the citizens. Four years later, upon the death of the congregation's bishop, Valerius, Augustine became the new bishop of Hippo. It was an office he held for the rest of his life.

Shortly after his consecration to higher office, Augustine began to write his most beautiful book, the *Confessions*.

The title meant, for Augustine, "accusation of oneself; praise of God"—a conception that made sustained self-examination central to the act of confessing. (It was only in later centuries that the Catholic Church formalized penance as a sacrament that required revealing one's sins to a priest for absolution.)

In the decade since his baptism, Augustine had moved steadily away from the self-reliant idealism that defined his conversion of 386. He remembered his rapturous visions of God. But as time passed, and his memory waned, he also took the full measure of the transience of these moments: "Sometimes you cause me to enter into an extraordinary depth of feeling marked by a strange sweetness. If it were brought to perfection in me, it would be an experience quite beyond anything in this life. But I fall back into my usual ways under my miserable burdens. I am reabsorbed by my habitual practices. I weep profusely, but still I am held. Such is the strength of the burden of habit. Here I have the power to be, but do not wish it. There I wish to be, but lack the power."

Habit fetters the will and cripples our capacity to reason. Augustine knew it too well. Even a sage such as himself, despite his visions of God and no matter how many times he renews his vows of moral purity, inevitably falls back, distracted by old routines. For several years after his conversion, he had supposed that "if they wish," all people who trust and believe God may "turn from a love of visible and time-bound things to the fulfillment of his commands."

But now he felt that the will, though free, is "prepared by God," and thus any man succeeds in fulfilling God's commandments only by the grace of God, not by the power of his will unaided.

A purity of will remained Augustine's most ardent desire. But a life of perfect integrity is not only exceptionally rare (as Stoics like Seneca readily conceded)—it is impossible. Man by nature is imperfect—a creature of gratuitous transgressions, epitomized by the boy who once stole a pear for the sheer pleasure of stealing.

A man cannot rely on himself, for his inward imperfections are as variegated as the fleeting desires and decisions that, taken together, constitute his unique past, the singularity of his prior life. The intractability of the past individuates and separates man from man, and man from God, and this individuality is no cause for joy, since it entails a life of disorder, disintegration, and disquiet: "The storms of incoherent events tear to pieces my thoughts, the inmost entrails of my soul, until that day when, purified and molten by the fire of your love, I flow together to merge into you."

A man of enlightened good faith, like Augustine, has to admit that he does not know even himself. "I cannot judge rightly," he confesses, "since I fear that the sin has just gone into hiding, where it is visible to you but not to me." It is only through a constant quest to achieve a unified self, through the kind of narrative he dedicates to God in confession, that Augustine has any hope of becoming whole.

The *Confessions* were also meant to allay suspicions about the character of the author, a man long publicly associated with heretics, someone clearly at home with the writings of the pagan Platonists, and someone who by his own account had experienced more than one dramatic conversion. Who was to say that his conversion to Catholicism was either genuine or lasting? (The senior bishop of Numidia had for a time refused to ordain Augustine as the new bishop of Hippo, accusing him of being a "crypto-Manichaean.")

In recounting his personal odyssey, Augustine thus goes out of his way to dramatize his conversion to Christianity, exaggerating the influence of Ambrose, and describing an improbably clean break with the past symbolized by his baptism in 387. For similar reasons, he downplays the philosophical wandering of his youth, minimizing his Manichaean phase, evoking his debt to

Plotinus through lyrical allusions rather than straightforward quotation, and omitting any mention by name of Mallius Theodorus.

Throughout, he stresses the role played by divine providence, in part by constantly addressing himself to God directly: "What then am I, my God?"

He represents a self that is protean, divided, and unreliable, because incomplete and unfinished, even after his conversion. It is only in contemplation, through thought, that he is able to collect himself.

"By thinking we, as it were, gather together ideas which the memory contains in a dispersed and disordered way . . . They have to be brought together [*cogenda*, from *cogo*] so as to be capable of being known; this means that they have to be gathered [*colligenda*] from their dispersed state. Hence is derived the word cogitate [*cogito*]."

Cogitation is required to produce, in retrospect, a *narratio*, a narrative that makes known (*narro*) the episodes of a life by forming them, through recollection, into a thoughtfully unified whole.

Hence the reflective form of the self-portrait in the *Confessions*: Augustine creates a narrative unity through a consistent interpretation of past events in the light of the author's unwavering love of God, and with a supervening awareness of the overriding role played by God's grace in shaping the course of the superficially chaotic events of his prior life. This retrospective reinterpretation manages to create a rational unity out of otherwise disparate elements, joining painful and joyful memories, of sinful deeds and of enraptured moments of vision, into a portrait of a Christian still struggling to become morally unblemished.

In the years after completing the *Confessions*, Augustine produced a torrent of prose, preaching countless sermons and publishing a stream of essays, in addition to composing two large works of systematic theology, *The Literal Meaning of Genesis* and *The Trinity*. In these works, the claims of reason are strictly limited, for the premises of their arguments are secured by faith alone.

While the detailed arguments he offered in support of his theology were often complex, the life he led as the bishop of Hippo was a model of simplicity. According to Possidius, "his clothes and food, and bedclothes also, were simple and adequate, neither ostentatious nor particularly poor." Eschewing displays of extreme asceticism, he enjoyed a good dinner with guests, mainly for the pleasure he took in conversing seriously about serious matters. Gossip, by contrast, was strictly forbidden. He guarded his chastity, in part by prohibiting all women from visiting his residence—even his sister, who had taken vows herself in order to become a prioress.

However humble his personal regimen, the bishop of Hippo was now forced by his public duties to put into play (as one biographer puts it) "emotions that affected him intimately: great ambition, a love of praise, a need to dominate others, an immense sensitivity to insult." Unlike a medieval bishop, Augustine did not inherit a clear mandate. He had to fight to establish his authority against rival religious sects and rival sources of local patronage. According to Possidius, he patiently tried to show heretics "by reasoned argument that they ought either to alter their perverse opinions, or else meet him in debate." But some heretics refused to debate, saying that the bishop of Hippo "was a wolf to be killed."

As the leader of an embattled church, Augustine was forced back into the cave of common humanity, where he felt increasingly compelled to instill various beliefs and habits that resembled, as closely as possible, the knowledge and virtues otherwise accessible to only a few wise men. If nothing else, Augustine's period of youthful skepticism had convinced him that some questions of importance, involving "things I could not see," could *not* be answered by reasoned argument. In such cases, it was "more modest and not in the least misleading to be told by the Church to believe what could not be demonstrated."

As he confided in a letter written to a colleague, he continued to be perplexed "as to the way in which we ought to live amongst men," feeling himself beset by "very great dangers," in the midst "of a great variety of manners and of minds having inclinations and infirmities hidden altogether from our sight," but also feeling certain of his goal: to "seek the interest of those who are citizens and subjects, not of Rome, which is on earth, but of Jerusalem which is in heaven," working, "with all the zeal of love," toward "the good of our neighbor, that he may rightly spend the present life so as to obtain life eternal."

In practice, "the zeal of love" could be a terrifying scourge.

During Augustine's episcopate, he and his fellow bishops ordered the destruction of pagan temples and the suppression of pagan rituals. In 405, he supported a so-called Edict of Unity, an Orwellian proclamation that in effect outlawed the Donatist Christian Church in Numidia. The former member of a persecuted sect became a persecuting sectarian. (Years later, he watched impassively when the defeat of his former foes produced an epidemic of religious suicides: "Seeing that God, by a hidden, though just, disposition, has predestined some to the ultimate penalty [of hellfire], it is doubtless better that an overwhelming majority of the Donatists should have been collected and reabsorbed [into the Catholic fold] . . . while a few perish in their own flames.")

A jealous shepherd, Augustine became perhaps the first major thinker to turn persecution itself into an intellectual art form, as ruthlessly effective in theory as it could sometimes be in practice. In his most combative texts, he wielded words like a scythe, slashing away at the enemies of the One True Church—Manichaeans, Donatists, Pelagians—heretics guilty of heresies paradoxically immortalized in Augustine's countless pages of invective and doctrinal quibbling, as unpleasant and dreary as anything to be found in the collected works of Lenin.

In the last years of his life, the followers of the British lay ascetic Pelagius piqued his special fury, perhaps because Pelagius himself had been inspired, in part, by the moral perfectionism expressed in Augustine's early Christian dialogues. While Augustine himself was moving steadily away from his youthful optimism in the power of human reason and will, embracing instead a darker vision, of man's abject dependence on the grace of God, Pelagius was confidently laying out "rules for behavior and the conduct of a holy life," arguing that the most exacting imitation of Christ was well within "the power and functioning of human nature" and hence an obligation for the true Christian.

The disagreement between Augustine and Pelagius erupted into a protracted dispute. The disagreement revolved around, among other things, how to read one sentence in Paul's Letter to the Romans: "Just as sin came into the world through one man, and death came through sin, and so death spread to all, because all have sinned."

Pelagius argued that Paul's passage could not be cited as proof that Holy Scripture barred the Christian pursuit of moral perfection, because baptism remitted the sin of Adam. With strenuous effort, a good Christian could aspire to live a life of perfect virtue, not unlike the pagan Stoics and Platonists.

Augustine (implicitly renouncing his similar arguments in early works like *The Blessed Life*) vehemently disagreed.

The baptized Christian, no matter how serenely contemplative and ascetic his way of life, remained an invalid. To live in harmony with the divine order was a matter not only of self-renunciation and reasoning rightly but also of having faith, of submitting to authority, of subordinating oneself to consecrated scriptures and rituals embraced by a community of the righteous. "That is why the Scripture says, 'The just man lives on the basis of faith.' For we do not yet see our good, and hence we have to seek it by believing; and it is not in our power to live rightly, unless while we believe and pray we receive help from him who has given us the faith to believe that we must be helped by him."

In a way, this was good news. After all, the life of philosophical contemplation and conversation that Socrates and Plato and Plotinus and the young Christian Augustine had all enjoined was not an option for most people. Few had the free time. And each differed greatly in his ability to reason rightly. But to search for wisdom through prayer and ritual professions of faith was a path open to everyone.

This was an egalitarian view—but it came with a disquieting proviso.

The intractability of original sin meant that the thirst for Christian wisdom could never be quenched in the lifetime of any mortal soul. Even the self-examination of the most sincere of Christian philosophers might reveal something about the truth and beauty of God—but only through a glass darkly: "For no one is known to another so intimately as he is known to himself, and yet no one can be sure as to his own conduct on the morrow ; . . . the minds of men are so unknown and so unstable that there is the highest wisdom in the exhortation of the apostle: 'Therefore do not pronounce judgment before the time, before the Lord comes, who will bring to light the things now hidden in darkness and will disclose the purposes of the heart.'"

In 410, Goths sacked Rome. "If Rome can perish," wrote the Catholic doctor Jerome, "what can be safe?" In the atmosphere of gathering panic that followed, Augustine increasingly came to believe that Christian doctrine, firmly inculcated, alone could rightly regulate the welfare of individual souls and the political communities they belonged to. "With God, the crimes in which many are banded together do not pass un-avenged, as is often the case with a king, or any other magistrate who is only a man."

Augustine did not shrink from the coercive spiritual discipline that such views implied. Even fear was a feeling he marshaled fearlessly, preaching that the Lord's "wrath shall come when you know not."

As Peter Brown, his greatest modern biographer, comments, "Fallen men had come to need restraint. Even man's greatest achievements had been made possible only by a 'strait-jacket' of unremitting harshness."

Although Augustine's career in the church went on for another two decades, and although he exercised growing influence within the councils of the Eastern Church, as many of his works were translated from Latin into Greek, it is not obvious that he can, or should, be regarded as a philosopher in the final years of his life. As bishop, he tried to curb and control the search for wisdom. And the very idea of "philosophy" now left him ambivalent.

On the one hand, in *The City of God*, he defines the "true philosopher" as the "lover of God," and he reaffirms his admiration for Plato and some of the Platonic teachings.

But he also ridicules the Neoplatonist Porphyry for criticizing Christianity, and for holding (in Augustine's gloss) "that no doctrine has yet been established to form the teaching of a philosophical sect, which offers a universal way for the liberation of the soul." Puffed up with pride, the Platonist cannot acknowledge the One True Way—even though it is right there, before his very eyes, in the Christian faith that he explicitly rejects. It is no wonder that Augustine now unfavorably compares the interminable disagreements among pagan philosophers with the "harmony of the Scriptures." And near the end of *The City of God*, he goes even further, speaking with characteristic sarcasm of the "impressive reasoning of the wise" and then hurling a quote from the Old Testament: "The LORD knows our thoughts, that they are but an empty breath."

Toward the end of his life, Augustine made a chronological survey of the books he had dictated and distributed, some written as a Christian layman, some as a priest, and some as a bishop.

Whenever he found anything in them that seemed to contradict his current understanding of Catholic doctrine, he censored himself and offered a revision or a retraction—hence the title *Retractiones*. "As far as man's nature is concerned," Augustine remarks in this work, reflecting on the dialogues he had written as a young Christian Platonist, "there is nothing better in him than mind and reason. Nevertheless, it isn't in accordance with mind and reason that one who wants to live happily should live; for, in that case, he lives in accordance with man, whereas to be able to attain happiness *one should live in accordance with God*. To reach happiness, our mind ought not to be content with itself, but rather subordinate itself to God."

In this passage, one senses that Augustine protests too much—as if struggling to subordinate himself, and to silence the part of himself that he had identified with "Reason" in the pages of his own Platonic *Soliloquies* decades before.

Augustine finished these commentaries on the corpus of his authorized works in 427. Two years later, "by God's will and permission," in the words of Augustine's biographer Possidius, "there poured into Africa from across the sea in ships from Spain a huge host of savage enemies armed with every kind of weapon and trained in war." After ravaging Numidia, the Vandals laid siege to Hippo. Over a meal held in the midst of the siege, Augustine said to his monks, "My prayer to God is that He will either consent to liberate this besieged city or, if He thinks otherwise, will give His servants strength to go through with what He wills for them or, so far as I am concerned, will take me from this world."

He had lived just long enough to see "cities overthrown and destroyed and, with them, their citizens and inhabitants and the buildings on their estates wiped out by a murderous enemy"; he had witnessed "churches denuded of priests and ministers; holy virgins and ascetics dispersed, some succumbing to torture, others perishing by the sword."

In the midst of this catastrophe, the bishop of Hippo consoled himself not just with Holy Scripture, according to Possidius, but also with "the maxim of a certain wise man"—Plotinus—who had asserted that the true philosopher will not despair if buildings tumble and men die, since his "estimate of death, we hold, must be that it is better than life in the body."

A few months later, in 430, Augustine fell ill. Sensing that he was dying, the seventy-six-year-old bishop asked to be left alone with copies of the Psalms displayed on a wall near his bed.

When awake, he would look up, "gazing at them and reading them, and copiously and continuously weeping as he read." And when he was not reading, he prayed.

According to Possidius, "he made no will because, as one of God's poor, he had nothing to leave." But he did leave "a standing order that the library of the church and all the books should be carefully preserved for posterity." Augustine had long retained a small army of scribes and stenographers to record his sermons and make copies of his letters; he had made certain that transcriptions of his key treatises were kept in the church library. Possidius thus inherited a vast corpus of texts, much larger than that left behind by Plato or Plotinus, and much more authoritatively codified (Augustine is one of the very few classical writers whose formal works a modern scholar can date with relative precision).

"No one can read what he wrote on theology without profit," concludes Possidius, who nonetheless thought it highly unlikely that any one man could ever read everything Augustine had written, ninety-three formal works in all, not counting the sermons and letters. "But I think that those were able to profit still more who could hear him speak in church and see him with their own eyes and, above all, had some knowledge of him as he lived among his fellow men. For . . . he was also one of those in whom is fulfilled the text, 'So speak and so act.'"

At the time of his death, Augustine exercised temporal authority over the spiritual life of a relatively small number of Catholics in a remote province of a disintegrating empire. But because the bishop had taken care, with the help of Possidius, to preserve his major works for posterity, his posthumous influence on Christianity proved to be profound, both in theory and in practice, laying out some of the conceptual grounds for creating perhaps the most powerful community of closed belief in world history—the Catholic Church that ruled over medieval Western Europe as an all-encompassing, if not quite totalitarian, theocracy, unrivaled before or since by any other religious or secular one-party state, be it Muslim or Communist.

It was, not coincidentally, a form of life unified through repressive force and structured along the lines not of Plato's wide-open Academy of inquiring minds but rather of the ideally just society imagined in Plato's *Republic*, administered by a specially trained elite of philosopher-kings.

"It was the tragic destiny of Christianity to extract the holiest experiences of the human heart from the quiet of the individual's life, and to evoke mechanistic morality and hierarchical hypocrisy in the process." So wrote the German historian Wilhelm Dilthey, lamenting what had been lost.

And it was the fate of Augustine, whose *Confessions* represent perhaps the most beautiful account of the holiest experiences of the human heart, to play a leading role in this lamentable process by helping to justify a monolithic spiritual discipline that, for nearly a thousand years in the Catholic West, stifled the older forms of the philosophical life—the very forms that had made possible Augustine's own spiritual odyssey.

MONTAIGNE

Sketch of Montaigne, pencil on paper, c. 1590, by François Quesnel (1543–1619). In an age of ruthless religious warfare, Montaigne argued for mercy: "There is no man so good that if he placed all his actions and thoughts under the scrutiny of the laws, he would not deserve hanging ten times in his life—even though it would be very harmful and unjust to punish and destroy him."

For a long time in the West, men of goodwill and strong faith, inspired in part by the example of Christian sages like Augustine, had built up a set of beliefs and ways of behaving that were maintained more or less rigorously within communities that tried to exclude any alternatives. Those aspiring to spiritual perfection were encouraged to aim high, in hopes of experiencing a moment of vision, a rapturous fusion with God.

"They want to get out of themselves, and escape from the man," remarked Michel de Montaigne of such aspiring saints. "That is madness." He made this acid remark in the book he called *Essays*, a sprawling record of his readings and reflections, meant to test, or "assay," the quality of various beliefs and practices: "Instead of changing into angels, they change into beasts; instead of raising themselves, they lower themselves."

Montaigne would know. He was a witness to the hecatombs provoked by the Reformation in France. On the one side stood Catholics loyal to the ecclesiastical authority of Rome and the spiritual leadership of the pope; on the other side stood a variety of "reformed" Christian congregations that rejected the authority of the Roman papacy as corrupt and recognized instead new forms of purified Christian worship associated with dissident Christian leaders, Protestants like Martin Luther and John Calvin. The sacrificial slaughters organized by these rival communities of the Christian faithful outraged Montaigne. With merciless clarity, they revealed the hard truth that in search of perfect virtue, a human being could become a perfect beast. And "there is no beast in the world," writes Montaigne, "so much to be feared by man as man himself."

Montaigne's biting commentary, contained in the one work he published, the *Essays* he composed between 1572 and 1592, earned him a reputation as the foremost French philosopher of his day. Consisting of 107 chapters grouped into three books, the earliest of the *Essays* are modeled, in part, on the short moral writings of Plutarch; on Niccolò Machiavelli's *Discourses on the First Ten Books of Livy* (1531), a series of historical reflections analyzing the civic and martial virtues proper to a free people; and finally on Erasmus of Rotterdam's *Adagiorum opus* (or *Adages*), a continuously expanding commentary on famous proverbs (such as "Know thyself") that was published in ten editions between 1500 and 1536, making it the most popular work by perhaps the most famous Christian humanist of the Renaissance.

As he began to write in earnest, and as he continued to add to his *Essays* as Erasmus had added to his *Adages*, Montaigne moved away from classical and modern precedents, and his work slowly turned into a novel search for self-knowledge, undertaken not through a close reading of canonic texts (though he quotes from many different kinds of texts), nor through adherence to any traditional set of virtues, whether pagan, Christian, or Machiavellian, but rather through an increasingly candid description and analysis of himself, and the world, as he directly experienced them.

"I am myself the matter of my book," he declares at one point. But his *Essays* reveal little about the outward course of his life, which led him from an undistinguished career in provincial politics to the centers of cultural and political power in Paris. Instead, Montaigne takes the famous Socratic maxim—"Don't you think that actions are more reliable evidence than words?"—and at one point characteristically inverts it. "My actions," he writes, "would tell more about fortune than about me . . . It is not my deeds that I write down; it is myself, it is my essence"—an essence he regards as synonymous with his own thoughts, inclinations, and intentions, which he supposes can be represented independently of his outward conduct.

It was only in the nineteenth century that scholars finally began to sort through the evidence of Montaigne's life apart from the *Essays*. The documents that survive include a journal of Montaigne's travels, first discovered in the eighteenth century, and a handful of letters (thirty-nine in all). Although our information is incomplete, the outlines of his life, both public and private, are reasonably clear.

Michel de Montaigne was born in 1533, at his family's estate in Gascony, the Château de Montaigne, located some thirty miles east of the French port city of Bordeaux. His paternal great-grandfather, a prosperous merchant who bought and sold wine, fish, and indigo dye, had bought the castle three generations earlier. The family flourished in the decades that followed. But the first member to fulfill the martial and civic virtues of a proper nobleman was Michel's father, Pierre Eyquem de Montaigne.

Pierre had fought with the French army in Italy before serving Bordeaux as a magistrate and, for two years, as the town's mayor. Montaigne's mother, Antoinette de Louppes de Villeneuve, belonged to an equally prominent and prosperous family. But unlike the Eyquems, the Louppes family were Marranos—Spanish Jews who had been forcibly converted to Christianity and then fled during the Inquisition to more welcoming European cities, from Bordeaux in France to Amsterdam in Flanders.

Michel was the third of ten children but the first to survive infancy. It was a large family and varied in its religious convictions. His brother Thomas, one year younger, and his sister Jeanne, who was three years younger, both converted to Protestantism in later years, while Michel remained an observant Catholic.

His siblings were part of a broader movement in Bordeaux and its environs. Criticism of corruption in the Roman Church fueled a rapid growth in the number of Calvinist congregations. By 1561, one historian estimates that there were seven thousand Protestants in a city of about fifty thousand.

By then, Calvinist congregations had spread widely throughout France. Attempts at reconciling doctrinal differences led to repeated failure, and efforts to repress the heresy only created martyrs and more violence. Catholics burned Calvinists at the stake. Protestants torched Catholic churches.

Alarmed by the apparent inability of the French Crown to control the mounting disorder, Catholic vigilantes led by François de Guise in 1562 took the law into their own hands and slaughtered twenty Protestants who were illegally worshipping together. Thus began a civil war between Catholics and Huguenots (as the French Calvinists were called) that would continue sporadically for the remainder of Montaigne's life and end only in 1629, with the so-called Peace of Alais.

Although Montaigne's parents were loyal Catholics, they agreed that religion was a matter of conscience and that one should be free to worship as one's personal conscience dictated. Despite their confessional differences, the extended family remained on friendly terms.

Since the good faith of a Marrano like his mother was often suspect—and there is evidence that other members of his mother's family later recanted their conversions to Christianity and returned to their ancestral faith—it is arguable that Montaigne, by the Jewish law of matrilineal descent, should be regarded as a Jew, even though there is no evidence that his mother was an insincere Christian, and even though by upbringing, custom, and long-held conviction, Montaigne himself was a Roman Catholic.

Montaigne certainly knew the basic facts of his mother's ancestry. But he felt the personal implications were moot. For, as he remarks in a barbed passage in the *Essays*—in a context where he is speaking explicitly of the atrocious suffering caused by the coerced conversion of the Jews of Spain and Portugal—"custom and length of time are far stronger counselors than any other compulsion."

His father, who personally supervised Montaigne's education, made sure that the boy was steeped in the classics of pagan antiquity. When Montaigne was old enough to start reading, his father hired a live-in Latin tutor, so the young boy was exposed only to Latin literature and learned the language "without artificial means, without a book, without grammar or precept."

After several years of this regimen, Montaigne was sent away to Bordeaux to study at a newly established school, the Collège de Guyenne, where Montaigne would imbibe the classical erudition and crusading introspective spirit ("we must wage war with ourselves") championed by Christian humanists like Erasmus (c. 1469–1536). Since his father was grooming his oldest son for a career as a magistrate as well as a soldier, Montaigne next studied law, probably spending most of his teen years at the University of Toulouse.

About the time that Montaigne turned twenty-one, he inherited a post that his father (or perhaps his uncle) had purchased at the Cour des Aides of Périgueux, recently established as a new arm of the king's judicial power. Lawyers in this position received a salary, supplemented by income from the taxes they levied on all parties to a judicial dispute. In 1557, the new court was dissolved and its members incorporated into the Parlement of Bordeaux, where Montaigne served for another thirteen years as a *conseiller*, or magistrate.

Bordeaux's parlement was one of eight similar institutions (located in Paris, Toulouse, Grenoble, Dijon, Rouen, Aix, and Rennes) that, together, formed the highest court of justice in France. As dissent over religion rose in these years, and the power of the king weakened, the magistrates of the various French parlements played a leading role not only in administering justice but also in executing royal edicts and formulating public policy.

As a young man, Montaigne seems to have been a loyal subject of his monarch. In the 1560s, he sometimes served as an ambassador from the Parlement of Bordeaux to the king's court in Paris. In his own portrait of himself in the *Essays*, he depicts a man of casual comportment, less than punctilious in matters of dress and etiquette. Restless by nature, he finds it hard to stand still. "I have a distaste for mastery," he writes, and his distaste extends to the self-discipline required for perfect self-control. He can be impulsive. And the freedom he most cherishes, candor in speech, sometimes makes him appear indiscreet.

As a magistrate with access to the court in Paris, Montaigne came to know from the inside how the administration of law worked—an experience that left him without illusions. "Now laws remain in credit not because they are just, but because they are laws," he tartly observes in the *Essays*. "That is the mystic foundation of their authority; they have no other. And that is a good thing for them. They are often made by fools, more often by people who, in their hatred of equality, are wanting in equity; but always by men, vain and irresolute authors."

Still, not every magistrate was a fool, as Montaigne discovered when he met the young man who would become the single most important figure in his life, Étienne de La Boétie (1530–1563). Two and half years older than Montaigne, La Boétie was a true Renaissance man, a scholar trained at the University of Orléans, where the study of law was regarded as an aspect of the larger search for wisdom (and where his primary teacher would end up being burned at the stake in 1559 as a Huguenot heretic).

At the age of eighteen, La Boétie had written the *Discourse of Voluntary Servitude*, a disquisition against tyranny that was remarkably learned, demonstrating a familiarity with Plato, Aristotle, Tacitus, Dante, Thomas More, Erasmus, and Machiavelli, among other authorities ancient and modern. In the years that followed, the text of La Boétie's discourse circulated widely among the magistrates of Bordeaux. Montaigne reports his own youthful admiration for its striking rhetoric.

It was, for its time, a quite radical piece of writing, filled with the kind of frank speech that Montaigne himself prized. Though La Boétie explicitly absolved the French monarchy of any taint of tyranny, his brief against despotic regimes was sweeping. As the title indicates, his target was not simply tyrants but also the servility of ordinary citizens—what Kant would later call their "self-imposed immaturity." Without the complicity of quiescent subjects, tyranny could not survive.

Sometime between the end of 1557 and the first months of 1559, Montaigne met La Boétie for the first time. The two became soul mates, joined in a shared love of wisdom, not unlike Seneca and Lucilius—and joined, too, in a shared love for the soul of the other, not unlike the Platonic love that Socrates expressed toward Alcibiades.

"Particularly in the matter of natural gifts, I know no one who can be compared with him," Montaigne remarks in the *Essays*. "If you press me to tell why I loved him, I feel that this cannot be expressed, except by answering: Because it was he, because it was I."

These remarks appear in the essay "Of Friendship," where Montaigne does not mince words about his feelings. The warmth of his sentiments was reciprocated by La Boétie, who addressed several poems to Montaigne. In one, he likens the younger man to Alcibiades—and implies that he, by playing the role of Socrates to Montaigne's Alcibiades, must help teach his younger friend how to have reason, rather than impulse, rule his life.

In this way, La Boétie turned Montaigne toward "philosophy" understood as a way of life rather than a catalog of doctrines.

For some, philosophy in Montaigne's day remained what it had become in the Middle Ages: a specialized vocation, normally pursued in universities under the direction of Catholic clergy, and organized around the close reading of a small set of consecrated texts (by Aristotle above all) and authoritative commentaries on them (by Thomas Aquinas above all). But for many others, "philosophy" was now associated with a rejection of this scholastic approach by leading figures in the Renaissance of the late fifteenth century. In Florence, Marsilio Ficino (1433–1499) appealed to the work of Augustine, Plotinus, and Plato, imagining it to represent a finer moral tradition than the Aristotelian approach championed by Aquinas. Erasmus, one of the first critical editors of the New Testament, had similarly argued that the true philosopher is not the scholar in his study but the person who seeks wisdom in practice, by trying to emulate Socrates—or Jesus.

The rebirth of the ability to read Greek among humanists like Ficino, Pico della Mirandola, Erasmus, and Thomas More led to the rediscovery in the Renaissance of the other great philosophical sects of classical antiquity: the Stoic school of Zeno and his Roman followers Seneca, Epictetus, and Marcus Aurelius; the Skeptical school of Pyrrho, who taught that a suspension of judgment about the truth or falsity of endlessly questionable core beliefs would produce tranquillity of soul; and the materialist school of Epicurus, whose disciples consoled themselves by contemplating the endless variety of the created cosmos while preaching an ethic of enjoying bodily pleasures in moderation (thus eschewing the more extreme forms of renunciation prized within the Christian and Platonic traditions). It was the ancient understanding of the philosophical life taught in these sects that La Boétie had set out to emulate—and to instill in his friend Michel.

But unlike Seneca at the end of his life, neither man at that moment had any interest in retiring from public life and worldly affairs. On the contrary, both La Boétie and Montaigne, as active members of the Parlement of Bordeaux, found themselves enmeshed willy-nilly in the political and religious troubles that increasingly beset the kingdom. More and more Frenchmen—including many people both men knew well—took up the Protestant cause.

The king vacillated between conciliation and repression. The result was a "confusing morass of court factions, countless leading actors and bit players, a seemingly unending series of peace agreements followed by renewed warfare, and the bizarre diplomatic intrigues of nearly every state in Western Europe."

La Boétie, who was already one of the most accomplished negotiators in the Parlement of Bordeaux, plunged directly into this messy situation. Like Montaigne, he was a moderate and a loyalist, a supporter of the monarchy and the established church. In order to deter any Huguenot attempt to seize power in Bordeaux, he had helped the Parlement muster an army of twelve hundred men. A few months after the king issued an edict in January 1562, one of a recurrent series of decrees meant to quell Protestant violence by granting the Huguenots greater freedom of worship, La Boétie composed a memorandum criticizing the edict. He warned that a nation that contained two different religious bodies would sooner or later fall into disorder and bloodshed. The only solution, he argued, was a Catholic Church reformed neither by Catholic leaders nor by dissenting Christians but rather by the king acting in concert with his Parlements. (It has often been conjectured that Montaigne largely agreed with La Boétie's pragmatic arguments for a parliamentary monarchy and religious unity.)

In 1563, La Boétie accompanied troops sent from Bordeaux to the town of Agen, in order to quell a Protestant uprising there. He persuaded the town's rebels to lay down their arms, thus preventing more violence. He also fell ill with dysentery.

When Montaigne invited La Boétie to dinner in August 1563, he learned that his friend was in failing health. In the days that followed, Montaigne was a constant companion at La Boétie's bedside. Realizing that he would not survive, La Boétie composed a will witnessed by his wife, his uncle, and Montaigne, in which he provided for his family and bequeathed his library to Montaigne.

In a letter to his father that was probably written soon after La Boétie's death, Montaigne recounts several of their last conversations. On one occasion, Montaigne, marveling at La Boétie's "greatness of soul" under duress, vowed that "this would serve me as an example, to play this same part in my turn." La Boétie begged Montaigne to emulate him in just this way, "to show in action that the talks we had had together during our health had been not merely borne in our mouths but deeply engraved on heart and in soul, in such a way as to be put into execution on the first occasions that offered; adding that this was the true object of our studies, and of philosophy."

La Boétie's death devastated Montaigne. Grief stricken, he began to prepare for publication everything that La Boétie had written. At the same time, Montaigne submitted to pressure from his father on two fronts: by consenting to an arranged marriage and agreeing to translate into French a lengthy treatise, *Natural Theology*, by a forgotten fifteenth-century monk named Raymond Sebond.

The externals of his life in these years leave an impression of decorum and propriety. When his father died in 1568, the thirty-four-year-old Michel, as the oldest son, became head of the family and inherited the family seat. For the rest of his life, he lived at the Château de Montaigne with his widowed mother. In the months that followed, Montaigne published his first texts: a dedication to his father of Sebond's *Natural Theology*, followed by six prefaces to six different works by La Boétie—two books of poems and four translations.

As a nobleman of independent means, Montaigne was now free to devote himself exclusively to the philosophical life. In 1570, he resigned from the Parlement. A few months later, he solemnized his decision to "retire" with a Latin inscription on a wall in his library: "In the year of Christ 1571, at the age of thirty-eight, on the last day of February, anniversary of his birth, Michel de Montaigne, long weary of the servitude of the court and of public employments, while still entire, retired to the bosom of the Muses, where in calm and freedom from all cares he will spend what little remains of his life now more than half run out. If the fates permit, he will complete this abode, this sweet ancestral retreat; and he has consecrated it to his freedom, tranquility, and leisure."

It is in this context—in isolation from his wife and family, alone in a library filled with the books of his friend La Boétie, and perhaps still grieving— that Montaigne embarked on a new project. "It was a melancholy humor," he later claimed, "that first put into my head this daydream of meddling with writing. And then, finding myself entirely destitute and void of any other matter, I presented myself to myself for argument and subject." According to this account, his *Essays* were meant to lift his spirits and to continue the quest for wisdom that he had started with La Boétie by his side.

Upon retiring to his library, one of the first things he did was inscribe a memorial to his friend on its walls: "[To the shades of Étienne de La Boétie], the tenderest, sweetest, and closest companion, than whom our age has seen no better, more learned, more charming, or indeed more perfect, Michel de Montaigne, miserably bereft of so dear a support of his life, remembering the mutual love and dear feeling that bound them together, wanting to set up some unique monument, and unable to do so more meaningfully, has dedicated this excellent apparatus for the mind."

Lacking a living companion to converse with, Montaigne initiated a kind of philosophical soliloquy, a sustained conversation with himself. "My trade and my art is living," he declares. And like Seneca counseling Lucilius through a series of letters, Montaigne began to write a series of short texts, embarking on a kind of correspondence with himself that might help him "to know himself and to die well and live well." One of his mottoes was *"Sapere aude"*—dare to know (a phrase from Horace, cited by Kant two centuries later in the famous opening of his essay "What Is Enlightenment?").

But dare though he might—and Montaigne, when he writes, is nothing if not daring—can a man truly "know himself"? And, if so, how?

If he is to live a life governed by reason, what set of reasonable beliefs and practices should he select from the philosophical alternatives on offer? What model shall he emulate? Socrates? Seneca? A Christian philosopher like Augustine? Or, nearer to hand, a beloved friend like La Boétie? "His mind was molded in the pattern of other centuries than ours," he remarks of La Boétie in the *Essays*. And in a letter to his father, he describes La Boétie's life as an exemplary Stoic, "lofty, virtuous, and full of very certain resolution."

Still, the more Montaigne read, and the more he wrote, the more doubts he had—about the power of reason to regulate human passions, about the virtues of Stoicism, and about the point of examining oneself in a Christian humanist framework in which salvation would be attained through unwavering faith in Holy Scripture and a progressively closer attunement of oneself with God through Neoplatonic spiritual exercises.

At the same time, world events were forcing him to ponder the implications of the renewed religious conflict that had flared up throughout France. In the late summer and fall of 1572, an unprecedented surge of religious violence swept across France. On August 22, a handful of assassins made an abortive attempt to kill the Huguenot leader Gaspard de Coligny. Fearful that Protestant forces might seek revenge, particularly in the south of France, Henri de Guise convinced King Charles IX and his mother, Catherine de Médicis, to authorize a preemptive second strike two days later, on Saint Bartholomew's Day. This time, a larger band of armed men succeeded in killing several dozen Huguenot leaders gathered in Paris for the dynastic wedding of the Protestant Henry of Navarre and Marguerite de Valois, the Catholic sister of the king.

As news of the massacre spread, more spontaneous killings of Huguenots by Catholics erupted, leaving some two thousand Protestants dead in Paris alone. Over the next two months, similar slaughters occurred in Orléans, Lyon, Rouen, Toulouse, and Bordeaux, claiming the lives of three thousand more Protestants.

The only Huguenot noble to survive was Henry of Navarre. In exchange for his life he was forced to abjure Calvinism publicly, and then was kept under house arrest with his new wife at the king's court.

In the weeks and months that followed, countless fearful Huguenots flocked to local priests and asked to be rebaptized as Catholics. But such coerced conversions inevitably provoked doubts, no different in kind from the doubts that had bedeviled Jewish converts to Catholicism such as Montaigne's own mother. In a world where survival demanded dissimulation, it became all but impossible to distinguish friend from foe—and even harder to secure an elemental sense of trust between individuals from rival religious communities.

The Saint Bartholomew's Day Massacre led to the resumption of civil war in France. As a titled member of the nobility, Montaigne had the right—and duty—to bear arms in his king's army. He undoubtedly served as a soldier in these years, though precisely where and when he fought is unknown.

According to the most reliable contemporary historian of the French wars of religion, Jacques-Auguste de Thou (1553–1617), Montaigne was also drawn into the fray as a negotiator. In later years, he was friendly with de Thou and once told him that he had tried to mediate between Henry of Navarre and Henri de Guise. Presumably his diplomatic efforts occurred in Paris sometime between 1572 and 1576, when Navarre was under house arrest.

Given the personalities at issue, Montaigne faced an all but impossible challenge as a mediator. Besides embracing Calvinism, Henry of Navarre was a distant cousin to the king and second in line to succeed him; as the ruler of Navarre, he also was nominally responsible for maintaining law and order in the southwest of France. Guise, unlike Navarre, was without royal blood; he had made himself irreplaceable to the monarchy by his militant anti-Protestantism and by his leadership, after 1576, of the Holy League, a grimly effective militia, loosely linked with the Crown (since Guise nominally served the king as his leading general). To complicate matters even more, Navarre's bride, Marguerite de Valois, was an observant Catholic who had once been fond of Henri de Guise; theirs was a marriage of dynastic convenience, marked by infidelity on both sides in the years that followed.

Montaigne had some experience as a diplomat. But given the bloodshed on Saint Bartholomew's Day, it was predictable that neither side would trust the other. More surprising is Montaigne's conviction, as reported by de Thou, that both Navarre and Guise were using religious belief "speciously as a pretext" for advancing their rival political agendas.

In any event, Navarre managed to escape from Paris in 1576. Shortly afterward, he converted back to Calvinism and took control of Huguenot forces from his stronghold in Gascony.

In the years that followed, Protestant manifestos and pamphlets began to pour from the presses. Huguenots circulated the text of a constitution that was antimonarchical, based on the free election of Protestant leaders in each region under Huguenot control. One of the most widely distributed Protestant books in these years was *Mémoires de l'état de France sous Charles neufièsme*, a collection of documents and sensational stories about the villains and martyred heroes of the Saint Bartholomew's Day Massacres edited by Simon Goulart (d. 1628), a French Huguenot exile in Geneva. This volume included a complete French text, published without attribution, of La Boétie's spirited *Discourse of Voluntary Servitude*—presumably because it represented such a cogent argument for resistance to a dictatorial sovereign who would repress freedom of worship as well as freedom of conscience.

Montaigne had long planned to include the complete text of La Boétie's *Discourse* in his *Essays*, in the chapter "Of Friendship." But after the Parlement of Bordeaux in 1579 burned copies of the *Mémoires de l'état de France*, Montaigne changed his plan. The chapter on friendship and its encomiums to La Boétie he published without revision. But instead of reprinting the *Discourse*, Montaigne composed a new and Delphic conclusion, telling readers that he had decided at the last minute to omit the text "so that the memory of the author may not be damaged." He declares that "there never was a better citizen, or one more devoted to the tranquility of his country, or more hostile to the commotions and innovations of his time" than the author of the *Discourse*. But he adds, gratuitously, that if La Boétie could have chosen where to be born, it would not have been in France, but rather in Venice—a republic, not a monarchy.

As this example suggests, Montaigne was a master of oblique criticism—in this case, of the burning in France of his friend's libertarian treatise. In appearance, Montaigne upholds conservative pieties while simultaneously sowing doubts about what he really believes.

This uniquely indirect style—marked by contradictory assertions, non sequiturs, and paradoxical lines of apparent argument—reaches its crescendo in the longest by far of Montaigne's *Essays*, his "Apology for Raymond Sebond." Modern scholars agree that this chapter was written at the behest of Marguerite de Valois, probably sometime after she had rejoined her husband Henry of Navarre in 1578 and found herself surrounded by Protestants hoping that she would abjure Catholicism.

In almost every conceivable way, Montaigne's extended essay is the antithesis of the most famous previous apology in the philosophical tradition. Socrates had defended himself by avowing his integrity and claiming to eschew mere rhetoric; he had pledged to represent himself as he really was and to show how his beliefs perfectly harmonized with his deeds, which were both blameless and completely consistent.

Montaigne, by contrast, offers himself as Sebond's self-appointed representative and pleads his case in writing; the defense he offers is ironic at best. Virtually every conceivable rhetorical device appears somewhere in the torrent of words, sometimes for no apparent reason; from moment to moment, it is unclear whether this apologia is offered in earnest or meant to damn with faint praise. It is a convoluted and often confusing piece of writing aimed not at a jury of peers but rather at readers clever enough to decipher its manifold contradictions and sophistries.

It is true, as modern scholars have pointed out, that one can reconstruct a variety of plausible outlines of Montaigne's apology for Sebond, presenting skeletal versions of more or less coherent arguments. Sebond's *Natural Theology*, which Montaigne had rendered from Latin into French, was meant to demonstrate the harmony of reason and faith, by marshaling logical arguments and immediate evidence from the "book of nature," in hopes of persuading even a man lacking knowledge of the Bible to acknowledge the divine order of the cosmos, thus blazing an independent and entirely rational path toward the truth of revealed Christianity.

In his own "Apology," Montaigne chooses to answer two main objections that had been raised against Sebond's treatise: first, that Christianity ought to be based not on reason or empirical evidence but on faith alone; and, second, that Sebond's actual arguments and evidence are weak and unconvincing.

One modern philosopher has crisply summarized the ironic nature of Montaigne's response to the first objection: "In order to 'defend' Sebond's thesis that the truths of faith can be demonstrated rationally, Montaigne first made pure faith the cornerstone of religion; then allowed Sebond's efforts second-class status as aids after, but not before the acceptance of God." The argument thus summarized is coherent but perverse, given that the premise of Montaigne's defense seems to undermine Sebond's whole project.

Similarly perverse is Montaigne's response to the second objection to Sebond's treatise. He starts by conceding the weaknesses of Sebond's arguments and empirical evidence, then proceeds to defend these weaknesses, by arguing that nobody else has better arguments or evidence, "and that no one can achieve any certainty by rational means."

Despite the ability of careful readers to extract coherent arguments from what at first seems a hopelessly woolly and rambling text, there is to this day no fixed consensus about what Montaigne hoped to accomplish by expressing himself in this very peculiar way.

Did he mean seriously to defend the Christian faith? Or does the convoluted character of the prose, and its skeptical cast, instead indicate that Montaigne in fact doubted *everything*, even Catholic orthodoxy—which he is therefore merely pretending to defend?

One thing, at least, is clear: Montaigne's style of writing produced a radically open text, one that could be read in multiple ways. A typical passage, which appears midway through the "Apology for Raymond Sebond," is embedded in a paradoxical warning, directly addressed to a single person—presumably Marguerite de Valois—entreating this reader to ignore the extraordinary arguments Montaigne himself has just rehearsed at such length:

> Our mind is an erratic, dangerous, and heedless tool; it is hard to impose order and moderation on it. And in my time those that have some rare excellence beyond the others, and some extraordinary quickness, are nearly all, we see, incontinent in the license of their opinions and conduct. It is a miracle if you find a sedate and sociable one. People are right to give the tightest possible barriers to the human mind. In study, as in everything else, its steps must be counted and regulated for it, the limits of the chase must be artificially determined for it. They bridle and bind it with religions, laws, customs, science, precepts, mortal and immortal punishments and rewards; and still we see that by its whirling and its incohesiveness it escapes all these bonds. It is an empty body, with nothing by which it can be seized and directed; a varying and formless body, which can be neither tied nor grasped. Indeed there are few souls so orderly, so strong and wellborn, that they can be trusted with their own guidance, and that can sail with moderation and without temerity, in the freedom of their judgments, beyond the common opinions. It is more expedient to place them in tutelage. The mind is a dangerous blade, even to its possessor, for anyone who does not know how to wield it with order and discretion.

What is Montaigne trying to say in this passage? On the one hand, he says that "they" (who are they?) "bridle and bind" the mind, and implies that "people are right" to do so. On the other hand, and implicitly speaking for himself, he describes the mind as "empty," with "nothing by which it can be seized and directed." If his last assertion is true, then it must call into question the practical value of trying to bridle and bind any such "formless body."

We are, moreover, told that the mind is a dangerous weapon if a person does not know how to "wield it with order." But we read this in a passage that is itself disorderly. Instead of providing a crisp summary of precepts, or a set of clear statements on core matters of faith—what one might expect from someone sincerely interested in placing the public "in tutelage" and reinforcing the "tightest possible barriers to the human mind"—the reader is offered a formless hodgepodge of contradictions and free associations, a passage full of "whirling" and "incohesiveness," signifying . . . what?

One recalls Montaigne's personal motto, *Que sais-je?* (What do I know?), a question that hangs over every page of the *Essays*. In order to answer it, the author slowly but surely discards his earlier efforts to model himself on ancient exemplars, or even on the Stoic rectitude of his humanist friend La Boétie.

He instead turns inward and decides to study himself, by describing frankly the variability and vicissitudes of his judgment and behavior, experimenting with different forms of thought, and conducting this research through writing, not as an end in itself but rather as a means to test his beliefs without any preconceptions or fixed narrative goal in mind, and in this way— through an unpremeditated representation of his thoughts—to compose himself anew: "I have put all my efforts into forming my life. That is my trade and my work."

Despite the novelty of his book's form and style, Montaigne had little trouble finding a publisher. The printing press was still a relatively new invention, but it had already created a new social group, a community of readers, joined by their interest in specific texts that could now be circulated far more widely than the hand-copied manuscripts that had served Aquinas as well as Augustine.

Montaigne's business associate for the production of the *Essays* was Simon Millanges, a printer based in Bordeaux who specialized in producing fine editions of work by new writers for a mainly affluent clientele of noble readers. Despite being based in Bordeaux rather than Paris, Millanges published works by three of the most important French writers of his generation: besides Montaigne, he published Guillaume de Salluste Du Bartas (1544–1590), an epic poet (and Huguenot) whose influential *La Sepmaine; ou, Création du monde*

(1578) formed one basis for Milton's *Paradise Lost*; and in 1582, he published the first book by Jacques-Auguste de Thou. Millanges was a shrewd judge of literary talent, and Montaigne entered into a partnership with him, possibly helping to finance the first printing.

Montaigne claimed to have written a work "dedicated . . . to the private convenience of . . . relatives and friends," but most of his friends, and many of his relatives, held public office. His first readers were Frenchmen of his own station and status: officeholders, trained lawyers, gentlemen soldiers, diplomats—men who presumably shared some of his own political and moral concerns about the catastrophic cruelty of the country's wars of religion and the public policies and personal virtues that might help stanch the bloodshed.

As one modern scholar aptly writes, "Montaigne responds to the contemporary crisis of a civil war by propounding in the *Essais* a new ethics to counter the model of heroic virtue that prevailed in his culture and his noble class. Against the hard-liner who never yields, even in the face of death—the constant Stoic, the honor-bound aristocrat, the religious zealot—he offers a pliant goodness that is the product not of heroic effort and philosophical discipline, not even of Christian charity or meekness, but rather of ordinary fellow feeling."

In theory—if one takes seriously the skeptical views expressed indirectly and discreetly in the pages of the *Essays*—Montaigne was a deep pluralist; that is, a man keenly aware of the variety, transience, and sheer contingency of all moral and political customs and conventions. Yet in practice—fearful as he was of bloody anarchy, which was a constant possibility—the pluralist was also an absolutist: ready on prudential grounds to submit to the dictates of his Catholic king.

In the complex logic of the *Essays*, a gap opens up, between inward belief and outward behavior: "Whom shall we believe when he talks about himself, in so corrupt an age, seeing that there are few or none whom we can believe when they speak of others, where there is less incentive for lying?" Eschewing sincerity of the sort exemplified by Socrates in Plato's *Apology*, Montaigne forges an oblique new style of writing suited to the world of witch hunts and religious persecution that he actually inhabited. "We owe ourselves in part to society, but in the best part to ourselves," he remarks.

Like the philosopher-kings Plato depicted in his *Republic*, Montaigne will search for the truth while sometimes deploying "noble lies." He may mislead deliberately, and he explicitly contradicts himself, but he also tries to register accurately "all the little thoughts" that come to his mind, however inconsistent they seem. And by writing down *everything* that he thinks, he will truthfully render the gap—the inconsistencies—between the "best part" of himself, his inward beliefs, and the part of himself he owes to society: his outward behavior and his various public professions of faith.

"I do not portray being. I portray passing . . . [These *Essays* are] a record of various and changeable events, and of irresolute and even contradictory thoughts . . . I may indeed contradict myself now and then; but truth . . . I do not contradict."

Having launched the first edition of his *Essays* in print, Montaigne embarked on a grand tour in June 1580, bringing along a small retinue of family, friends, and servants. The group first journeyed to Paris, where tradition has it that Montaigne presented a specially bound copy of the *Essays* to King Henry III, who had ascended the throne after the death of Charles IX in 1574.

At the time, the king was planning to lay siege to a French town then held by Huguenot troops, and Montaigne agreed to join his army. Despite abhorring the cruelty of war, he did not mind fulfilling his martial duties: "There is no occupation so pleasant as the military one," he avers in one of the essays he added to his book in later years; it is "an occupation both noble in execution (for the strongest, most generous, and proudest of all virtues is valor) and noble in its cause: there is no more just and universal service than the protection of the peace and greatness of your country."

By early September, with the king's army on the verge of breaking the resistance of the Protestant rebels in La Fère, Montaigne and his entourage were free to continue on their tour. He was now forty-seven years old. A newly minted author and retired nobleman with firsthand experience of law, politics, and war, he was increasingly prey to the ailments of age and especially to recurrent bouts of kidney stones, which left him in excruciating pain.

No matter. He was eager to experience the larger world. Over the next fourteen months, his party journeyed from France to Switzerland, and then on to Germany. But they spent most of their time traveling in Italy. The group stayed for many weeks at the mineral baths of La Villa, where Montaigne tried to cure his kidney stones and restore his health, and they also stopped in Venice, Verona, Florence, Siena, Pisa, Lucca, and Rome for more than five months, to explore various places of historical interest.

Everywhere the group went, Montaigne explored the local forms of religious practice. At Basel, Baden, and Augsburg, he visited Protestant churches, attended services, and met with ministers to discuss their views, carefully taking notes on the doctrinal differences among Lutherans, Calvinists, and Zwinglians. He visited Catholic churches in Italy and took notes on how the priests and cardinals conducted services, concluding that Italians in general seemed more lax than French Catholics. He watched a Roman exorcist try to drive a demon out of a possessed man and described how the priest threatened the devil "in the loudest and most magisterial voice he could." He and his group were granted an audience with the pope, who may have helped Montaigne become an honorific "citizen of Rome." At Rome, he met several times with the Jesuit Juan Madonado, a learned theologian who had also participated in the conversion of Henry of Navarre from Calvinism to Catholicism after the Saint Bartholomew's massacre in Paris. He met with the papal censor in charge of reviewing the *Essays*, who let the author off lightly, merely admonishing him to let his conscience "redress what I should see was in bad taste." In Verona, Montaigne visited a synagogue and talked with the rabbi. After visiting a synagogue in Rome, he witnessed a ceremony of circumcision. He was insatiably curious about the varieties of religious experience.

Meanwhile, back in France, the *Essays* had struck a nerve. The book had made its author famous. Legend has it that when King Henry III complimented Montaigne on the virtues of his work, he replied that if His Majesty liked the essays, then he should like him, too, "as they were simply an account of his life and actions."

The first edition of his book was quickly followed by a second, slightly revised edition in 1582, also printed by Simon Millanges in Bordeaux; a third edition in 1584, printed in Rouen; and then a fourth, reproducing the second edition but printed by Jean Richer in Paris in 1587; and then a fifth and thoroughly revised edition, "enlarged by a third book and by six hundred additions to the first two," printed by one of the best-known publishers in France,

Abel L'Angelier in Paris in 1588.

Montaigne's growing reputation as a writer, combined with his experience as a magistrate in the Parlement of Bordeaux, and his service to the king's court in Paris as a diplomatic go-between, made his political skills and opinions of interest to a growing array of French notables. At the end of November 1581, Montaigne learned from King Henry III that in his absence he had been elected mayor of Bordeaux, apparently the unanimous choice of town officials and the relevant outside authorities, including not just Henry III but Henry of Navarre as well.

Montaigne hurried home to assume his new responsibilities. Most of Bordeaux's elite were Catholic loyalists, but the surrounding countryside was largely Protestant and under the control of Navarre. Bordeaux's mayor had at his disposal a company of lords and was expected to represent the interests of the region to the court in Paris. The historian de Thou, who first came to know Montaigne in these years, described the new mayor as "a man free in spirit and foreign to factions."

Because he professed loyalty to the French Crown, it is not surprising that Montaigne had become a gentleman-in-ordinary—an official aide—at the court of King Henry III in 1573. But four years later, he had also been made a gentleman-in-ordinary at the court of Henry of Navarre. One of the rare noblemen trusted by both sides as a counselor and envoy, the mayor entered into a series of diplomatic missions in 1583 and 1585, trying to broker a cease-fire between Navarre and the king, in what proved a successful effort to isolate militants from the Holy League in Bordeaux who were loyal to Guise. The future of the French monarchy was also at issue in these negotiations, since the death of the king's younger brother in 1584 had made Henry of Navarre the king's heir apparent.

It was a merciless time, but Montaigne was a discreet advocate of clemency and of mercy, themes that recur in his *Essays*. As a result of his diplomacy in these years, he became friends with Philippe du Plessis Mornay, one of Navarre's closest advisers and the Huguenot's foremost philosopher (he was reputed to be the author of the *Contra Vindiciae Tyrannos*, A Defense of Liberty Against Tyrants, a radical justification of rebellion published in 1579 that was not dissimilar in substance to arguments advanced a generation earlier by

Montaigne's old friend La Boétie).

But Montaigne himself continued to eschew radical rhetoric of any kind. As he saw it, his job was not to defend to the death abstract principles but rather to secure local law and order, by keeping Bordeaux and its environs peaceful and its citizens obedient to the monarchy. He was successful in this, even if his moderate policies—and his willingness to negotiate with Protestants—inevitably struck militant Catholics as a failure of nerve.

Max Horkheimer, the founder of twentieth-century critical theory, in the 1930s attacked Montaigne and what he took to be his "skepticism" as an insidious if genteel form of spineless irrationalism, the perfect philosophy for a complacent bourgeois—a man of comfortable means, free in spirit, conformist in practice, and constitutionally incapable of taking sides in a struggle that demanded hard choices. (Horkheimer of course had in mind the complacent German burghers of his own day, who were paralyzed into indecision by the looming showdown between fascism and communism in Weimar Germany).

This is a caricature, in part because it serves a polemical purpose. But Horkheimer was right to remark that Montaigne "saw his role essentially as that of a negotiator rather than an antagonist." And what Montaigne certainly did do was to give voice, in both theory and practice, to a ruthlessly unsentimental sort of realpolitik, one that justified the wiles and willingness to bend principles characteristic of enlightened diplomats in search of peaceful ways to resolve violent disputes.

This is doubtless one reason why Montaigne in the *Essays* goes out of his way to say nice things about the notorious Alcibiades, the Athenian chameleon and "madcap" (in Montaigne's words) whose charm as a negotiator nevertheless secured, however briefly, the trust of Athenians, of Spartans, even of Persians, and whose life—if we disregard his notorious treachery and focus instead on his obvious capacity to negotiate cultural differences—contains, as Montaigne writes with mischievous generosity, some of "the most rich and desirable qualities."

Like much in the *Essays*, this apparently nonchalant passage is a carefully crafted provocation. After all, in the accounts of Plato and Plutarch, Alcibiades functions as the antithesis of Socrates, long *the* image of the good man—and a recurrent touchstone for Montaigne himself. And as the author well knew, a classical criterion of the philosophical life properly lived was the sort of steadfast rational unity and reliable integrity that Socrates himself claimed to embody: "throughout my life, in any public activity I may have engaged in, I am the same man as I am in private life."

Yet Montaigne, in this respect like Alcibiades, pointedly, and repeatedly, avowed just the opposite: "We are all patchwork, and so shapeless and diverse in composition that each bit, each moment, plays its own game." Unlike Socrates, Montaigne holds the changeability of human beliefs and behavior to be sometimes a virtue and not invariably a vice. He thought it possible to "love virtue too much." The "fairest souls," he suggests, are supple, flexible, prepared to negotiate complex and changing circumstances. Montaigne will parley with Catholics, and he will parley with Protestants, too. Anyone wishing to judge the author of the *Essays* by traditional norms of integrity will find him wanting (as the most fervent Catholics and Protestants often did). He took seriously one of Saint Paul's maxims: "Be not wiser than you should, but be soberly wise." Sobriety entails moderation in belief and conduct, the opposite of the kind of unyielding conviction and resolute consistency epitomized by a Stoic hero such as Cato.

Montaigne is skeptical of the real motives of defiant martyrs: "I do not know if the ardor that is born of spite and obstinacy against the pressure and violence of authority, and of danger, or the concern for reputation, has not sent some men all the way to the stake to maintain an opinion for which, among their friends and at liberty, they would not have been willing to burn the tip of their finger." For the sake of maintaining civil peace, he generally urges submitting to traditional institutions: "the best and soundest side" in an aggravated conflict between rival forms of life "is undoubtedly that which maintains the old religion and the old government of the country." But this does not mean that Montaigne himself believes that the old religion and the old government harmonize with some "universal and natural reason," since he elsewhere makes it clear that he believes no such thing.

In 1585, Montaigne stepped down as mayor and retired again to his château, where he resumed reflecting on himself and writing more chapters for his *Essays*. His work was interrupted briefly that year and the next, after King

Henry III capitulated to the Catholic militants of the League and, joining forces with them, renewed war against the Protestants. In 1586, a Catholic army laid siege to the Protestant town of Castillon, five miles from Montaigne's castle. On this occasion, Montaigne did not volunteer to join the king's army, as he had in 1580. "I was belabored from every quarter," he later wrote. "To the Ghibelline I was a Guelph, to the Guelph a Ghibelline." From now on, the most militant Catholics suspected he was unreliable, a man too friendly to Henry of Navarre; while in the eyes of militant Protestants, he was widely distrusted as a Catholic too friendly to King Henry III.

The virulent plague that broke the siege of Castillon also left a large number of Montaigne's neighbors dead. In this somber setting, he renewed work in 1587 on the final additions to his book. Although his style and his views continued to evolve, at no point in the *Essays* does Montaigne elaborate a reasoned theory of justice, or offer logical arguments that defend clear views about how to think about truth, about the good, about God, etc. Montaigne moreover continues to stress that he lacks the sort of rational unity that Socrates exemplified, and that a number of other ancient philosophers had, in different ways, struggled to attain. Given these facts, one has to wonder: Is Montaigne really a "philosopher" at all?

Characteristically, Montaigne vacillates in his own answer to that question in the final chapters of his book.

"I am no philosopher," he writes at one point—but the context is his essay on vanity, and perhaps he is trying to appear modest.

"What rule my life belonged to, I did not learn until after it was completed and spent," he writes in another context, and then exclaims, almost exultantly: "A new figure: an unpremeditated and accidental philosopher!"

Accidental in his philosophy or not, Montaigne generally represents himself as a sincere seeker after self-knowledge: "It is a thorny undertaking, and more so than it seems, to follow a movement so wandering as that of our mind, to penetrate the opaque depths of its innermost folds, to pick out and immobilize the innumerable flutterings that agitate it. And it is a new and extraordinary amusement, which withdraws us from the ordinary occupations of the world, yes, even from those most recommended."

His dilemma vis-à-vis "philosophy" as it had been understood by most of the classical schools was simple: looking for a stable core, a coherent self with a resolute will, consistently capable of executing the commands of reason, his search had revealed instead what Augustine called "the abyss of human consciousness."

But unlike Augustine (or the Renaissance humanists who followed in his footsteps), Montaigne conspicuously lacked a compensatory faith in an indwelling God. At no point does Montaigne entertain the hope that a man suffused with pure intellect might transform himself into "an angel and the son of God," as Giovanni Pico della Mirandola had put it in his famous *Oration on the Dignity of Man* (1486). He seems never to have experienced a rapture, or been graced with anything like a divine revelation, and thus lacked the sublime certainty characteristic of Augustine and of Pico's brand of Neoplatonic Christian humanism.

Quite the contrary: the longer he pondered the facts of history, the sheer variety of social customs, and the many odd things he had personally seen and experienced, the more Montaigne felt forced to acknowledge that every man was inevitably a changeling, a bundle of inescapable pains and pleasures, with an intellect that was incurably impure and a mind that more often than not was uninformed by logic, unregulated by clear ideas, and filled instead with countless "flutterings."

In response, he chose to compose himself through his writing rather than through Stoic austerities or Christian asceticism: "I have not, like Socrates, corrected my natural disposition by force of reason," he declares. "I let myself go as I have come." Although it is "himself" that he hopes to fathom by writing, he has no faith in his own divine provenance and no confidence that the force of reason can make him a better man; as a result, it is inconceivable that he should craft an account of exemplary episodes from his life, as Plato does of Socrates, or a providential narrative, such as that presented by Augustine in his *Confessions*. Instead, he hopes to offer a portrait of his thinking as it actually unfolds.

As the years passed, and his experience of the world widened, Montaigne restlessly kept revising and rewriting, piling words upon words, building up an emblematic collage, stitching new sentences into existing essays, amassing more historical and political vignettes, more quotes from quarreling sages both ancient and modern, and more of his own miscellaneous and generally inconclusive thought experiments concerning matters large and small, both abstract and concrete. Defiantly unsystematic, the style of the whole is as novel as the philosophy it expresses, revealing a new inner world as confounding as anything the conquistadors had unearthed beyond the sea: *"If we could view that expanse of countries and ages, boundless in every direction, into which the mind, plunging and spreading itself, travels so far and wide that it can find no limit where it can stop, there would appear in that immensity an infinite capacity to produce innumerable forms."*

The protean potential of human beings is not simply (as in Pico della Mirandola's famous speech) clinching evidence of "the dignity of man." It is also evidence of the infinite folly of human beings: a source of amusement that may also provoke horror. The mind of man is capable of anything.

And in his *Essays*, Montaigne proves it, repeatedly, in passages that are cumulatively chastening: because they meticulously record the cruelties and atrocities of his age; because they recount the horrors as well as the glories of the ancients, as attested by Plutarch; because they endlessly quote the contradictory maxims quite reasonably put forward by a discordant lot of philosophers, from Plato to the devil's advocate Machiavelli; and humbling, too, because he records with unflinching honesty his ordinary vices as well as his virtues, his flights of fancy as well as his considered convictions.

But for all his stress on the vanity of human beings, the *Essays* are not, finally, an exercise in humility. For Montaigne's unprecedented method—a sort of "free association" *avant la lettre freudienne*—also reveals two sorts of positive truths: about some universal limits to the variability of human beings (since "each man bears the entire form of the human condition"), and about Montaigne himself as a unique individual, who embodies a singular pattern of natural impulses, recurring fantasies, and reasoned beliefs, self-consciously at odds with the codes of conduct and idealized images of perfect virtue promulgated by the classical schools of philosophy.

Montaigne is sometimes foolish. But his follies take a shape that is unmistakably his own. And by acknowledging what is distinctive about himself, as well as by describing the limitations he shares with every man—his ignorance, his susceptibility to pain, the unruliness of his animal appetites and desires—

Montaigne manages to console himself. He thus attains one of the chief goals of the first philosophers: tranquillity—though one has to wonder if his success results from his eccentric approach to philosophy or from the naturally equable disposition that the author of the *Essays* both reveals and commends.

In any case, his characteristic imperturbability doubtless served Montaigne well in his ongoing diplomatic sorties. To the end of his life, he remained an intermediary trusted by both Protestants and Catholics. Henry of Navarre stayed with Montaigne at his château in October 1587. The following year, Montaigne journeyed to Paris, where he helped to negotiate an alliance between Navarre and King Henry III against the militants of the Catholic League.

Henry III proceeded to recognize Navarre as his legitimate successor. But after arranging the murder of Henri de Guise in 1588, King Henry III was himself assassinated by a monk in 1589. A renewed civil war broke out, pitting the forces of Navarre, now King Henry IV, against the forces of the Catholic League, which refused to accept Navarre as France's lawful king.

For his part, Montaigne supported Navarre unconditionally and would presumably have joined his retinue of advisers had his health permitted. But the author of the *Essays* spent the last two years of his life largely confined to his château. He did not live to see King Henry IV abjure Protestantism in 1593, nor to see him dictate the terms of an uneasy religious modus vivendi between Catholics and Huguenots in the Edict of Nantes in 1598: policies shaped by expedience and a sincere desire to avoid more violence.

In 1592, Montaigne contracted quinsy. For several days, his throat infection left him unable to talk. Sensing that death was near, according to one contemporary account, he wrote a note asking his wife and some neighbors to join him for a Mass in his bedroom. "When the priest came to the elevation of the *Corpus Domini*, this poor gentleman rose up as best he could in his bed, with a desperate effort, hands clasped; and in this last action gave up his spirit to God."

One friend lamented the passing of "the true pattern and mirror of pure philosophy."

Another friend, the prominent French jurist and historian Étienne Pasquier, more accurately expressed the peculiar nature of his dead friend's achievement. Trying to express his mixed feelings, he hailed him as "another

Seneca in our language," but also described how Montaigne, unlike his classical precursors, "took pleasure in being pleasantly displeasing." Like many of the book's first admirers, he had pillaged its pages for various classical maxims and aperçus while passing over in silence the more puzzling autobiographical passages and deploring the ramshackle design of the whole: Montaigne's book of *Essays*, as he piquantly put it, "is not really a flower bed, arranged in various plots and borders, but a sort of diversified prairie of many flowers, pell-mell and without art."

Montaigne was the matter of this book. But his book, like its author, was inimitable, and (as Pasquier grasped) a bit wild, despite the repeated praise of moderation. By writing about himself as he really was—without shame, without inhibition, without deception—Montaigne revealed a singular personality and elaborated a style of thought that was unconstrained by either moral prohibitions or a demand for overarching logical consistency. He deplored novelty, yet his *Essays* were indisputably novel: a new form of self-expression, giving rise to a new kind of philosophy—uneasily at home in a world of deceptive appearances and religious bloodletting.

DESCARTES

Queen Christina of Sweden (1626–1689) and her court, detail showing Descartes tutoring the Queen in 1649, oil on canvas, by Pierre-Louis Dumesnil (1698–1781). An intellectual prodigy and one of the most powerful sovereigns in Europe, Christina had first contacted Descartes three years earlier, asking him: "What can cause more harm, if misused? Love or hate?" (Château de Versailles, France/The Bridgeman Art Library International)

istorians have often depicted René Descartes as the father of modern philosophy, because he was the first to free reasoned inquiry from the shackles of traditional authority, the first to demand that everyone, no matter the topic, think for himself or herself. A mathematical genius who made important contributions to calculus, algebra, and analytical geometry, Descartes was also the first to publish the law of refraction, which describes how light rays are deflected when they pass from one optical medium to another, and he was the first to advance "the very idea of a law of nature in print." Perhaps best known today for a single declarative sentence—*Cogito, ergo sum*, I think, therefore I am—he was renowned in his own day for arguing that any ordinary man or woman, if properly trained, could become educated and independent.

Descartes, in short, was in many respects just what most writers of the eighteenth-century Enlightenment made him out to be: a hero of unfettered intellect.

Paradoxically, Descartes knew that his own quest for knowledge had resulted from more than just a logical chain of clear and distinct ideas. Equally crucial was the revelation that he experienced on the night of November 10–11, 1619, in the course of three enigmatic but transformative dreams.

"The Lord has made three marvels," he wrote at the time, in a private notebook that never left his possession in the years that followed. "Something out of nothing; free will; and God in Man."

On the evidence of this notebook, Descartes regarded himself as a visionary, as certain as Augustine of the truths that God had revealed to him. He ardently believed that "all those to whom God has given the use of . . . reason have an obligation to employ it principally in the endeavor to know Him and to know themselves." Seneca supplied him with one of his favorite epigrams: "Death weighs on him who is known to all, but dies unknown to himself." Shortly after Descartes's death, a hagiographic myth sprung up around his memory, and the early biographies all recount his wayward youth, his conversion to the life of the mind, a meeting in the presence of the papal nuncio, etc.—always stressing the orthodoxy of his religious views.

A product of a Catholic upbringing who offered two famous (and famously unconvincing) proofs that God exists in the *Meditations* (1641), Descartes described a magisterial vision of a material world explained by applied mathematics, which laid the basis for later innovations in physics by Christiaan Huygens and Isaac Newton. At the same time, as he put it in a letter to the monk and mathematician Marin Mersenne (1588–1644), Descartes supposed that "the mathematical truths which you call eternal have been laid down by God and depend on him entirely," and he said that he had discovered "the foundations of physics" only because, by earnestly trying to know himself, he had come to know God. He furthermore assumed that it was his God-given duty to render, to the best of his ability, a true account of everything he had come to know in terms that would be "to the largest extent possible independent of the local perspectives or idiosyncrasies of enquirers" (to borrow the words of an eminent modern admirer).

Like some other Renaissance philosophers, he episodically dreamed of elaborating a *mathesis universalis*—"a general science that explains all the points that can be raised concerning order and measure irrespective of the subject matter." To some Christian critics, this dream, in its preoccupation with taking the measure of the physical world, was a form of blasphemy, a symptom of the sin of pride. And even though Descartes repeatedly professed his good faith in the few texts that he cautiously chose to publish in the last years of his life, he left a number of important works prudently unpublished in his lifetime and spent most of his adult life in Protestant countries, at a safe distance from the papal censors who had condemned the writings of Galileo.

This was not the comfortable life of riches and honor that Descartes's patrician father had planned for his son. René was born near Tours in the Loire Valley of France, on March 31, 1596, the third of three children who survived infancy. His father, Joachim Descartes, was a Catholic magistrate in the Parlement of Britanny, which convened in Rennes to the north. After his mother, Jeanne Brouchard, died in childbirth a year later, his father left the three children with their maternal grandmother, Jeanne Sain, who raised René until 1606, when he entered the college of La Flèche at Anjou. Like Montaigne two generations earlier, and like his elder brother Pierre, Descartes was being groomed for the career of a proper gentleman, as a magistrate in the Parlement.

This was a time of relative peace and prosperity in France. In 1598, after almost thirty years of civil war, King Henry IV—formerly Henry of Navarre, a Huguenot turned Catholic—had promulgated the Edict of Nantes, granting religious freedom to his Protestant subjects in order to restore law and order to his primarily Catholic kingdom. Descartes's school, La Flèche, was itself a product of Henry's enlightened policies.

Opened just two years before Descartes entered, and housed in a former palace donated by the king, La Flèche was meant from the start to be the most prestigious of the Catholic schools organized in these years under the auspices of the Society of Jesus. The society was a new Catholic order, founded by Ignatius Loyola and authorized by Rome in 1540, with hopes of reforming Catholicism from within, through a renewed emphasis on introspective self-examination, the creation of rigorously classical institutions of humanist education, and an unwavering fealty to the pope.

At La Flèche, Descartes was trained in Latin, Greek, classical literature, rhetoric, mathematics, logic, physics, metaphysics, and, in later years, theology. Life at the school was regulated in every detail, from the timing of worship to the language of instruction—Latin exclusively. Among classical philosophers, Aristotle as interpreted by Aquinas enjoyed pride of place; in addition, the Stoics and Cicero were studied as models of casuistry, the art of resolving moral problems without recourse to universal principles.

Perhaps the most distinctive feature of the school's curriculum was the requirement that *collegiens* not only study the admonitory writings of Loyola (for example, in thinking about hell, "smell the smoke, the brimstone, the corruption, and rottenness") but also put these admonitions into practice during retreats under the direction of a spiritual adviser. These retreats revolved around a meticulously regulated set of spiritual exercises involving silent prayer, meditation, the examination of conscience, and the visualization in solitude of specific biblical scenes, from the birth of Jesus to his ascension.

This routine was shattered on May 14, 1610, by the assassination of Henry IV by a fanatical Catholic, a death that traumatized all of France. Under the terms of his bequest to the Jesuits—and to express the seriousness of his gift— Henry IV stipulated that the college receive his heart after his death. Thus in late May the heart of the fallen king was conveyed in a chalice by stages from Paris to La Flèche, where the young Descartes would have attended a memorial service, along with the entire community.

The following year, the school commemorated the king's death with a ceremony. Students were asked to compose works in honor of Henry, and the contributions were bound under the title *Tears from La Flèche* and deposited in the school's library, where the manuscript can be seen today. The volume includes a poem in French that some scholars speculate was written by the young Descartes: "Sonnet on the death of the king Henry the Great, and on the discovery of some new Planets, or Stars wandering around Jupiter, made this Year by Galileo Galilei, famous Mathematician of the Grand Duke of Florence."

After leaving La Flèche in 1614, the eighteen-year-old math whiz became a cardsharp in Paris, according to his first biographers, capitalizing on his ability to calculate, and thus beat, the odds. In 1616, he took a Baccalaureat and Licence in Law at the University of Poitiers. Apart from sowing some wild oats, he seemed poised to follow in his father's sober footsteps, by becoming first a soldier in the king's army and then a magistrate in a provincial parlement.

Leaving Poitiers, the twenty-year-old next journeyed to the Netherlands. Armed religious conflict had flared up again throughout Europe, as had the long-standing rivalry between the Catholic empires of France and Spain. In the Netherlands, Descartes volunteered to join a French regiment stationed at Breda under Prince Maurice of Orange, the commander in chief of the armies of the Calvinist United Provinces, which had gained their independence by defeating the Spanish army. Besides being a Protestant ally of France against Spain, Maurice had hired mathematicians and physical scientists to teach enlightened officers the arts of military engineering: fortification, sieges, encampments, etc. Descartes did not see action in Breda, but he did meet Isaac Beeckman, a brilliant engineer and scientist.

At the time, Descartes was twenty-two years old, and Beeckman was twenty-nine. A candlemaker who also designed water conduits for breweries, Beeckman was a doctor of medicine who in his free time studied physics and mechanical engineering. Like many of his contemporaries who also were interested in "natural philosophy" (as such areas of inquiry were often described), Beeckman carried on a discreet but active research program with a variety of fellow researchers and interested onlookers. Discretion was essential, since neither the heliocentric teachings of Copernicus nor the mechanical philosophy of Galileo was easily reconciled with the views of orthodox Christians, both Calvinist and Catholic.

Though Beeckman published nothing in his lifetime, he and his friends met in his own private *het collegium mechanicum*—a kind of salon for engineers, where merchants, bankers, and natural philosophers could discuss practical applications of new inventions. When Beeckman's journals were eventually published (between 1939 and 1953), they showed that he had elaborated the law of falling bodies independently of Galileo and formulated the first known approach to the law of inertia; he also had elaborated a thoroughly mechanistic view of the world, speculating that the atomic construction of matter held the key to understanding all natural phenomena, from water pumps to musical sound.

Though his apprenticeship to Beeckman lasted only briefly, these were pivotal months for Descartes. Beeckman exemplified an alternative way of life. He was a philosopher devoted primarily to research, rather than a gentleman concerned with augmenting the status and standing of his family. Awed by his intellect and infatuated with his personality, Descartes wrote and dedicated a short treatise on music to his new friend. "It was you alone," he wrote Beeckman in April 1619, "who roused me from my state of indolence, and re-awakened the learning which by then had almost disappeared from my memory; and when my mind strayed from serious pursuits, it was you who led it back to worthier things."

The two men soon went their separate ways, but the encounter with Beeckman convinced Descartes that great discoveries could be expected from the application of mathematics to the problems of physics. He remained ambivalent about what path in life to take. Still on track to become a proper French gentleman, he enlisted in the Catholic army of Maximilian I, another ruler keen to use the latest scientific research for military ends. As winter approached, the army was stationed in Ulm at Neuburg, where a college of army engineering was located, and where Descartes may have made the acquaintance—and come under the influence—of a talented local mathematician, Johannes Faulhaber.

Unlike Beeckman, Faulhaber was a mystagogue. Four years earlier, he had published *Mysterium Arithmeticum*, addressed to the Brethren of the Rose Cross, or Rosicrucians. Like the Pythagorean sects in classical Greece, the Rosicrucians mixed mathematical research with mystical rites, promising an occult knowledge of nature based on a comprehensive numerology. And like some neo-Platonic philosophers of the Renaissance (such as Heinrich Cornelius Agrippa, 1486–1535), the brethren proclaimed the existence of a "science of sciences" that, starting from absolutely certain first principles, offered the key to the ordering of all knowledge.

Most modern scholars doubt that Descartes ever met Faulhaber—though Adrien Baillet describes in some detail how the two men conducted a long and substantive conversation about geometry. One thing is clear: "The great ferment of alchemists, astrologists, and magicians fed the desires of young men like Descartes to penetrate the mysteries of the natural world," in the words of a modern biographer. And in this period Descartes, to judge by his private journals, seems for a while to have fancied himself some sort of Rosicrucian.

The events of November 10–11, though rarely given a central role in modern accounts of Descartes, remain one of the most dramatic conversion scenes in the history of philosophy.

Three different sources document the event: There is Descartes's own rather discreet account of the winter of 1619 in the autobiographical passages that open *Discourse on the Method*, the first important text that he published, almost twenty years later, in 1637. There are Descartes's much more vivid private notes from the relevant months in his personal journal, which survives only in a few fragments transcribed in 1676 from the manuscript by the German mathematician and philosopher Gottfried Wilhelm Leibniz (1646–1716) and first published two hundred years later. And there is a more detailed paraphrase of the contents of the same personal journal given in perhaps the first comprehensive modern philosophical biography—filling two substantial volumes, it is a long-form hagiography, really—*La Vie de Monsieur Des-Cartes* by Adrien Baillet, published in 1691. (The journal that Baillet and Leibniz both saw has since vanished.)

"I stayed all day shut up alone in a stove-heated room," Descartes writes in *Discourse on the Method*, "where I was completely free to converse with myself about my own thoughts."

He recalls how his reading of philosophy had left him uncertain about its value, since it seemed that "nothing can be imagined which is too strange or incredible to have been said by some philosopher." Abandoning the study of letters, he acquired a law degree and set out to survey the larger world. Perhaps in hopes of fulfilling his father's wish that he enter politics, he "considered the customs of other men," only to find "almost as much diversity as I had found previously among the philosophers."

He had spent some time learning from "the book of the world."

Now he resolved to "study also myself" and "to use all the power of my mind to choose the paths I should follow."

Alone in his stove-heated room and free to meditate at will, Descartes first thought about how much more perfect were the works created by one man: a sole city planner, a single architect, a solitary lawgiver such as Sparta's legendary Lycurgus. "And so I thought that since the sciences contained in books . . . is amassed little by little from the opinions of many different persons, it never comes so close to the truth as the simple reasoning which a man of good sense naturally makes concerning whatever he comes across."

He concluded that it might be wise to jettison his prior beliefs "all at one go, in order to replace them afterwards with better ones, or with the same ones once I had squared them with the standards of reason."

This was a risky resolution. After making it, he felt "like a man who walks alone in the dark." Proceeding with due caution, and after further meditation alone in his room, Descartes resolved to adopt as well what he called a "provisional moral code."

This code consisted of three practical maxims and one general rule. The maxims were, first, to obey the laws and customs of the country one lives in; second, to act according to the most probable opinion whenever there is a lack of time to discern what is true; third, to try to subordinate one's wishes to the world, rather than the other way around.

As a general code of conduct, and as "the sole basis of the forgoing three maxims," he would persevere in quiet self-examination and constantly strive to cultivate reason, in order that he might advance as far as possible toward knowledge of the truth.

This was the account of his conversion to philosophy that Descartes chose to publish as the preface to his first major work. It omits any mention of the immediate sequel, as recorded in Descartes's personal journal, which he took pains to pass on, along with other unpublished papers, to his literary executors.

With access to that journal, Descartes's biographer Adrien Baillet described what happened next, after Descartes had ended his diurnal meditations with the pragmatic conclusion that, in his conduct of life going forward, "nothing was left but the love of Truth."

As a result of his cogitations,

his mind was thrown into violent agitations, which were amplified by an unceasing intensity of feeling, which left him unable to divert himself with a walk or human companionship. This so exhausted him that his brain took fire, and he fell into a sort of enthusiasm, which so affected his mind that it left him in a condition to receive the impression of dreams and visions.

He tells us that on 10 November, 1619, having gone to bed *completely filled with his enthusiasm*, and wholly preoccupied with the thought of *having found that very day the foundation of the wonderful science,* he had three consecutive dreams in the same night, which he imagined could only have come from on high.

In the first dream, he pictured himself having such difficulty walking on a windy day that he could not reach a church to pray, even though the people around him seemed to have no difficulty at all walking. He awoke feeling a "real pain," which made him wonder about the origin and meaning of the dream.

After spending two hours pondering "the goods and evils of this world," he fell asleep and began to dream again. He heard a loud clap of thunder. Terrified, he woke up. When he "opened his eyes, he noticed many sparks of fire scattered around the room." It was a startling sight, and he began to think of different possible physical explanations for the phenomenon. Calming himself by reasoning in this way, he fell asleep again—and experienced a third dream.

He was in a room, perhaps a study. He saw two books before him. One was a dictionary, the other an anthology of poems. Curious to see what the anthology contained, he opened that book at random and read: "What way in life shall I follow?" He stopped reading, looked up, and saw a man, someone he didn't recognize. The stranger handed him a piece of paper—it was a poem. The first line was, "Yes . . . And no . . ."

For the third time that night, Descartes woke up. Before he was even fully awake, he set to work trying to decipher the meaning of his latest dream. Perhaps the dictionary had symbolized "all the Sciences gathered together." Perhaps the poem in the anthology represented "the good advice of a wise person." The anthology as a whole, he decided, was a sign of "Revelation and Enthusiasm." And the Yes and No of the stranger's poem must have referred to the teachings of Pythagoras and the difficulties a seeker after wisdom faced in trying to unravel "Truth and Falsehood in human understanding and the profane sciences."

As dawn broke, and Descartes took the measure of his meditations and reveries, he finally concluded that the third dream was not a product of "his human mind." Instead, a good angel, or "Spirit of God," had visited him in order "by this dream" to open "unto him the treasures of all the sciences."

In practice, the upshot was simple: Descartes would defy his father and abandon any pretense that he would return home to become a proper French *gentilhomme*. Henceforth, he was on his own. The rest of his life he would dedicate to a ceaseless search for truth.

But the theoretical and theological implications of his long day's night were more complicated. "'God separated the light from the darkness,'" Descartes remarks in a journal entry shortly afterward. "This text in Genesis means that God separated the good angels from the bad angels." Descartes hastens to add that "God is pure intelligence"—a comforting thought, since how could a pure intelligence possibly disdain "the treasures of all the sciences"?

Descartes took care to record the content of his dreams in a little journal bound in parchment that he titled the "Olympia." But he kept the journal to himself. As Descartes remarks in another passage in the same journal, "So far, I have been a spectator in this theatre which is the world, but I am now about to mount the stage, and I come forward masked."

As a student of the Jesuits, Descartes had to wonder: Had he really been visited by a good angel? Or were his revelations the work of a "malicious demon"? The Augustinian orthodoxy on this matter was not reassuring. In *The City of God*, in the chapter in which Augustine attacks the false theurgy of the Platonists and seeks to distinguish the bad, deceiving demons from the good kind, the divine messengers he called "angels," Augustine avers that "the good angels hold cheap all the knowledge of material and temporal matters, which inflates the demons with pride." Since Descartes's Olympian visions seemed to revolve around acquiring knowledge "of material and temporal matters," a good Augustinian would have to wonder about the provenance of his purportedly divine revelation. And Loyola himself had warned that "it is characteristic of the evil one to transform himself into an angel of light, to work with the soul in the beginning, and in the end to work for himself."

This was an era of witch hunts and exorcisms dark arts presided over by subtle theologians, often Jesuits who had thought long and hard about when testimony in a trial might be admitted from someone possessed by satanic forces. By Descartes's day, such cases of possession, previously rare in Christian societies, had become so commonplace that one modern historian refers to a "witch-craze."

Under these circumstances, a public claim of divine inspiration might leave the new method that Descartes wished to advocate open to misunderstanding. It might suggest that he had in some way come under the occult influence of Rosicrucians, or lead to claims that he was trying to promulgate his own brand of heretical science. Better, then, to proceed with indirection and due caution, and to formulate independent reasons for undertaking the quest for truth. Better to take his time and decide how best to acknowledge, and try to answer directly, the possibility that "some malicious demon of the utmost power and cunning has employed all his energies in order to deceive me."

In the months that followed "the wonderful discovery" of November 1619, Descartes remained with the Catholic army of Maximilian I and probably also composed early drafts of the first eleven "rules" for the direction of the mind that survived in his private papers (the incomplete manuscript of *Regulae ad Directionem Ingenii* was published posthumously in Dutch in 1684, with the Latin original appearing only in 1701). Where the schools of his day stressed axiomatic demonstration, showing how a solution can be derived from first principles, Descartes was interested in specifying useful ways to solve mathematical problems and mechanical puzzles. He starts with "intuition," by which he means an immediate mental apprehension of a clear and distinct idea. Intuition in this sense allows almost anyone, if freed from prejudice, to apprehend a number of perfectly simple truths that, put together, constitute all knowledge. It is just a matter of exercising a steadfast mental gaze and carefully analyzing the available evidence. (The egalitarian implications of this new approach to learning became clear in later years, when Descartes emerged as a leading advocate for the education of women and also supported efforts to found a new college that would teach the arts and sciences to the children of artisans, and not just those of noble birth.)

On March 31, 1621, Descartes turned twenty-five and came into his maternal inheritance, which consisted of four small farms and a house in Poitiers. Instead of selling this property in order to purchase a sinecure, Descartes chose to invest some of the proceeds and use the interest to support his research.

What else he did in these years is not entirely clear. He had already glimpsed (when he was with the Catholic army of Maximilian I) some of the first maneuvers in the great tragedy that later historians call the Thirty Years

War—a series of bloody military campaigns that occurred between 1618 and 1648 and that involved almost every state in Europe, pitting armies of Protestants against armies of Catholics, and turning parts of Central Europe into a charnel house.

Descartes traveled through large stretches of the war zone. In 1628, according to his first biographers, he witnessed the surrender of the Huguenot redoubt of La Rochelle to King Louis XIII after a long and brutal siege that had left more than twenty thousand people dead from starvation, disease, and combat injuries. He certainly knew something at firsthand about the wages of religious warfare. But unlike Montaigne, he never saw combat himself.

Instead, he preferred the freedom of the study to the responsibilities (and risks) of public life. Setting aside his first, halting efforts to elaborate a *mathesis universalis*, Descartes spent much of his time trying to discover solutions to specific problems in mathematics, mechanics, meteorology, and optics. It was in this period that he most fully explored his intuition that spatial relations could always be mapped in numerical terms, and conversely, that numerical truths could be represented spatially—the crux of analytical geometry (a field of inquiry that he helped to create, in part by devising what is still known as the Cartesian coordinate system).

Between 1625 and 1628, he spent most of his time in Paris as an independent researcher. While there, he came into contact with a variety of inventors and philosophers, above all Marin Mersenne. A monk committed to living a life of Christian piety, Mersenne was equally committed to fostering new forms of inquiry, helping to promote (and, sometimes, helping to shield from religious persecution) a large number of prominent contemporaries, including the British materialist and political philosopher Thomas Hobbes (1588–1679) and the French astronomer and mathematician Pierre Gassendi (1592–1655). Instead of embarking on an impossible quest to know the world as God may know it, Mersenne argued that the Christian trying to understand the glory of God's creation is better off analyzing piecemeal and patiently the parts of the world as they appear to us, and pursuing research projects—in mathematics, mechanics, and optics—that have a demonstrable value in practice. Mersenne also advocated a strong doctrine of matter as being completely inert, because such a doctrine facilitates a quantitative understanding of nature and, even more important, because such a doctrine clearly separates the natural from the supernatural, by assigning the powers of motion, volition, and will only to God. Nature consists only of matter, but it is matter in motion—God is necessary to give matter a push.

One apparent result of Descartes's friendship with Mersenne was that he returned to the manuscript of *Regulae ad Directionem Ingenii* and added a new set of rules, meant to show how our perception of the physical world can be explained in purely mechanistic terms.

According to Baillet's biography of Descartes, another result of his friendship with the erudite monk was a meeting in Paris with the papal nuncio, Monsieur de Bagni, and a number of other important religious figures, including Cardinal Pierre de Berulle, a Catholic hard-liner who favored using force to purge France of Protestant infidels. Legend has it that Descartes mesmerized this group by demonstrating his ability to pass off the truth as false, and vice versa, by deploying arguments that were merely probable rather than certain. When the group asked how to avoid being duped in this way, Descartes, the story goes, briefly explained his own scientific method. Floored by the Frenchman's genius, the cardinal supposedly demanded that Descartes, as "an obligation of conscience," continue his researches—and Descartes in turn supposedly said that he would renounce "high society" and instead "retire forever to a congenial place to procure perfect solitude in a moderately cold land where no one would know him."

Although some such meeting may well have occurred, it seems unlikely that the cardinal—a ruthless and doctrinaire man—ever advised the philosopher to continue his quest for truth, and improbable that Descartes would have taken his advice seriously. Still, the story served an apologetic purpose in Baillet's narrative and helped to insulate his subject from doubts about his good faith as a Catholic.

These were fraught years for advocates of open inquiry. In 1624, the Parlement of Paris had prohibited anyone, on pain of death, from "holding any public debate other than those approved by the doctors of the Theology Faculty" of the Sorbonne. Just two years earlier, Parisian authorities had burned at the stake a philosopher accused of paganism. At the same time, a network of informal institutions had begun to spring up in Paris, bringing together merchants, magistrates, and philosophers, to discuss discreetly how the new theories of mathematics and mechanics might be usefully applied in practice, in fields like medicine and engineering. By sponsoring important new scientific research, wealthy patrons could boost their status, while researchers in return received a stipend and some protection against accusations of heresy.

In this context, Descartes's renewed interest in showing how the methods of formal logic and geometry could resolve physical, moral, *and* metaphysical problems was, as one modern author has put it, "more than a worthwhile experiment in philosophical method. It was also a smart political move." (Just as usefully, it abstracted the project of pure inquiry from the most questionable element in its genesis, the dreams in 1619.)

But Descartes was taking no chances. He rejected the support of patrons and, while living in Paris, tried to conceal his work and whereabouts, instructing Mersenne on more than one occasion to lie about his activities. At the end of 1628 or start of 1629, he took an even more dramatic step to protect his privacy: he moved to the Netherlands, where (as he wrote in 1637) "I have been able to lead a life as solitary and withdrawn as if I were in the most remote desert." He stayed in the Netherlands for two decades, regularly moving from place to place, as if he were a fugitive on the run: "The good life Descartes maintained by remaining well hidden required a lot of dissimulation."

He arrived with little furniture and few books, apart from his Bible. But once resettled, Descartes set a new and grandiose goal for himself. "Rather than explaining any one phenomenon by itself," he wrote to Mersenne, "I have resolved to explain all the phenomena of nature, that is to say all of physics. I like my present plan better than any other I have ever had, for I think I have found a way of unfolding all my thoughts which some will find satisfying and which others will have no cause to disagree." At the same time, he had begun to think about how to establish the existence of God and the immortality of the soul. In another letter to Mersenne, he wrote that he had "found a way of proving metaphysical truths that is more evident than the truths of geometry"—a claim almost as startling as his ambition to explain all the phenomena of nature.

From the start, Descartes ran into difficulties. He titled one part of his projected treatise *The World* (or, in French, *Le Monde*) and another part *Trea-*

tise on Man. But it was not clear how to turn the findings of specific inquiries—about optics, meteorology, and the behavior of light rays—into the promised general explanation of nature. Nor was it clear how to organize and structure a treatise that would present solutions to both physical and long-standing metaphysical questions about the soul and intellect. He hoped to explain in sequence inanimate nature, animate nature, and mind.

In these years, he studied anatomy and physiology. He also busied himself by designing a new machine to cut lenses and also became fascinated with "automatons," machines that seemed to move spontaneously—for example, clocks and water pumps. For the purposes of analysis, he proposed treating the human being as "nothing but a statue or machine made of earth." In 1632, he wrote to Mersenne that he had become "caught up in the heavens. I have discovered their nature and the nature of the stars we see there and many other things which a few years ago I would not even have dared to hope to discover; and now I have become so rash as to seek the cause of the position of every fixed star." The tone of his letters vacillated between elation at fresh discoveries and despair that his increasingly ambitious project could ever be completed.

Then disaster struck. "I had intended to send you *Le Monde* as a New Year gift," Descartes wrote Mersenne in November 1633, "but in the meantime I tried to find out in Leiden and Amsterdam whether Galileo's *World System* was available . . . I was told that it had indeed been published, but that all copies had been burned at Rome, and that Galileo had been convicted and fined. I was so surprised by this that I nearly burned all my papers, or at least let no one see them."

He considered revising *Le Monde* in an effort to avoid offending the censors but rejected the idea, since Galileo's teaching was "such an integral part of my treatise that I couldn't remove it without making the whole work defective. But for all that, I wouldn't want to publish a discourse which had a single word that the Church disapproved of; so I prefer to suppress it rather than publish it in a mutilated form."

The vehemence of Descartes's reaction is revealing. The Netherlands was beyond the reach of papal authority, and France itself had no Inquisition. Descartes could probably have published and distributed *Le Monde* in Amsterdam and Paris without incident, given the help of highly placed Catholic friends like Mersenne.

But his doubts and suspicions could not be assuaged. And Descartes was not interested in picking a fight with the Vatican. "I desire to live in peace," he explained to Mersenne in April 1634, "and to continue the life I have begun under the motto 'to live well you must live unseen.' And so I am more happy to be delivered from the fear of my work's making unwanted acquaintances than I am unhappy at having lost the time and trouble which I spent on its composition."

Unfortunately, Descartes came under religious censure once again, this time because of his personal conduct. In August 1635, he appeared in a church at Deventer to acknowledge that he was the father of the girl being baptized. She was named Francine and had been born to Helene Jans, a maid in the house in Amsterdam where Descartes was then staying. After 1637, Francine (and perhaps Helene, too) lived with, and was cared for, by Descartes. That the girl had been conceived out of wedlock disconcerted Adrien Baillet, who went out of his way to put the affair in a piously Christian perspective, as if Descartes, like Augustine, should be seen as some kind of saint. "The mistake that he had made one time in his life against the honor of celibacy," writes Baillet, "is less a proof of his inclination for sex than of his weakness: and God, having promptly set him back on his feet, arranged that the memory of his fall would cause him endless humiliation, and that his contrition would be a salutary remedy for the haughtiness of his spirit."

Chastened or not, Descartes experienced a great burst of creative energy, publishing in 1637 the first of his books to reach a wide audience. Having decided to shelve *The World* and his *Treatise on Man* (though taking care to preserve the manuscripts among his personal papers, in hopes, as he later wrote, that "those who get them after my death can make the most appropriate use of them"), Descartes settled on a fresh approach. He would salvage parts of the longer treatise that did not broach the sensitive subject of the earth's movement and offer a selection of scientific texts, modestly, as *"essais"*—attempts to solve a variety of specific problems in three domains: optics (telescopes, how to cut lenses, etc.), meteorology (the origin of rainbows, the cause of lightning, etc.), and geometry (constructions using only circles and straight lines, the nature of curved lines, etc.). In addition, he would compose a preface to these scientific essays, a *Discourse on the Method of rightly conducting one's reason and seeking the truth in the sciences*, in which he, like Montaigne, would write in the first person—though unlike Montaigne, he would eschew any hint of humanist erudition, preferring direct address and a plain style largely devoid of ornament or literary allusion.

This was not the first time that Descartes had floated the idea of composing a self-portrait. In 1628, he had promised some friends that he planned to write a "History of My Mind." After Galileo's condemnation, he may well have thought that he might disarm Catholic skeptics by composing a personalized "history or, if you prefer, a fable"—an exemplary narrative rehearsing acts worthy of emulation—combined with short proofs that God exists and that the soul is immortal.

He did not suffer criticism gladly, but in his fictive self-portrait, he paints himself as humble, even self-effacing: "I always try to lean towards diffidence rather than presumption in the judgments I make about myself; and when I cast a philosophical eye upon the various activities and undertakings of mankind, there are almost none which I do not consider vain and useless." As if to underline the kinship of the author with Everyman, his self-portrait is written not in the Latin still primarily used for scholarly communication but rather in the vernacular French of Descartes's native land.

He recounts his prior life in disarmingly modest terms: Leaving behind the book learning of his school years, he endeavors as a young man to learn about the world from experience. Humbled by what he learns, and in "recognition of my ignorance," though still in search of wisdom, he resolves to "undertake studies within myself." Implicitly referring to the events of November 10–11, 1619, he then recounts the meditations he undertook and how they led him to embrace a few simple rules for further inquiry, modeled on the "long chains of very simple and easy reasonings, which geometers customarily use to arrive at their most difficult demonstrations."

Descartes is often depicted as a solipsist, a monster of egocentric intellection, an impression left by some passages in his *Meditations*, published shortly after the *Discourse*. But in his original autobiographical narrative, Descartes recalls how he had entered into conversation and correspondence with other researchers, having concluded that he could root out any remaining errors in his thinking "more readily by talking with other men than by staying shut in the stove-heated room where I had had all these thoughts." He also recounts how, having established his maxims for inquiry into the physical universe, he "set them on one side together with the truths of faith, which have always been foremost among my beliefs"—thus avowing the orthodoxy of his Catholic faith, even as he goes on to describe how he proceeded to "rid myself of all the rest of my opinions."

Moving beyond mere declarations of good faith, Descartes in part four of the *Discourse* offers—for the first time in his surviving works—metaphysical arguments for justifying the various beliefs he feels absolutely certain about. He disarms his own doubts by remarking that "*I think, therefore I am*" (*Je pense, donc je suis*, a proposition more famous in its Latin form, *Cogito, ergo sum*)—deploying a phrase used before him by Augustine, as contemporaries instantly recognized.

Years later, the French poet Paul Valéry shrewdly observed that *Je pense, donc je suis* "is not a piece of reasoning. It's a fist coming down on a table, to corroborate words in the mind."

Descartes believed that other key convictions could be corroborated in a similar fashion: Whatever one can conceive as "clearly and distinctly" as one can conceive the proposition "I think, therefore I am," one ought to accept as true. This view allows Descartes to argue that *anyone*, after a little more reflection, could in a similar fashion uphold two key "truths of faith": the immateriality of the mind, and hence its absolute distinction from the (mortal) body; and the existence of God, which, he writes, is "at least as certain as any geometrical proof."

He apologizes to the reader for the sketchiness of his account in the *Discourse*, on the grounds that many of his inquiries concern "questions that are being debated among the learned, and I do not wish to quarrel with them" (a prudent decision, given the fate of Galileo). At the same time, Descartes boldly promises that "through this philosophy we could know the power and action of fire, water, air, the stars, the heavens and all the other bodies in our environment, as distinctly as we know the various crafts of our artisans; and we could use this knowledge—as the artisans use theirs—for all the purposes for

which it is appropriate, and thus make ourselves, as it wer
ters of nature."

Taken as a whole, the *Discourse* functions as an artfully ren
for the life of inquiry that Descartes had actually led since 1619, when he
barked on what he regarded as his divinely ordained search for truth. As the
twentieth-century Cartesian Edmund Husserl aptly remarked, "The Delphic
motto, 'Know Thyself!' has gained new significance. Positive science is a science
lost in the world. I must lose the world"—through radical doubt—"in order to
regain it by a universal self-examination." The God that Descartes, like Plotinus,
finds through self-examination guarantees the clear and distinct ideas that animate his scientific inquiries. One is reminded of one of Augustine's maxims:
"Do not go out. Go in to yourself. Truth dwells in the inner man."

By laying out the singular origins of his quest for universal wisdom, and
by trying to demonstrate the divine provenance of his basic convictions, Descartes endeavors to persuade readers that his scientific projects not only conform to the "truths of faith" but also offer new tools for vindicating these
truths. And by explaining how the truths of science are secured only by the
demonstrable existence of God within, Descartes is able to conclude by sum-
marizing some of the "general notions in physics" that he could not keep secret
"without sinning gravely against the law which obliges us to do all in our power
to secure the general welfare of mankind."

By writing in French, Descartes signaled that he was addressing his *Discourse* primarily to lay readers open to new ideas, to artisans as well as scho-
lastics, to women as well as men. And among such readers, the *Discourse* was
an extraordinary success: as one modern historian remarks, it "became the
most famous text that Descartes ever wrote, probably the most famous and
widely read document of the Scientific Revolution."

Descartes was already well known in mathematical and scientific circles.
But the publication of the *Discourse* made him more renowned than ever—
and turned him into an inviting target for public criticism. Despite the active
interest of monks like Mersenne in the new science, a growing number of
theologians both Protestant and Catholic took issue with the brisk new approach in the *Discourse* to traditional problems in metaphysics. Some of the
book's critics suggested that Descartes was a diabolically clever sophist who

ιad deliberately jettisoned well-known arguments for the existence of God and replaced them with a novel argument of his own that was so transparently unconvincing that readers were meant to conclude that God in fact does *not* exist.

In the decade that followed, Descartes found himself drawn willy-nilly ever more deeply into religious controversy. The most notable result was the *Meditationes de Prima Philosophiae*, or *Meditations on First Philosophy*, published in 1641. Written in Latin and taking the superficial form of a set of six spiritual exercises of a sort familiar to anyone trained by the Jesuits, the *Meditations* were aimed squarely at Christian scholars. According to the subtitle of the second edition of 1642, the primary purpose of the meditations was to demonstrate "the existence of God and the distinction between the human soul and body." Going beyond the autobiographical account he had offered in the *Discourse*, Descartes now offers independent philosophical proofs, using "natural reason" alone, for propositions that a good Catholic like himself will also accept on faith alone.

In the first of these *Meditations*, he tries to meet directly the kind of doubt a Catholic skeptic might feel about the project of pure inquiry that Descartes had embarked upon as a result of his ostensibly divine revelation on that night more than twenty years ago. Suppose that the source of this revelation was "not God, who is supremely good and the source of truth, but rather some malicious demon of the utmost power and cunning" who has "employed all his energies in order to deceive me." This of course was not just a rhetorical worry for Descartes; it was a worry he had felt the night of his revelatory dreams.

In this context of the *Meditations*, his response to the possibility that he has been deceived by an evil demon is delayed until he restates (in the third of his *Meditations*) his conviction that God exists. In his private journals, Descartes had briefly sketched the process by which he had convinced himself after his night of dreams that he had been graced with a true vision of how one could acquire reliable knowledge of God and nature. In the remainder of the *Meditations*, he argues at greater length that only God (and not an evil demon) could be the source of his clear and distinct ideas, including his ideas about a perfect God, as well as his ideas about the truths of mathematics and of nature.

As long as he is certain that he is contemplating "the true God, in whom all the treasures of wisdom and the sciences lie hidden," Descartes is equally certain, he says, that "it is impossible that God should ever deceive me." Since God is not a deceiver, and since he gives to Descartes "a strong propensity" to believe that the ideas he has of nature are "produced by corporeal things," it follows that corporeal things exist, and that "they possess all the properties which I clearly and distinctly understand, that is, all those which, viewed in general terms, are comprised within the subject-matter of pure mathematics." In this way, Descartes in the *Meditations* vindicates anew his original revelation of a science of sciences, founded on a mathematical understanding of matter—though whether this argument is coherent, or just a flagrant example of circular reasoning, has been a subject of debate ever since.

A number of contemporary readers were certainly not persuaded. The French Jesuit Pierre Bourdin didn't see how Descartes could answer the suspicion that Satan had, in fact, tricked him, for example, into his unexamined assumption that no harm will come from the disavowal, however temporary, of traditional beliefs. As one modern philosopher has pointed out, taking the idea of a deceiving demon seriously, as Bourdin did, raises the "startling possibility" that "whether we know it or not, we may all be victims of demonism and be unable to tell that we are victims, because of systematic delusion caused by the demonic agent."

One thing seems clear: through the exercise of writing, again, about his meditative epiphany in 1619, Descartes is able to confirm, again, his own monumental sense of self-confidence—and also to offer independent reasons for upholding his core convictions.

In an additional gesture of open-minded engagement with his critics, Descartes asked Mersenne to solicit and compile a variety of responses from a range of theologians and natural philosophers, from Thomas Hobbes, a materialist, and Pierre Gassendi, a skeptic, to Antoine Arnauld (1612–1694), a theological determinist and coauthor of the *Port Royal Logic*. Although Descartes was thin-skinned, he took the occasion to enter into precisely the sort of learned disputation that, in the *Discourse*, he had said he hoped to avoid.

Descartes may have made a strategic mistake. Hoping to shield his discovery of "the foundation of [a] wonderful science" from religious criticism, he had provoked an endless debate, involving theologians as well as philosophers, that focused not on the foundations of his wonderful science but on a series of metaphysical propositions. (Near the end of his life, Descartes even warned one visitor that he "should not devote so much attention to the *Meditations* and to metaphysical questions . . . They draw the mind too far away from physical and observable things, and make it unfit to study them. Yet it is precisely these physical studies that it is most desirable for men to pursue.")

As the debate over Descartes's religious views simmered, rumors about his private life began to circulate as well. It was whispered that Descartes, besides being a godless materialist, was an immoral man who had fathered an illegitimate child. (Francine had died of scarlet fever in 1640, leaving Descartes bereft. Under Dutch law, she was not technically "illegitimate," since the father had publicly acknowledged his paternity.)

Despite settling in a remote farmhouse facing sand dunes leading to the ocean, Descartes had to cope with a steady stream of visitors. When one such pilgrim asked to see the great man's library, Descartes supposedly said, "Come with me"—and took his guest to a shed where he showed him a dead calf ready to dissect. Another myth spread that Descartes in these years always traveled with an automaton of his own design, a life-size female doll that he had built for companionship and also to prove that even human beings are only machines.

As his fame grew, it became fashionable for educated young ladies to seek out Descartes to ask his advice on the conduct of life, as well as to hear more about the results of his physical studies. Those who were unable to meet him face-to-face wrote him letters instead. The most important of these correspondents was Princess Elizabeth of Bohemia (1618–1680), a scion of Protestant royalty (who ended her days as the abbess of a Lutheran monastery in Westphalia).

They first exchanged letters in 1643, when Elizabeth was twenty-five years old and living in The Hague. Growing up she had learned German, French, English, Dutch, Italian, and Latin. She was skilled at mathematics and schooled in metaphysics, and in her first letter to Descartes she raised a problem with the accounts he had offered in the *Discourse* and *Meditations* of the mind and the body.

If, as Descartes had asserted, all bodies are machines, purely material substances, that work the way they do in response to external stimuli, in accord with the laws of physics; and if, as Descartes had also asserted, the human mind is an immaterial and immortal substance that, through its free will, puts the human body into motion; then how can the mind, which is immaterial, get a grip on the machinery of the body, and how do external stimuli enter our consciousness, as they clearly do?

Descartes had to concede that experience shows us that mind and body *are* interrelated, but just how, God only knows. The inadequacy of this kind of response helped kindle a correspondence that lasted until the end of Descartes's life.

Their epistolary exchange—after his death, it was sometimes published separately as an introduction to a properly Cartesian way of life—revolved around metaphysical puzzles but also around practical problems like those discussed by Seneca in his letters to Lucilius. For example, Elizabeth in November 1645 presses Descartes on his claim in a prior letter that there is more good than evil in the world. Disputing his assertion, she notes that human beings have more occasions for distress than delight, and that "there are a thousand errors for one truth." In response, Descartes in effect admonishes Elizabeth to keep a stiff upper lip. With a little practice in premeditating the worst evils, errors, and distress that might befall a soul, he assures her that she, too, might inure herself to whatever misfortune may bring and learn to focus instead on the many goods, truths, and delights of life, just like a good Stoic.

"We should pay little attention," Descartes advises, "to all the things outside of us that do not depend on our free will, in comparison with those things that do depend on it, which we can always make good, when we know how to use our will properly; by this means, we can prevent the evils that come from elsewhere, however great they may be, from penetrating our soul any more deeply than the sadness that actors can arouse when they perform various morbid acts; though to respond in this way, I agree, one must be very philosophical indeed."

Their epistolary friendship had its ups and downs. Elizabeth was under standably upset by the nonchalance of Descartes's response to her expression of distress at learning that her brother had converted from Lutheranism to Catholicism. As a Catholic himself, Descartes replied, he could not help but approve of her brother's decision; in any case, God works in mysterious ways, and someone who makes a religious vow for the wrong reasons may nevertheless "lead a life of great holiness." Besides, "in all affairs where there are different sides, it is impossible to please one without displeasing the other." While it is hard to doubt the fervor of Descartes's own sense of divine mission, intimate documents like this suggest that he (not unlike Montaigne) prized peace and quiet more than vehement professions of faith, whether Protestant or Catholic.

Descartes's next book was dedicated to the princess. His *Principia Philosophiae* (*Philosophical Principles*), first published in Latin in 1644, offered a textbook summary of his views, using the terminology and format of a traditional treatise on metaphysics. And his last book, *Les Passions de l'Ame* (*Passions of the Soul*), grew out of his correspondence with Elizabeth. First published in French in 1649, and thus aimed at secular readers, it explored at length how the passions linked body and soul.

A few months later, Descartes accepted an offer to move to Stockholm from Queen Christina of Sweden. The queen was only twenty-three years old, but like Princess Elizabeth, she was highly educated and widely read. Christina planned to have Descartes join her court; in return, he was expected to serve as her teacher and tutor. Descartes had grown tired of his endless arguments with Dutch divines, and he may have hoped as well to secure some similar post in Sweden for Princess Elizabeth.

Soon after taking up the position in the queen's court, early in 1650, Descartes fell ill. Refusing treatment from the queen's doctors, he dosed himself on wine flavored with tobacco. The home remedy didn't work, and Descartes died on February 11, 1650.

In the days that followed, the rumor spread that Protestant courtiers who feared Descartes's influence over the queen's religious views had poisoned him. (Four years later, Christina in fact shocked her compatriots by abdicating her throne, after secretly converting to Catholicism.) Another rumor had it that Descartes had not actually died but simply gone into hiding, the better to conduct his nefarious research. If to some Protestants he seemed an agent of the pope, to many Catholics he seemed simply a heretic, perhaps even a secret Rosicrucian. In Holland, "Cartesian" became a synonym for subversion, both religious and moral. And in 1663, the Roman Church placed all his works on the *Index Librorum Prohibitorum*.

Still, his stature continued to grow, and by 1666, his reputation had sufficiently improved in France that arrangements were made to exhume his remains from their Swedish grave and send them home for reburial. Before the skeleton was packed, the French ambassador was allowed to cut off a forefinger to keep as a relic, and a Swedish guard surreptitiously removed the skull.

Throughout the first half of the eighteenth century, Descartes loomed large as a patron saint of modern science and the culture of Enlightenment, as new accounts of the natural world slowly replaced the Aristotelian accounts long taught in the schools. In France, Holland, and England, groups of devoted Cartesians kept his method and his memory alive. But as time passed, Newton replaced Descartes as the preeminent avatar of the scientific method in the public mind, and new findings made Descartes's scientific and mathematical discoveries of dwindling interest. At the same time, the story of his life faded from view. As a result of all these trends, his name became synonymous less with the new physics than with a metaphysics of the *cogito*, connected with an implausibly sharp distinction between body and mind—even as the Cartesian project of pure inquiry was severed from the revelations of 1619.

Descartes is a transitional figure. In the accounts given by his first biographers, as in the autobiographical passages of his *Discourse*, philosophy is still conceived as a spiritual exercise with a constitutive code of conduct, expressed in narratives that exemplify the pure moral ethos of a model researcher. But in his presentation of his mathematical approach to understanding nature, Descartes laid the groundwork for an entirely different approach to philosophy—a quest for certainty, based on a system of clear and distinct ideas about the world as it really is, formulated, to the largest extent possible, independently of the idiosyncrasies of any particular inquirer. As Michel Foucault put it, "before Descartes, one could not be impure, immoral, and know the truth." After him, by contrast, "direct evidence is enough . . . Evidence has been substituted for *askesis* [spiritual discipline]."

Descartes did inspire the work of one significant twentieth-century philosopher, the German phenomenologist Edmund Husserl (1859–1938). "Anyone who seriously intends to become a philosopher," Husserl declared, "must 'once in his life' withdraw into himself and attempt, within himself, to overthrow and build anew all the sciences that, up to then, he has been accepting. Philosophy—wisdom (*sagesse*)—is the philosopher's quite personal affair." An "*all-embracing self-investigation*" would, Husserl believed, encompass "all self-accountable science."

But Husserl's stress on "self-acquired knowledge" as the only sure ground of scientific thought has proved to be an anomaly. Since Descartes, most philosophers have developed their views within one of two divergent traditions.

The mainstream tradition of modern philosophy in the West has elaborated increasingly impersonal forms of inquiry, often inspired by contemporary research in the natural sciences, frequently associated with logical analysis, and sometimes based on Descartes's original quest to represent "the world as it really is." Thus, in his *Tractatus Logico-Philosophicus* of 1921, Ludwig Wittgenstein (1889–1951) used modern symbolic logic in an effort to represent "all that is the case" in a set of elementary propositions.

A rival tradition, which harks back to the classical understanding of philosophy as a way of life, has laid stress on a renewed practice of self-examination, often represented as frankly hostile to the primacy of logic and the standards of reason (as in Nietzsche), and sometimes based (as in Heidegger's more obscure analysis in *Being and Time*) on the conclusion that the Cartesian formula *Cogito, ergo sum* has laid the basis for a catastrophic occlusion of "the *meaning of the Being of the 'sum.'*"

Descartes himself would presumably have been horrified by this division within philosophy. For it would mean that most subsequent philosophers had failed to fulfill the whole of what Descartes took to be their God-given duty—to use their reason not just to know the world as it really is but also to know themselves, and not just to analyze one's individual existence but also to understand all that exists.

ROUSSEAU

Bust of Jean-Jacques Rousseau, terra-cotta, by Jean-Antoine Houdon (1741–1828). The most renowned sculptor of his day, Houdon was allowed to make a death mask as the basis for this posthumous portrait of a profound moral philosopher: "His piercing gaze seems to penetrate the most hidden twists and turns of the human heart," marveled one admirer of the bust. (Musée Lambinet, Versailles, France/Lauros/Giraudon/The Bridgeman Art Library International)

On an unseasonably warm fall day in 1749, Jean-Jacques Rousseau, a struggling thirty-seven-year-old musician, went on a long walk to visit a prison where his friend Denis Diderot was under arrest, charged with subverting the teachings of the Catholic Church through his writings. Unlike Rousseau, the thirty-six-year-old Diderot was already well-known for his unorthodox views on morality and religion. While walking along the road from Paris toward Vincennes, Rousseau was leafing through a copy of *Mercure de France*, one of the most prominent journals of the French cultural elite. He was stopped in his tracks, he later recalled, when he came to the announcement that a prize was being offered for the best essay on the topic "Whether the restoration of the sciences and arts has tended to purify morals."

"If anything ever resembled a sudden inspiration," he later wrote, "it was the motion that was made in me as I read that." He felt dizzy, faint, overcome. "At the moment of that reading, I saw another universe and I became another man."

Gasping for breath, he collapsed under a tree, weeping in agitation. "Suddenly I felt my mind dazzled by a thousand lights; crowds of lively ideas presented themselves at once, with a force and confusion that threw me into inexpressible turmoil . . . Oh, Sir, if ever I could have written a quarter of what I saw and felt under that tree, with what clarity would I have revealed all the contradictions of the social system, with what force would I have exposed all the abuses of our institutions, with what simplicity would I have demonstrated that man is naturally good and it is through these institutions alone that men become bad."

Rousseau's epiphany led him to change his outward conduct immediately, and in ways that friends like Diderot could not help but notice. "I gave up gilt and white gloves, I put on a round wig, I took off my sword, I sold my watch, saying to myself with unbelievable joy, 'Thank Heaven, I will no longer need to know what time it is.'" Temporarily setting aside his musical ambitions, he began to write like a man possessed, submitting a response to the question posed by the Academy of Dijon. His response won the jury's prize, and when Rousseau's first *Discourse on the Sciences and the Arts* was published the next year, it turned him overnight from an obscure composer into a public figure of commanding stature.

But in the years that followed, as gaps began to appear between Rousseau's actual conduct and his stirring philosophical ideals, critics began to question his integrity. As an erstwhile friend jibed, Rousseau was "a moral dwarf on stilts"—a man hardly worthy of the large and often enthusiastic readership his works attracted in the years after his alleged conversion to philosophy.

In response to such critics, Rousseau conceded that he was a complex, even contradictory character, memorably declaring that he "preferred to be a man of paradoxes than a man of prejudices." Although he claimed that human beings were animated by an innate sense of pity, his own conscience proved a pitiless interlocutor. And so he spent a great deal of time in his final years bearing witness against himself, laying bare the contradictions between his life and his work. Like Seneca at the end of his life, he made his personal weaknesses an explicit object of his philosophizing. And like Augustine, he wrote a series of autobiographical *Confessions*, in which he acknowledged a number of shameful acts—above all, his abandonment to an orphanage of all the children he conceived with his longtime companion Thérèse Levasseur.

Rousseau was born in Geneva in 1712. Bordered by Savoy and France, Geneva was an anomaly in eighteenth-century Europe, a Calvinist republic in the midst of Catholic kingdoms. It was a self-governing city-state, its borders confined, its population of twenty-five thousand far smaller than that of classical Athens. Even when compared with its Swiss neighbors, the cantons of Vaud and Valais, Geneva was unusual. While they were rugged and rural and dependent on farming, Geneva, standing at the crossroads of the Alps, was cosmopolitan and commercial, a city rich in trade—and riven by chronic conflict between a prosperous ruling elite and a larger group of artisanal laborers who yearned for a larger voice in the city's government.

It was this volatile political climate that surrounded the young Jean-Jacques Rousseau, who grew up in the faubourg de Saint-Gervais, a quarter of Geneva known for the political activism of its artisans. His mother, from a wellborn family, died a few days after his birth, leaving him to be raised by his father, Isaac, a journeyman watchmaker who owned a small library of books and whose "love of his fatherland was his strongest passion," according to his son. Unable to afford a formal education, the father encouraged his son to read Ovid, Plutarch, and Plato, besides the epistolary novels that had become popular in the eighteenth century, which he enjoyed as well. At home in the pages of these books, Rousseau "felt before thinking"—an autodidact, inspired by idealized accounts of classical virtue and romantic love.

When Rousseau was ten, his father was forced to flee Geneva, and the boy was apprenticed first to a lawyer and then to an engraver who treated him so brutally that he finally ran away in 1728. Thus began a picaresque adventure that would take Rousseau from the Kingdom of Savoy to Turin in Italy, and from Lyon in France to the cultural capital of eighteenth-century Europe, Paris.

For more than a decade, the most constant presence in Rousseau's life was Françoise-Louise-Éléanore de la Tour, baroness de Warens, whom he met as a fifteen-year-old. Thirteen years older than Rousseau, Mme. de Warens had left a Protestant husband in Lausanne to seek refuge in Savoy, where she had converted to Catholicism and had accepted a government pension in return for helping to convert other Protestant refugees to Catholicism. Mme. de Warens offered the adolescent Rousseau shelter and spiritual guidance—and, in the years that followed his conversion to Catholicism, she also offered him a pietist form of faith that stressed devotion to the divine voice of conscience within.

Rousseau called Mme. de Warens his *maman*. For several years they were lovers, and he ascribed to her (in the words of a modern biographer) all "those qualities of sweetness, grace, and beauty, which, as a motherless child, he longed to find in all the women under whose spell he was later to fall."

With support from Mme. de Warens and her patrons, Rousseau received instruction in modern literature, philosophy, and—above all—music. He trained his voice, committed cantatas to memory, and learned how to play the flute, violin, and keyboard instruments. Impressed by his musical gifts, Mme. de Warens encouraged him to organize musical events for her and to support himself on the side by teaching and copying music. In 1737, when Rousseau was twenty-five, the *Mercure de France* published a song that he had composed. Two abortive operas followed—only the libretti survive.

Convinced that the current system of musical notation was needlessly cumbersome, Rousseau devised a new system, in which numbers replaced the visual representation of notes. In 1742, the thirty-year-old struck out on his own, eventually to settle in Paris, where he hoped he might convince the French musical establishment to adopt his new notational system. He got a respectful hearing from the Academy of Science but no endorsement. He met the greatest living French composer and musical theorist, Jean-Philippe Rameau (1683–1764), who was even more lukewarm about Rousseau and his invention.

He also met a variety of other young artists and intellectuals. The most important was Denis Diderot (1713–1784), who had recently been named the editor of the new French *Encyclopedia*. An audacious publishing venture, subsidized by a handful of affluent subscribers, the *Encyclopedia* was meant to offer a comprehensive summary of contemporary knowledge in all areas of human endeavor and inquiry in a series of alphabetically arranged essays on various topics, from the "Acts of the Apostles" and "Artichoke" to "Zenicon" ("Name of a poison that the hunters of Celtic Gaul used in olden days"). The contributors to this venture included a number of Diderot's friends, most of them struggling artists and intellectuals like Rousseau, who were unattached to any academic institution.

A few years after arriving in Paris and joining Diderot's circle, Rousseau entered into what would become a lifelong liaison with Thérèse Levasseur. Barely literate, and nearly ten years Rousseau's junior, she was a simple soul with a sweet disposition and considerably more common sense than Rousseau himself. She offered him companionship as well as sexual gratification, and though he kept his promise that he would never abandon her, he refused for many years to marry her.

Whenever Thérèse got pregnant—as she did several times between 1746 and 1752—Rousseau arranged for her to stay with a midwife and for the child to be consigned after birth to a foundling home, the Hôpital des Enfants-Trouvés in Paris, a religious charitable institution that received roughly six thousand infants a year. This was not an uncommon practice: in these years, roughly 20 percent of the children baptized in Paris were consigned to a foundling home. "I said to myself: since this is the practice of the country, when one lives there one can follow it," he wrote. "I made up my mind cheerfully and without the least scruples." As so often in Rousseau's autobiographical writing, it is hard to know whether he was being disingenuous or self-deceiving: he must have known that most of the babies given to the Enfants-Trouvés were dead within a year.

Rousseau in these years eked out a living by copying music and writing articles for Diderot's *Encyclopedia*, most of them on musical topics. His compositions were starting to attract a bit of attention; Rameau even accused him of plagiarism. Still, there was no indication that he was ever going to amount to much.

This all changed abruptly after the publication in 1750 of Rousseau's *Discourse on the Sciences and the Arts*, which turned its author into an intellectual cause célèbre—an ironic turn of events, since this essay was, among other things, a scathing critique of the sort of civilization that would lavish honors and attention on a few famous writers.

The main thesis of what came to be known as the *First Discourse*, which grew directly out of Rousseau's revelation on the road to Vincennes, was that "our souls have been corrupted in proportion to the advancement of our sciences and our arts toward perfection."

This was a provocative assertion, since it flatly contradicted the main drift of enlightened opinion in Paris. The mid-eighteenth century was a time of mounting enthusiasm for the new gospel of material progress, a faith rooted in real changes, since the mechanical and financial arts were developing rapidly. Diderot's *Encyclopedia* was meant to be a *Reasoned Dictionary of the Sciences, Arts, and Trades*, and many of its entries and illustrations showed how the findings of modern science were being fruitfully applied in trades such as cloth dying, mirror making, and the manufacture of watches. Rousseau, moreover, was well informed about these developments: his father had been a watchmaker, and he had spent time as a young man in Lyon, one of the biggest centers of manufacturing and commerce in eighteenth-century France. In a poem written in Lyon in 1741 (one of his earliest surviving works), Rousseau himself had sung the praises of "innocent industry," which "multiplies the comforts of life and, beneficial to all through its useful services, satisfies need by the route of luxury."

Such sentiments, most famously expressed a generation later by Adam Smith in *The Wealth of Nations*, were typical of what subsequent intellectual historians called "the Age of Enlightenment"—but Rousseau now rounded on that conventional wisdom. Luxury bred vice, he argued in his *First Discourse*, undermining the sorts of integrity and perfect goodness prized by Socrates, Plato, and Seneca. A faith in progress was insidious when it hid how corrupting civil society really could be: "Suspicions, offenses, fears, coldness, reserve, hate, and betrayal will hide constantly under that uniform and false veil of politeness."

Perhaps assuming that Rousseau was merely trying to be provocative, some of his friends—Diderot, for one—found it hard to take Rousseau's new views seriously. Others displayed less equanimity. A bitter controversy erupted, with Rousseau at its center.

Before his epiphany and the controversy produced by his subsequent essay, Rousseau had been an aspiring musician, a writer, and perhaps even a *philosophe*, as that word was used in eighteenth-century French (as a synonym for what an American today might call an "intellectual"). But Rousseau had not yet become, by his own estimate, a *real* philosopher in the ancient sense—someone who tries to live his life in harmony with his professed principles. "How sweet it would be to live among us if exterior appearance were always the image of the heart's disposition," he now declared, "if our maxims served as our rules; if true Philosophy were inseparable from the title of Philosopher!"

In the eyes of many contemporary readers, the author of the *First Discourse* seemed like a throwback, a premodern philosopher, closer in spirit to the ancient Greeks and noble Romans than to the savants who frequented the salons of Paris. His most influential German admirer, Immanuel Kant (1724– 1804), called him a "subtle Diogenes." Like Diogenes of Sinope, Rousseau in his prize-winning essay represented the highest good as a product of nature, not of art: the good man, having few needs, will by nature be content with little, but since modern societies multiply our needs, the minds of most men become disquieted and uneasy. Rousseau, like Diogenes, renounced modern society as corrupting and went in search of a truly good man.

The uproar over Rousseau's *First Discourse* lasted for nearly a year and secured his status as the most controversial and best-known thinker of his generation. Since he was unabashed about offering himself as a living exemplar, curiosity about his conduct naturally began to grow. And by April 1751, at the latest, Rousseau's most shameful secret had been revealed by Thérèse Levasseur's mother to a few of Rousseau's influential friends.

Fearing for his newfound reputation as a paragon of ancient virtues, Rousseau responded with a lengthy letter of justification to one of these influential friends, a copy of which he kept among his papers in a rudimentary cipher, as if to confirm the extent of his feeling of guilt over its contents. The encrypted letter was in fact a feeble attempt to rationalize what he had done to his children. He pleaded that poverty and ill health had made him unfit to be a proper father, and that he wished to avoid dishonoring the unwed mother (never mind that he had refused to marry her), and that a foundling home was in fact a perfectly respectable place for children to grow up, since it would force its charges to become tough and self-sufficient, prepared for every conceivable hardship (never mind that most of them died). He even cited Plato in his defense, as if the Hôpital des Enfants-Trouvés were in some way comparable to the scheme laid out in the *Republic* for the public education of all children independently of their parents.

It would take a decade before Rousseau's secret became general knowledge. In the meantime, he had to fend off public criticism of his moral integrity for a completely different reason: the stunning popularity of his short opera *Le Devin du Village* (The Village Soothsayer), performed in Paris for the first time on March 1, 1753. In the months and years that followed, French audiences could not hear enough of Rousseau's overture and arias. Even the king of France, though tone-deaf, was overheard trying to hum the melodies. But colleagues and rivals were left feeling more jealous—and skeptical—than ever. It was hard to see how the author of the *Discourse on the Sciences and the Arts* could possibly reconcile his vehement criticism of the arts with his stunning popularity as a purveyor of the arts. Perhaps this was yet another case, all too typical among moralists in any age, of sheer bad faith.

In his *Confessions*, written between 1764 and 1770 but published only after his death in 1778, Rousseau recalled how awkward and out of place he had felt at the gala premiere of his opera. Offered a pension by the king, he amazed his critics by turning it down. Despite the enviable success of *The Village Soothsayer*, Rousseau gave up composing music. From now on, he made a point of deliberately scorning—in fact, ostentatiously rejecting—the outward trappings of worldly success, choosing to live a life of voluntary poverty, earning a modest income as a music copyist, trying to personify the independent ethos of an upright artisan.

In the autumn of 1753, the Academy of Dijon announced another essay competition. This time, contestants were invited to address the question "What is the origin of inequality among men, and is it authorized by natural law?"

Still feeling a need to express his newfound convictions in writing, and feeling increasingly confident about his talents as a writer and thinker, Rousseau once again decided to submit an essay. He had already begun privately to elaborate his principles in various manuscripts and notebooks that would, in time, be worked up into his two greatest works, his treatise on education, *Émile*, and his essay on legitimate political institutions, *On the Social Contract* (both published in 1762). In the meantime, the Academy's new question supplied a perfect pretext for clarifying publicly the character of his emergent philosophy.

Resolving "to think this great matter out at my leisure," he arranged to spend a week in the small village of Saint-Germain. There he went on long strolls, as if to summon in a more controlled fashion the spirit of rapturous illumination that had overtaken him on the road to Vincennes:

> Deep in the forest, I sought and found the image of the first times, the history of which I proudly traced. I made a clean sweep of the petty lies of mankind; I dared to strip naked their nature, to follow the progress of time, and trace the things which distorted it; and by comparing man as he has made himself with natural man I showed him in his pretended perfection the true source of his misery. Exalted by these sublime meditations, my soul raised itself close to the divinity, and seeing my fellow men pursuing the blind path of their prejudices, of their errors, of their misfortunes and their crimes, I cried to them in a feeble voice that they could not hear, "Madmen who ceaselessly complain of nature, learn that all your evils arise from yourselves!"

In composing his new *Discourse on the Origin of Inequality*, Rousseau also consulted a wide variety of scholarly books, trying to obtain more "accurate notions" about the human being in its presocial state. Yet, as he insists at the outset of his text, one must set "aside all the facts," approaching with skepticism most scientific books—which naturally raised the question: How, then, *can* one "judge properly" about the original constitution of the human being?

Rousseau's apparent answer is laconic. By "meditating on the first and most simple operations of the soul"—and perhaps by inviting a certain kind of rapturous illumination, not unlike what Rousseau experienced during his walks in the woods at Saint-Germain—anyone, so he implies, may yet honor the Delphic precept discreetly alluded to in the first sentence of the preface to his new essay: "Know thyself."

At the end of his life, Rousseau was perfectly candid: "Where could the painter and apologist of nature, today so disfigured and slandered, have found the model if not in his own heart?" Throughout these productive years—from his epiphany in 1749 until the completion of *Émile* and the *Social Contract* thirteen years later—Rousseau wrote as a man inspired, drawing strength from his certainty that he, a naturally good man, had been graced by a rapturous vision of natural goodness. Everything from his pen "during this period of his effervescence," Rousseau later avowed, "bears a stamp that is impossible to mistake, and more impossible to imitate. His music, his prose, his verse, everything during those . . . years had coloration, a hue that no other will ever match."

This almost mystical element in Rousseau's way of thinking was something he evidently wished in some way to communicate. Hoping to provoke and convert—and inspire—his readers, Rousseau filled the *Second Discourse* with outrageous epigrams and startling assertions: "The mind perverts the senses." "Reason is what engenders egocentrism and reflection strengthens it." "All ran to chain themselves." But the implicit aim of the exaggerated rhetoric is spiritual, inviting a reader to jettison received truths and to grapple with fundamental questions. It is Rousseau's attempt to provoke a reader into examining himself or herself and to acknowledge natural sentiments that have been obscured by the sediments of civilization, for example, the instinctive sympathy one feels when beholding another's bodily suffering—what Rousseau called "pity."

Above all, a meditation on "the first and most simple operations of the soul" reveals the primordial power of free will. As Rousseau explains in a key passage from the discourse on inequality, "It is not so much understanding which constitutes the distinction of man among the animals, as it is his being a free agent. Nature commands every animal, and the beast obeys. Man feels the same impetus, but he realizes that he is free to acquiesce or to resist, and it is above all in the consciousness of this freedom that the spirituality of his soul is shown."

Rousseau generally accepted the conception of nature held by modern scientists like Buffon (1707–1788), who explained the intrinsic attributes of the different species of animals through "the laws of mechanics" rather than the old Aristotelian teleology. Pity, for example, was an attribute of men that Rousseau believed was instinctive and hence amenable to a purely mechanical explanation. Like Diderot and such British philosophers as John Locke (1632–1704), Rousseau similarly assumed that our direct knowledge of the world grows out of sense perceptions: a great many of our beliefs about the world can be explained as a necessary outcome of physical impressions.

But unlike Diderot, Rousseau never concluded that, as a result, "the word freedom is void of sense." When it came to freedom, Rousseau was unapologetically a Cartesian—even though he laid out the radical implications of free will for morality and politics in ways that surely would have shocked Descartes himself.

Rousseau took freedom to be a mysterious and God-given power, revolving around an inexplicable spontaneity, the miraculous ability to initiate an act without a physical or material cause. "Every motion not produced by another can come only from a spontaneous, voluntary action. Inanimate bodies act only by motion, and there is no true action without will . . . The principle of every action is in the will of a free being."

Because Rousseau thinks that every one of us has a free will, the human being is "not simply a sensitive and passive being but an active and intelligent being." Or, to borrow an analogous formulation in Kant, "There is in man a power of self-determination, independently of any coercion through sensuous impulses."

Hence the practical significance of the Cartesian metaphysical doctrine in Rousseau's account: As a result of its innate power of self-determination, the human being is a creature not simply of instinct, but also of choice. The choices one freely makes over time take the form of habits. Whereas instincts are invariably fixed, habits, as an issue of will, are changeable. Whereas instincts belong to the involuntary and immutable realm of physics, habits are mutable: they belong to the voluntary and essentially indeterminate realm of what Rousseau calls "Morals." Freedom, in short, gives human beings, whether in isolation or in concert, the capacity to start over, to form new habits, even to establish spontaneously a new constitution of the soul or of society.

In the *Second Discourse*, Rousseau does not present any empirical evidence at all for his bald assertion that humans have free will. Indeed, in asserting his principle of freedom, he must "set all the facts aside," as he notoriously said he would do earlier in the *Discourse*. That is because the freedom that he describes does not belong to the natural realm of sensible phenomena; it is not an observable part of the animal essence of the human being. Because it is a part of one's "metaphysical side," the concept of freedom cannot be illuminated by the natural sciences.

So how can we know that our will is really free? Rousseau's considered answer to this obvious question is both simple and disarming: We don't know. And we can't.

"*We do not know*," declares the Savoyard Vicar, Rousseau's fictive spiritual alter ego in *Émile*, his great bildungsroman on education. The Savoyard Vicar echoes the skepticism of Montaigne: "We are ignorant of ourselves; we know neither our nature nor our active principle." If a skeptic argues that the will is predetermined, there is no way to refute him. One can only represent the inward feeling of spontaneity that accompanies the exercise of one's will—and one can invite another to look inward and see whether he discovers a similar feeling within. Anyone averse to such a spiritual exercise is likely to mistake or misunderstand—or not recognize at all—a sentiment that is anything but self-evident.

In our own society, after all—as Rousseau's narrative of social and political catastrophes makes clear in the *Second Discourse*—the feeling of freedom has been all but lost. It has been perverted and concealed, deeply hidden, hence hard to acknowledge. Born free, man is everywhere in chains.

As a consequence of this inscrutably "spiritual" capacity to resist the commands of nature, a human being, once able to exercise freedom in concert with others, develops the capacity that Rousseau, coining a new word, calls "perfectibility." And as this *Discourse* and Rousseau's other works make plain, the implications of mankind's pliable and "perfectible" free will are dizzying. Most of the classical thinkers—especially Plato and Aristotle—turn out to be in error, according to Rousseau's account. They were wrong to think that the ability to reason was innate, and they were wrong to think that the human being was naturally directed, by its inborn capacity to embody an invariant form of reasoning, toward one final and universal state of perfection, a proper telos.

The principle of freedom and its corollary, perfectibility, rather suggest that the possibilities for being human are both multiple and, literally, endless. Faced with chance obstacles, a person's habits or a people's mores can spontaneously change—perhaps for better, but also for worse. Supervised carefully by a tutor or regulated through a shared code of laws, habits and mores can be deliberately formed and re-formed—again, perhaps for better, but also for worse. In effect, the intrinsically uncertain and indeterminate power of freedom has turned the human being into an animal destined not to contemplate eternal truths, but rather to grapple in ever-changeable ways with ever-changeable habits and mores, in time producing a unique *history*, which paradoxically appears as an unrelenting record of evils.

But that is not the end of the story. At precisely the most intolerable stage in his narrative in the *Second Discourse*, just when things seem hopeless, Rousseau brings dramatically back into play his own great principle for "judging properly," the principle of freedom. Evil is essentially artificial, a product of society. As a result, there is no reason to suffer evil at all.

Instead, one can strengthen one's will, in order to resist the snares of civilization, and in this way attain a measure of *virtue*, a word that Rousseau, like Seneca, makes central to his moral philosophy. We can also exercise our free will virtuously in concert with others, in order to change the laws and mores that lead a people to acquiesce in living under conditions of grotesque inequality. For this reason, the last chapter of the story Rousseau tells in the *Second Discourse* has yet to be written. The ending is up to us. Our historical destiny is, to an uncertain but critical extent, in our own hands—such is the significance of being free. By rising up against a regime that would instill only "the blindest obedience," Rousseau reminds us, a people acts only according to the natural order, by reasserting its essential freedom. "And whatever the outcome of these brief and frequent revolutions"—a new beginning, or a relapse into bad habits—"no one can complain about someone else's injustice, but only of his own imprudence or his misfortune."

A new way of thinking about the human condition had appeared in the *Second Discourse*—a rare event, and one reason why Rousseau's writing conveys such an infectious air of agitated discovery, despite the gloomy description of mankind's decline and fall. As Hegel put it two generations later, "The principle of freedom dawned on the world in Rousseau, and gave infinite strength to man, who thus apprehended himself as infinite."

Hegel's generous assessment was fiercely disputed at the time. Not only did Rousseau lose the Academy's competition for 1754, his new discourse also earned the undying enmity of Voltaire, the most powerful and prominent representative of the French Enlightenment.

A generation older than Rousseau and Diderot, Voltaire (1694–1776) had first become famous as an outspoken critic of superstition and Christian bigotry in the *Philosophical Letters* he published in 1734. Born François-Marie

Arouet, he had given himself a new name after becoming independently wealthy through shrewd investments. In the years that followed, Voltaire wrote poetry, plays, fiction, histories, and innumerable essays on philosophical, scientific, and political topics, glorying in his status as a tribune of enlightened justice, marshaling public opinion in polemical broadsides that commanded a wide readership. In 1755, he settled in Switzerland, first in Geneva and then just outside the city limits at a lavish estate where he could stage his plays for his friends and admirers.

In his *First Discourse*, Rousseau had obliquely criticized Voltaire, taunting him with his real name: "Tell us, celebrated Arouet, how many strong and masculine beauties you have sacrificed to our false delicacy, and how many great things the spirit of gallantry, so fertile in little things, has cost you!" Yet he continued to profess his admiration for Voltaire's talent and sent him a copy of his *Second Discourse*—which provoked a famous response: "I have received, Sir, your new book against the human race . . . Never has so much intelligence been used in seeking to make us stupid."

A testy correspondence ensued. Rousseau insisted that his discourse had been in earnest, despite the paradoxes ridiculed by Voltaire: "If I had pursued my first vocation and had neither read nor written, I would doubtless have been happier. However, if letters were abolished now, I would be deprived of the only pleasure remaining to me." A year later, Rousseau followed up with a long letter in which he defended his idiosyncratic belief in divine providence and made plain his own conviction that a good society would never tolerate intolerance, including those "intolerant unbelievers"—such as Voltaire— "who wished to force the people to believe nothing."

The points of disagreement were manifold. Rousseau insisted on publishing his books under his own name, while Arouet had donned the mask of Voltaire. Irony was Voltaire's forte, while Rousseau was painfully earnest. A bon vivant at home in high society, Voltaire could not comprehend Rousseau's taste for solitude and his modest way of life. Rousseau upheld the claims of faith even as he undermined the claims of common sense and reason. And to top it all off, Rousseau was indiscreet, even reckless in expressing his political views: as Voltaire tartly put it, he had "judged kings and republics without being asked to." That fame and popular influence in Voltaire's adopted hometown of Geneva should be one of Rousseau's rewards for his pious eccentricity was the last straw.

Geneva and its political prospects increasingly preoccupied Rousseau. Ever since he had published the *Discourse on the Sciences and the Arts* in 1750, he had identified himself publicly as "a citizen of Geneva"—even though he had been stripped of his citizenship years before, as a result of converting to Catholicism. After he completed his *Discourse on the Origin of Inequality* in 1754, Rousseau decided to compose a dedicatory preface, hymning the virtues of Geneva, which he depicted as the democratic homeland of his dreams. Shortly afterward, he returned to Geneva, abjured Catholicism, and became again a real citizen of Geneva.

His homeland was as polarized as ever. On one side stood the established ruling class, committed to preserving its aristocratic privileges and keen to savor the urbane theatrical fare on offer at Voltaire's château; on the other side stood a popular party consisting of clergymen and artisans, adamant that ordinary citizens play a more robust role in the city's government and aghast at the elite's conspicuous consumption of French entertainments.

Rousseau was warmly welcomed in some quarters, more coolly in others. To some magistrates and members of the ruling elite, he was automatically suspect for being a man of the lower classes, and a religious traitor as well. But professors and pastors flocked to his side, and he became a hero to the watchmakers of the faubourg de Saint-Gervais, the artisan district where his father had worked and lived.

After this brief homecoming, Rousseau retired again to France. In practice, he preferred a philosopher's leisure to the responsibilities of active citizenship. By choosing exile on the outskirts of Paris, he remained free to think for himself without having to worry about censorship or the difficulties and dangers of political action. "There are some circumstances in which a man can be more useful to his fellow citizens outside of his fatherland than if he were living in its bosom," Rousseau later remarked.

Living in bucolic seclusion, and counting on the goodwill of a few wealthy friends to supplement what money he made from copying music and, more erratically, from sales of his books, Rousseau alternated intense bursts of concentrated writing with long periods of relaxed meditation. While daydreaming on his solitary walks, Rousseau found his spirit exalted. Images of modern men and women who embodied Stoic virtues arose within, forming "a genuinely new spectacle" and a picture of perfect love. "I made a golden age at my whim," he recalled. "The impossibility of reaching real beings threw me into the land of chimeras, and seeing none that existed worthy of my delirium, I nurtured it in an ideal world which my creative imagination soon peopled with beings according to my own heart."

Thus began his work on *Julie, or the New Héloïse*, an epistolary romance largely set in Switzerland. It featured correspondents who, as Rousseau pointedly remarked in a preface, "are not French, not sophisticates, not academicians nor *philosophes* but rather provincials, foreigners, recluses, young people, almost children, who in their romantic imaginations take the innocent frenzy of their minds to be philosophy" (not unlike Rousseau himself, one could argue).

Rousseau had never been more productive. Besides working on his novel, he continued to gather notes for a treatise on political right and intermittently worked on another text imagining how one might ideally prepare a child for a life of virtue.

Then, in 1758, he was distracted by the appearance of the seventh and latest volume of the *Encyclopedia*. The lengthy entry on Geneva, by Diderot's colleague and coeditor d'Alembert, contained the provocative suggestion, made in passing, that the city ought to build a municipal theater, in order to "add the urbanity of Athens to the prudence of Sparta." Fearing the possible impact of such misguided ideas on his homeland, Rousseau composed an impassioned response in three weeks of furious writing.

Although his overt target was d'Alembert, Rousseau was implicitly attacking Voltaire as well, for Voltaire had been staging plays at his house for the local gentry, catering to their recently acquired taste for Parisian forms of entertainment. Even though Rousseau had written plays and had tried to get one staged in Paris, he felt compelled, in this period of moral effervescence, to write "against my own interest. *Vitam impendere vero* [consecrate life to truth]: that is the motto I have chosen, and of which I feel myself worthy." Theatrical frivolities might do no harm in a decadent metropolis like Paris, but in an upright republic like Geneva, they were disastrous and corrupting.

Better, argued Rousseau, to encourage ordinary citizens to participate in inclusive civic festivals, or, even better, to debate civic virtue in one of the political clubs frequented by artisans—never mind that many of the city's leading citizens enjoyed their exclusive evenings chez Voltaire and rather disapproved of the informal political circles Rousseau was praising.

When Rousseau's *Letter to d'Alembert* was published in 1758, Voltaire was predictably furious. In his own (private) letter to d'Alembert, Voltaire complained about "this arch-madman" and disingenuous hypocrite who "writes against the theater after having written a bad play, he writes against France which nourishes him, he has found four or five rotten staves from Diogenes' barrel and he gets inside to bark."

To add insult to injury, Rousseau's *Letter* included a veiled attack on Diderot, at a time when his old friend was coming under the fiercest criticism yet from the French clergy. From now on, Rousseau fancied himself an exile from the Republic of Letters, a self-avowed outcast from the community of friends that had helped launch his literary career in the first place.

To his former friends, his latest pose was insufferable. But Rousseau still found patrons who were willing to protect and shelter him. He may have been the most subversive author of his day, but he never could have survived without the support of a series of sympathetic dukes, princes, and earls who left him alone to resume his routine of reverie and writing.

The controversy over his *Letter to d'Alembert* had kept him in the public eye, as did the continuing popularity of his opera. But it was the publication in 1761 of *Julie, or the New Héloïse* that transformed Rousseau from a celebrated philosopher into a cynosure of virtue in the eyes of countless readers.

"One must suffocate, one must abandon the book, one must weep," declared one correspondent. "One must write to you that one is choking with emotion and weeping." "Your divine works, Monsieur, are an all-consuming fire," wrote another. "Ever since I read your blessed book, I have burned with the love of virtue, and my heart, which I had thought extinguished, beats harder than ever. Feeling has taken over once again: love, pity, virtue, sweet friendship have for ever conquered my soul."

In a preface to *Julie* acknowledging the paradox that the author of the *Letter to d'Alembert* had simultaneously written an impassioned romance about "two lovers who live in a small town at the foot of the Alps," Rousseau argued that even novels can have some usefulness—as long as they "set aside everything artificial; bring everything back to nature"; and "give men the love of a regular and simple life," such as that depicted in *Julie*.

Julie was swiftly translated into English and German, going into multiple printings in multiple editions and becoming one of the best-selling books of the eighteenth century. Rousseau had never been more famous.

Yet even as his romantic novel was converting readers to a newfound love of classical virtue and such natural sentiments as pity, and even as the author did nothing to discourage readers from supposing that "I myself was the Hero of this novel," Rousseau was busy finishing the two texts that he regarded as the capstone of his lifework. He was more committed than ever to communicating as clearly and cogently as he could the content and implications of his revelation "that man is naturally good and it is through [their] institutions alone that men become bad."

The first and by far the longer text was *Émile*, an implicit critique of the institution of education in the form of a fantasy, an account of an imaginary young man being raised under ideal circumstances by a solitary tutor. The second, and more consequential in Rousseau's own mind, was *The Social Contract*. "Of the diverse works that I had in hand," he later confessed, "the one which I had meditated on for the longest time, the one which I had devoted myself to with the greatest relish, the one on which I wanted to work all my life, and the one which, in my opinion, ought to put the seal on my reputation was my *Political Institutions*."

Once again, a conception of free will played a key role, both in *Émile*, where a properly cultivated good will is what enables an individual to withstand the temptations of a corrupt society, and in *The Social Contract*, where what Rousseau called a "general will"—good wills exercised in concert—enables a people to regulate itself rightly, in a self-governing community. Moral freedom requires developing one's strength to resist distracting external events beyond one's control, thus perfecting what Rousseau (like Seneca) defined as "virtue," while political freedom requires participating actively in public affairs. Both forms of freedom augment and artificially reinforce the strength of a human being's will, in such a fashion that he "wants only what he

can do, and only does what pleases him"—Rousseau's most concise description of the "truly free man" in *Émile*.

Once again, Rousseau downplays the claims of reason in a life properly
lived. He maintains that it is the proper elaboration of a free will—and not
reason or the acquisition of knowledge—that enables the human being to do
good and to forbear doing wrong. In place of the Platonic idea that knowledge
of the good can be possessed (or approximated) by only a few—which ostensibly justifies a regime governed by philosopher-kings—Rousseau elaborates
his own idea of the good as the unhampered and uncorrupted exercise of the
free will inherent in every single soul, which justifies popular sovereignty. The
key to securing this form of liberty is the collective free will of a people—an
impersonal form of power limited by the extent of their shared interests, as
expressed in periodic assemblies where all citizens could meet face-to-face.

This was a radical notion, a prescription for democracy in a context where
kings still exercised unbounded power in the government of most states in
Europe. It was even a subversive idea in Rousseau's native Geneva, where effective political power lay in a small town council controlled by a wealthy
elite.

In April 1762, *The Social Contract* and *Émile* were published almost simultaneously. Rousseau did not even try to get official approval to distribute *The
Social Contract*. Since the appearance of his *First Discourse*, he had been living
something of a charmed life as a very public contrarian, quite unlike his former friend Diderot. (After his arrest in 1749, Diderot had kept his most incendiary writings to himself, leaving them to be published after his death.) But by
publishing the two books together, Rousseau had badly misjudged the tolerance of church and government officials not only in France but also in Geneva.

In both places, the source of the problems was not primarily *The Social
Contract* but rather the long passage in Book IV of *Émile* in which Rousseau's
tutor recounts to his imaginary pupil how a "Savoyard Vicar" had long ago
shared with him an idiosyncratic "Profession of Faith."

Rousseau's fictive vicar holds that a powerful and wise will moves the
world; *God* is his name for this "Being that wills." The vicar, like Rousseau in
the *Discourse on Inequality*, furthermore represents the will as a metaphysical

aspect of the human being, which separates man from the other animals and makes each one akin to God, so that "I [can] sense Him in me," in part through the sentiment of freedom. What is singularly human about human nature is thus something *super*natural, something divine. But how, then, to explain the endless series of evils that human beings obviously suffer? Why would a God who is wise leave his divine creation free, yet everywhere in chains?

The vicar's approach to this quandary, like Rousseau's in his *Second Discourse*, seems fairly conventional at first: "Everything is good as it leaves the hands of the author of things; everything degenerates in the hands of man." When evils befall mankind, man has only himself to blame. Whereas "a beast cannot deviate from the rule that is prescribed to it," a man may deviate freely, and "often to his detriment." The "first depravity" of men "comes from their own will," when human beings out of weakness fall into bad habits in conformity with evil laws.

But on another level, Rousseau's theology of freedom resurrects one of the oldest heresies in Christendom, that associated by Augustine with the name of Pelagius. It was Pelagius, writing in the fifth century A.D., who famously advanced the proposition that "God has conferred upon men liberty of their own will, in order that by purity and sinlessness of life they may become like unto God." A very similar thought appears in the pages of *Émile*. "To prevent man from being wicked, was it necessary to limit him to instinct and make him a beast? No, God of my soul, I shall never reproach You for having made him in Your image, so that I can be free, good, and happy like You!"

Like Pelagius, Rousseau insists on the innate goodness of the will. The "right" of freedom—taking the French word *droit* in the twofold sense of "justice" and "straightforwardness"—arises from freedom itself: "I am not free to want what is bad for me." Even in our most abased state, insists Rousseau, "all our first inclinations are legitimate." So long as it is strong enough and does not stray, free will can do no wrong.

All wrongdoing must therefore be considered involuntary, a product of external causes: "I have always the power of will," says the vicar, "but not always the strength to execute it." If the will in itself is innocent, then the source of evil must be sought not in the metaphysical or spiritual realm but in the physical realm: in the frailties of the body; in the overriding attraction of tempting external objects; or in prejudices, needless passions, and the kind of corrupt society that engenders both in the vast majority of human beings.

That is the bad news.

The good news, according to both Rousseau and Pelagius, is that the divine power of free will gives the human being the power to start over. Defining evil as an issue of bad habits, rather than an unavoidable effect of the original sin of Adam, reduces sin to a problem of human "negligence," one curable through an act of human free will. Furthermore, if the causes of evil are exclusively to be found in the physical realm of material cause and effect, then "the Fall, and any possible redemption from it, can be explained in terms that are purely natural."

It is precisely the claim that human beings possess such an independent power to reform themselves that Augustine and the mainstream Christian tradition condemned as heresy. "Since man could fall by will, by free choice," argued Augustine, "he could not rise again" by an exercise of will alone: "No man can be freed from evil . . . except by the Grace of God."

Rousseau's similar heresy was swiftly reproved by the ecclesiastical authorities, first in Catholic Paris and then in Protestant Geneva. In both cities, his books were burned, his theology condemned. And in Geneva, officials censored his political theory as well, declaring that an "extreme freedom is the deity of the author" and deploring his support for "periodic assemblies—which are expressly prohibited by our laws, and which would render freedom even more crushing than servitude."

In order to avoid arrest, Rousseau was forced to flee Paris on June 8, 1762. Shortly afterward, Genevan authorities issued a warrant for his arrest if he set foot in the city. Rousseau found refuge in Môtiers, a village in the Swiss province of Neuchâtel that was under the protection of Prussia's king Frederick the Great, an absolute monarch with little to fear from either Rousseau's unorthodox theology or his radical theories about politics.

Facing official censure almost everywhere in Europe, Rousseau was defiantly unrepentant. "The fundamental principle of all morality about which I have reasoned in all my writings and developed in [*Émile*] with all the clarity of which I was capable, is that man is a naturally good being, loving justice and order; that there is no original perversity in the human heart, and that the first movements of nature are always right." At the end of 1764, after re-nouncing his Geneva citizenship, he addressed his enemies in his homeland directly, declaring that "the democratic constitution is certainly the master-piece of the political art"—an incendiary remark in the eighteenth-century context.

With Geneva on edge because of the latest Rousseau controversy, an anon-ymous eight-page pamphlet titled *The Sentiment of the Citizens* appeared. Purporting to be the work of a concerned Calvinist divine, it was in fact writ-ten by Voltaire, who had allied himself with the oligarchy in the uproar over *The Social Contract*. ("Punish him with the full severity of the laws," he wrote privately to one Genevan friend, urging him to treat Rousseau "as a blasphe-mous subversive who blasphemes Jesus Christ while calling himself a Chris-tian, and who wants to overturn his country while calling himself a citizen.") Voltaire's screed made a number of false allegations about Rousseau, but it also took dead aim at his Achilles' heel, describing how this supposed paladin of truth and virtue had surreptitiously abandoned the children he had con-ceived out of wedlock "at the door of an orphanage."

For years, only a few people had known Rousseau's secret. Now, thanks to Voltaire, the world knew.

More trouble followed. Rousseau's latest publications defending himself and his ideas were banned and burned in city after city throughout Europe. In Môtiers itself, his daily walks became the occasion for public ridicule, and a local minister preached against his iniquities so forcefully that parishioners felt justified in pelting his residence with stones. In late October 1765, he left Neuchâtel, his destination unclear. Old friends in France offered their sup-port, but he didn't dare accept it. After several weeks of wandering, he finally sought refuge in England, arriving in January 1766, escorted by Britain's cel-ebrated historian, essayist, and philosopher, David Hume (1711–1776), then chargé d'affaires at the British embassy in Paris.

Hume's first impressions of Rousseau were favorable:

M. Rousseau is of small stature, and wou'd be rather ugly, had he not the finest physiognomny in the world, I mean, the most expressive countenance. His moed-esty seems not to be good manners; but ignorance of his own excellence: As he writes and speaks and acts from the impulse of genius, more than from the use of his ordinary faculties, it is very likely that he forgets its force, whenever it is laid asleep. I am well assurd, that at times he believes he has inspirations from an immediate communication with the divinity. He falls sometimes into ecstasies which retain him in the same posture for hours together. Does not this example solve the difficulty of Socrates's genius and of his ecstasies? I think Rousseau in many things very much resembles Socrates.

But the relationship between Hume and the French Socrates was bound to be strained: Hume spoke French, but Rousseau could neither speak nor understand English (though he could read it). Hume was gregarious and sociable by nature, whereas Rousseau was shy and awkward. Hume was famously poker-faced and impassive, and prided himself on "great moderation in all my passions," while Rousseau wore his heart on his sleeve and was prey to wild mood swings. Still, most of literary London followed Hume's lead and welcomed the famous exile to their fabled land of civil liberties.

Wishing to settle down someplace that was rural and remote, Rousseau accepted an offer from a wealthy admirer to live in a Midlands mansion. It proved to be a gloomy retreat, and as the months went by, Rousseau, isolated as never before, became convinced that he was the target of a vast and shadowy "plot" designed to destroy his reputation and to make his life miserable.

Rousseau's paranoia was all the more pitiable because he was, in fact, being persecuted. He had been expelled from one country after another, and he had been formally denounced not just by governments and churches but also by old friends and former associates. But when he guessed, correctly, that Hume was secretly opening letters addressed to him (in order, Hume explained to friends, to spare Rousseau the expense of forwarding correspondence that Hume thought unimportant), Rousseau began to think, incorrectly, that David Hume was one of his greatest enemies.

What followed was tragic farce. On a trip to London, Rousseau visited with Hume. After supper, he noticed Hume staring at him and became alarmed. Suddenly disgusted at his own paranoia, he threw his arms around Hume and said, "No! No! David Hume is no traitor! If he is not the best, he would have to be the worst." Hume uncharacteristically returned the embrace

246 THE PHILOSOPHICAL LIFE

and tried to calm his friend, saying "*Quoi donc, mon cher monsieur,*" How now, my dear sir. But as he explained in a subsequent letter rehashing the event, Rousseau took offense at what he regarded as Hume's coldness and reserve.

Increasingly accusatory letters were exchanged, and, at the suggestion of some of Rousseau's enemies in Paris, Hume arranged to publish the entire correspondence in both France and England. The publication made Rousseau look ridiculous. As one London satirist wrote, Rousseau's evidence for treachery "apparently amounted to Hume's staring at Rousseau and then saying 'My dear sir' while patting him on the back."

In a panic, Rousseau abruptly returned with Thérèse to France, traveling incognito in order to evade arrest. Unable to trust anyone, more convinced than ever that he was the victim of a vast conspiracy, he traveled from place to place, resuming the transient way of life he had known as a young man. In this rootless state, he started to write about his childhood and adolescence—an autobiography that grew in the months and years that followed into several books of *Confessions* meant to rival those of Augustine.

Some of his memories consoled him, but others were painful to recall. Inevitably, he would have to expiate what had become his most notorious sin, by recounting the circumstances in which he had consigned his children with Thérèse Levasseur to a foundling home: "By abandoning my children to public education for lack of power to bring them up myself; by destining them to become workers and peasants rather than adventurers and fortune hunters, I believed I was performing an action of a Citizen and father." But try as he might, he obviously was unable to lift or even shift the burden of guilt. The best he could do was to pretend that he had no regrets and to claim at the end of his life that he had found "compensation for my sacrifice" in the insights about the raising of children he was able to elaborate in his books, wanly asserting that "it would assuredly be the most unbelievable thing in the world that the *Héloïse* and the *Émile* were the work of a man who did not love children."

In 1770, having finished a draft of his *Confessions* and having belatedly arranged to marry Thérèse, Rousseau moved back to Paris with his wife. There he hoped to repair his tattered reputation. The couple moved into an apartment, and Rousseau began to give public readings from the *Confessions*. At least three such readings occurred between December 1770 and May 1771.

On one occasion, according to an eyewitness (who may or may not be credible), Rousseau read for seventeen hours, with only brief pauses for refreshment. When he came to the subject of his abandoned children, he recounted his version of events, and then paused, as if daring someone to criticize his conduct. "The only response was a gloomy silence," broken only when members of the audience rose to console the author: "He wept, and all of us wept hot tears."

Rousseau did not exactly invite disagreement at these public appearances. He finished his final reading by declaring that he had told the truth, and that "if anyone knows some things contrary to what I have just set forth, even if they are proven a thousand times, he knows lies and impostures, and if he refuses to get to the bottom of them and clear them up with me while I am alive he does not love either justice or truth," and is someone who "ought to be choked."

There were no more public appearances after the chief of police ordered Rousseau to stop. Thwarted in his latest effort to exonerate himself, he felt ever more isolated, alone, hopelessly misunderstood.

He worked fitfully over the next few years on a different kind of justification of himself, a set of three interior dialogues he titled *Rousseau, Judge of Jean-Jacques*. This is a very peculiar text, in which the author imagines an anonymous "Frenchman" in conversation with an imaginary character named "Rousseau," both of whom debate how to evaluate the moral character of the man who wrote *Julie*, *Émile*, etc., who is referred to throughout as "Jean-Jacques." The Frenchman, based on the gossip he has heard, believes Jean-Jacques is a monster; "Rousseau," based on his reading of the books, believes that Jean-Jacques must be a good man. The Frenchman challenges "Rousseau" to visit Jean-Jacques and to observe the man's conduct; "Rousseau" challenges the Frenchman to read the books.

In the *Confessions*, Rousseau, writing as himself, had invited his readers to be the judge of his character. In these dialogues, the author, through the fictional character called "Rousseau," passes judgment on the man who wrote the *Confessions*: "He is a man without malice rather than good, a soul healthy but weak, who adores virtue without practicing it, who ardently loves the good and does hardly any. As for crime, I am as persuaded as I am of my own existence that it never came near his heart, nor did hate. That is the summary of my observations on his moral character." "Rousseau" even tells the Frenchman that Jean-Jacques is in the midst of composing a series of dialogues, "rather like the one that may result from our conversation."

During his "period of effervescence," from 1749 until the appearance of the *Letters Written from the Mountain* more than fifteen years later, Rousseau tried to share his glad tidings about the natural goodness of the human being, inviting others to embark on a Promethean quest, to rid mankind once and for all of the evil institutions that had created universal slavery in place of universal freedom.

But as Rousseau himself had shown in *Émile*, this was not the only honorable response to his salvific teaching, since a human being is always free, not only to act but also to refrain deliberately from action, like a Stoic who would prefer *otium* to the obligations of public life. Indeed, he who endeavors to live a life of public virtue makes himself a hostage to fortune, to a host of external forces and factors that are well beyond the power of one man's will, or even a society's general will, when it is not strong, to control and direct toward a good end.

"A motive for virtue," confides Rousseau in his last will and testament, the *Reveries of a Solitary Walker*, which he was writing at the time of his death, "is nothing but a trap . . . I know that the only good which might henceforth be within my power is to abstain from acting, from fear of doing evil without wanting to and without knowing it."

This is a stunning volte-face. Rousseau now has to concede that the " 'Know Thyself' of the temple of Delphi was not as easy a maxim to follow as I had believed in my *Confessions*," and that "to dare to profess great virtues" without the courage and strength needed in practice to live a life in true harmony with those great virtues "is to be arrogant and rash."

At the same time, he confesses that "to act against my inclination was always impossible for me"—he simultaneously understands and resents the need for feats of Stoic self-restraint. Transcending his resentment, he announces that he has chosen for himself a new ethos, a new way of life: "In my present situation, I no longer have any other rule of conduct than in every-thing to follow my propensity without restraint." But this does not imply that Rousseau is now prepared to act on his every passing whim. Unwilling to bri-dle his will, yet fearful of the consequences of acting on a will that is unbri-dled, he finally chooses to will *not* to will and simply to exist in a state of perfect indolence.

And that, more or less, is where Rousseau's own odyssey ended: in serene isolation and tranquil passivity. He spent the final months of his life at a châ-teau in Ermenonville, twenty-five miles north of Paris, where an admirer, the marquis de Garardin, had installed extensive gardens in the natural style Rousseau had described in *Julie*. There Rousseau was content to botanize, and to record in writing his daydreams, and to savor select episodes from his past in the pages of his *Reveries*. By restricting the play of his will to imagining and remembering, Rousseau was in his last days finally able more or less con-stantly to follow his propensities without restraint—an ostensibly good man lost in his thoughts, savoring anew those moments, fleeting yet sweet, when he had felt most "perfectly free."

He died on July 2, 1778, four days after his sixty-sixth birthday, with only Thérèse present. A rumor spread that Rousseau had committed suicide by shooting himself with a pistol. But the doctors who examined the corpse shortly after his death declared the cause of death to be a stroke—a finding corroborated in 1897 when authorities, hoping to dispel the lingering rumors, reexamined his skeleton and found no trace of a gunshot wound.

Rousseau was buried on the château's grounds, on a small island in the middle of an ornamental lake. Shortly afterward, Thérèse Levasseur was re-ported to have said, "If my husband is not a saint, who will ever be one?"

In the years that followed the posthumous publication of the *Confessions* in 1781, Rousseau became the object of a quasi-religious cult. Pilgrimages to his tomb on the Isle of Poplars at Ermenonville became so frequent that a guidebook to the place was published in 1788. Visitors held séances with the departed and demonstrated their solidarity by sacrificial burnings of Dider-ot's criticisms of Rousseau. After one such séance, a devotee exclaimed, "It is he himself who has talked with me; . . . the divine Rousseau, a man so good, so simple, and sublime." The simplicity of the citizen was palpable in such relics as the wooden clogs he had worn. A visiting duchess spent an afternoon at Ermenonville hobbling about in them, presumably to participate, however vicariously, in the plebeian goodness of the simple artisan's son.

In 1794, five years after the storming of the Bastille and the start of the French Revolution—an epochal event that many felt Rousseau had inspired—the philosopher's body was exhumed and transferred to Paris in a public procession that lasted three days. The French legislature honored Rousseau with a special session, and then a cortege bearing his body wound through the streets of Paris, toward the Panthéon, a church that the revolutionaries had transformed into a mausoleum for the interment of great Frenchmen.

There Rousseau was laid to rest—an ironic apotheosis for the picaresque philosopher who had come to realize, belatedly, that he could never live up to the images of the perfectly virtuous man and citizen that he had bequeathed to posterity in the pages of his books.

KANT

Portrait of Immanuel Kant, oil on canvas, unknown artist of the German school, eighteenth century. Although Kant revered the classical ideal of "true philosophy" as a way of life, his own life consisted largely of composing scholarly lectures and carefully pondered treatises in an effort to elaborate maxims based on pure reason and abstract moral principles. (Private collection/The Bridgeman Art Library International)

The man widely regarded as the greatest philosopher of modern times was, in the sour estimate of one close friend, a "little schoolmaster." A professor by trade, Immanuel Kant was a small man with a frail body and a capacious mind; his forehead was broad, his gaze penetrating. He had a talent for conceptual gymnastics and had labored long and hard to refine two notions that were largely of his own invention: the autonomy of the will and the limits of pure reason. A paragon of self-renunciation, Kant never married and almost never traveled, rarely leaving the city of his birth, Königsberg, in East Prussia. Instead, Kant let his mind roam freely, keeping his imagination in check through a stern sense of moral duty and an equally stern sense of intellectual probity.

For a half century, the University of Königsberg was the center of his universe. Year in and year out, he lectured from sixteen to twenty-five hours a week on many different topics: logic, metaphysics, anthropology, physical geography, moral philosophy, natural law, natural religion, theoretical physics, mathematics, pedagogy, mechanical science, mineralogy, a course under the title Philosophical Encyclopedia, and possibly even pyrotechnics. In the four months of the academic year when he wasn't giving lectures, he was writing scholarly essays and books, most of them in German, many aimed exclusively at a small circle of professional peers. Kant is the first modern philosopher to work entirely within an academic context, and the heart of his contribution to philosophy is to be found in the treatises he wrote.

The book that secured his reputation for posterity is *The Critique of Pure Reason*, published in 1781. As Michel Foucault put it, the world after Kant's critique "appears as a city to be built, rather than as a cosmos already given." But that heady prospect is expressed in prose that is nothing if not austere.

The poet Heinrich Heine (1797–1856) notoriously asserted that "it is difficult to write the history of the life of Immanuel Kant, for he had neither life nor history." Because Kant's many volumes of published texts are characteristically impersonal—no *Confessions* for him—one biographer decided to recount his life by describing in detail "how his individuality blends ever more closely with his work, and seemingly vanishes entirely."

Yet Kant admired Rousseau and appreciated his strenuous effort to exemplify his maxims in his way of life according to the ancient understanding of the true philosopher. Kant also recognized the limits of the modern project of pure inquiry, if divorced from the classical conception of the philosophical life. "If we take the ancient Greek philosophers—such as Epicurus, Zeno, Socrates," he declared in one of his lectures, "we discover that the principal object of their science has been the destination of man, and the means to achieve it. They thus remained much more faithful to the true Idea of the philosopher than has been the case in modern times, when we encounter the philosopher only as an artist of reason."

Like Rousseau, Kant came from a modest background—his father, Johann Georg Kant, was a master harness maker. He was born in Königsberg in April 1724, the fourth child born to Johann and Anna Regina. He was baptized Emanuel, and for the rest of his life prized the meaning of his name in Hebrew: "God is with him." (He later changed the spelling on the grounds that Immanuel was a more faithful rendering of the original Hebrew.) The Kants would have a total of nine children, but only five survived infancy. Immanuel was the oldest son.

Kant's father was an artisan in a guild who took pride in his status as a self-reliant laborer. Both his parents were adherents of Protestant Pietism, a fierce form of Lutheranism that was influential in Prussia in the first half of the eighteenth century. The religion was founded on daily soul-searching and aimed at spiritual rebirth—a conversion, born of abjection, to a holier form of life. The chastened children of men, born again as "children of God," were henceforth expected to renounce worldly pleasures and perform acts of public charity. Despite its self-sacrificing ethos, Pietism appealed not only to hard-working commoners like Kant's mother and father but also to King Frederick William I, who turned what had been a reforming movement into a state religion.

"One may say about Pietism what one will," Kant remarked to an associate late in life, long after he had ostensibly abjured the gloomy creed of his parents. "Enough! The people who took it seriously were distinguished in a way that is worthy of honor. They possessed the highest qualities that a human being can possess, namely a calmness and pleasantness, an inner peace that can be disturbed by no passion." Their example left a lasting impression on the young man, despite his equally lasting distaste for systematic self-examination.

After a short time in a local elementary school, Kant was sent at the age of eight to the Collegium Fridericianuum, a strictly Pietist school where students were groomed for careers in the church or the civil service. It was a regimented institution, with a curriculum organized around the study of the Old and New Testaments, Luther's small and large catechisms, and Hebrew, Greek, and Latin; Kant in addition learned French, a little mathematics, and some philosophy. Learning was often rote, a matter of repetition and recitation. Introspection was obligatory. Every student who hoped to receive Communion at church services had to compose a report on the "state of his soul" beforehand, to be submitted to a spiritual supervisor.

In later years, Kant warned that such exercises could produce "enthusiasm and insanity." He shuddered when he recalled his "slavery" at the hands of teachers who were religious fanatics. But not every aspect of the experience left him cold: Kant admired his Latin teacher, and for a while was enamored with Seneca, whose words he happily memorized. He was a model student, earning top marks in almost all of his classes.

Königsberg in these years was a thriving port city with a population of around forty-five thousand. Founded in 1255, and a member of the Hanseatic League since 1340, it had been the capital of Prussia until 1701. It still housed a large garrison of Prussian soldiers as well as various state offices; along with Berlin, it was one of the most important cities in Prussia. A regional center of trade, it attracted merchants from neighboring countries like Lithuania, Poland, and Russia, and also from maritime nations like Holland and England. There was a significant Jewish community, and also a large number of Huguenot refugees from France. Despite its remote location on the eastern frontier of East Prussia, it was far less provincial than most other German university towns.

In 1740, Kant entered the Albertina University of Königsberg. The only university in the area, it was one of the premier institutions in Prussia and attracted a cosmopolitan body of students from neighboring countries. A Lutheran institution, reformed according to Pietist principles, the Albertina did not admit Catholics or Jews, even though applicants had to submit an analysis of some part of the Hebrew Pentateuch, in addition to interpretations of the Greek text of at least two gospels in the New Testament.

All entering students were obliged to study philosophy, which was regarded as a "lower" discipline that served as an introduction to the school's three "higher" faculties—medicine, law, and theology. Most students moved on quickly to the study of theology, in hopes of being ordained as a pastor or professor of theology. But not Kant: even though the university was weak in physics and mathematics, he became preoccupied with natural philosophy and was eager to publish his research. Instead of concentrating his efforts on completing a thesis in Latin, which would have qualified him to begin teaching at a high school or at the university, Kant took the unusual and precocious step of writing and publishing a book in German, *True Estimation of the Living Forces* (1749), in which he tried to mediate an arcane dispute between the followers of Leibniz and of Descartes over how to measure kinetic energy.

Shortly after the appearance of Kant's book, he left the Albertina without submitting the required theses or taking his final examinations. For the next several years, he earned money by tutoring the children of local noblemen. At the same time, he continued to write, working to fulfill the requirements to graduate from the university, and also completing a second book in German, which appeared in 1755: *General Natural History and Theory of the Heavens, or an Essay on the Constitution and Mechanical Origin of the Whole Universe,*

Treated in Accordance with Newtonian Principles.

In this *Natural History*, Kant argued that laws of physics, not chance, govern the cosmos, and that God has created these laws so that the universe may unfold harmoniously without any subsequent need for divine intervention. His commitment to the scientific principles of Newton did not keep him from speculating wildly about the nature of the solar system: assuming the likelihood that there was life on other planets, he conjectured that the creatures inhabiting Jupiter and Saturn had cognitive capacities so vastly superior to those of human beings that their intellects would make Newton seem like a child.

A decade earlier, the publication of such a book would have been a defiant, even suicidal gesture for anyone hoping for an academic career at the university, given its divergence from Pietist orthodoxy. But by 1755, Kant's materialist approach to physics was perfectly consonant with the views held by the monarch to whom Kant dedicated his *Natural History*: Frederick William II, better known as Frederick the Great.

Frederick the Great had become king of Prussia in 1740, after the death of his father. Raised with punishing rigor according to strict Pietist precepts, he became a lifelong anticleric. One of his first acts as king was to disestablish Pietism as the de facto state religion. He favored religious tolerance, remarking that every man had the right to be saved according to his own lights. He also abolished judicial torture and tried to establish (with limited success) a system of universal public education. A connoisseur of the novel theories and open inquiry associated with the philosophes of Paris, he installed Voltaire as an intellectual ornament in Berlin (where the Frenchman lived for three years, from 1750 to 1753).

Besides being a Francophile, Fredrick the Great was an omnipotent sovereign who proved to be a brilliant commander in chief. He doubled the size of Prussia's armed forces and, in a series of bold military campaigns, capped by the Seven Years War (1756–1763), greatly expanded the territory under Prussian control. By the end of his long reign in 1786, Frederick had transformed Prussia from a minor principality into a rising continental power with a distinctive ethos of unfettered enterprise and an unflagging sense of discipline and duty, which left no aspect of Prussian life untouched.

Frederick's influence was certainly felt at Albertina University. Philosophical perspectives that had been taboo under Prussia's previous monarch could now be explored with impunity. The range of views open to dispute—and the language in which they could be articulated—began to expand, as foreign works were quickly translated into German. (For example, David Hume's *Enquiry Concerning Human Understanding*, published in England in 1748, appeared in translation seven years later—and Kant promptly added references to Hume in his lecture courses.) But one thing about the intellectual milieu was slow to change: the scholastic climate of debate, which demanded (and rewarded) hair-splitting disputes over doctrinal subtleties that were completely unintelligible to the uninitiated (anyone who had never mastered the techniques of philosophical dispute as taught at the Albertina).

Following the publication of *Natural History*, Kant defended three dissertations at the university, all of them composed (as required) in Latin: the first was on fire, the second on the first principles of metaphysical knowledge, and the third on the relation between the philosophy of Leibniz and the physics of Newton. Completing the theses and passing the oral exams qualified him to become a *Privatdozent*, or adjunct lecturer, entitled to offer lectures to students for a fee (the sole income he received—only full-fledged professors received a salary directly from the university). In these years, Kant was no more immune to economic pressures than any other *Privatdozent* aspiring to become a professor. Though it is a little hard to believe when one reads the lecture notes that survive, Kant was livelier and less stilted than most of his young colleagues. As a result, he quickly developed a following. With a steady income, he was able to rent more spacious rooms for himself.

In 1758, two years after Frederick the Great had marched into Saxony and triggered what became the Seven Years War, Prussia had to cede Königsberg to Russia for what turned out to be a five-year-long occupation. Some residents were resentful, but others, including Kant, found that their fortunes improved. The Russians had money and a taste for the finer things of life. Officers began to attend Kant's lectures, and he was now in demand at dinner parties where drinking punch was the new fashion. He became something of a dandy, relaxing over billiards or a card game, telling his students that it was "better to be a fool in style than a fool out of style." He wore coats with golden borders and a ceremonial sword to the dinner parties he attended with Russian officers and the Königsberg elite—it was a "duty," he said, "not to make a distasteful or even unusual impression on others."

Women reportedly enjoyed Kant's company. But even though Kant in his lectures praised the virtues of marriage as a civil institution, conjugal bliss and sexual congress were two of the many common pleasures he apparently never experienced firsthand.

Legend has it that he once met a beautiful widow who struck his fancy. "He calculated income and expenses and delayed the decision from one day to the next." By the time he had completed the cost-benefit analysis, the widow had picked another suitor. On another occasion, a young woman visiting from Westphalia pleased him greatly, but again he dithered—and by the time he resolved to propose marrying her, she had packed her bags and gone home.

Kant meanwhile busied himself with a variety of technical disputes with academic rivals who were competing for the same small pool of paying philosophy students. Among the topics were determinism and the limits of free will; and whether human beings lived in the best of all possible worlds, as Leibniz had maintained and as Kant in this period was inclined to agree, even after the calamitous earthquake in Lisbon in 1755 (the event that led Voltaire to poke fun in *Candide* at Leibniz's optimism).

As one of his most sympathetic biographers sums up Kant in this period, "Real radicalism is absent from his thinking and his life alike." When he tried to address everyday concerns—and his students in these years had begun to turn to him for advice—he ended up dispensing platitudes:

"Every human being makes his own plan of his destiny in the world," he proclaimed in an essay on the meaning of life, written shortly after one of his students had died suddenly at the age of twenty-two. "Happiness in conjugal life and a long list of pleasures or projects make up the pictures of the magic lantern, which he paints for himself and which he allows to play continuously in his imagination. Death, which ends this play of shadows, shows itself only in the great distance . . . While we are dreaming, our true destiny leads us on in an entirely different way. The part we really get seldom looks like the one we expected, and we find our hopes dashed with every step we take . . . until death, which always seemed far away, suddenly ends the entire game." Sententious and fairly banal—such was the *Magister*'s moral style at this point in his career.

In 1762, the Russians withdrew their troops from Königsberg. When Prussia's garrison returned to the city, the king ordered his officers to improve themselves by taking classes at the city's *école militaire*, where Kant sometimes lectured. His social circle continued to expand, and his academic reputation continued to grow. In 1764, his essay on the *Principles of Natural Theology and Morality* was published in the Proceedings of the Berlin Academy, which made his name known outside Prussia.

Kant's professional prospects had never looked brighter. He earned enough from his lectures that he was able to retain a personal servant, Martin Lampe, who would spend the next forty years at Kant's side, making sure that his master had clean clothes and tidy rooms, and woke up on time.

Yet in this very period, as a result of a profound immersion in the philosophy of Jean-Jacques Rousseau, worries about his bodily health that would prove chronic, and, not least, a budding friendship with a scholarly English merchant, Joseph Green, Kant decided to revise dramatically "his own plan of his destiny in the world."

Sometime in the mid-1760s, he began to adhere to a new regimen, both theoretical and practical, in hopes of forging a new moral character for himself, based on what he would later call—in a typically cumbersome formulation—an "absolute unity of the inner principle of conduct as such."

Joseph Green epitomized for Kant just such an "absolute unity" of precept and practice. He was "a rare man of strict righteousness and true nobility," in the words of one of Kant's first biographers, and in his everyday life he "followed an invariable and odd rule"—he worshipped punctuality.

Green, like Kant, was a bachelor. A creature of inflexible habit, Green resolutely followed "maxims"—rules of personal conduct. Besides attending to his business interests, Green was a polymath, an aficionado of contemporary philosophy and the vagaries of its leading living exponents: in the letters he wrote to Kant from England in 1766, he relayed all the latest gossip about Rousseau's ill-fated visit to Hume that year.

Before meeting Green, Kant had led a fairly conventional life. He worked hard but let himself relax, too. He enjoyed nights on the town and sometimes drank too much. But after Green became his best friend, Kant settled into a more sober fixed routine. Most days he got up at 5:00 a.m. and drank one or two cups of weak tea. He then smoked a pipe—he allowed himself only one bowl of tobacco a day, though visitors reported that the bowls of his pipes grew larger as he got older. He then prepared to deliver his lectures. From 1771 on, his first lecture was at 7:00 a.m. (a time set by the ministry of education), with additional one-hour lectures lasting until eleven or twelve. He worked on his writings until he went out to a local pub to have his main meal of the day. After lunch, he took a walk, ending up at Green's house for their daily afternoon conversation. He left Green's house at 7:00 p.m. sharp. Back home, he did some more work, reading, preparing for his classes, or writing.

It was a perfectly predictable schedule, and Heinrich Heine gibed that when Kant walked by at the proper time, the citizens of Königsberg "gave him friendly greetings and set their watches." Kant's punctual conduct reflected a "constant striving," according to his friend Louis Ernst Borowski, one of his first biographers, "to act in accordance with thought-out maxims, which—at least in *his* opinion—were well-founded principles, and by his eagerness to formulate maxims in all the greater and smaller, more and less important matters, from which he always began and to which he always returned."

Kant soon discovered that this rigid regimen was a tonic for his "somewhat fragile health." In a rare autobiographical passage in one of his last works (*The Conflict of the Faculties*, 1798), Kant confided, "I myself have a natural disposition to hypochondria," giving as a reason "my flat and narrow chest, which leaves little room for the movement of the heart and lungs." When he was younger, his physical complaints "made me almost weary of life."

In more than one passage from lectures and theoretical works he conceived after his reform, Kant explicitly discusses hypochondria, defining it as an ailment "of the cognitive faculty"—a mental illness. Those afflicted with this form of mental illness risked misunderstanding the real state of their bodily health by constantly complaining of imaginary ailments. The remedy that Kant proposed for his own hypochondria was an inflexible code of conduct organized around strict maxims and "distracting occupations." He believed that complaints about ill health might disappear altogether if a hypochondriac habitually devoted himself to "intentional abstraction."

In this way, Kant, like a good Stoic, upheld "the power of the mind to master its morbid feelings by sheer resolution." The more soberly he applied himself to "intentional abstraction," the less unwell he felt, he said. In later years, Kant credited his longevity to the rigid routine he had followed after he turned forty. Although he continued to suffer from recurrent feelings of anxiety about his health, he wrote that "I have mastered its influence on my thoughts and actions by diverting my attention from this feeling, as if it had nothing to do with me."

Believing as he did that predictable habits were a cure for imaginary ailments, Kant had found a powerful motive for applying maxims as rigidly as his friend Green. But Kant also believed that a carefully regulated life could produce a rational unity of belief and behavior. "Character," he claimed, "requires maxims, which proceed from reason and from moral and practical principles." In the same context, Kant goes on to assert that the creation of a "character" that is truly virtuous "comes about only through an explosion." It amounts to a "kind of rebirth, like a certain solemn kind of promise to oneself," which "follows all at once upon dissatisfaction with the state of vacillation of instinct."

Although there is no evidence that Kant ever enjoyed any such explosive epiphany—unlike Augustine in the garden, or Descartes during his night of dreams, or Rousseau on the road to Vincennes—there is some indication that he did experience "a kind of rebirth," not just because of his friendship with Joseph Green but also because of his fascination with Jean-Jacques Rousseau.

Kant had read most of Rousseau's books as they were being published, from the *First Discourse* in 1751 to *The Social Contract* in 1762. Legend has it that Kant only once interrupted his daily schedule: while reading *Émile* for the first time in 1762. A portrait of Rousseau was the only picture in his study. "I am by inclination an inquirer," Kant wrote in the copious "Remarks" he attached to his own copy of *Observations on the Feeling of the Beautiful and the Sublime* (1764). "I feel in its entirety a thirst for knowledge, and a yearning restlessness to increase it, but also satisfaction in every forward step. There was a time when I thought that this alone could constitute the honor of mankind, and I despised the people, who know nothing. Rousseau set me right."

By 1765, when he jotted down these "Remarks," Kant had come to know much of Rousseau's work by heart, perhaps in an effort to overcome his initial enthusiasm: "I must read Rousseau until the beauty of expression no longer moves me, and then I can look at him rationally." His reflections at the time circled around an interconnected series of thoughts raised by his reading of Rousseau: the corruption of contemporary morals, the limits of knowledge, the power of free will, the potential goodness of the will when it is free to act spontaneously, the evils that result from subjecting the will—and the conviction that "there is a perfect world (the moral) in accordance with the order of nature."

Like Rousseau, Kant entertained the prospect that we might discover a science of morals that would show a man how "properly to fulfill the place which was allotted to him in creation." Like Rousseau, he acknowledged the profound obstacles to establishing such a science: "Everything goes by us in a flux, and the varying tastes and differing shapes of man make the whole game uncertain and delusive. Where do I find the fixed points of nature that man cannot displace?" Because human nature has been corrupted, "natural first principles become dubious and unrecognizable." More complications result from the indeterminate spontaneity of the free will, which both Kant and Rousseau regard as the metaphysical essence of the human being. Although Kant associates Rousseau with Newton in one passage, he notes as well the stark difference between the objects of physical and of moral inquiry. Physical inquiry yields determinate knowledge, while moral inquiry is potentially indeterminate, because it is inescapably *meta*physical: "The movements of matter do indeed maintain a certain definite rule, but human self-will is without rule."

As an eminent German scholar has put it, "one can describe Kant's entire philosophy as the result of an attempt to transform this philosopher's thoughts into a scientifically respectable and universally applicable theory." This was a tall order, since Rousseau's reflections were rhapsodic, and his flights of introspection were impassioned as well as lyrical: Rousseau worked within a recognizably French tradition of moral reflection established by Montaigne. Although Kant admired Montaigne, his own conception of what was "scientifically respectable" was drawn from the German tradition of Leibniz and

Christian Wolff, who both strove for a dry precision in their use of speculative reason and tried to explain the intelligible universe as a whole. Working up his reflections on Rousseau into a "universally applicable theory" thus presented Kant with challenges that were simultaneously substantive and "architectonic"—to use Kant's term of art for what he (like Leibniz and Wolff) assumed to be the systematic structure of knowledge.

It would take him years to resolve all the challenges. But in the meantime, he settled into his new routine, carving out a part of each day for disciplined reflection. As Kant explained to a former student, "the gentle but sensitive tranquility" of the philosopher was infinitely preferable to the rapturous flights "dreamed of by the mystics." His would be a philosophical life devoted to calm reasoning, impervious by design to the vagaries of strong feelings and unruly impulses.

In 1769 and 1770, he received offers to teach in Erlangen and in Jena. Unwilling to disrupt his regimen, Kant rejected both. "All change frightens me, even one that might offer the greatest prospect of improvement in my circumstances," he admitted to a friend a few years later. "All I have wanted is a situation in which my spirit, hypersensitive but in other respects carefree, and my body, more troublesome but never actually sick, can both be kept busy without being strained—and that is what I have managed to obtain."

Finally, in March 1770, a full professorship opened up at the Albertina, and Kant was appointed to teach logic and metaphysics, which ensured him a steady if modest salary, over and above his lecture fees. Unlike some of his colleagues, Kant was conscientious about collecting the money he was due and investing it prudently. He took attendance at the free lectures he was obliged to give as a full professor and wouldn't allow anyone to attend the same free lecture course twice (though he was willing, for a fee, to welcome repeat customers to his other courses).

On August 21, 1770, Kant delivered his inaugural dissertation in Latin, "On the Form and Principles of the Sensible and Intelligible World." It offers the first public indication of how his thinking had been transformed by his reflections on Rousseau. Like the author of the *Second Discourse* and the Savoyard Vicar in *Émile*, Kant stipulates a sharp distinction between two worlds. But where Rousseau separated a natural world of cause and effect, to be explained through physics, from the moral world of the free will, to be under-stood through metaphysics, Kant counterposes a *mundus sensibilis*, associated with "phenomena," things as they appear, and a *mundus intelligibilis*, associated with "noumena," or things as they are in themselves. The "*perfectio noumenon*," Kant argues, is in its theoretical sense "the Supreme Being, God," and in its practical sense "moral perfection."

At the same time, his inaugural dissertation makes it plain that Kant has also revised key parts of Rousseau's original philosophy. Where Rousseau stressed pity, Kant aims instead to "determine maxims and first principles that hold objectively and tell us how we should approve or reject something, or act or refrain from acting," independently of any putatively natural moral sentiments. For the rest of his life, Kant's primary question would be, "What are the *principia prima diiudicationis moralis* . . . , i.e., What are the highest maxims of morality, and what is their highest law?" Unlike Rousseau, who regarded the ability to reason with suspicion and eventually resigned himself to acting on whim and impulse, according to what he believed were his natural inclinations, Kant was moving in the opposite direction, emphasizing, as one modern scholar puts it, "the *dependence* of moral feeling on a logically prior and independent rational principle," eventually going on to argue that only acts done out of a deliberate sense of duty have moral value.

In December 1770, one of Kant's few philosophical peers in Prussia, Moses Mendelssohn, after reading the inaugural dissertation, expressed reservations about Kant's style that have since been echoed by more than one critic: "The ostensible obscurity of certain passages is a clue," Mendelssohn remarked in a letter to Kant, "that this work must be part of a larger whole . . . Since you possess a great talent for writing in such a way as to reach many readers, one hopes that you will not always restrict yourself to a few adepts who are up on the latest things, and who are able to guess what lies undisclosed behind the published hints."

Mendelssohn's hopes would be frustrated. Kant's self-imposed requirement that his new philosophy be presented as a comprehensive deductive system crippled his ability to express himself clearly. His letters and his later short essays prove that he could write with epigrammatic concision. Glimpses of spontaneous wit also break out occasionally in his most popular lecture course, on anthropology. But his major works have what Heine called "the grey, dry style of a paper bag." And his lectures on logic and metaphysics became notorious for their opacity. "The method of my discourse," Kant remarks in a diary note, "has a prejudicial countenance; it appears scholastic, hence pettifogging and arid, indeed crabbed and a far cry from the note of genius."

As one of his auditors, the historian Adolph Franz Joseph Baczko, recalled, "I attended his lectures right away and did not understand them. Given the estimation of Kant's name and the suspicions that I have always entertained about my abilities, I came to believe that I had to put more time into my own studies . . . I worked through entire nights, labored uninterrupted for twenty hours and more over a book and learned nothing . . . I began to be convinced that some of Kant's students knew even less than I did. I began to believe that they went to Kant's lectures in order to gain a reputation."

Insulated by his daily routines and preoccupied with thinking through his new philosophy, Kant increasingly appeared to students as an unapproachable sage, often inscrutable in his ex cathedra declamations. Kant himself confided to a friend that he had "almost no private acquaintance with my auditors." Though he had reason to believe that many of his students had no idea what he was talking about, he refused to modify his manner of presentation. (Many years later, writing to a correspondent who asked for clarification on a subtle point of doctrine, Kant confided that "I do not understand myself. Such overly refined hairsplitting is no longer for me.") In this way, Kant became complicit in creating around himself a strange cult of unintelligibility, choosing to speak only to the converted and leaving the uninitiated to gape in awe at the oracle with the powdered wig behind the lectern.

In 1778, Kant was nominated by Prussia's minister of education to become professor of philosophy at Halle, a prestigious post at an eminent institution. Once again, Kant turned down the offer, remarking that he needed carefully "to spin out to greater length the thin and delicate thread of life which the Fates have spun for me."

He was by now settled in his habits, and he wished to maintain his intimate friendship with Joseph Green. He was also loath to give up his standing among the local nobility. When the famous astronomer Johann Bernoulli

(1744–1807) passed through Königsberg that year, he recorded his impressions of the professor, whom he met over lunch at the home of a count: "This famous philosopher is in his social intercourse such a lively and polite man, and he has such an elegant way of life that one would not easily expect such a deeply searching mind in him. But his eyes and his face betray a great wit."

As Bernoulli remarked, many years had gone by since Kant had published anything significant. For more than a decade, Kant kept promising the appearance of new work "soon," but the anticipated work was repeatedly delayed. At last, in 1781, the long-promised work finally appeared: a massive new treatise of more than eight hundred pages, *Critique of Pure Reason*.

The book's publisher, Johann Georg Hartknoch, lived in Riga but had the book printed in Halle; Kant had first offered the book to a Königsberg publisher, who turned it down for fear that the sales of such a massive tome would not allow him to recoup his costs.

Perhaps the first person to read the *Critique* was one of Kant's oldest Königsberg friends, Johann Georg Hamann, who convinced Hartknoch to send him printed sheets of the book as they became available. "There will probably be few readers who can master its scholastic contents," Hamann remarked to one correspondent, though he conceded that "there are charming oases after one has long been wading in the sand." In private, he was harsher: he dubbed the *Critique* "Sancho Panza's transcendental philosophy."

Given the ponderousness of the new book's style, it is no wonder that its reception was not immediately favorable. One reviewer declared the *Critique* to be "a monument to the nobility and subtlety of the human understanding" but went on to caution that it was written for "the teachers of metaphysics" and that its contents would be "incomprehensible to the great majority of the reading public."

The book revolves in part around a deceptively simple premise: that it is only from a human standpoint (and not from some imaginary God's-eye point of view) that we can speak of space, time, and the existence of physical things. What we can know about anything we perceive is determined by the categories and concepts we construct to use in our inquiries, as well as by our sentient experience of the world. Both parts are essential: in the formula of the first *Critique*, "thoughts without content are empty, intuitions without concepts are blind."

Kant had developed his new approach in part in an effort to secure the findings of modern natural science (as exemplified by Newton) against skeptical attack. In trying to establish the limits of trustworthy knowledge, he felt compelled to draw a sharp line between the empirical knowledge that arose in the course of experience and what he called "transcendental ideas," formed by speculative reason alone, concerning what lay beyond all possible experience: for example, ideas about the existence of God, the immortality of the soul, and freedom of the will. "Human reason," as he puts it in the very first sentence of the *Critique*, "has the peculiar fate . . . that it is burdened with questions that it cannot dismiss, since they are given to it as problems by the nature of reason itself, but which it also cannot answer, since they transcend every capacity of human reason."

Several of the most influential parts of the *Critique* are thus purely negative: they demonstrate why all attempts to prove the existence of God, the immortality of the soul, and the like are doomed to failure. It was these passages that earned Kant a reputation for radical skepticism among his earliest readers and provoked Moses Mendelssohn to call him the "all-destroyer."

Kant himself had a subtler view of the implications of his critique. Take, for example, his treatment of the speculative idea that the will is free. Of all the "Ideas of Reason" that Kant analyzed in the *Critique*, the idea of the free will is perhaps the most important—and certainly the most paradoxical. This idea, as he defines it, "stands only for the absolute spontaneity of an action," independent of physical causation or "of any coercion through sensuous impulses." Because Kant thought that there was no way to demonstrate with certainty that the will is free, he concedes that the correlative idea of freedom is, literally, inexplicable. But he also conjectures that "a constitution allowing *the greatest possible human freedom* in accordance with laws by which *the freedom of each is made to be consistent with that of all others*" is a "necessary idea" that cannot be dismissed through an appeal to experience or empirical evidence: "For what the highest degree may be at which mankind may have to come to a stand, and however great a gulf may remain between the idea [of a free society] and its execution [in practice]," he writes in the *Critique*, "no one can or should try to determine this, just because it is freedom that can go beyond every proposed boundary."

Hence the second aspect of what some called Kant's "Copernican revolution": his suggestion that human beings (as Rousseau had suggested) are able in practice to construct a moral and political world for themselves, over and above the facts they learn about the physical universe. Philosophy cannot content itself with an inventory of the formal limits to what we can know. It must also create what Kant calls "a science of the highest maxim of the use of our reason," in part by elaborating "transcendental ideas" that will enable human beings to choose wisely between different ends, and in part by showing how an abstract variant of the Golden Rule ("Do unto others as you would have them do unto you," which became Kant's famous categorical imperative: "Act on a maxim which also holds as a universal law") offers an infallible moral compass that enables every human being "to distinguish in every case that comes up what is good and what is evil, what is in conformity with duty or contrary to duty."

Every human being is thus enjoined to realize a perfectly moral world through a carefully regulated exercise of one's rational will: "The saying, *Perfect yourself*—when it is taken to say simply 'Be good, make yourself worthy of happiness, be a good man, and not merely happy'—can be seen as the *principle* of ethics." And in certain contexts, Kant seems to hold out the Promethean prospect that the human race, properly enlightened, may yet attain its "highest possible perfection," which will be "the kingdom of God on earth," when "conscience, justice and equity will then hold sway, rather than the power of authority."

As even a brief summary of the *Critique of Pure Reason* may suggest, it is "a rich mine with various ores and many veins," as one of his first biographers put it, "and it has often happened that persons of the most diverse tendencies have found, or imagined that they found, just the ore they sought, because each one worked only a particular vein or mistook the nature of the metal which he discovered."

Kant had fixed views about how to understand his magnum opus. Since he was thin-skinned by temperament—and since he assumed that his was a systematic theory that had to be grasped as a whole—he reacted with irritation to criticism, and with a renewed sense of literary zeal to the sheer variety of responses that the *Critique* initially provoked. In the years that followed, essays and books poured from his pen, as he made a concentrated effort to clarify once and for all his original intentions, as well as to elaborate the full implications of his new way of thinking for morality, natural science, history, politics, religion, art, logic—the whole range of human experience.

Fifty-seven years old when the first *Critique* appeared, Kant crammed a lifetime of writing into the fifteen years that followed, producing many of the works for which he is best known. His astonishing productivity in these years doubtless cost Kant dearly. In order to write his books, the great theorist of freedom felt more compelled than ever to limit his own spontaneity, to keep a tight leash on his life. To a remarkable extent, he turned himself into a kind of thinking machine, duty bound to conquer "sensuous impulses," the better to devise categories and build arguments with brisk efficiency.

His routine mainly consisted of teaching and writing, and in this manner he became a quintessential modern philosopher, a salaried professor who was largely known for his books. Like Rousseau, Kant acknowledged the classical ideal of "true philosophy" as a way of life. But the mature way of life Kant himself chose was narrowly focused on systematic inquiry. In effect, he reinvented himself in these years as an exemplary "artist of reason"—a paradigmatic practitioner of philosophy as a unified science, striving to give an integrated and accurate account of everything he had come to know in terms that would be, to the largest extent possible, independent of his own personal idiosyncrasies.

In 1783, he published a short *Prolegomena to Any Future Metaphysics*, meant to answer his critics and clarify the intentions of his *Critique*. The following year he published two essays in a journal, aimed at a relatively wide audience, "Idea for a Universal History of Mankind" and "What Is Enlightenment?" More treatises followed: *Groundwork of the Metaphysics of Morals* in 1785, the *Metaphysical Foundations of Natural Science* in 1786.

In that year, a literary journal published a series of letters about Kant's *Critique of Pure Reason*, which for the first time sparked popular interest in the new system of thought. A colleague wrote from Jena, "You can tell how diligently the students here are studying your *Critique of Pure Reason* from the fact that, a few weeks ago, two students fought a duel because one of them had said to the other that he didn't understand your book and that it would take another thirty years of study before he would understand it and another thirty before he would be able to say anything about it."

In 1787, Kant published an extensively revised second edition of the *Critique of Pure Reason* and suddenly, for reasons that aren't entirely clear, his philosophy was in vogue. High officials in Berlin debated its merits, and merchants sang its praises. His book began to sell. One correspondent told Kant that he had met a man on a trip to The Hague who spent hours alone in his hotel room, poring over the pages of the *Critique*. The praise now heaped on Kant knew no limits. In Prussia, he was hailed as the modern Socrates, the German Plato, and Aristotle rolled into one. One admirer wrote, "God said, Let there be light; and there was—Kant's philosophy."

Capitalizing on the popularity of the first *Critique*, Kant published a second *Critique of Practical Reason* in 1788, and a third *Critique of Judgment* in 1790; two other major works followed: *Religion Within the Bounds of Mere Reason* in 1792 and *The Metaphysics of Morals* in 1797. All these books appeared in large printings and reached a broad audience in the German-speaking lands.

In the course of producing this torrent of prose, Kant modified or qualified a number of the views expressed in the *Critique of Pure Reason*. In the first iteration of his moral philosophy, the *Groundwork of the Metaphysics of Morals*, he had declared that "autonomy of the will" is "the supreme principle of morality," and that freedom, not the contingent dictates of priests or kings, was the source of morality, properly understood. Since freedom of the will, according to the *Critique*, is a "metaphysical" assumption that cannot be proved, Kant had to concede that his "supreme principle of morality" puts philosophy in "a precarious position." In his subsequent essays on morality, politics, and history, he nevertheless seeks to articulate rational principles for the proper exercise of free will, placing duty over desires, obligations over emotions, and formulating precepts that sometimes defy common sense (as, for example, when he solemnly decrees that "carnal enjoyment" outside of marriage "is *cannibalistic* in principle").

Unlike Rousseau, Kant never seriously entertained the idea that "man is naturally good." On the contrary, Kant cautions that "man is an animal," with unruly wants and passions, and that "only the descent into the hell of self-cognition can pave the way to godliness." Such self-examination reveals "an evil will actually present" in the human being. As a result, our wicked impulses must be restrained and regulated by self-imposed rules of conduct. Unfortunately, man "abuses his freedom with respect to other men, and although as a reasonable being he wishes to have a law which limits the freedom of all, his selfish animal impulses tempt him, where possible, to exempt himself from them. He thus requires a master, who will break his will, and force him to obey a will that is universally valid, under which each can be free." In any case, a uniform solution to the riddles posed by Kant's radical new principle of freedom is "impossible, for from such crooked timber as man is made, nothing perfectly straight can be built"—a remark prized by the twentieth-century liberal philosopher Isaiah Berlin, who took it as a warning against "single, all-embracing systems, guaranteed to be eternal."

Unwilling to see his views censored or dismissed as subversive, Kant in these years tried to express his philosophy in a variety of ways that were broadly compatible with the moral and political opinions current in Prussia. For example, his remarks about "crooked timber" and man's need for a "master" sharply qualify his conception of the free will and make his essay on universal history broadly consistent with Lutheran teachings about the "bondage" of the human will and also with Prussian norms of discipline and obedience.

In addition, as Kant well knew, human beings vary greatly in their ability to live with uncertainty. As a result, different people need different types of beliefs to regulate their lives. In the conduct of his own life, Kant personally felt no need to believe that God exists or that the soul is immortal. In this he behaved according to the strict precepts of the *Critique of Pure Reason*: like a latter-day Socrates, he knew only that he did not know, and that he could *never* know whether the soul is immortal or if God exists.

But he had to concede, based on experience, that most people have different needs. Such common souls as his servant Lampe yearn for compelling answers not just to the question "What can I know?" but also to three other key questions: "What ought I to do? What may I hope? What is man?"

As if to compensate for the joyless aspects of his teaching, Kant postulated a life after death, where an ordinary man of good will may reasonably assume that he shall enjoy life eternal. In a characteristically convoluted passage in his *Critique of Practical Reason*, Kant baldly asserts that freedom, immortality, and God are "concepts to which real objects belong, because practical reason unavoidably requires the existence of them for the possibility of its object, the highest good, which is absolutely necessary practically, and theoretical reason is justified in assuming them"—even though, he quickly warns, no further use of this fine piece of wishful thinking may be made "for theoretical purposes."

Kant's recourse to such tortuous casuistry provoked a derisive commentary from Heinrich Heine.

> Tragedy is followed by farce . . . Immanuel Kant has played the merciless philosopher, he has stormed the heavens, he has routed the whole garrison, the supreme ruler lies unproved, no fatherly love, no reward in the other world for the restraint shown in this one, the immortality of the soul is breathing its last—there is groaning and moaning—and the old Lampe stands there with his umbrella under his arm, a mournful observer, cold sweat and tears running down his cheeks. Then Immanuel Kant takes pity and shows that he is not only a great philosopher but also a good man, and he ponders, and then, half in earnest and half in jest, he says, "the old Lampe must have a God, otherwise the poor man will never be happy— man should be happy on this earth—so practical reason tells us—oh, well, let practical reason guarantee the existence of God." In consequence of this argument, Kant draws the distinction between theoretical reason and practical reason, and with the latter, as with a magic wand, he resurrects the corpse of deism, which theoretical reason had put to death.

Heine has a point. But Kant's views on religion also recall the egalitarian substance of his original response to Rousseau ("I learned to honor human beings"), which is confirmed by a remark he makes near the end of *Critique of Pure Reason*: "In regard to the essential ends of human nature even the highest philosophy cannot advance further than the guidance that nature has also conferred on the most common understanding." To "honor human beings," as Kant understood the task, in part meant framing a philosophy that can answer the spiritual needs of a man like his servant Lampe.

Despite these concessions, Kant simultaneously continued to insist, qui-

etly but firmly, that no true philosopher will rest content with mere postulates, or ritually instilled beliefs and habits, however necessary such postulates
or rituals might be to orient the "most common understanding." He never
promised himself a rose garden—only the "intellectual contentment" of acting
resolutely on coherent maxims for himself and doing what he should in accordance with the laws of morality his inquiries disclosed. As he explained in a
letter to a friend who asked for his views on faith and prayer, he was "a man
who believes that, in the final moment only the purest candor concerning our
most hidden inner convictions can stand the test and who, like Job, takes it to
be a sin to flatter God and make inner confessions, perhaps forced out of fear,
that fail to agree with what we freely believe."

One of Kant's favorite mottos was *Sapere aude!*—Dare to know! He criticized the extent of mankind's "self-imposed immaturity" and conjectured
that the sorts of beliefs that human beings find it reasonable to postulate must
inevitably change, as freedom of thought spreads more widely, and that our
most cherished "Ideas of Reason" are liable to change as well, since it is of the
essence of freedom that it can broach "every proposed limit."

But Kant was nothing if not prudent when it came to testing such limits.
In his essay on enlightenment, he expresses his admiration for a motto of
Frederick the Great: "Argue as much as you will, and about what you will—
only obey!" Only gradually could the common understanding become "capable of managing freedom." To "enlighten an *age*" was a "very slow and arduous"
process, and he cautioned his colleagues against impatience and what he
called a "presumptuous" assertion of intellectual independence, for fear that
the censors would crack down.

In 1786, when he issued these warnings, Kant had good reason to be worried. Frederick the Great, a champion of the German enlightenment, had recently died, and it was anticipated that civil liberties would be rolled back
with the accession to power of Frederick William II. For better or worse, Kant
had begun to view himself as an avatar of reason, a public figure who was
properly concerned not just with freedom of thought but also with helping to
justify limits on that freedom—through self-censorship, if necessary. His
prudence—which sometimes verged on pusillanimity—was duly noted: the
new king gave Kant a yearly stipend and smoothed the way for him to become

a member of the Academy of Sciences in Berlin.

He cut a regal figure in these years. "His head was adorned with a finely powdered wig," one visitor to Königsberg recalled, and his "silk stockings and shoes also belonged to the usual outfit of a well-dressed gentleman." The visitor also noticed that when an academic procession ended at the cathedral of Königsberg, Kant, who had marched with the other professors, proceeded to walk right "past the entrance of the church." He did little to hide his disinterest in the institutions and rituals of organized religion.

When the French Revolution broke out in 1789, Kant also did little to hide his admiration for the revolutionaries. "He lived and moved in it," according to one of his confidants in these years, "and, in spite of all the terror, he held on to his hopes so much that when he heard of the declaration of the republic he called out with excitement: 'Now let your servant go in peace to his grave, for I have seen the glory of the world.'" Old friends made excuses for his vicarious political zealotry, which they took to be a "peculiarity" of his character rather than a more serious moral defect.

Although open among friends in his contempt for organized religion and his admiration for the French Republic, he was guarded with strangers. If he knew a visitor was opposed to the revolution, he would suggest they avoid the subject. And in 1793, he went even further, publishing an essay in which he denounced rebellion of any sort: tacitly answering recent charges in Germany that "metaphysics" had helped bring about the revolution in France, Kant argued that "any resistance to the supreme legislative power" of a state, "any insurrection that breaks out in rebellion, is the highest and most punishable crime within a commonwealth, because it destroys its foundations. And this prohibition is *unconditional*."

(In a private notebook written at around the same time, Kant argued that the king of France had transferred the supreme legislative power to the Estates-General in 1789. This was a fine piece of sophistry, suggesting as it did that the French Revolution was not, technically speaking, a rebellion. But it was a line of reasoning that doubtless helped Kant convince himself that he was not being a complete hypocrite when he declared his "*unconditional*" opposition to rebellion.)

Kant was also concerned about continuing insinuations that he was an atheist, or that his philosophy led to immorality. He put pressure on some of his academic friends to defend him against such charges. Yet he also toyed with the censors in Berlin, and in his book *Religion Within the Boundaries of Mere Reason*, he boldly asserts that *"Apart from a good life-conduct"*—the primary focus of his own practical philosophy—*"anything which the human being believes he can do to become well-pleasing to God,"* for example, by slavishly following some catechism, *"is mere religious delusion and counterfeit service of God."*

By the time *Religion* appeared early in 1794, the French revolutionaries had executed King Louis XVI, and Kant, nearing his seventieth birthday, was being treated as if he were a "king in Königsberg." His philosophy had become the touchstone for a new generation of German philosophers, and countless books and articles appeared for and against Kant, as these younger thinkers—Fichte, Schelling, Hegel—embarked on their own careers.

It was in these circumstances, on October 1, 1794, that an adviser to King Frederick William II belatedly wrote at his behest to Kant, reporting that "our most high person has long observed with great displeasure how you misuse your philosophy to distort and negatively evaluate many of the cardinal and basic teachings of Christianity . . . We demand that you give a conscientious vindication of your actions."

For a long time, Kant's lofty reputation had helped to shield him from royal censure. But faced with this letter, he composed a brief apologia for himself before completely capitulating. "As Your Majesty's loyal subject," he wrote in a letter dated October 12, "I find that in order not to fall under suspicion, it will be the surest course for me to abstain entirely from all public lectures on religious topics."

Though lacking in courage, Kant's abject response was entirely consistent with an ethos he had established for himself long before. As he had confided nearly thirty years earlier to Moses Mendelssohn, "Although there are many things that I think with the clearest conviction and utmost satisfaction, but shall never have the courage to say, I will never say anything that I do not think." Like many famous philosophers before and since, Kant above all craved peace and quiet, and he had elaborated an extraordinary repertoire of ways to convince himself of his own moral integrity and the correctness of his own views, no matter the circumstances.

When Frederick William II died in November 1797, Kant regarded his previous promise not to lecture or publish on religious topics as vacated, since it had been very carefully tendered to one person alone ("As Your Majesty's loyal subject") and not to the institution of the monarchy. He promptly published a new work on religious matters, *The Conflict of the Faculties*, in 1798 and included in the preface the complete correspondence between himself and Frederick William II, followed by obsequious words of praise for the new king, Frederick William III—"an enlightened statesman" who will "secure the progress of culture in the field of the sciences."

By the time this volume appeared, Kant had largely retired from the university. Scholars continued to consult the great man, and some were shocked to find that his mental faculties had greatly diminished. One visitor reported that "Kant does not read his writings any longer; does not right away understand what he has written himself before." These were the first symptoms of the senile dementia that reduced the philosophical "king in Königsberg" to a shadow of his former self in the final years of his long life.

His habits became increasingly rigid, his behavior more solipsistic, his rationalizations for his conduct more bizarre. He was certain that his health depended on the weather, and he obsessively consulted his weather vane, thermometer, barometer, and hygrometer. He was convinced that perspiration was an evil to be rigorously avoided. If he felt himself on the verge of breaking a sweat during a walk on a summer day, he would stand stock-still in the shade until the danger passed. "Going to sleep became a fixed, elaborate ritual, as part of which his watch was hung on a nail between his barometer and thermometer." The table talk of the great proponent of free thought grew bitter: "If a man were to say and write all he thinks," one visitor recalled him saying, "there would be nothing more horrible on God's earth than man."

Unlike his hero Rousseau, who seemed to have achieved a measure of serenity in his last days, Kant was reduced to fear and trembling by dreams that had grown violent: "Almost every night he imagined himself surrounded by thieves and murderers," and almost every morning he would, on first awakening, mistake his servant, "who was hurrying to calm him and help him," for a killer.

During Kant's long decline, loyal associates continued to prepare new books based on old lecture notes: *Anthropology from a Pragmatic Point of View* in 1798, *Logic* in 1800, *Physical Geography* in 1802, and *On Pedagogy* in 1803. Kant himself, amazingly enough, continued fitfully working on a new treatise he had planned, jotting notes, sketching outlines, and drafting fragments. The project had various working titles: "Transition from Metaphysics to Physics," "The Highest Point of View of Transcendental Philosophy in the System of Ideas." In one section, Kant claimed to establish a priori the existence of an original moving force in nature, a kind of ether, without which there could be no objects of experience. Scholars continue to dispute the value of these final manuscripts, though one thing seems clear: Kant's account of ether is just the sort of speculative theory that he had tried to discourage in the *Critique of Pure Reason*.

On February 11, 1804, Immanuel Kant uttered his last words. During a visit from a friend, Kant accepted a glass of wine mixed with water, saying only, "*Es est gut*"—It is good. He died the next day, less than two months before his eightieth birthday.

Many years later, funds were raised in Königsberg to build a proper monument to Kant's memory for the centenary of the *Critique of Pure Reason*. In 1870, his remains were exhumed, in preparation for their transfer to the new resting place. Two professors on the medical faculty of the University of Königsberg used the occasion to photograph Kant's skull and to measure it carefully. The exhumation itself was a festive public event, observed with pomp and ceremony. Precise measurement confirmed that Kant's forehead was high and broad, and that the unusual size of the skull suggested that his brain had been significantly larger than that of the "average German male."

The following year, Kant was reburied outside Königsberg Cathedral, in a rather grand chapel with an enormous rose-colored porphyry portico. The chapel was one of the few structures in Königsberg to survive World War II and the subsequent Soviet annexation of the city, renamed Kaliningrad. Since the fall of the Soviet Union, it has become the custom for bridal parties to flock to Kant's monument rather than Lenin's in order to celebrate their vows, drink champagne, and leave flowers. On the monument is a bronze plaque with an inscription in both German and Russian of a passage from the *Cri-*

tique of Practical Reason:

"Two things fill the mind with ever new and increasing admiration and reverence, the more often and more steadily one reflects on them: *the starry heavens above me and the moral law within me.*"

ÉMERSON

Portrait of Ralph Waldo Emerson, photographer unknown, America, nineteenth century. One of the most popular public orators of his day, Emerson had a meditative manner that helped persuade a broad public that every man, whatever his station in life, might appreciate, and perhaps even emulate, the spiritual accomplishments of a uniquely self-made poet and thinker.
(Private collection/The Bridgeman Art Library International)

The institutionalization of philosophy in the modern research university was an achievement of the nineteenth century, first in Europe and subsequently in the United States. Kant's first heirs in Germany, scholastic by training and ambition, wrote treatises so abstract, dryly reasoned, and defensive that they were generally accessible only to experts. These professors generally purged their vocabulary of poetry, even when limning the Promethean potential of the imagination and the free will, or joining Kant in anticipation of that "*philosophical chiliasm*, which hopes for a state of perpetual peace based on a federation of nations united in a world republic."

At the same time, first in England and then in New England, there arose a contrasting but allied movement of letters and thought that, taking heart from the German idealists, hoped to turn philosophy into a species of poetry, or a new form of post-Christian prophecy, or both. In a work published in 1834, the British writer Thomas Carlyle coined the term "Natural Supernaturalism" to describe this movement's romantic tendency to divinize the human and to humanize the divine, in part through the appropriation, whether warranted or not, of German philosophers like Kant.

The result, in America, was the emergence of a phenomenon presaged in many ways by the Rousseau cult in late-eighteenth-century France: the philosopher as a popular hero.

In the person of Ralph Waldo Emerson, philosophy for the first time offered itself to all members of a large democratic society in the form of an egalitarian "self-culture." So profound was the revolution Emerson wrought in American thought that John Dewey (1859–1952), perhaps his greatest heir, hailed him as "the philosopher of democracy," adding that he was "the one citizen of the New World fit to have his name uttered in the same breath with that of Plato."

Whereas the modern biographer of Kant can credibly claim that the author's individuality "blends ever more closely with the work, and seemingly vanishes entirely," a contemporary biographer of Emerson can make no such claim. The opposite is true. As one of his first biographers, Oliver Wendell Holmes (1809–1894), put it, "He delineates himself so perfectly in his various writings that the careful reader sees his nature just as it was in all its essentials, and has little more to learn than those human accidents which individualize him in space and time."

Emerson moreover documented a great many such accidents, the externals of his daily life, and registered as well his feelings and thoughts, in a series of diaries, journals, and notebooks that he kept throughout most of his life. In addition, a large number of his letters survive. The contents of this spontaneous and unprecedented month-by-month autobiography currently fill thirty-eight volumes in modern scholarly editions, making it possible to reconstruct in minute detail the unvarnished life of "the sage of Concord."

In his astonishingly uninhibited embrace of introspective forms of writing, Emerson renews older patterns of the philosophical life deliberately ignored by Kant and his followers: for all their talk about autonomy and (in Kant's case) even about self-examination, the German idealists generally refused to indulge in any sort of writing that might be construed as confessional.

Emerson, by contrast, used his journals as a medium not just for self-reflection and self-criticism but also for self-transformation. In their pages, a reader can watch as the author reinvents himself—an extraordinary spectacle, with no real parallel in the lives of previous philosophers. (The only journal that Montaigne kept recorded his trip to Germany, Switzerland, and Italy in 1580–1581; Rousseau in his *Confessions* offered readers only a retrospective narrative account of his self-in-the-making.)

Emerson's singular odyssey began in Boston in 1803. The fourth of eight children (and the third of six boys) born to Ruth Haskins and the Reverend William Emerson, he had "in his veins the blood of several lines of 'painful preachers,'" to borrow a phrase from his first authoritative biographer, James Elliot Cabot.

Emerson's father had been ordained at the age of twenty-three to become a minister at the Congregational Church in Harvard, Massachusetts, twelve miles from the extended family's first home, in Concord. Like his forebears, the father had literary as well as religious interests, and he moved in a Boston circle that was generally conservative in its politics and liberal in its religious views (tending toward what would become the Unitarian view, that God was one, that Jesus was a being distinct from and inferior to God, and that the most important purpose of the religious life was not penance but cultivation of the mind).

William Emerson died when Ralph Waldo was eight, leaving the family destitute and the children to be raised by his mother with the help of their father's sister, Mary Moody Emerson, who became a commanding influence. An exacting mentor and prominent gadfly who expected great things from the Emerson children, Mary Moody was a visionary and a mystic, an autodidact and self-described "deistic pietist" who read voraciously—from Plato and Plotinus to Rousseau and Coleridge. Admonishing the children to "scorn trifles" and aim high, she preached a stern form of Protestant Christianity that brooked neither opposition nor irresoluteness from her charges: as she said of herself, "I love to be a vessel of cumbersomeness to society."

A year after the death of his father, Emerson began to attend the Boston Public Latin School, where he learned Greek as well as Latin, and also learned how to speak in public with force and eloquence. An avid reader, he came to know the classics—Plato, Cicero, Tacitus—and modern English literature from Shakespeare and Milton to Doctor Johnson. He wrote some poems. And in 1817, he had no difficulty winning entrance to Harvard University, even though he was only fourteen years old, below the average age of his class.

Harvard in these years forced its students to adhere to an austere regimen. Rules mandated participation in public prayer in the morning and evening, as well as strict observance of the Sabbath. Spontaneous expressions of merriment might be punished with fines. As at the Latin School, memorization and declamation were the preferred tools of teaching. Emerson seems to have been remarkable mainly for his self-restraint, which kept him out of trouble. He was elected to a student club that met weekly to debate various set questions, for example, "Whether deep researches into abstruse metaphysical subjects be advantageous to the student" and "Whether theatrical representations be advantageous to morality"—a question that Emerson (like Rousseau before him) answered in the negative.

A major turning point for Emerson came midway through his junior year. Shortly after dropping his first name, in order to call himself simply Waldo, he decided to begin a journal, which he titled "The Wide World"—a place for him to record old ideas and "new thoughts," to discuss various philosophical and literary issues on his mind, and to experiment with his growing interest in poetry. The writing of diaries, a rare practice until the seventeenth century, had become a central component of everyday life in Emerson's spiritual milieu. As he well knew, many of his forebears and relatives had kept a running record of their personal experience, or an "Almanack," as Mary Moody Emerson called her daily record.

At first, his journals allowed Emerson to engage directly in the sort of soul-searching that Mary Moody prized and that would become a defining feature of Emerson's private life and, eventually, his public personality as well. As time went by, the journals grew more disorganized and more capacious. In private, he let himself go, recording (as he later described the contents of his journals) "disjointed dreams, audacities, unsystematic, irresponsible lampoons of systems, and all manner of rambling reveries, the poor chupes and berries I find in my basket after endless and aimless rambles in woods and pastures." For virtually the rest of his life, Emerson religiously maintained his journals, creating an unpremeditated mosaic portrait—in more than 260 notebooks—of "Man Thinking."

At roughly the same time that Emerson began to keep a diary, he was also studying in depth the lives of various ancient philosophers, reading Diogenes

Laertius and also Xenophon and Plato on Socrates, in order to complete "A Dissertation on the Character of Socrates." This was the first time that he reviewed the different accounts of Socrates' daimon, a topic that became a lifelong interest. He also read for the first time "the most extraordinary book ever written," Montaigne's *Essays*.

After graduating from Harvard at the age of eighteen, Emerson took a job teaching at a school for girls that his older brother William had established in Boston. His journals show that the prospect of spending the rest of his life as a "schoolmaster" filled him with horror. He continued to read widely—novels, history, Shakespeare, the *Moral Letters* of Seneca, and David Hume, whose skepticism about the value of religious faith Emerson felt had to be answered in some way. At the same time, a new ambition stirs in the pages of his diary.

"Mistrust no more your ability," he exhorts himself on March 23, 1823. "God has put into our hands the elements of our character, the iron & the brass, the silver & the gold, to choose & to fashion them as we will."

On May 1823, shortly before his twentieth birthday, Waldo joined William in signing a "Declaration of Faith"—in God, in Jesus Christ, in the sanctity of Holy Writ—long circulated among members of the First Church of Christ in Boston. William subsequently went abroad to study theology and philosophy in Germany, leaving Waldo to run the girls' school. But he was already saving money in order to enter Harvard Divinity School. With some qualms, but preferring the prospect of preaching to that of teaching, he was preparing to follow in his father's footsteps.

In private, he recorded more than one wave of exultation in his sheer existence, as if, like Descartes before him, he would rout skepticism through sheer self-assertion: "Why may not I act & speak & write & think with entire freedom? . . . I say to the Universe, Mighty one! thou art not my mother; Return to chaos, if thou wilt, I shall still exist. I live. If I owe my being, it is to a destiny greater than thine. Star by star, world by world, system by system shall be crushed,—but I shall live."

Like his aunt Mary, Emerson was willing to take his moral bearings from such epiphanies. But his mood was more often depressed than elated, and accounts of rapture were supplemented by other, more gimlet-eyed entries in the growing account he was keeping of his life. In one extraordinarily detailed journal entry written a few months later, Emerson evaluated his strengths and weaknesses with merciless precision.

He has, he thinks, a "strong imagination & consequently a keen relish for the beauties of poetry," but, he confesses, "my reasoning faculty is proportionately weak." He itemizes various vices: he doesn't warm to social situations, he is "a lover of indolence" (a favorite self-deprecating theme), he lacks self-confidence, and he says and does too many things born of shame rather than conviction.

Still, "in Divinity I hope to thrive," he writes, since "the highest species of reasoning upon divine subjects" is "the fruit of a sort of moral imagination" rather than a product of the " 'Reasoning Machines,' " as he calls philosophers like Locke and Hume. Preaching will play to one of his strengths, for he has inherited "a passionate love for the strains of eloquence," and burns after "the *aliquid immensum infitumque*"—something great and immeasurable—"which Cicero desired."

Emerson formally entered the Divinity School in February 1825, and on October 10, 1826, he received a formal license to preach. Three years later, he became junior pastor of Boston's Old North Church. Although the need to write a new sermon every week burdened him, he was handsomely compensated for his labor.

In 1827, Emerson fell in love with Ellen Tucker, an aspiring poet and a woman of independent means, whom he would marry two years later. In his journals, he describes how their union had awakened in him "a certain awe: I know my imperfections: I know my ill-deserts; & the bounty of God makes me feel my own sinfulness the more. I throw myself with humble gratitude upon his goodness. I feel my total dependence."

His prospects seemed promising, yet Emerson was beset by misgivings and a variety of physical complaints. His eyesight and lungs troubled him, and he may well have suffered from some form of the tuberculosis pandemic ravaging Boston at the time, which more gravely would afflict his wife. "I am embarrassed by doubts in all my purposes," he wrote in his diary. In public, he delivered the kind of sermons his flock expected, but in private, in the pages of his journal, his doubts about his proper vocation multiplied.

At first, it was Hume's arguments against the existence of an all-powerful and beneficent God that preoccupied him, and his aunt Mary worried that he had become "so imbued with his manner of thinking that you cannot shake him off." In search of new sources of conviction, he supplemented his required study of biblical commentary with renewed reading in Plato, whom he understood as invoking "the idea of the divine unity"—a helpful idea for a Unitarian divinity student struggling with doubts about the existence of the divine.

He had a model of spiritual eloquence ready to hand in the person of William Ellery Channing (1780–1842), the most influential Unitarian orator of his generation and a friend of the Emerson family who supplied Waldo with lists of books to read. From Channing, too, he imbibed the tenets of "self-culture," which the older man described as "the care which every man owes himself, to the unfolding and perfecting of his nature," by "acting on, determining, and forming" a soul that is, by divine design, free and "illimitable."

In the spring of 1826, supplementing his readings in English and American spirituality, Emerson rediscovered Montaigne. In the *Essays*, he found a form of skepticism that could lay the basis for religious faith—and also found a type of "self-culture" that was unconstrained by either moral inhibitions or a demand for overarching logical consistency. "It seemed to me as if I had myself written the book, in some former life, so sincerely it spoke to my thought and experience."

He was similarly electrified by Coleridge's *Aids to Reflection*, a collection of aphorisms and spiritual exercises meant to marry German idealism with a Christian-Platonic ascent of the soul toward God. More sharply and less carefully than Kant, Coleridge distinguished between two faculties of the mind: the Understanding, which was limited by its dependence on sensory impressions, and Reason, which transcended such limitations and hence enabled a man to intuit, and become attuned to, supersensory mysteries (thus vindicating, in Coleridge's own opinion, the essentials of his own quite orthodox Anglican faith). "His eye," Emerson later remarked of Coleridge, "was fixed upon Man's Reason as the faculty in which the very Godhead manifested itself or the Word was anew made flesh. His reverence for the Divine Reason was truly philosophical and made him regard every man as the most sacred object in the Universe, the Temple of Deity."

Coleridge's ecstatic prose reinforced Emerson's confidence that he harbored within himself "*that image of God*" manifest in man's divine powers of "*reason* and *free-will*," a conviction consistent with the Christian moral perfectionism of Channing. Montaigne at the same time had showed him how one might deploy a supple language for expressing an ideal of "self-culture" that was responsive to the soul's "fluxions and mobility." Plato offered him a vision of transcendent unity. And Ellen made him blissful, offering him an existential anchor, a partner in prayer.

Emerson's core convictions were taking shape. In his journals, he sketched out his understanding of conversion, the turning of the soul toward the truth that Plato had depicted in his *Republic*, that Augustine had experienced in the garden at Milan, that Rousseau had experienced on the road to Vincennes: it was, he explained to himself, "like day after twilight. The orb of the earth is lighted brighter & brighter as it turns until at last there is a particular moment when the eye sees the sun and so when the soul perceives God."

He preached to his congregation the glad tidings of his newfound faith in the divine capacities of Reason and the human soul, in 1830 delivering an important sermon titled "Trust Yourself": "In listening more intently to our soul, we are not becoming in the ordinary sense more selfish, but are departing farther from what is low and falling back upon truth and upon God. For the whole value of the soul depends on the fact that it contains a divine principle, and the voice of the eternal inhabitant may always be heard within it."

But Emerson's own self-trust was about to be shaken by "the complete wreck of earthly good." Ellen fell ill in the fall of 1830, coughing blood and confined to bed with chronic tuberculosis. When she died, on February 8, 1831, Emerson was unstrung.

As he put it in a poem written in June,

The days pass over me
And I am still the same
The Aroma of my life is gone
Like the flower with which it came.

His vocational crisis now came to an abrupt head. God might be intuited in moments of vision, but he privately admitted that "God cannot be intellectually discerned"—his existence cannot be demonstrate͏̈

be proved beyond a reasonable doubt to anyone who choose.

ing more voraciously than ever—in chemistry, zoology, and astru.

Emerson developed an enduring interest in the natural sciences. But his new

readings wakened old doubts. "In my study my faith is perfect," he wrote in

his journal on December 28, 1831. "It breaks, scatters, becomes confounded in

converse with men."

"It is the best part of the man, I sometimes think," he recorded a few days

later, "that revolts most against his being the minister." The difficulty, he con-

tinues, "is that we do not make a world of our own but fall into institutions

already made & have to accommodate ourselves to them to be useful at all. &

this accommodation is, I say, a loss of so much integrity & of course of so much

power."

Unwilling to sacrifice his own growing sense of intellectual freedom—the

source, for him, of his increasing confidence in his unique capacities—he

resolved to express openly the conclusions that he had drawn from his recent

readings about the modern scientific understanding of nature. In a sermon

delivered on May 27, 1832, he said publicly what he had already written in

private: "I regard it as the irresistible effect of the Copernican astronomy to

have made the theological scheme of redemption absolutely incredible." And if

this were not provocation enough, he followed up with a letter to his church,

explaining that he could no longer in good conscience administer Commu-

nion, since he had come to regard the prescribed form of the Eucharist as a

ritual debasement of what ought to remain an intensely inward and entirely

spiritual experience, of being at one with God.

In June, his church met and agreed that the junior preacher was free to

believe what he would, but that Communion must remain a part of the church

service.

Emerson retreated into himself, spending several weeks that summer in

the White Mountains of New Hampshire.

"The good of going into the mountains," he remarked, "is that life is re-

considered." In his journal entry on July 6, Emerson speculates that "religion,"

properly understood, is a matter neither of "credulity" nor of empty ritual, but

rather "is a life. It is the order & soundness of a man. It is not something else *to be got*, to be *added*, but is a new life of those faculties you have. It is to do right. It is to love, it is to serve, it is to think."

A week later, he writes, "I would think—I would feel. I would be the vehicle of that divine principle that lurks within & of which life has afforded only glimpses enough to assure of its being."

He imagined becoming a "modern Plutarch," by recounting the lives of great men divinely inspired, like Socrates, like Plato—and like George Fox, the sixteenth-century religious visionary who had founded the Society of Friends in England.

He felt himself similarly inspired: "God is, & we in him." Enthusiasm—to feel filled with God—was the mark of genius: Socrates, Jesus, Luther, Milton, "every great man, every one with whose character the idea of stability presents itself had this faith." "We want lives," he wrote a month later. "We want characters of worthy men, not their books nor their relics."

Alone in the mountains, he had made his personal leap of faith. Abandoning the institution of the church, he would follow his own enthusiasm wherever it led, "and then will our true heaven be entered, when we have learned to be the same manner of person to others that we are alone."

In September, he made it official, by asking the Second Church to dismiss him from "the pastoral charge."

"I would be free—I cannot be," he wrote in a poem shortly afterward:

Henceforth, please God, forever I forego
The yoke of men's opinions. I will be
Lighthearted as a bird & live with God.

More than once, he inscribed as a motto, "The true philosophy is the only true prophet." A few weeks later, in the pages of a notebook, he summoned the ghost of Martin Luther: "Here stand I, I cannot otherwise. God assist me. Amen!"

Defrocked, he was born again, this time, as a philosopher—a very peculiar sort of philosopher, someone who was also a prophet, someone defiantly poised to protest his unique understanding about how to "live with God." Emerson is a mystic like Plato but with no patience for reasoned dialectic; a restless seeker like Augustine but unwilling to place his trust in God's grace rather than himself; an essayist of himself like Montaigne but without his distrust of moral perfectionism; an idealist like Kant but uninterested in crafting a system of thought out of his various reflections. "At each step, or level, explanation comes to an end," perhaps Emerson's greatest philosophical proponent, Stanley Cavell, observed. "There is no level to which all explanations come, at which all end. An American might see this as taking the open road. The philosopher as the hobo of thought."

Emerson gave up his house, sold his furniture, and on Christmas Day 1832, he set sail for Europe. In the months that followed, he journeyed from Naples to Rome to Venice; to Paris and then on to London and Scotland; and then to Liverpool, whence he set sail for America in September. During his travels, he went out of his way to introduce himself to various philosophers, poets, writers—John Stuart Mill, Wordsworth, Coleridge, Carlyle—and (in part by using Socrates as his touchstone for evaluating each great man he met) he gained a new confidence in his own talents and his convictions.

"What is it that is to convince the faithful & at the same time the philosopher? Let us hear this new thing," he writes in his journal near the end of his European sojourn. "It is very old. It is the old revelation that perfect beauty is perfect goodness"—an offhand reference to a Neoplatonic equation that he took on trust, or faith. He continues:

A man contains all that is needful to his government within himself. He is made a law unto himself. All real good or evil that can befall him must be from himself. He only can do himself any good or any harm. Nothing can be given to him or taken from him but always there is a compensation. There is a correspondence between the human soul & everything that exists in the world,—more properly, everything that is known to man . . . The purpose of life seems to be to acquaint a man with himself. He is not to live to the future as described to him but to live to the real future by living to the real present. The highest revelation is that God is in every man. I

The final "I" floats free in this passage, with no period to anchor the train of thought. The whole passage, of course, is not a proper piece of reasoning, any more than is Descartes's *cogito, ergo sum*. It is a spontaneous proclamation of a core conviction, with no basis other than sheer faith. But this ungrounded faith was unwavering: the essentials of this core conviction, once asserted, remained unchanged for the rest of Emerson's life. It was a part of the purity of his will to preach this peculiarly democratic and egalitarian belief—that God is in *every* man—with resolute constancy, using every available medium.

Still, and no matter how firm his faith was in himself, a man had to make a living. The anticipated inheritance from Ellen's estate would almost enable Emerson to live the life of a genteel man of letters, but he needed to supplement this income. He started to preach occasionally in churches around the Boston area, feeling himself "pledged if health & opportunity be granted me to demonstrate that all necessary truth is its own evidence; that no doctrine of God need appeal to a book"—even the Bible; and "that Christianity is wrongly received by all such as take it for a system of doctrines," for "it is a rule of life not a rule of faith."

He also decided to try something new, by preparing lectures to deliver before a lay audience, mainly by working up thoughts and ideas and observations he had recorded in his journals and notebooks.

"A lecture is a new literature," Emerson later remarked, "which leaves aside all tradition, time, place, circumstance, & addresses an assembly as mere human beings,—no more—It has never been done very well. It is an organ of sublime power, a panharmonicon for variety of note. But only then is the orator successful when he is himself agitated & is as much a hearer as any of the assembly. In that office you may & shall (please God!) yet see the electricity part from the cloud & shine from one part of heaven to the other."

He was thirty years old when he delivered his first public talk, on natural history, to Boston's Natural History Society at the Masonic Temple in November 1833. More talks quickly followed, organized by various associations dedicated to the spread of knowledge, including the Boston Mechanics Institution, the American Institute of Instruction, a number of local congregations and colleges, and the American Society for the Diffusion of Useful Knowledge, which sponsored his first planned series of public lectures in 1835 on biography, in which he briefly recounted a series of exemplary lives, from Michelangelo and Martin Luther to Edmund Burke.

By then, the so-called lyceum movement in the United States had created a large and growing network of local lecture bureaus in virtually every town and city in New England. As envisaged by the movement's founder, Josiah Holbrook, the lyceum would narrow the gulf between rich and poor by offering a form of community education through weekly lectures, libraries, debates, and traveling exhibits, often organized in collaboration with local schools and cultural associations. By the early 1840s, there were probably between thirty-five hundred and four thousand communities in the United States that contained a society sponsoring public lectures—in the Midwest, such societies were sometimes among the first institutions established in a newly formed town, if only as a sign that its residents were receptive to the "culture" that a public lecture represented.

For nearly a half century, Emerson made his living mainly by lecturing, rather than by teaching or writing (his first book to turn a modest profit, *English Traits*, was published in 1856, long after the author had become famous for his oratory).

Between 1833 and 1881, besides giving 64 lectures in England and Scotland, Emerson gave at least 1,469 lectures in at least twenty-two American states and Canada, appearing in at least 283 towns. He delivered an average of 47 lectures a year. Reiterating onstage thoughts that had occurred to him spontaneously and in private, and generally "speaking in a voice not much exalted above a whisper," Emerson offered himself to his audience as a fellow soul who could think for himself, a man not different in kind from themselves, but one who had escaped—as they could, too, if they tried—from the benighted state of intellectual indolence that Kant had described as a kind of "self-imposed immaturity."

In order to reach a popular audience that expected to be entertained as well as enlightened, Emerson resorted to a variety of rhetorical devices on the lecture circuit, some of them similar to those taught to aspiring preachers in divinity school classes on homiletics. Regularly mining material from his journals—in 1834, he had vowed that "I will say at Public Lectures & the like, those things which I have meditated for their own sake & not for the first time with a view to that occasion"—he polished the prose and kept his sentences short. He elaborated his views by implication and allusion rather than direct statement. Generally eschewing reasoned arguments, he became a master of sustained metaphors. For example, instead of justifying the proposition that a beautiful whole is greater than the sum of its parts, he evoked the general idea in an early speech (first delivered in 1834) with a series of concrete—and ecstatic—examples: "The smell of a field surpasses the scent of any flower and the selection of the prism is not comparable to the confusion of a sunset. A hillside expresses what has never been written down."

Challenging the ability of listeners to imagine where he was going, he rarely presented a specific "moral" to his remarks. "The intellect is stimulated by the statement of truth in a trope," he declared, "and the will by clothing the laws of life in illusions." He consistently refused to address directly the questions inevitably raised by his elliptical, disjointed style. Instead, the sentences he strung together often seemed like non sequiturs, creating a style that was simultaneously concrete and abstract, epigrammatic yet elusive, all but guaranteeing a puzzled reaction from listeners who were nevertheless generally enchanted by what they heard, perhaps because they felt in some way inspired by his words.

In 1835, having come into his portion of Ellen's estate, and having banked some of his earnings from the lectures and sermons, Emerson bought a house in the village of Concord, roughly a two-hour ride by stagecoach from Boston. In January of that year, he had become engaged to Lydia Jackson of Plymouth, whom he married in September. He had resolved "not to utter any speech, poem, or book that is not entirely & peculiarly my own work" and now worked hard to deliver on that deceptively simple promise.

Apart from his growing repertoire of public lectures—that fall, he prepared a series on English literature to deliver in Boston—he began to sift through his journals and notebooks, looking for material that he could work up into a book, intended to serve as a sort of New World "New Testament," conveying his philosophy of life. He took as his starting point some paragraphs from his first public lecture, "The Uses of Natural History," delivered on November 5, 1833.

"You are impressed by the inexhaustible gigantic riches of nature," he had told his audience on that occasion. "The real is stranger than the imaginary."

Taking the measure of nature in all its teeming diversity, the speaker feels "impressed with a singular conviction" that there is "not a form so grotesque, so savage, or so beautiful" that it is not "an expression of something in man the observer. We feel that there is an occult relation between the very worm, the crawling scorpions, and man. I am moved by strange sympathies. I say I will listen to this invitation. I will be a naturalist."

Written twenty-five years before Darwin's *The Origin of Species*, Emerson's words show a keen appreciation for the chaotic unity of nature as a whole, which he beholds with the serenity of a mystic contemplating the One. Indeed, a passage from Plotinus, the great Neoplatonist who provided a template for Augustine's ascent toward God, prefaces the first edition of Emerson's *Nature*. From the Swedish mystic Emanuel Swedenborg (1688–1772), whose theology was a fusion of Christianity and Neoplatonism, Emerson borrowed the intuition that "Man is a kind of very minute heaven, corresponding to the world of spirits and to heaven"—a microcosm of the One, uniting in himself the worlds of spirit and nature, mind and matter. In the beauty of nature as a whole, Emerson found an outward mirror for God within. He could elaborate this core belief without any direct recourse to Holy Scripture or the authority of an existing church—and also without any recourse to empirical evidence or logical argument.

"I am born a poet," he explained in a letter to his future wife, Lydia. "That is my nature & vocation. My singing, be sure, is very 'husky,' & is for the most part in prose. Still am I a poet in the sense of a perceiver & dear lover of the harmonies that are in the soul & in matter, & specially in the correspondences between these & those. A sunset, a forest, a snow storm, a certain river-view, are more to me than many friends & do ordinarily divide my day with my books."

He was not alone in his impatience to get beyond the forms of worship and spiritual questing on offer in New England. As he worked on his personal—and hence heretical—new testament through the summer of 1836, Emerson came into regular contact with a growing circle of kindred spirits—Margaret Fuller, Orestes Brownson, Theodore Parker, Bronson Alcott, and others—who shared his chagrin at established institutions and who had been similarly electrified by the American publication of Coleridge's *Aids to Reflec-*

tion.

"Do not be conformed to this world, but be transformed by the renewing of your minds," wrote Paul to the Romans, "so that you may discern what is the will of God." In the pages of *Nature*, Emerson similarly enjoined his own generation to look at the world with new eyes: "I am nothing; I see all; the currents of the Universal Being circulate through me; I am part or parcel of God."

Nature sold briskly in Boston, where the extravagance of the rhetoric divided readers. Some admired its "poetry," while those more orthodox in their religious and philosophical views deplored the dangers of such fuzzy thinking: "The reader feels as in a disturbed dream, in which shows of surpassing beauty are around him, and he is conversant with disembodied spirits, yet all the time he is harassed by an uneasy sort of consciousness, that the whole combination of phenomena is fantastic and unreal."

Nine months later, when the Harvard members of Phi Beta Kappa needed a last-minute speaker to deliver the chapter's annual lecture, they turned to Emerson, whose fame had been bolstered by the controversy over his first book. Founded in 1776, and introduced at Harvard three years later, Phi Beta Kappa was the first collegiate society to have a Greek letter name, a badge, mottoes in Latin and Greek, a code of laws, an elaborate form of initiation, a seal, and a special handclasp. As an initiate of the club, Emerson knew its traditions and admired the oratory of such previous speakers as Edward Everett, who had delivered a rousing speech that helped him win election to Congress. Delivering the speech was an opportunity but also a challenge: appearing in the college chapel, invited in part as a representative of a new voice in American letters, he would be facing critics within the Harvard community but also speaking to friends and allies.

Emerson generally abhorred confrontation. But days before he was to speak, he had a dream of a duel, a trial by wager of battle. After noting the dream in his journal, and remarking on its possibly prophetic implications, he went on to rehearse what would be an uncharacteristically combative speech. The key theme would be hope, "the voice of the Supreme Being to the Individual," and the need to marshal it against the forms of despair perforce produced by institutionalized Christianity, and especially the Calvinist stress on sin: "Man is fallen, Man is banished; an exile; he is in earth whilst there is a heaven."

On August 31, 1837, the day after Harvard's commencement, Emerson addressed an overflow audience, speaking on the topic "The American Scholar." One eyewitness, eighteen-year-old James Russell Lowell, described "an event without any former parallel in our literary annals . . . What crowded and breathless aisles, what windows clustering with eager heads, what enthusiasm of approval, what grim silence of foregone dissent!"

Emerson spoke as the partisan of hope, and he presented his hopes in the form of a fable. Once upon a time, man was neither banished nor fallen, but experienced himself as part or parcel of a greater Unity: "One Man." Today, by contrast, the state of society is "one in which the members have suffered amputation from the trunk, and strut about so many walking monsters,—a good finger, a neck, a stomach, an elbow, but never a man." Restored to his proper estate in the cosmos, the American scholar is *Man Thinking*. In the degenerate state, he tends to become a mere thinker, or, still worse, the parrot of other men's thinking."

Moreover, culture as it was dispensed by the guardians of Harvard College formed an impediment in its own right to creativity, originality, the capacity to behold the world with fresh eyes—the hallmarks for Emerson of *Man Thinking*. Would he resurrect these slumbering capacities, a man should contemplate the wonder of Nature, learn to emulate the authors of great books rather than parrot the doctrines in the books, and observe how the whole of experience, even the most ordinary perceptions, might be "converted into thought as mulberry leaf is converted into satin . . . Life is our dictionary . . . I will not shut myself out of this globe of action, and transplant an oak into a flower pot."

Surveying his estimable audience, the orator described the American scholar as he actually existed—"decent, indolent, complaisant. See already the tragic consequence." Imagining the alternative, Emerson concluded with an exhortation, returning to the image of his opening fable: "In yourself slumbers the whole of Reason. It is for you to know all, it is for you to dare all . . . We will walk on our own feet; we will work with our own hands; we will speak our own minds . . . A nation of men will for the first time exist, because each believes himself inspired by the Divine Soul which also inspires all men."

Years later, Oliver Wendell Holmes described the impact of Emerson's speech on his generation of students. "This grand Oration was our intellectual Declaration of Independence," he recalled. "The dignity, not to say the formality of the Academic assembly was startled . . . These domestic illustrations had a kind of nursery homeliness about them which the grave professors and sedate clergymen were unused to expect on so stately an occasion. But the young men went out from it as if a prophet had been proclaiming to them, 'Thus saith the Lord.' No listener ever forgot that Address, and among all the noble utterances of the speaker it may be questioned if one ever contained more truth in language more like that of immediate inspiration."

In his style as well as substance, Emerson divided his audience, just as he did with the publication of *Nature*. What Holmes found prophetic, others found "misty, dreamy, unintelligible." But a first printing of five hundred copies of Emerson's oration sold out within a month. In Cambridge and Boston, Emerson was more discussed than ever. And less than a year later, capitalizing on his newfound notoriety, Emerson chose to drive the divisiveness of his philosophy home, in an address delivered again to a throng crowded into the chapel at Harvard.

His audience on this occasion was the senior class of the Harvard Divinity School, assembled to hear the annual discourse delivered to graduates entering the active Christian ministry, and his target this time was the spiritual complaisance specifically of contemporary Christian ministers: "Men have come to speak of the revelation as somewhat long ago given and done, as if God were dead." Because "the soul is not preached," the church is hastening the "death of faith." Redemption may come, Emerson said, but only by preaching the soul: "Yourself a newborn bard of the Holy Ghost,—cast behind you all conformity, and acquaint men at first hand with Deity. Look to it first and only, that fashion, custom, authority, pleasure, and money, are nothing to you,—are not bandages over your eyes, that you cannot see,—but live with the privilege of the immeasurable mind."

Rising to Emerson's bait, the Unitarian elite closed ranks with the conservatives of other denominations to excommunicate the apostate and censure his manifold heresies. In the pamphlet war that followed, Emerson was denounced as a man with "neither good divinity nor good sense," an "infidel and an atheist," a freelance mystic whose message would weaken entrenched bulwarks of social order.

Rallying to his defense, more liberal divines hailed his effort "to induce men to think for themselves on all subjects, and to speak from their own full hearts and earnest convictions," as Orestes Brownson charitably summed up "The Divinity School Address" a few months later. But divisions for the moment had hardened: Emerson would not be invited to speak at Harvard again for nearly thirty years.

In these months, a professor at the Divinity School who had spent a night at Emerson's house described his demeanor in his diary: "He is perfectly quiet amidst the storm. To my objections and remarks he gave the most candid replies. Such a calm, steady, simple soul, always looking for truth and living in wisdom, in love for man and goodness, I have never met."

In private, in his journals, Emerson registers his disappointment at the quality of the scholarly response to his oration. "It is a poor-spirited age," he remarks. "The great army of cowards who bellow & bully from their bed chamber windows have no confidence in truth or God. Truth will not maintain itself, they fancy, unless they bolster it up & whip & stone the assailants; and the religion of God, the being God, they seem to think dependent on what we say of it." Speaking of himself, and his new way of looking at the world, he writes of "a believer, a mind whose faith is consciousness," and whose faith is "never disturbed because other persons do not yet see the fact which he sees."

Letting others pick over the theological implications, Emerson in public sailed on serene. Unchurched, he was liberated to teach "the doctrine of the perpetual revelation"—and teach it freely he did, in lecture after public lecture.

The controversy having turned Emerson into an object of popular curiosity, the audience for his talks kept growing. As James Elliot Cabot, his first literary executor, observed of the crowd that gathered at the Masonic Temple on December 5, 1838, to witness the first in a series of lectures on the general topic of human life, "the attendance was large, and of the same class of persons as before, most of them, no doubt, Liberal Christians, but of liberality that was not disturbed by his departure from the Cambridge platform." According to Cabot, they came not to hear his views—these most people found "too airy and indistinct to be identified with any of the solid inhabitants of earth." Still, his growing public "liked to put themselves under the influence of one who obviously had lived the heavenly life from his youth up, and who made them feel for the time as if that were the normal mode of existence."

"The true preacher," Emerson had declared, "can be known by this, that he deals out to the people his life,—life passed through the fire of thought." His experience offered him the raw material for the meditations in his journals, and the meditations became the basis of the lectures, and the lectures allowed him to make his own thought public, exemplifying in practice the cardinal virtue he called "self-trust" or "self-reliance."

This virtue, as Emerson elaborated it, entailed a kind of seesaw motion of the soul, proclaiming the divine spark within every man, yet simultaneously humbling his audience by reminding them of the lofty achievements of his own preferred beacons of hope and paragons of the philosophical life, from Plato to Montaigne, and beyond: "Accept the hint of shame, of spiritual emptiness and waste, which true Nature gives you," he preached, proclaiming his own brand of asceticism, a stoic ethos as self-critical as anything in Seneca, "and retire, and hide; lock the door; shut the shutters; then welcome falls the imprisoning rain,—dear hermitage of nature. Recollect the spirits. Have solitary prayer and praise. Digest and correct the past experience. Blend it with the new and divine life, and grow with God."

Like Plato, Emerson held out the hope of a turning of the soul, a conversion from a world of shadows to one of pure vision. Also like Plato, he toyed with the idea of founding a new school. But unlike his great predecessor, he had no patience with institutions, no passion for politics, no interest in cultivating disciples—indeed, to encourage anyone to follow his lead would undermine, rather than strengthen, the core virtue of self-trust. These were some of the reasons why he kept a certain distance from his friends in the so-called Transcendental Club (the members at various times included George Ripley, Bronson Alcott, Theodore Parker, Henry David Thoreau, and Margaret Fuller), and also why Emerson turned down an offer to establish his own school and join a utopian commune that George Ripley had established at Brook Farm, in West Roxbury, Massachusetts, along with a number of other reformers inspired by Emerson's teachings. (Moreover, unlike many of his friends and most of his favorite forerunners, Emerson had a wife and three kids. He had a conventional household to maintain, above and beyond his vaulting vision of Man Thinking.)

By now, Emerson was the most visible representative of a new spirit of reform in New England. His public appearances were turning into a kind of collective séance, with the gaunt orator a medium, as if conjuring a ghostly spirit. Doubtless buoyed by his growing fame on the lecture circuit, Emerson now laid plans to publish a book of essays that could bear comparison with the *Essays* of Montaigne. For this purpose, he refused to take the easy way out and publish a selection of his best lectures. Instead, he decided to mine his journals anew, using for this purpose an index of their contents that he had begun to compile in 1838. He would systematically cull the best passages from the journals on a given topic, representing the spontaneity of his most inward and idiosyncratic reflections in the form of written essays meant to inspire a reader to undertake reflections of his or her own. "The way, the thought, the good, shall be wholly strange and new," as Emerson in one essay would sum up his efforts to communicate the goal of the examined life, carefully choosing his words in order silently to revise, repudiate, and radicalize Christ's representation of himself (in the Johannine formulation) as "the way, and the truth, and the life."

In late October, while working on his *Essays*, Emerson had another prophetic vision, which he recorded in his journal. "I dreamed that I floated at will in the great Ether, and I saw this world floating also not far off, but diminished to the size of an apple. Then an angel took it in his hand & brought it to me and said 'This must thou eat.' And I ate the world."

In its very biblical symbolism—which evokes simultaneously a pantheist Eucharist and the consumption of forbidden fruit—his dream had to raise anew the kinds of nagging doubts experienced by Augustine, and by Descartes, and by every philosopher in thrall to such enigmatic revelations received as if from on high. For what if the vision came from below? What if it were a satanic trap?

In "Self-Reliance," the keynote essay in his first book of *Essays*, Emerson raises precisely this sort of objection to his project, only to dismiss it with a defiant, almost flippant aside: "If I am the Devil's child, I will live then from the Devil."

Emerson was by now impaled on the horns of many dilemmas, and enmeshed, in the very warp and woof of his writing, in incoherence and contradiction, as he cheerfully acknowledged, famously quipping that "a foolish consistency is the hobgoblin of little minds." His command of the suggestive non sequitur in the *Essays* rises to the sublime level of a past master like Montaigne.

More strenuously than almost any previous philosopher, he advocated self-examination as the key to liberation and well-being, the precondition for human flourishing. But for Emerson in his *Essays*, the philosophical life had become almost as incredible as that exemplified by Diogenes the Cynic with his public tub and cryptic wisecracks: despite the recurrent paeans to Reason, Emerson's thinking was untethered from empirical evidence, from logical argument, from sacred Scripture, from any fixed set of spiritual exercises meant to prepare adepts to intuit the truth in a moment of revelation.

As Emerson presented the search for wisdom, the old Delphic admonition to "Know thyself" was to be honored by a perfectly idiosyncratic quest that required, above all, the courage to obey a deceptively simple commandment: that each individual should continuously plumb the depths of his unique, and literally unfathomable, experience of the world, neglecting neither the singular nor universal, neither the commonplace nor the visionary, neither inward reason nor outward nature, in ceaseless search of, yet without any convincing proof of ever finding, God within.

He was no conventional preacher, but his manner of address won real converts. As the transcendentalist writer and pioneering feminist Margaret Fuller put it in a review of Emerson's second series of *Essays*, published three years later, Emerson's original *Essays* "made to themselves a circle of readers attentive, thoughtful, more and more intelligent, and this circle is a large one if we consider the circumstances of this country and of England also, at this time."

The first series of *Essays* had been published in England with an introduction from Emerson's friend Carlyle and were perhaps even more widely noted there than at home. Even though most contemporary English reviewers were put off by the book's fractured, elliptical style, Emerson was widely hailed as a distinctively American "Teacher of Wisdom." And after a triumphal lecture tour of England in 1847, Emerson returned home as a conquering hero, a New World genius consecrated by the Old World arbiters of Anglophone high culture.

As his fame spread, audiences throughout North America flocked to hear Emerson speak. In the decades that followed, Emerson ventured ever farther afield, from New York, Philadelphia, and Baltimore to Montreal and Toronto, from Chicago and St. Louis to San Francisco, crisscrossing the continent and delivering countless talks even in smaller towns. Almost everywhere he went, he drew large and mixed audiences of men and women, young and old, clergymen, teachers, and local worthies, but also laborers, clerks, salesmen, migrants from rural America—all of them drawn by the chance to see the great man and hear him declaim on topics like "Instinct and Inspiration," "England," and "Eloquence."

What they got was an oration delivered without fireworks, larded with a few memorable maxims, but otherwise elusive and impossible to sum up in a sentence. "The lecture," reported the *Cincinnati Daily Enquirer*, describing one of Emerson's lectures in that city, "was listened to with profound attention, though, from its epigrammatic and somewhat abrupt and disconnected style, it was a matter of extreme difficulty to follow the thread of the discourse." The baffled correspondent focused instead on the Sage of Concord's sheer *look*: "Mr. Emerson is a tall man, full six feet high, but slender and bony," and he wore a "plain suit of ill-fitting black." His nose was "large, and his eyebrows highly arched and meeting. He rarely looks his hearers full in the face," making no effort to pretend to speak extemporaneously. "He stands at an acute angle towards his audience . . . and has barely a gesture beyond the motion of the left hand at his side, as if the intensity of thought were escaping, like the electricity of a battery, at that point." Reading his prepared text with a deliberate and imperturbable air, he "has a habit of turning his eyes backward as though he desired to look in at himself."

In a context where Emerson was performing alongside the likes of P. T. Barnum (who in these years toured the lyceum circuit with lectures such as "The Advantages of Temperance" and "Success in Life"), his meditative appearance—lost in thought, even on stage—seemed to reassure a democratic public that every man, whatever his station in life, could appreciate and applaud the accomplishments of a model philosopher.

It was an irony, perhaps unavoidable, that by exemplifying in this manner "Man Thinking," Emerson risked turning his idea of self-reliance into a kind of common coin, inspiring the cultivation en masse of superficially self-reliant souls, made complacent by pseudotranscendentalist slogans ("Be all that you can be")—a characteristic feature of America's popular culture to this day. His lectures, he acknowledged, risked turning into "a puppet show of Eleusinian Mysteries."

On the other hand, the effervescence, and evanescence, of Emerson's rhetoric to some extent forestalled vulgar misunderstandings. As the reporter for the *Cincinnati Daily Enquirer* put it, summing up the contents of an Emerson lecture "would be like carrying soda-water to a friend the morning after it was drawn, and asking him how he relished it." And though he, like most lyceum lecturers, generally steered clear of controversy and current affairs in his appearances, Emerson in the 1850s felt compelled to speak more and more bluntly about a matter of growing urgency in the country at large: the institution of slavery and the need to abolish it in the United States. When the abolitionist and homegrown terrorist John Brown was captured after his abortive and bloody armed attack on Harpers Ferry, Emerson caused a minor furor by declaring that Brown's death "will make the gallows as glorious as the cross."

Four months after the South started the Civil War by firing on Fort Sumter, Emerson published *The Conduct of Life*, his sixth volume of collected prose and his last major publication (though two additional anthologies of lectures would appear subsequently). Throughout the war, he kept up an active schedule of lectures, speaking mainly in New England but also in the Midwest and Canada. His national reputation continued to grow. And in the aftermath of the war, Emerson was more popular than ever.

In 1867, he was at last invited back to Harvard—fittingly enough, to give the annual Phi Beta Kappa lecture. The same year marked the peak of his career on the lyceum circuit: he delivered eighty lectures, traveling from Massachusetts to New York, Ohio, Michigan, Illinois, Iowa, Minnesota, Kansas, Missouri, Pennsylvania, Maine, and New Hampshire. Outside the South (where his paeans to John Brown were long regarded as unforgivable), he had become

America's sage.

But his powers were already starting to flag. He began to mine unpublished earlier lectures to come up with new material to deliver on the road. In 1872, he suffered lapses of memory while lecturing, and in 1875 he stopped writing in his journals.

Like Kant, Emerson was fated to live his last years in a thickening mental fog. He spent most of these years at home in Concord, breaking the monotony of his days by attending church services with his pious wife, provoking speculation that the old heretic might be returning to the Unitarian fold—a misunderstanding that he instructed his son Edward to correct. In 1880, astonishingly, he mustered the energy to deliver his one-hundredth lecture in Concord before friends and neighbors at the city's lyceum—where his entrance was greeted with a standing ovation.

Two years later, in April 1882, Emerson contracted pneumonia. He was confined to his bed and in rapidly failing health when a friend watched over him shortly before his death. "He kept (when awake) repeating in his sonorous voice, not yet weakened, fragments of sentences, almost as if reciting. It seemed strange and solemn in the night, alone with him, to hear these efforts to deliver something evidently with a thread of fine recollection to it; his voice as deep and musical almost as ever." When the old orator died on April 27, the bells of the Concord town church tolled seventy-nine times; had he lived a month longer, Emerson would have been seventy-nine years old.

NIETZSCHE

An idealized replica of Nietzsche's death mask, plaster, 1910, by the Czech sculptor Rudolf Saudek (1880–1965). "Around every profound spirit," claimed Nietzsche, "a mask is growing continually, owing to the constantly false, namely *shallow*, interpretation of every word, every step, every sign of life he gives." (Private collection/Archives Charmet/The Bridgeman Art Library International)

N ear the end of his life, Friedrich Nietzsche boasted, characteristically, about the protean cast of his written works. "Considering that the multiplicity of inward states is exceptionally large in my case," he wrote, "I have many stylistic possibilities—the most multifarious art of style that has ever been at the disposal of one man." He was in fact a stylist of rare range, and in the fourteen books he produced between 1872 and 1889, his manifold ways of writing—with exaggeration, with irony, with humor, in earnest, in polemics, in essays, in poems, in fictions, and in fragmentary collections of aphorisms that incorporate contradictions and inconsistencies as a matter of intellectual scruple—Nietzsche, deliberately it seems, left his written corpus open to endless disputes over how to understand it. "Tell me what you need," a German satirist quipped, "and I will supply you with a Nietzsche quote."

But if the meaning of Nietzsche's written work is ambiguous, the arc of his life is anything but. By 1864, when the twenty-two-year-old Nietzsche entered the University of Bonn to study philosophy and theology, he had clearly embarked on what would become a lifelong quest to formulate answers to a handful of straightforward, if intractable, questions: "Why am I alive? What lesson should I learn from life? How have I become what I am, and why do I suffer from so being?"

The quest to answer these questions would lead the student of philosophy and theology away from Augustine and Luther, and toward the sorts of open-ended inquiry favored by Socrates and his followers, some of whom impressed Nietzsche deeply. He was struck by the unashamed conduct of Diogenes and the improvised written forays of Montaigne. But he was also enamored with the hortatory rhetoric of Emerson—and it was, finally, a similarly prophetic voice that he would assign to his proudest fiction, the itinerant preacher he named Zarathustra.

Most of the books that Nietzsche wrote in the seventeen years that he was productive found few readers until after he was silenced by dementia paralytica in 1889. But by 1900, the year of his death, he was probably the most famous philosopher in the world: a mythic figure of Promethean self-invention.

He was born in Prussia in 1844, the son of a minister who tended a small Lutheran flock in a country church in the rural town of Röcken. When Nietzsche was four years old, his father, age thirty-six, died blind and insane, suffering from a brain tumor (what the doctors of the day called "softening of the brain"). The experience left Nietzsche wondering if he, too, was "destined to spend only a short time on this earth, a memory of life, rather than life itself."

An introspective prodigy, he wrote his first autobiographical essay when he was twelve. He fitfully kept a journal and faithfully filled notebooks with his ideas throughout his creative life, and he episodically took stock of his spiritual progress. "How can we set about painting a picture of the life and character of a person we have come to know?" he asked in 1863, when he was nineteen, in yet another autobiographical essay. By then, he was already thinking in terms of "fate" and "free will," and weighing how these metaphysical ideas might apply to his life, but in these adolescent notes, searching for clues to his own nature, he also turned unexpectedly to an organic metaphor. It "is in the world of plants," Nietzsche writes, "that we find the most detailed characteristics for a comparative study of nature." He recalled the physical location where he had been born, a house "in the shadow of three spreading acacias," beside a church and a cemetery "full of crosses and fallen gravestones." He reckoned that he was morbid by organic nature but spiritually self-conscious, as a constitutive part of a divine calling: "I was born as a plant near a graveyard, and as a man in a rectory."

His absent father was a constant presence, palpable like a phantom limb, even after the young boy moved with his mother and younger sister to the city of Naumburg in 1850. He confessed that he still sometimes heard his father's voice, whispering ghostly admonitions. "All my yearnings," he confided in another adolescent autobiographical essay, "go back to the home of my dear father, and on wings of longing and nostalgia, I often fly to the place where my first happiness once blossomed." He suffered from chronically poor health—a school infirmary's sick book lists countless visits and at one point describes the invalid: "He is a strong stout man with a peculiarly piercing look, short-sighted, and frequently plagued with pains in many parts of his head."

At the age of fourteen, Nietzsche left home to attend a boarding school located near Naumburg. Schulpforta was famous for training a number of Germany's most prominent poets, philosophers, and scholars. The school's curriculum was rigorously classical, with required course work in Latin and ancient Greek literature. Students were up by five, and prayers and Bible readings began at five thirty. Each boy was required to reflect earnestly on his conduct and course of life, in part by composing essays on a variety of prescribed topics: for example, could a soul filled with envy ever be truly happy? "Envy," Nietzsche wrote in his response, "is not compatible with love, and without love there exists no goodness of character." By the time he was asked to write this essay, Nietzsche had become a virtuoso of moral judgment, exquisitely attuned to feelings of shame and guilt, because invited constantly to compare himself against the Christian ideals of a pure heart and a perfectly good will.

An aspiring poet and composer, the young man was irresistibly drawn toward the ideal of romantic genius exemplified by Beethoven. Like Goethe, whose work he had also studied closely, he understood creativity in quasi-Socratic terms, as a quest that entailed uncovering, and coming to grips with, one's unique daimon. As he wrote in one youthful poem,

> I want to know thee, O unknown power,
> That thrusts its hand into my soul,

314 THE PHILOSOPHICAL LIFE

Raging through my life like a storm,
O unfathomable One, my kinsman!
I want to know thee and serve thee.

His training in ancient Greek literature left him enamored with the *Oedipus Rex* of Sophocles and the *Symposium* of Plato. Like Alcibiades in Plato's dialogue, he was besotted by the idea that seeking the truth was an intrinsically erotic activity—an intoxicating antidote to the dourness of Luther's catechism. At the same time, he was reading the maverick theologian Ludwig Feuerbach, who had argued that the idea of God was a projection by mankind of its own divine powers of self-creation, and also reading Emerson's essays, whose secularizing doctrine of godlike self-reliance he equally took to heart. "As soon as it becomes possible for a strong will to overturn the whole past of the world," he wrote in one of his school essays in 1862, "we would immediately join the ranks of independent gods, and world history would mean nothing else to us but a dreamlike state of rapture; the curtain falls, and man finds himself like a child, playing with worlds—like a child who awakens at dawn and wipes away all nightmares with a smile."

By the time he left Schulpforta, Nietzsche was more pagan than Christian, more of an aesthete than a priest in waiting. Still, his family hoped against hope that he would follow in his father's footsteps. And when he entered the University of Bonn in the fall of 1864, he did keep his options open, enrolling as a student of theology but continuing course work in classical Greek literature.

"Certainly, faith alone brings salvation," he explained in a letter to his sister Elisabeth in the spring of 1865. But what *sort* of faith? Must it take the form of Christian piety? Or "is it not certain that we would have experienced the same blessings if we had, from childhood on, held the belief that all salvation comes from someone other than Jesus—say, from Mohammed?"

When Nietzsche transferred to the University of Leipzig several months later, he decided to change his path and enroll only as a student of philology. He quickly impressed the most prominent of his professors, Friedrich Wilhelm Ritschl, who in collaboration with Theodor Mommsen had edited the *Priscae Latinitatis Monumenta Epigraphica* (1862; Epigraphical Records of

Ancient Latin), an edition of Latin inscriptions from the earliest times to the end of the Roman Republic, and a work that established Ritschl as one of the founders of modern epigraphy.

Nietzsche joined a fraternity and tried hard to blend in with the other students. But his journals and notebooks tell the story of a tormented young man who was frequently ill and subject to hallucinatory visions. "What I fear," he wrote in one journal entry, "is not the fearful character behind my chair," apparently referring to his daimon, "but his voice: and not his words, but the terrifyingly inarticulate and inhuman tone of this character. If only it spoke as humans speak!"

Shortly after arriving in Leipzig, Nietzsche experienced a more welcome epiphany. While browsing in a secondhand bookshop, "I saw this book," he recalled in an autobiographical essay, and "I took it down and began to turn the pages. Then a demon whispered in my ear: 'Take this book home with you.'"

The book was by Arthur Schopenhauer, at the time the most fashionable philosopher in Germany. Born in 1788, Schopenhauer had an abortive career as an academic, writing a dissertation on *The Fourfold Root of the Principle of Sufficient Reason*, and winning a teaching post in Berlin. But in 1831, he had resigned his professorship in order to become an independent man of letters. He belatedly won a wide readership when in 1850 a collection of his short essays, *Parega and Paralipomena*, became a surprise best seller in Germany and turned the previously unknown author into a celebrity for the last decade of his life.

Schopenhauer had a talent for boiling down complicated ideas into arresting maxims: "Style is what gives value to thoughts." "Our first ideas of life are generally taken from fiction rather than fact." "Monotheism is the personification of the whole of nature at one blow." The human condition, he taught in his magnum opus, *The World as Will and Representation* (1819), was unavoidably painful:

> Willing and striving are its whole essence, and can be fully compared to an unquenchable thirst. The basis of all willing, however, is need, lack, and hence pain, and by its very nature and origin it is therefore destined to pain. If, on the other

hand, it lacks objects of willing, because it is at once deprived of them again by too easy a satisfaction, a fearful emptiness and boredom come over it; in other words, its being and its existence itself become an intolerable burden for it. Hence its life swings like a pendulum to and fro between pain and boredom, and these two are in fact its ultimate constituents.

Nietzsche recalled taking Schopenhauer's book home, hoping "for the spirit of this powerful, mysterious genius to work its miracles on me." He was not disappointed. In the pages of Schopenhauer, he "found a mirror in which was reflected in terrifying grandeur the world, life, and my own character." He felt himself gripped "by a desire for self-knowledge, even self-mortification," and pondered "the deification and transformation of the very heart of mankind."

Despite this inward metamorphosis, most of Nietzsche's energy for the next three years went into conventional research and academic writing. Hoping to win a prize for his scholarship, he wrote a paper on the sources that Diogenes Laertius had used in composing his *Lives of the Eminent Philosophers*. Through his close study of this text, he became familiar with the whole range of ancient Greek philosophers, including Heraclitus, whose "extraordinary power to think intuitively" (rather than logically) he admired; and also Diogenes the Cynic, whose notoriously "Dog-like" shamelessness became another kind of model for him.

He was proud of his scholarly discipline. But in private, he acknowledged that he was no longer wholeheartedly committed to philology as a vocation. "Perhaps I do not belong at all among the specific philologists on whose brows nature with a stylus of bronze has set the mark, This Is A Philologist," he wrote in 1869. "When I look back and see how I have come from art to philosophy and from philosophy to a science, and here again into an increasingly narrow field, then it"—his choice to pursue a scholarly career in philology—"almost looks like a conscious renunciation."

In these months, Nietzsche was treated by a doctor for syphilis—how he contracted the disease is unclear. It is also unclear how he reacted to his diagnosis, if he was told. For syphilis in the nineteenth century was not just any disease but an affliction that seemed a kind of tragic curse—impossible to cure, hard to treat, and raising the prospect of years of debilitating illness. After an onset marked by sores, rashes, and a fever, syphilis enters an uncertain period of latency, when the disease silently begins to destroy blood vessels, bones, and neurons. New symptoms episodically appear—violent headaches, vomiting, vertigo, seizures, outbreaks of mania—eventually climaxed by dementia paralytica.

One thing is clear: Nietzsche from now on was prey to chronic pain and haunted by the prospect of madness—a fear reinforced by his knowledge of how his father had died.

Despite his poor health—he had especially bad eyesight—Nietzsche learned in the fall of 1867 that he would not be exempt from military service. Joining an artillery regiment stationed in Naumburg, he discovered that "my philosophy now has the chance to be of practical use to me." After a month of training, he wrote to a friend, "I have not felt a moment's depression . . . Sometimes hidden under the horse's belly I murmur, 'Schopenhauer, help!'" He was in the army for only a few months. In March 1868, he injured himself in a riding accident; six months later, he was discharged. (When war broke out between Prussia and France two years later, he enlisted and briefly served in the army again, only to fall ill and be discharged as before.)

A turning point in Nietzsche's life came in January 1869, when he was called to the chair of Greek language and literature at the University of Basel. He was only twenty-four years old and hadn't even completed his dissertation; the University of Leipzig, on Ritschl's recommendation, rushed to award him a doctorate on the basis of a few previously published scholarly essays. Among the Swiss cantons, the city of Basel was unique, because of its proximity to both Germany and France, because of its prosperity as a cosmopolitan commercial center, and because of the welcome the city-state had extended to such free-spirited senior scholars as Johann Jakob Bachofen, a pioneering social anthropologist, and Jacob Burckhardt, one of the first great historians of art and culture, best known for his book *The Civilization of the Renaissance in Italy*.

Among his younger colleagues, the most important would become Franz Overbeck. A heterodox thinker as iconoclastic as Nietzsche himself, Overbeck elaborated a kind of negative theology: "Whoever stands truly and firmly on his own two feet in the world must have the courage to stand on nothing," Overbeck wrote in one of his notebooks. "Only without God can he live as a free individual."

Nietzsche cut a curious figure in these years, as Overbeck's wife, Ida, later recalled. He had expressive hands and carefully manicured fingernails that suggested to her "a trace of femininity." He was a bit of a fop, paying careful attention to his coats and scarves, and sporting a thick handlebar mustache that he kept neatly trimmed and waxed. Despite his exquisite grooming and refined manners, "he gave the impression," Ida wrote, "of a very introverted, somewhat ailing man. He tended to avoid encounters and conversations; but if they took place, then he was striking for the cordiality and earnestness he developed and seemed to direct to his counterpart. One immediately felt challenged to tell him something that one felt to be important."

In addition to enjoying serious talk about serious matters, the Overbecks shared with Nietzsche a love of music. During their first encounter, they played a four-handed piano piece by Brahms, and Nietzsche responded by playing a piece composed by one of his current idols, Richard Wagner.

Already a renowned figure in German music circles, Wagner was living at the time near Basel, at Triebschen, in an isolated villa near Lake Lucerne. Born in 1813, a generation before Nietzsche, Wagner had first become well known in Dresden in the 1840s, thanks to the popularity of his operas *Rienzi*, *The Flying Dutchman*, and *Tannhäuser*. Like many intellectuals and artists, Wagner was electrified by the European popular uprisings of 1848, and he was forced to flee into exile after he was caught taking part in a revolt in Dresden in 1849.

In a hortatory essay published that same year, Wagner called for a German cultural revolution. Taking as his model the tragic drama of ancient Greece, he proposed creating a new, neopagan art form that might displace what he regarded as the crippling effects on the German spirit of Christianity, a pernicious form of life that "adjusts the ills of an honorless, useless, and sorrowful existence of mankind on earth, by the miraculous love of God." Not simply dreaming of a "perfect Art-work, the great united utterance of a free and lovely public life," Wagner went on to spend two decades composing a "total" artwork that would combine word and image, music and theater, and bring back to life the pre-Christian ethos of the Teutonic peoples, as expressed in the *The Nibelungenlied*, an epic poem from the Middle Ages, portraying the Germanic ideals of fate and loyalty, and distinguished by violent emotion and acts of bloody vengeance.

By the time he met Nietzsche in 1868, Wagner had completed five additional operas, and, thanks to an amnesty, had been able to see them produced in Munich: *Lohengrin, Tristan and Isolde, Die Meistersinger, The Rhinegold,* and *The Valkyrie*. But because he had also become the lover in these years of Cosima von Bülow, the young daughter of the composer Franz Liszt and wife of the famous German critic and conductor Hans von Bülow, he went into exile again, this time under the patronage of the young king of Bavaria, who had installed him with Cosima at Triebschen.

Nietzsche had first met Wagner in Leipzig, where the two men had discussed Schopenhauer and philosophy, and Wagner had invited the younger man to visit him again. After Nietzsche moved to Basel a few months later, such visits became a routine. The villa at Triebschen where Wagner and Cosima lived was a rococo shrine to its master's eccentric genius, decorated with pink satin curtains and various busts and portraits depicting Wagner as well as his royal patron. Every Sunday—the one day of the week he was free—Nietzsche traveled to Lake Lucerne. And every Sunday night, as one of his Basel friends recalled, "he came back full of his god and told me of all the splendid things he had seen and heard."

Wagner in these years was completing his great cycle of four operas based on the German legend of *The Ring of the Niebelung*, and already planning to build a new theater at Bayreuth, meant to become the cynosure of a neopagan cult that would rally a regenerated body of strong and beautiful souls, forging them, through their ritual appreciation of a total artwork, into a unified national community. Old enough to be Nietzsche's father, Wagner was a formidable presence. Nietzsche could scarcely hope to meet the composer on his own ground (though Nietzsche did continue to compose music). Instead, the young professor rose to the challenge of his example by throwing scholarly caution to the winds and composing a kind of prose poem, a paean to the revolutionary cultural ideals that Wagner claimed to embody.

Finished in 1871 and published the following year, *The Birth of Tragedy* was a bold, even reckless work for an aspiring philologist to publish, praising as it did the art worlds of dream and intoxication, and postulating a direct link between the cultural achievements of the ancient Greeks and the cultural challenges facing contemporary Germany—challenges met, he declared, by Wagner's *Ring*, a modern "tragic myth, reborn from music." Most of Nietzsche's colleagues at the University of Basel—including Bachofen and Burckhardt—admired the audacity of Nietzsche's argument. Wagner himself was naturally flattered.

Still, Nietzsche had to contend with the criticism of his academic peers. His old mentor, Ritschl, privately heaped scorn on the book, calling it in his correspondence "a piece of pseudo-aesthetic, unscholarly religious mystification produced by a man suffering from paranoia"—which would not be the last time that Nietzsche would find former friends impugning his sanity. Another academic critic, this time in a published review, spoke of Nietzsche's "ignorance and lack of love of truth."

In 1871, feeling estranged from philology and ever more interested in becoming a philosopher, Nietzsche had presented himself as a candidate for a chair of philosophy at the University of Basel. He was summarily rejected on the grounds that he lacked the proper academic training.

In the months that followed, as hostile criticisms of his book began to appear, he was plunged into self-doubt. Who was he? What should he become? Should he remain a professor of classics and live the life of an academic scholar? Should he focus instead on writing more polemical essays on culture and art in the style of his book on tragedy? Or, despite the rebuff from his colleagues at Basel, should he try to live the life of a philosopher?

And just what kind of life would that be?

In the summer of 1872, Nietzsche began to sketch his answer to such questions, thinking that he might write an entire book on the topic. Although over the next several months he drafted dozens of different outlines for a text to be titled "The Philosopher," Nietzsche ultimately abandoned his plan—but not before composing a large number of notes that reveal how he was groping toward a new goal for himself.

In these notebooks, he wrote lovingly about the first philosophers, though with scant hope at first that he could ever follow in their footsteps. He admired

Thales—the Greek sage who had defended "the absurd notion . . . that *water* is the primal origin and womb of all things"—because Thales had renounced superstition by offering a physical explanation, however erroneous, for the origin of the world, and because he had simultaneously explored the metaphysical hypothesis that "all things are one." But he admired Socrates even more as the apotheosis of ancient Greek philosophy: "From him proceeds a moral flood, an incredible force of will directed toward an ethical reform . . . *Knowledge* as the path to virtue differentiates his philosophical character: *dialectic* as the *single* path, induction and definition. The struggle against desire, drives, anger, and so on directs itself against a deeply-lying ignorance. He is the first philosopher of *life* . . . A life ruled by thought!"

What drove Thales was what, according to Nietzsche, would drive every subsequent true philosopher (doubtless including himself): "a metaphysical theorem, taken on faith, which had its origin in a mystic intuition." And what drove Socrates was a purity of will—a will to know, the will to truth—that, according to Nietzsche, also would distinguish every subsequent true philosopher. The result was an unstable amalgam of two competing drives: one aimed at a life ruled purely by thought, purged of superstition, attuned to the scruples of discursive reason, yet paradoxically, and simultaneously, another drive aimed at obtaining some sort of mystical intuition, an experience that might provoke something like a leap of faith. Taken together, these traits defined all true philosophers.

"If all goes well," Nietzsche remarked, "the time will come when one will take up the memorabilia of Socrates rather than the Bible as a guide to morals and reason, and when Montaigne . . . will be used as [one of the] forerunners and signposts to an understanding of this simplest and most imperishable of predecessors."

Still, to emulate Socrates, or Montaigne, was no simple matter, particularly in the circumstances that Nietzsche felt that he was facing: "An era which suffers from a so-called high general level of education but which is devoid of culture in the sense of a unity of style which characterizes all of its life, will not quite know what to do with philosophy, even if the genius of truth itself were to proclaim it in the streets and market places . . . No one may venture to fulfill the law of philosophy—no one can live philosophically—with that simple human faithfulness that compelled an ancient, no matter what he was doing, to deport himself as a Stoic, once he had pledged fealty to the stoa."

On this quite classical view, a philosopher's essential creation was "his *life* (which occupies the most important position, *before* his [written] *works*). His life is his work of art"—and every philosophy worthy of the name "must be able to do what I demand: it must be able to concentrate a man," equip him with a purity of will and a great goal. But due to the circumstances of life in a modern commercial society, with its specialization and division of labor, and its concomitant lack of a unifying common culture, "no philosophy can do this today." When he surveys his surroundings, Nietzsche writes in his notebooks, "I see nothing but spiritual cripples: their partial education has turned them into hunchbacks."

Becoming a genuine philosopher, in Nietzsche's sense, was complicated still further, he conceded, by a "horrible consequence of Darwinism, which, by the way, I consider to be correct." Nietzsche, unlike many of his nineteenth-century peers (including, for example, Karl Marx and Herbert Spencer), grasped the real implications of Darwin's scientific theory of natural selection: that the natural cosmos of living organisms, of which human beings are inextricably a part, is itself a chance product of random variations. Thus, the will, far from representing some sort of supernatural and inexplicable essence, itself had to be "a highly complex end product of nature." Contrary to Kant and such successors as Hegel, there was no rational goal to history: "For a long time, human beings did not exist . . . They have no further mission and no purpose." If Darwin was correct, then even the most basic tools of reason itself—dialectical questioning, the methodical deployment of induction and definition, empirical research and logical analysis—also had to be regarded as unintended outcomes of natural selection. As Nietzsche put it, writing with characteristic hyperbole, "*The human being became a knowing being by accident.*"

If the culture one shares with others is devoid of a unifying style, and if there is no goal to history, Nietzsche concludes that anyone aspiring to live a thoughtful life must learn to live a life of self-reliance (not unlike that prescribed by Emerson a generation before): "He must organize the chaos within by thinking back to his real needs. His forthrightness, the strength and truthfulness of his character, must at some time or other rebel against a state of things in which he only repeats what he has heard, learns what is already known, imitates what already exists."

A circumscribed ambition, perhaps, but one with consequences for the larger culture as potentially revolutionary as any piece of music composed by Wagner. "'Beware,'" writes Nietzsche, quoting Emerson with approval. "'When the great God lets loose a thinker on this planet. Then all things are at risk. It is as when a conflagration has broken out in a great city, and no man knows what is safe, or where it will end. There is not a piece of science but its flank may be turned tomorrow; there is not any literary reputation, not the so-called eternal names of fame, that may not be revised and condemned; the things which are dear to men at this hour are so on account of the ideas which have emerged on their mental horizon, and which cause the present order of things, as a tree bears its apples. *A new degree of culture would instantly revolutionize the entire system of human pursuits.*'"

The first fruit of Nietzsche's changing conception of his proper vocation was a sequence of four essays in cultural criticism. The first, published in 1873, was a polemical attack on David Strauss, the author of a popular *Life of Jesus*; the second, which appeared in 1874, was an attack on conventional views about the value of historical knowledge epitomized by philosophers like Hegel and scholars like Leopold von Ranke; the third, also published in 1874, was a hymn to Schopenhauer as a contemporary example of a true philosopher; and the last, published in 1876, was a new essay about his old idol, Wagner.

The essays on history and Schopenhauer both indirectly broach the issue of the philosophical life. But Nietzsche in his written work had yet to forge a philosophical voice uniquely his own; he had yet to experience the sort of "mystical intuition" that might supply him with "a metaphysical theorem, taken on faith."

On May 22, 1872, on the occasion of Wagner's fifty-ninth birthday, Nietzsche traveled to the Bavarian town of Bayreuth, to participate in the laying of the foundation stone for the new opera house there. The Wagners were in the midst of moving from Lucerne to their new villa in Bayreuth. Desperate to remain a member of their inner circle, Nietzsche volunteered to move to Bayreuth and become Wagner's personal publicist. It was a crazy idea, and

Wagner talked him out of it.

When Nietzsche returned to Basel in the fall, he discovered that nobody had enrolled in one of his seminars, and that no one was registered for his lecture course on Homer; his third class, on classical rhetoric, attracted only two people.

Despite a lack of students, Nietzsche was not intellectually isolated in these years. In the summer of 1873, Nietzsche met Paul Rée, who would become perhaps his single most important interlocutor over the next decade. Five years younger than Nietzsche, Rée was an aspiring author. Impressed by *The Birth of Tragedy*, Rée showed Nietzsche a manuscript of the book he was working on, which would be published anonymously two years later as *Psychological Observations*. When Nietzsche read the published book—audaciously composed as a sequence of aphorisms, modeled on those of the seventeenth-century French moralist La Rochefoucauld—he recognized it as Rée's work and wrote him a letter of praise. The two men shared a passion for Schopenhauer and a conviction that Darwinism had to be the basis of any modern attempt to provide a naturalistic account of the origin of the moral sensations. This was the subject of Rée's second book, which would be published in 1877.

Nietzsche's ongoing philosophical investigations were complicated by his continuing poor health. He suffered from crippling migraines. His eyesight grew worse and left him functionally blind for long stretches of time, forcing him to depend on others to read to him and take dictation. "My father died of an inflammation of the brain at age thirty-six," he wrote to a friend early in 1876, when he was thirty-two. "It is possible that it will happen to me even faster." Worried about his health, he was also concerned about the diminished impact of his writing: none of his new essays had reached as many readers as *The Birth of Tragedy*. At the same time, he was under constant pressure from his mother to settle down and find a suitable wife.

Of the handful of memoirs that describe Nietzsche in these years, the most revealing was written by his former student Ludwig von Scheffler. A protégé of Jacob Burckhardt, von Scheffler became an expert on the work of August Graf von Platen (1796–1835), a German dramatist and poet whose homosexuality was made a matter of public scandal by Heinrich Heine, and

whose great theme of suffering, with a homoerotic subtext, was set to music by
Franz Schubert in "Du liebst, mich nicht" (You love me not).

Nietzsche "was of short rather than medium height," recalled von Scheffler, "his head deep in the shoulders of his stocky yet delicate body." Instead of
the shabby coats worn by many other professors in the university, "he was
wearing light-colored pants, a short jacket, and around his collar fluttered a
delicately knotted necktie, also of a lighter color," as if "to suggest something
artistic in his appearance. The long hair framing his face not with curls but
only with strands of hair also suggested this."

Lecturing on Plato, Nietzsche "spoke slowly, often haltingly, not so much
seeking an expression as checking the impression of his dicta to himself. If the
thread of his thought led him to something particularly extreme, then his
voice also sank, as if hesitatingly, down to the softest *pianissimo*." He appeared
to be in pain, stoically enduring a fate that would be crushing were it not for
his palpable yearning to express himself lucidly. "The warmth of his presentation, the manner in which this worldview took shape before us in his words,
nonetheless gave the impression of something new and completely individual.
It lay like a cloud on this man's entire being. And over and over the question
came to me as I listened: 'Who is he? Where is he heading, this thinker?'"

Midway through the semester, after the professor had delivered one of his
gloomiest lectures, he surprised von Scheffler by inviting him to have tea at
his apartment the next day. Since von Scheffler had been a frequent visitor to
Burckhardt's home, he expected to find Nietzsche in a study like the historian's, stuffed with books stacked on shelves and crowding the floor. Instead,
Nietzsche ushered him into a sunny apartment furnished with "soft large
armchairs" that were decorated with "white lace coverlets with delightful
flower patterns." There were freshly cut flowers everywhere, "in glasses, in
bowls, on tables, in corners, on walls! Everything airy, aromatic and delicate!
Lightly curtained windows, filtering the glare of daylight, made one feel like a
guest invited not to a professor's house but to a beloved girlfriend's."

In the weeks that followed, the two men conversed regularly after class,
until one day von Scheffler rebuffed Nietzsche's invitation to join him on va-
cation in Italy. "I looked down dejectedly and gave a negative excuse which
must have sounded cold enough. Nietzsche's hands immediately slid from my

arm." Years later, reflecting on what had happened, he felt that the philosopher, like the poet Platen, had been tormented by his sexuality: "In Platen's case the evidence is in his memoirs, which say everything. In Nietzsche's case, I learned it from life, from direct experience."

There certainly seems to be an echo of such torments in one of Nietzsche's most impassioned autobiographical outbursts, evoking this period in his life when he was struggling to liberate himself, to become a "free spirit." In one passage, written shortly after his conversations with von Scheffler, Nietzsche speaks of the soul in quest of freedom "convulsed, torn loose, torn away—it itself does not know what is happening. A drive and impulse rules it like a command," provoking

> a lightning-bolt of contempt for what it had called "duty," a rebellious, arbitrary, volcanically erupting desire for travel, strange places, estrangements, coldness, soberness, frost, a hatred of love, perhaps a desecrating blow and glance *backwards* to where it formerly loved and worshiped, perhaps a hot blush of shame at what it has just done and at the same time an exultation *that* it has done it, a drunken, inwardly exultant shudder which betrays that victory has been won—a victory? Over what? Over whom? An enigmatic, question-packed, questionable victory, but the *first* victory nonetheless: such bad and painful things are part of the history of that great liberation. It is at the same time a sickness that can destroy the man that has it, this first outpouring of strength and will to self-determination, to evaluating on one's own account, this will to *free* will: and how much sickness is expressed in the wild experiments and singularities through which the liberated prisoner now seeks to demonstrate his mastery,

in part through an "unslaked lasciviousness."

Pleading continuing poor health, Nietzsche arranged for a leave from his teaching duties in the fall of 1876 and winter of 1877. He invited Paul Rée to join him for him the duration. For five months, the two men were in daily contact, living mainly in Sorrento on the Bay of Naples, swapping ideas while Rée completed his treatise *On the Origin of the Moral Sensations* and Nietzsche worked on his first book of aphorisms, *Human, All Too Human: A Book for Free Spirits*. It was in this context that Nietzsche for the first time imagined that human beings might be inhabitants of a completely predetermined world of cause and effect that left no room for free will, and hence offered no reason to feel "remorse or pangs of guilt." This thought experiment was as radical in its implications as Descartes's doubt. For Nietzsche, it had the effect of wiping the ethical slate clean: at the end of his thought experiment, there were no self-evident moral sentiments left standing.

Close as Rée and Nietzsche were on many matters, there remained profound differences between them. Nietzsche was keen to cast off conventional moral claims, Rée was not. Like Darwin in *The Descent of Man* (1871), Rée traced the origin of morality to the essentially good-natured aspects of the higher primates, stressing how the need to nurture helpless offspring creates an evolutionary basis for altruistic behavior and a biological foundation for the subsequent elaboration by human beings in many different social settings of something like the Golden Rule.

Nietzsche was more impressed by the survival of aggressive instincts and the element of compulsion in many customs, evidence of what he would soon be calling "the will to power." Nietzsche vehemently rejected Rousseau's, Darwin's, and Rée's view that human nature was essentially benign. He saw cruelty where one might least expect to find it, in the most spectacularly self-abnegating forms of human behavior, for example, the ascetic renunciations of the Christian saint: "He scourges his self-idolatry with self-contempt and cruelty, he rejoices in the wild riot of his desires, in the sharp sting of sin, indeed in the idea that he is lost . . . and when, finally, he comes to thirst for visions, for colloquies with the dead or divine beings, it is at bottom a rare kind of voluptuousness that he desires."

In addition, Nietzsche, unlike Rée, felt that human beings had a need for myths, illusions, mystic intuitions. He even speculated that evolutionary forces may have given to the human being "a double-brain, as it were two brain ventricles, one for the perceptions of science, the other for those of non-science: lying beside one another, not confused together, separable, capable of being shut off; this is a demand of health. In one domain lies the power source, in the other the regulator: it must be heated with illusions, prejudices, passions, and the perilous consequences of overheating must be avoided with the aid of the knowledge furnished by science."

After spending the summer of 1877 working on *Human, All Too Human*, Nietzsche returned to Basel and resumed his duties as a professor. In constant pain and still bothered by headaches and poor eyesight, he consulted a new doctor, one close to Wagner, who in turn asked the composer for his diagnosis. As Nietzsche later discovered, Wagner's response was devastating: he explained his personal conviction that Nietzsche's deteriorating health was a result of "unnatural perversions, with allusions to pederasty." (This was an especially vicious episode in a series of betrayals, both real and perceived, that led Nietzsche in the years that followed to turn violently against his former idol.)

The same doctor also apparently told Nietzsche a few months later that he was suffering from a serious brain disease (perhaps suspecting that his patient in fact was showing early symptoms of the sort of dementia associated with syphilis). In Basel, rumors about Nietzsche's sanity began to spread.

In the fall of 1878, Nietzsche's old student Ludwig von Scheffler found himself back in Basel for the first time in several months and decided to visit his old professor, to see for himself how he was doing. Warned that Nietzsche was not receiving visitors, he stood on a street in a drab suburb of Basel and peeped through a window. He saw Nietzsche hunched over a disorganized desk, in a small room cluttered with cooking utensils. Von Scheffler was aghast: "Was this still the same man who had once sat before me on the delicate lace furniture, whose femininely delicate sense tolerated only beauty around him?"

In the spring of 1879, Nietzsche formally submitted his resignation to the University of Basel, on grounds of failing health. He was granted a small annual pension, his primary source of income as he embarked on a new phase of his life.

From now on, he was a nomad with no settled residence, drifting back and forth between Germany, Switzerland, and Italy, in chronic pain, suffering from repeated sudden seizures that struck him like bolts of lightning and left him paralyzed, his eyes clouded over, his spirit sometimes spent, yet still hoping, if only in his writing, to express some new, hitherto undiscovered possibility of the philosophical life.

In reply to New Year's greetings for 1880 from his doctor, Nietzsche confided that "my existence is a fearful burden. I would have thrown it off long ago if I had not been making the most instructive tests and experiments on mental and moral questions in precisely this condition of suffering and almost complete renunciation . . . On the whole, I am happier than ever before. And yet, continual pain; for many hours of the day a feeling closely akin to sea-sickness, a semi-paralysis which makes it difficult to speak, alternating with furious attacks."

He was by now on a regimen of various painkillers, some of them powerful opiates. But in between the migraines and seizures, he also experienced moments of intense euphoria. He carefully chronicled his thoughts, and when he was able to compose himself, he wrote furiously.

In the summer of 1881, Nietzsche traveled by rail from Recoaro Terme in the Veneto region of Italy to the eastern Swiss canton of Graubünden, not far from the border with Italy. He eventually settled into a hotel in Sils-Maria, a small village located amid lakes in a wooded Alpine valley. For the first time, he began seriously to read the philosopher Spinoza (1632–1677), an independent Dutch thinker, conversant with the main currents of Cartesianism and suspected, like Descartes, of being a secret atheist. "Not only is his whole tendency like my own," he wrote to his old friend Franz Overbeck, "to make knowledge the *most powerful passion*—but also in five main points of his doctrine I find myself; this most abnormal and lonely thinker is closest to me in these points precisely: he denies free will, denies purposes, denies the moral world order, denies the non-egoistical, and denies evil."

A few days later, on one of his daily walks through the nearby meadows, inspiration struck, apparently out of the blue. On a scrap of paper, Nietzsche recorded the moment: "Beginning of August 1881 in Sils-Maria, 6,000 feet above sea level, and far higher above all earthly things!" In haste, under the heading "eternal recurrence," he jotted down a few cryptic thoughts: "The passion for knowledge . . . The innocent. The individual as experiment. The alleviation of life, humiliation, relief—transport. The new *heavy weight: the eternal recurrence of the same.*"

He relayed the glad tidings to one of his closest associates: "On my horizon, thoughts have arisen such as I have never seen before . . . Ah, my friend, sometimes the idea runs through my head that I am living an extremely dangerous life, for I am one of those machines that can explode. The intensities of my feeling make me shudder and laugh; several times I could not leave my room for the ridiculous reason that my eyes were inflamed—from what? Each time, I had wept too much on my previous day's walk, not sentimental tears, but tears of joy; I sang, and talked nonsense, filled with a glimpse of things that put me in advance of all other men."

Beside himself, he conjured up a new alter ego, a character he named Zarathustra, who might serve as a fictive vessel for communicating his latest revelations. His model for Zarathustra was Zoraster, the legendary Persian poet, prophet, and founder of the Zoroastrian religion. Scholars now think he flourished roughly a thousand years before the birth of Christ; in ancient Greek, the prophet's very name, a conjunction of the word *zoros*, meaning "undiluted," with *astra*, or "stars," was evocative. The Greek poets and philosophers alike regarded Zoroaster as a font of orphic wisdom. They depicted the Persian as prophesying a universe rent asunder, in a cosmic struggle between truth and lies, a struggle not unlike the one Nietzsche imagined he was waging with himself. He conceived of a new series of aphorisms, to introduce the character of Zarathustra and to present his newest convictions in fragmentary form.

The first result was *The Gay Science*, a work largely written between October 1881 and March 1882, and published later that year with an epigraph from Emerson: "To the poet, to the philosopher, to the saint, all things are friendly and sacred, all events profitable, all days holy, all men divine."

At the end of Book Four of *The Gay Science*, under the heading "*Incipit tragoedia*" (The Tragedy Begins), Nietzsche's Zarathustra makes his debut. Perhaps the most famous of Nietzsche's aphorisms also appears in this context. Titled "The Madman," it describes how a fool carrying a lit lamp in broad daylight (evoking Diogenes) incessantly cried, "I seek God! I seek God!" (In the first draft of this aphorism, the fool is named Zarathustra.) He goes on to declare that "God is dead," and then, more enigmatically, he asks, "Is not the greatness of this deed too great for us? Must we ourselves not become gods simply to appear worthy of it?"

In April 1882, after finishing a draft of *The Gay Science*, Nietzsche traveled alone to Sicily, where he soaked in the sun and toured Greek ruins. He re-

turned via Rome, where his old friend Paul Rée introduced him to an exotic
young Russian, Lou Andreas-Salomé. As another mutual friend explained to
Nietzsche before he arrived, the young woman seemed to have "reached the
same results in philosophical thinking as you, i.e., practical idealism, with a
discarding of every metaphysical assumption." Though she was only twenty-
one years old, Salomé was already well versed in Western philosophy and
theology, world religions, and French and German literature. (She would go
on to become a prolific writer of novels and essays, a psychoanalyst, and the
mistress of the poet Rilke, as well as a friend of Sigmund Freud.)

Although Salomé was a striking beauty who would later in life become a
femme fatale, in 1882 she was an avowed virgin who dressed like a nun, in a
black gown buttoned up to the neck. Sensing a rare opportunity to play the
matchmaker for his spiritual master, Rée suggested that Nietzsche marry her:
for reasons of propriety, she needed an intelligent consort, just as Nietzsche
did, to silence his mother's unrelenting demand that the confirmed bachelor
take a wife. Nietzsche hesitated before falling for Salomé's charms, but by
then Rée had fallen for Salomé himself, and in any case Salomé had no interest in a marriage of convenience to Nietzsche. So the trio cooked up a new
idea, to set up a household together in Paris as a platonic ménage à trois.

Infatuated with Salomé, Nietzsche became miraculously garrulous. Suddenly, he felt able to converse tirelessly about his deepest intuitions. He told
her about his moment of vision in Sils-Maria and his plans for a sequel to *The
Gay Science*, regarding her as "uniquely ready for the till now almost undisclosed part of my philosophy." And she shared her own nascent conviction
that philosophical systems could profitably be reduced to the status of "personal records of their authors"—a project that Nietzsche had endorsed years
before as his own, in his notebooks and lectures on the pre-Platonic philosophers.

And that was not all. According to Salomé, they also talked about sex. "To
the extent that cruel people are also masochists, the whole situation has a rel-
evance to the question of bisexuality," she wrote years later, in a diary she kept
in 1912 and 1913, after she had become conversant with the work of Freud and
while she was training to become a psychoanalyst. She continued: "The first
person with whom I talked about the matter was Nietzsche, himself a sado-

masochist. And I remember that afterwards we did not dare to look each other in the eye."

In October, Salomé and Paul Rée left Nietzsche in Rome. They were ostensibly looking for an appropriate apartment in Paris for their planned trio. But it soon became clear that Salomé had run off with Nietzsche's old soul mate. Sometime in December, having moved for the winter to a room in a boardinghouse in Rapallo, an Italian seaport near Genoa, the humiliated suitor sent an abject letter to the couple: "Consider me, the two of you, as a semi-lunatic with a sore head who has been totally bewildered by a long solitude. To this, I think, *sensible* insight into the state of things I have come after taking a huge dose of opium—in desperation. But instead of losing my reason as a result, I seem at last to have *come* to reason."

Alone again, Nietzsche retreated deep into himself. Unable to achieve equanimity through a platonic ménage, he returned to the character of Zarathustra. Listless weeks were followed by euphoric outbursts of inspiration: writing feverishly, as if in a trance, he poured out the first part of *Thus Spoke Zarathustra* in ten days early in 1883, promptly sending the revised text off to be published.

For the next few months, he seesawed between mania and depression. But whenever the euphoria returned, he was able to think with clarity and write with abandon. In two additional ten-day outbursts of sustained productivity, he completed a second and a third part of *Zarathustra*. He had never felt happier, explaining in one letter to Franz Overbeck that his new work "contains an image of myself in the sharpest focus, as I am, *once* I have thrown off my whole burden."

In these months, Overbeck remained a faithful correspondent and friend, all too painfully aware of Nietzsche's wild mood swings. "Nietzsche was already inhabited by Zarathustra," Overbeck remarked years later, adding that "Nietzsche always really took himself with religious seriousness as an individual, and that explains the otherwise incomprehensible phenomenon of the two faces he presented to those who knew him: the wild tempestuous nature, the fanatic (which he himself from time to time acknowledged he was), and the model human being." Overbeck spoke of his "*worship* of self" with good reason. As Nietzsche had confided to him in a letter written late in 1882, the writing of *Zarathustra* would give him "the most splendid chance to prove that for me"—as for Emerson—"'all experiences are useful, all days holy and all people godlike'!!!"

Nietzsche felt himself in uncharted waters. He no longer was a scholar, and he no longer lectured in a classroom. He was no longer aiming at some sort of tranquil balance, like Montaigne before him, content to analyze the follies and foibles of the human animal with bemused forbearance. He was a man possessed.

"When I was younger," he wrote in a notebook from this period, "I worried about what a philosopher really was . . . Finally I realized that there are two different kinds of philosopher." One kind was like Kant, someone who hoped to "hold fast some large body of valuations," by making all moral valuations "up to now easy to survey, easy to think through, to grasp, to manage." This was a "great and wondrous" achievement, Nietzsche conceded—but it was no longer Nietzsche's kind of philosophy. "The real philosophers *command and legislate*, they say: this is how it *shall* be! And it is they who determine the Where to and What for of man."

In *Thus Spoke Zarathustra*, Nietzsche struggled to give a definitive poetic form to what Lou Andreas-Salomé called "the deep movement of the godseeker . . . who came from religion and was heading towards religious prophecy." What the god seeker found is, in effect, what his fictive mouthpiece, Zarathustra, proclaims: nothing less than a new gospel of self-reliance, conveyed in a mythic narrative meant to rival Wagner's musical mythmaking in the *Ring* and based on his new master idea of eternal recurrence.

The gist of the idea itself he had first broached publicly in the penultimate aphorism of the first edition of *The Gay Science*, under the title "The Greatest Heavy Weight": "This life as you now live it and have lived it, you will have to live once more and innumerable times more; and there will be nothing new in it, but every pain and every joy and every thought and sigh and everything unutterably small or great in your life will return to you, all in the same succession and sequence."

The idea was, in part, a thought experiment, a spiritual exercise: Imagine having to live your life over again. How does that thought make you feel? If the prospect fills you with horror, you have not yet become reconciled to what is unalterable about yourself, you have not yet become what you are—you have not yet managed to say "*Yes* to the world as it is, to the point of wishing for its absolute recurrence and eternity: which would mean a new ideal of philosophy and sensibility."

But the idea of eternal recurrence was not merely a spiritual exercise; it was also a metaphysical theorem, taken on faith, no different in kind from Thales' proposition that "everything is one."

In his notebooks, Nietzsche tried to convince himself that the idea made sense in terms of natural science. But ultimately he had to fall back on the account he gives in *Ecce Homo* of the idea's indisputable origin in a mystic intuition: "Has anyone at the end of the nineteenth century a clear idea of what poets of strong ages have called *inspiration*? If not, I will describe it.—If one had the slightest residue of superstition left in one's system"—and the son of a Lutheran minister could not help having *some* such residue—"one could hardly reject altogether the idea that one is merely incarnation, merely mouthpiece, merely a medium of overpowering forces. . . . One hears, one does not seek; one accepts, one does not ask who gives; like lightning, a thought flashes up, with necessity, without hesitation regarding its form,—I never had any choice . . . Everything happens involuntarily in the highest degree but as in a gale of a feeling of freedom, of absoluteness, of power, of divinity."

It is easy to imagine that *Thus Spoke Zarathustra* is a product of some sort of divine inspiration. Febrile and sometimes gnomic, the prose is frequently overwrought, despite the comic relief offered by countless parodies of passages from the Bible. But Zarathustra does not come down from his mountain with a tablet of commandments. Nor does he behave like his historical namesake, who, as Nietzsche remarks, "was the first to consider the fight of good and evil the very wheel of the machinery of things." Instead, Nietzsche's mouthpiece will atone for the follies of Moses and Zoroaster by crafting a code of values that is avowedly beyond monotheistic conceptions of good and evil.

Thus, in the climactic part three of *Thus Spoke Zarathustra*, in the longest single chapter in the entire book, Nietzsche's prophet speaks about "Old and New Tablets." Zarathustra reiterates his three key metaphysical theorems. He reviews the idea of eternal recurrence. He recalls the insight into the "will to power," revealing that all things, including all human beings, want more power—in effect a daimonic (and Darwinian) revision of Aristotle's teaching that all human beings in their actions strive for *eudaimonia* or "happiness." And he preaches again the *Übermensch*, or "overhuman," a naturalized version of Emerson's preaching of the "Oversoul," a word meant in both cases to offer every single individual a unique challenge, namely (in Nietzsche's words), "to compose into one and bring together what is fragment and riddle and dreadful chance in man."

Not content only to assert his metaphysical theorems, Nietzsche's prophet also reiterates, with an exclamation point for emphasis, a series of new commandments: "Precisely this is godliness, that there are gods but no God!" "Shatter the old law tables!" "*Do not spare your neighbor!*"

Like Socrates, Nietzsche had examined himself. Like Plato, he was willing to legislate for others, if only as a ventriloquist speaking through his fictive prophet Zarathustra. But unlike the ancient philosophers from Aristotle to Augustine, Nietzsche's transparently fictive prophet will not command obedience to any single set of positive precepts and beliefs, embodied in word and deed. For like Montaigne, Nietzsche had found himself to be a creature in flux, a pure potentiality for being, uncertainly oriented toward what had previously been held to be the good, the true, and the beautiful. And as a result, he will have his Zarathustra, like Emerson, preach a gospel of self-reliance.

After finishing part three of *Zarathustra* early in 1884, Nietzsche was more convinced than ever that he was an epochal thinker, the great legislator of a new and liberating dispensation. "It is possible for the first time the idea has come to me that will split mankind in two," he wrote Franz Overbeck in March. "Everyone who has lived in [the pages of *Zarathustra*] will return to the world seeing things differently," he added in another letter to Overbeck, sent a few weeks later.

But his months of inspired creativity ended as abruptly as they had begun. And as time passed, and the volumes of *Zarathustra* rolled off the presses, Nietzsche was forced to acknowledge that his prophecy had fallen on deaf ears—that he now had to contend with "the gruesome silence one hears all around one." When Nietzsche's publisher, on the verge of bankruptcy, tried to raise cash by selling the rights to publish Nietzsche's works, he failed to find a buyer.

336 THE PHILOSOPHICAL LIFE

Even though his books weren't selling, Nietzsche kept writing. He produced a fourth and final part of *Zarathustra*, a parody, as if to imply that Zarathustra was more clown than prophet.

A visitor who came to see him in the summer of 1884 in Sils-Maria found a sick and disheartened soul. Nietzsche "immediately began to speak about the unbearableness of his ailment. He described to me how, when he closed his eyes, he saw an abundance of fantastic flowers, winding and intertwining, constantly growing and changing forms and colors in exotic luxuriance . . . Then, with his large, dark eyes looking straight at me, he asked in his weak voice with disquieting urgency, 'Don't you believe that this condition is a symptom of incipient madness? My father died of brain disease.'"

He kept moving from place to place, Switzerland in the summer, Italy in the winter. Done with *Zarathustra*, he resumed work on his core concepts, hoping to produce a more systematic account of his worldview. He laid plans for a large new book, *The Will to Power*, and began to fill his notebooks with passages to include. While working on *Power*, he produced another book of aphorisms on the moral sentiments, though he had trouble finding a new publisher for *Beyond Good and Evil*, which finally appeared in 1886.

When Nietzsche visited Basel that summer for the first time in years, old friends were shocked by what they saw. "An indescribable atmosphere of peculiarity emanated from him," wrote Erwin Rohde, "something that deeply unsettled me . . . as though he were from a country in which no one else lives."

Convinced that readers had misunderstood the significance of *Beyond Good and Evil*, Nietzsche tried to clarify his position in a series of three essays titled *On the Genealogy of Morals*, published as a book in 1887. He spent time that year in Nice, traveled from Italy to Switzerland, stayed in Sils-Maria for the summer, before returning to Nice via Venice. The scale and scope of *Power* kept growing; he had embarked on the fullest elaboration of his metaphysical theorems that he could manage, but he was struggling to shape his material.

Then, in the summer of 1888, he abruptly changed his plans. Revising material from his notebooks, he quickly prepared for publication two brief volumes of aphorisms, *Twilight of the Idols* and *The Antichrist* (both eventually published, in 1889 and 1895, respectively). The tempo of his work accelerated. In September he moved to Turin for the winter and began writing an autobiographical *apologia pro vita sua* that he titled *Ecce Homo*, an allusion to a passage in the passion of Christ, as recounted in John 19:4–5: "Jesus, therefore, went forth, wearing the crown of thorns and the purple garment; and he saith unto them, Behold the Man." He also quickly wrote and prepared for publication a polemical essay, *Nietzsche Contra Wagner*; though the composer had died five years earlier, he still felt him to be a thorn in his side.

In his correspondence, he grew ever more grandiose. On December 7, 1888: "I am strong enough to break the history of mankind in two." On December 18: "The world will be standing on its head for the next few years: since the old God has abdicated, *I* shall rule the world from now on." On December 21: "I have real geniuses among my admirers—today no other name is treated with so much distinction and reverence as mine." On December 25: "In two months I shall be the foremost name on earth." On December 29: "The most remarkable thing here in Turin is the complete fascination that I exert—over all classes of people. With every glance I am treated like a prince."

On the morning of January 3, 1889, when Nietzsche saw a cabdriver beating his horse, the philosopher embraced the horse, collapsed, and had to be carried back to his lodgings. A few days later, his landlady, alarmed by his increasingly erratic behavior, peeped through the keyhole to his room and discovered that he was singing "and capering around in the nude."

After Jacob Burckhardt had received a note from Nietzsche signed "Dionysus," and another, even more insane letter on January 6, he anxiously called on Franz Overbeck to ask him to go immediately to Turin to fetch their old friend.

Overbeck arrived in Turin the next day. He found Nietzsche "huddled up reading in the corner of a sofa . . . the incomparable master of expression is incapable of conveying even the delights of his merriment in anything but the most trivial expressions or by dancing and jumping about in a comical manner."

Under the care of doctors and his family, Nietzsche would live for eleven more years, suffering from dementia paralytica, unable to speak or write. With each passing year, his fame grew. A well-known photograph taken in these years shows the philosopher in profile, with a striking walrus mustache and a stony visage—the very image of the stern prophet, as if fixed under the gaze of eternity.

After the death of his mother in 1897, his sister moved Nietzsche to a villa in Weimar, where a steady stream of pilgrims came to behold the great man and to ponder the irony (as one visitor put it) that "only a miracle could save Zarathustra, the godless one." His life as a philosopher had ended in 1889—but when he died on August 25, 1900, his legend was still taking shape.

It was a legend that Nietzsche himself had helped to forge, above all through the character of Zarathustra. But his interest in mythmaking is obvious from the start; and as early as 1872, in one of the notes for his unfinished book "The Philosopher," written long before Zarathustra was a gleam in his eye, he had conjured a soliloquy for Oedipus that makes an eerily fitting epitaph for Nietzsche himself:

I call myself the last philosopher because I am the last human being. I myself am the only one who speaks with me, and my voice comes to me as the voice of someone who is dying. Let me commune with you for just one hour, beloved voice, with you, the last trace of the memory of all human happiness; with your help I will deceive myself about loneliness and lie my way into community and love; for my heart refuses to believe that love is dead; it cannot bear the shudder of the loneliest loneliness, and it forces me to speak as if I were Two.

EPILOGUE

N ietzsche, of course, was not the last philosopher, nor was he, despite his own grandiose conception of his uniqueness, the last philosopher to feel challenged by the example of Socrates. In the twentieth century, philosophers as different as Martin Heidegger and Ludwig Wittgenstein would keep alive the idea of philosophy as a way of life—and so would Michel Foucault, whose final lectures at the Collège de France helped to inspire the short biographies of the twelve philosophers that form this book.

As someone who was raised within a Lutheran community that prized introspection and sincere professions of good faith, and then was initiated into the study of academic philosophy through the reading of such key existentialist texts as Heidegger's *Being and Time* and Jean-Paul Sartre's *Being and Nothingness*, which encouraged a reader to live a life of "authenticity," I had long assumed, like Socrates in Plato's *Apology*, that "the unexamined life is not worth living."

But as a historian who has finished telling the stories of twelve different men who labored to live up to the Socratic ambition in very different times and places, I confess that some of my old assumptions about the value of an examined life have been shaken, in part because recounting these particular philosophical lives has provoked a variety of unexpected reactions—not just awe and admiration, but also pity, chagrin, and, in a few instances, amused disbelief.

In antiquity, living an examined life was not generally thought to be an end in itself. For some of the classical philosophers, it was a means to attain happiness and tranquillity; for others, a preparation for wisely wielding political power; and for still others, a necessary precondition for eternal salvation. Most of the ancient authors envisioned it as a quest that harmonized well with both rigorous inquiry and an overriding faith in God or the Good.

Yet for Montaigne and for many of those moderns who have struggled to describe honestly the motley character of one's inner experience, the quest for self-knowledge no longer fits easily with either a confidence in science or belief in a divinely ordered cosmos. Indeed, the effort to know oneself in some cases—Nietzsche is an example—seems to have ended in failure, as if to vindicate Nietzsche's remark that "we are necessarily strangers to ourselves." Even worse, the very practice of self-examination, given the protean and transient character of inner experience, seems in modern times to have become a potential source of depression—Montaigne speaks of his "melancholy humor"—and, in the cases of Rousseau and Nietzsche, perhaps even of madness.

Some may welcome such a chastening result—for the conflicted self plumbed by philosophers from Seneca to Nietzsche stands revealed as wretched, vain, and all too human, because it is guilty of falling short in an effort to lead a life of perfect integrity or wisdom.

In some moods, Montaigne, as a good student of Augustine, shared this humbling view. But Montaigne explicitly rejected those forms of moral perfectionism that entailed a chronic feeling of guilt, and he was fortunate, like Emerson, to have found for himself, in part through his introspective essays, an equable temperament, which enabled him to behold his failings and the follies of others with an enviable equanimity.

Nietzsche, by contrast, was unable to lift the burden of guilt he scrutinized and relentlessly criticized in his writing, perhaps because his character proved to be indelibly marked by the practices of punishing self-examination he had learned from his Lutheran father, and learned again from those ancient philosophers who were as obsessed as he became with fearlessly answering "the question of truth—the truth concerning what one is, what one does, and what one is capable of doing."

The moral of these philosophical biographies is therefore neither simple nor uniformly edifying. For anyone hoping for happiness, or political wisdom, or salvation, philosophical self-examination seems in practice to have led to self-doubt as often as self-trust, to misery as often as joy, to reckless public acts as often as prudent political conduct, and to moments of self-inflicted torment as often as moments of saving grace.

No wonder Montaigne spoke of the philosopher in search of wisdom as "the investigator without knowledge, the magistrate without jurisdiction, and all in all, the fool of the farce."

Surveying some of Montaigne's predecessors, we also have to wonder whether we might understand philosophy as a way of life differently if we could know as much about the lives of Socrates and Plato as we evidently know about the lives of Emerson and Nietzsche. It is hard to believe that the ancient philosophers were as rationally consistent in word and deed as they appear in the surviving lore about their lives. The myths are certainly charming—but they also make Socrates, Plato, and Diogenes feel somewhat remote, more like polished marble statues than fallible creatures of flesh and blood.

With Seneca and Augustine, on the other hand, we begin to feel a sense of kinship, because we see glimpses of what seem to be more realistic life stories, full of incident, accidents, successes, and failures, a cacophony of competing beliefs and codes of conduct. Instead of defining an essential self primarily informed by an intuition of some ruling Form of the Good, Seneca inventoried a wide range of feelings, emotions, and sentiments, from anger and grief to joy and happiness. Augustine acknowledged a similarly varied interior landscape, which served to mark the gulf between the fallen self of actually existing human beings and the perfectly rational unity and goodness of God.

When Montaigne tried, and failed, to emulate the stoic composure of Seneca, and chose instead to describe himself as he really was in his *Essays*, he was able finally to step outside the tradition of moral perfectionism that had linked the philosophical ideals of Socrates and Plato to those articulated by Seneca and Augustine. And when Rousseau subsequently, and even more spec-

344   THE PHILOSOPHICAL LIFE

tacularly, proved unable to live up consistently to his own daunting standard of virtuous conduct, he was unafraid to draw one possible conclusion: "You want people always to be consistent"—the classical ideal of rational unity. "I doubt that is possible for man; but what is possible is for him always to be true: that is what I mean to try to be."

"The love of truth is terrible and mighty," wrote Nietzsche—and the outline of his life, like that of the lives of several other modern philosophers, suggests the wisdom of that maxim. To consecrate oneself to truth—and to examine oneself and others—appears if anything harder and less potentially rewarding than it seems to have been for Socrates more than two thousand years ago.

Perhaps that is why in scientific and pragmatic societies like our own, which reinforce skepticism about the value of cultivating an inward contemplativeness, "philosophy," as Nietzsche complained, "remains the learned monologue of the lonely stroller, the accidental loot of the individual, the secret skeleton in the closet, or the harmless chatter between senile academics and children."

If we want to get a grip on "the world as it really is," then we should probably try (like Aristotle, Descartes, and Kant) to study the most general and abstract features of the world and the categories with which we think, in terms as impersonal as possible. Some contemporary evolutionary biologists and cognitive scientists have gone even further, arguing that modern science alone will yield useful knowledge about the human condition.

Moreover, if we mainly seek happiness or tranquillity or a transcendent meaning for life, then it may in fact be simpler to abandon both the search for unconditional scientific knowledge and the philosophical search for the truth concerning what we are, in order to uphold instead a certain faith, by either joining in some form of traditional religious worship or exploring one of the various contemporary alternatives. As the popular American preacher Rick Warren has put it, in terms that amount to a repudiation of philosophy as a way of life, "You won't discover your life's meaning by looking within yourself . . . You didn't create yourself, so there is no way you can tell yourself what you were created for!"

Yet within this contemporary context, dominated as it is by the struggle between the pragmatic power of applied science and the equally evident power of faith-based communities to give meaning to life, the classical conception of philosophy as a way of life survives, almost miraculously. It continues to offer a real alternative—but *only* if one is willing to take pains to elaborate one's *own* pondered thoughts, in response to such large questions as: "What can I know? What ought I to do? What may I hope?"

Of course, a "history starting from the problem of the philosophical life" cannot, by itself, suggest how best to approach any of these questions. Each one of the avowedly philosophical lives recounted in this book, exemplary though some of the lives may seem, is literally inimitable—defying imitation or emulation, in part for inalterable historical reasons. At the start of the twenty-first century, we lack the specific spiritual resources and cultural contexts that made feasible the characteristic nineteenth-century quests of Emerson and Nietzsche—never mind the early modern lives of Montaigne and Descartes, or such ancient exemplars as Socrates, Plato, Seneca, and Augustine.

As a result, for us today there can be no ideal form of philosophy as a way of life, "identical for all," as the twentieth-century German philosopher Karl Jaspers remarked in a cryptic image: at best, the philosophical life "is like a star-shower, a myriad meteors, which, knowing not whence they come nor whither they go, shoot through life."

It may nevertheless have been useful to have recalled some key episodes in a philosophical history that still haunts those of us who were irrevocably formed by rituals of introspection and who remain attracted, however fitfully, to the possibility of realizing a better or more "authentic" life for oneself and for others.

For whether we acknowledge it or not, we still live in the shadow of the Delphic injunction "Know thyself" and the Socratic ambition to examine oneself and others, even if taking these ideals seriously in the wake of Rousseau, Kant, Emerson, and Nietzsche seems now to entail an unending quest, with no firm goal and no certain reward, apart from experiencing, however briefly, a yearning for wisdom and a desire to live a life in harmony with that yearning—come what may.

NOTES

Works cited frequently here are identified by the following abbreviations:

AK   Immanuel Kant, *Gesammelte Schriften*, 34 vols. (Berlin: Preussichen Akademie der Wissenschaften, 1902–).

AT   René Descartes, *Œuvres de Descartes*, ed. Charles Adam and Paul Tannery, revised edition, 11 vols. (Paris: Vrin/C.N.R.S., 1964–76).

CC   Jean-Jacques Rousseau, *Correspondance complète de Jean Jacques Rousseau*, ed. R. A. Leigh, 52 vols. (Geneva: Institut et Musée Voltaire, 1965–98).

EJ   Ralph Waldo Emerson, *Emerson in His Journals*, ed. Joel Porte (Cambridge, MA: Harvard University Press, 1982).

EL   Ralph Waldo Emerson, *Essays and Lectures* (New York: Library of America, 1983).

ET   Immanuel Kant, *Anthropology from a Pragmatic Point of View*, English trans. Victor Lyle Dowdell and Hans H. Rudnick (Carbondale: Southern Illinois University Press, 1978).

JMN   Ralph Waldo Emerson, *The Journals and Miscellaneous Notebooks*, ed. William H. Gillman et al., 16 vols. (Cambridge, MA: Harvard University Press, 1960–82).

KSA   Friedrich Nietzsche, *Sämtliche Werke, Kritische Studienausgabe*, ed. Giorgio Colli and Mazzino Montinari, 15 vols. (New York: W. de Gruyter, 1980).

OC   Jean-Jacques Rousseau, *Oeuvres complète*, Pleiade ed., 5 vols. (Paris: Gallimard, 1959–95).

PW   René Descartes, *Philosophical Writings*, trans. John Cottingham et al. (New York: Cambridge University Press, 1984–91).

SL   Ralph Waldo Emerson, *The Selected Letters of Ralph Waldo Emerson,* ed. Joel Myerson (New York: Columbia University Press, 1997).

INTRODUCTION

6   "the study of the most general and abstract features of the world": Simon Blackburn, *Oxford Dictionary of Philosophy,* 2nd ed. (New York: Oxford University Press, 2008), an indispensable reference work.

6   "Philosophical theories make claims": Seyla Benhabib, "Taking Ideas Seriously," *Boston Review,* December 2002/January 2003, p. 40.

7   "the kind of person": Alexander Nehamas, *The Art of Living* (Berkeley: University of California Press, 1998), p. 2.

7   "philosophical, discourse . . . originates in a choice of life": Pierre Hadot, *What Is Ancient Philosophy?,* trans. Michael Chase (Cambridge, MA: Harvard University Press, 2002), p. 3.

7   "If I don't reveal my views": Xenophon, *Memorabilia,* IV, iv, 10.

7   "To him belongs the proverb": Diogenes Laertius, *Lives of the Eminent Philosophers,* I, 39.

7   "It is said that once": Ibid., 34.

8   From the start—in the Socratic dialogues of Plato: Aristotle famously classified Plato's *Sokratikoi logi* as a species of poetry in his *Poetics,* 1447b11.

8   In such dramatic dialogues: Cf. Plato, *Laws,* 903b: "We need to find words to charm . . ."

8   "experimented in biography": Arnaldo Momigliano, *The Development of Greek Biography* (Cambridge, MA: Harvard University Press, 1993), p. 46.

9   To separate what is fact from what is fiction: Nietzsche, *Untimely Meditations,* "On the Use and Abuse of History for Life," 6, *KSA* #1, p. 288.

9   potentiality for being: Translating *Seinkönnen,* a term coined by Martin Heidegger in *Being and Time.*

9   "I for one prefer reading Diogenes Laertius": Nietzsche, *Untimely Meditations,* "Schopenhauer as Educator," 8, *KSA* #1, p. 417.

10   our modern "negligence": Michel Foucault, Collège de France lecture, March 14, 1984.

10   Toward the end of that work, Sartre went even further: See Sartre, *Being and Nothingness,* trans. Hazel Barnes (New York: Philosophical Library, 1956), p. 568, an approach that Sartre called "existential psychoanalysis."

11   "our own pondered thoughts": Robert Nozick, *The Examined Life* (New York: Simon & Schuster, 1989), p. 15.

11   "What can I know?": Immanuel Kant, *Logik,* AK, 9:25.

12   Some now said: Diogenes Laertius, *Lives,* Preface, 12.

12   Aristotle, in his *Metaphysics*: Aristotle, *Metaphysics*, 982b20.

12   "to live the life of a philosopher": Plato, *Apology*, 28e.

12   "I am still unable": Plato, *Phaedrus*, 229e–230a.

13   It omits: I have written about the case of Heidegger in a long biographical essay, "Heidegger's Guilt," *Salmagundi* 109–110 (Winter–Spring 1996).

13   "natural to believe in great men": Emerson, *Representative Men*, I, "Uses of Great Men," *EL*: 615.

13   "to see whether one can live in accordance with it": Nietzsche, *Untimely Meditations*, "Schopenhauer as Educator," 8, *KSA* #1, p. 417.

14   "we are necessarily strangers to ourselves": Nietzsche, *Genealogy of Morals*, Preface, 1, *KSA* 5, p. 247.

SOCRATES

18   "I was Socrates": Henry Crabb Robinson, *Blake, Coleridge, Wordsworth, Lamb, Etc.* (London: Longman, 1922), p. 3.

19   "believed themselves to be a priestly nation": Jacob Burckhardt, *The Greeks and Greek Civilization*, trans. Sheila Stern (New York: St. Martin's Press, 1998), p. 217.

20   In some situations, the voice: Plato, *Apology*, 31c–d.

21   There are also stories, all of them unreliable: See Debra Nails, *The People of Plato* (Indianapolis: Hackett, 2002), pp. 264, 299, 218.

21   "he was so orderly in his way of life": Diogenes Laertius, *Lives*, II, 25.

21   "used to say that he most enjoyed the food": Ibid., 27.

21   "the sculptors of marble statues": Ibid., 33.

21   The association of the word *philosophy* with Socrates: The evidence for this claim has recently been marshaled exhaustively by Andrea Wilson Nightingale, *Genres in Dialogue: Plato and the Construct of Philosophy* (New York: Cambridge University Press, 1995). Cf. Michael Frede, "The Philosopher," in Jacques Brunschwig and Geoffrey E. R. Lloyd, eds., *Greek Thought*, trans. Catherine Porter (Cambridge, MA: Harvard University Press, 222), pp. 3–19.

22   According to Plato, it was Socrates' dissatisfaction: Plato, *Phaedo*, 96a.

22   But Aristotle claimed: Aristotle, Fragments 1–3.

22   "know yourself, and make compliant your youthful ways": Aeschylus, *Prometheus Bound*, 309–10. See also Eliza Gregory Wilkins, *The Delphic Maxims in Literature* (Chicago: University of Chicago Press, 1929), and Pierre Courcelle, *Connais-toi toi-même de Socrate à Saint Bernard* (Paris: Études Augustiniennes, 1974).

23   There were two ways to consult the Delphic oracle: Following the speculative ac-

counts given in C.D.C. Reeve, *Socrates in the* Apology (Indianapolis: Hackett, 1989), pp. 21–32, and Gregory Vlastos, *Socrates: Ironist and Moral Philosopher* (Ithaca: Cornell University Press, 1991), pp. 288–89.

23   he ceased "to engage in public affairs": Plato, *Apology*, 23b; *useless* is the word Pericles used in his famous funeral oration, according to Thucydides, *The Peloponnesian War*, II, 40.

24   "He sometimes stops and stands": Plato, *Symposium*, 175b.

24   "One time at dawn he began to think": Ibid., 203d.

24   his avowed humility seemed obnoxious: Following the account in George Grote, *History of Greece* (London, 1869–70), 8:211–12, who stressed the publicity of Socrates' way of life and the public criticism it provoked.

24   This was perhaps the most disturbing aspect: Aristotle, *Nichomachean Ethics*, 4.7, 1127b25, mentions Socrates in the context of discussing boastfulness and false modesty.

24   "Often when he looked at the multitude of wares": Diogenes Laertius, *Lives*, II, 25.

25   "They relate that Euripides gave him": Ibid., 22.

25   "Frequently owing to his vehemence": Ibid., 21.

25   In busts erected shortly after his death: See Paul Zanker, *The Mask of Socrates* (Berkeley: University of California Press, 1995), p. 43.

26   his friends compared him with Silenus: Plato, *Symposium*, 216d–e.

26   "A foreigner who knew about faces": Nietzsche, *The Twilight of the Idols*, "The Problem of Socrates," 3. Zopyrus was the subject of a Socratic conversation by Phaedo, once famous, now lost. See Charles Kahn, *Plato and the Socratic Dialogue* (New York: Cambridge University Press, 1996), p. 11.

26   "I am a poor man": Diogenes Laertius, *Lives*, II, 34.

26   Socrates was walking on a narrow street in central Athens: Ibid., 48.

26   "Aristippus, when he met Ischomachus at Olympia": Plutarch, *De curiositate*, 2, 516c.

27   "the high priest of subtlest poppycock": Aristophanes, *Clouds*, 359.

27   "You strut around like a grand gander": Ibid., 363.

27   When his school goes up in smoke: Ibid., 1508; and see the classic essay by K. J. Dover in his Greek edition of the play (New York: Oxford University Press, 1989).

28   "Soon a large number of high-born men": Plutarch, "Alcibiades," 4.

28   There is no Greek or Latin word: See K. J. Dover, *Greek Homosexuality* (Cambridge, MA: Harvard University Press, 1978).

28   "The fact that Socrates was in love with him": Plutarch, "Alcibiades," 4.

28   "When I arose after having slept with Socrates": Plato, *Symposium*, 219c–d.

29   How Socrates set about trying to effect this transformation: See, e.g., R. S. Bluck, "The Origin of the Greater Alcibiades," *Classical Quarterly* 3, no. 1/2 (1953):

46–52.

29   "You want your reputation and your influence": Plato, *Alcibiades*, 105c.

29   "I must be in some absolutely bizarre condition!": Ibid., 116e.

29   "Don't you realize that the errors": Ibid., 117d.

29   "trust in me": Ibid., 124a–b.

29   "The command that we should know ourselves": Ibid., 130e.

30   What Alcibiades needs to prosper: Cf. Plutarch, "Alcibiades," 2. As Plutarch puts it, he needs to forge a character (*ethos*) strong enough to master the strength of his passion (*pathos*).

30   "I will never forsake you now": Plato, *Alcibiades*, 132a.

30   "I should like to believe that you will persevere": Ibid., 135e.

30   " 'He crouched down in fear' ": Plutarch, "Alcibiades," 4.

30   In Plutarch's account: Ibid., 6.

30   "it was by pandering to his ambitious longing": Ibid., 6.

31   "He could change more abruptly than a chameleon": Ibid., 23.

31   "the notable men of Athens": Ibid., 16.

32   After he set sail with the Athenian fleet: For the whole story, see Thucydides, *The Peloponnesian War*, VI–VIII.

32   According to Xenophon: Xenophon, *Memoirs*, I, 2.36.

32   According to Plato, Socrates refused: Plato, *Letter VII*, 324e–325a.

33   "Socrates does injustice": Diogenes Laertius, *Lives*, II, 40. Cf. Plato, *Apology*, 24b–c.

33   "What does the god mean?": Plato, *Apology*, 28e.

33   "This began when I was a child": Ibid., 31c–d. Cf. Xenophon, *Apology*, 12–13.

34   "Do you know anyone who is less a slave to bodily desires?": Xenophon, *Apology*, 18.

34   It is they who should stand trial: Cf. Miles Burnyeat, "The Impiety of Socrates," *Ancient Philosophy* 17 (1997): 1–12.

35   He insisted instead on fulfilling the letter: Plato, *Crito*, 51b.

35   "aped the manners of Sparta": Aristophanes, *Birds*, 1280–83. The verb *socratize* was a coinage of the comedian.

36   "a Socrates idealized and made new": [Plato?], *Letter II*, 314c.

36   The Socratic conversations mark one of the first important experiments: See Momigliano, *Development of Greek Biography*, pp. 46–48, and Kahn, *Plato and the Socratic Dialogue*, pp. 1–35.

36   the genre itself, as Aristotle observed: Aristotle, *Poetics*, 1447b11.

37   The "Socrates" of Antisthenes: Most of this paragraph is paraphrasing Kahn, *Plato and the Socratic Dialogue*, p. 4.

38   "a paradise of inconclusive guesswork": Burnyeat, "The Impiety of Socrates," p. 1.

38   And skeptical though he may be: Cf. the discussion in Kahn, *Plato and the Socratic Dialogue*, pp. 88–95.

38   His enemies suspected Socrates: See the discussion in Nehamas, *The Art of Living*, pp. 46–98.

38   "Throughout my life, in any public activity": Plato, *Apology*, 33a.

39   "From me you will hear the whole truth": Ibid., 17b–c.

39   "neglected what occupies most people": Ibid., 36b.

39   He consistently says only what he thinks to be true: Ibid., 32d.

39   In his landmark study *The Great Philosophers*: Karl Jaspers, *The Great Philosophers: The Foundations*, ed. Hannah Arendt, trans. Ralph Manheim (New York: Harcourt, 1962).

39   "there is no greater evil one can suffer": Plato, *Phaedo*, 89d.

40   After all, to be prepared constantly to question: This paragraph is indebted to Michael Frede, "Plato's Arguments and the Dialogue Form," in James C. Klagge and Nicholas D. Smith, eds., *Methods of Interpreting Plato and His Dialogues*, *Oxford Studies in Ancient Philosophy* 10 (1992): Supplement, 215. For a contemporary attempt to explain what "rational unity" means in practice, see Graham Hubbs, "The Rational Unity of the Self" (Ph.D. dissert., University of Pittsburgh, 2008), http://etd.library.pitt.edu/ETD/available/etd-04052008-144828/unrestricted/Hubbs5April2008.pdf.

41   "I know of no better aim of life": Nietzsche, *Untimely Meditations*, "On the Uses and Disadvantages of History for Life," 9.

PLATO

46   "He was originally called Aristocles": Diogenes Laertius, *Lives*, III, 2. Cf. Anonymous, *Prolegomena to Platonic Philosophy*, trans. and ed. L. G. Westerink (Amsterdam: North-Holland Publishing, 1962), I, p. 2.

46   "Plato was a divine man": Ibid.

46   In the same biography: Ibid., I, pp. 4–6.

46   He was raised on a strict regimen: Ibid., I, p. 6.

46   As a child, he was "so modest": Diogenes Laertius, *Lives*, III, 26.

46   He trained in gymnastics: Ibid., 5.

46   He learned to write: Ibid., 4.

46   He painted and wrote poetry: Ibid., 5.

47   "You cannot step into the same river twice": See the translations of Heraclitus in John Burnet, *Early Greek Philosophy* (London, 1892), pp. 130–68.

47   "It is stated that Socrates in a dream": Diogenes Laertius, *Lives*, III, 5.

47   "Come hither, O fire-god": Ibid., 5, 63.

47   "When I was a young man": Plato, *Letter VII*, 324b–d.

48   His family's nobility and wealth: Following the speculation of George Grote, *Plato and the Other Companions of Sokrates* (London, 1865), 1:117, and G. C.

Field, *Plato and His Contemporaries* (London: Methuen, 1930), p. 5.

48 "certain happenings": Plato, *Letter VII*, 324d.

49 In his epistolary account of these events: Ibid., 325a.

49 "All existing states" and "The ills of the human race": Ibid., 326ab.

49 "he set out in quest of the best state": Paul Friedländer, *Plato: An Introduction*, trans. Hans Meyerhoff (Princeton: Princeton University Press, 1969), p. 6.

49 His first stop: Diogenes Laertius, *Lives*, II, 106; III, 6.

50 The ancient biographers represent Plato: *Prolegomena to Platonic Philosophy*, I, p. 8.

50 The colony of Croton in these years: See Charles Kahn, *Pythagoras and the Pythagoreans* (Indianapolis: Hackett, 2001), pp. 6–7.

50 "Let reason, the gift divine," etc.: From "The Golden Verses of Pythagoras," 40ff, in Kenneth Sylvan Guthrie, ed., *The Pythagorean Sourcebook and Library* (Grand Rapids: Phanes, 1987), p. 164.

51 "Do I participate in the divine?": Plato, *Phaedrus*, 230a.

51 the content of the Pythagorean teaching was supposed to be secret: See the maxims in Guthrie, *Pythagorean Sourcebook*, pp. 159–61; also in Kahn, *Pythagoras and the Pythagoreans*, pp. 8–10.

51 Archytas, according to Diogenes Laertius: See *Lives*, VIII, 79–83. On Plato and Philolaus, see *Lives*, III, 6, and VIII, 84–85.

52 In some of his later dialogues: For the influence of Archytas on Plato, see Kahn, *Pythagoras and the Pythagoreans*, pp. 39–62.

53 some of the ancient sources imply: Iamblichus, *The Life of Pythagoras*, 31, in Guthrie, *Pythagorean Sourcebook*, p. 105.

53 According to the account given in the *Seventh Letter*: Plato, *Letter VII*, 327a–b.

53 "the general theme of the conversation": Plutarch, *Lives*, "Dion," 5.

53 "And you like a tyrant": Diogenes Laertius, *Lives*, III, 18.

53 Your quest has been futile: Plutarch, *Lives*, "Dion," 5.

53 Some say it was only a personal appeal: Diogenes Laertius, *Lives*, III, 20; VIII, 79.

53 For example, according to Diogenes Laertius: Ibid., III, 9.

54 Elsewhere, Diogenes Laertius reports: Ibid., 20.

54 "true lover of wisdom": Plato, *Letter VII*, 340c, d.

55 "That is what happened": Aristoxenus, *Elementa Harmonica*, II, 1, quoted in John Patrick Lynch, *Aristotle's School: A Study of a Greek Educational Institution* (Berkeley: University of California Press, 1972), p. 90.

55 The capstone of the curriculum was dialectics: In the last part of this sentence, I am paraphrasing the contemporary British philosopher Bernard Williams, defending his own conception of the value of scientific inquiry.

56 Recounting the ascent toward true knowledge: Plato, *Republic*, 522–34.

56 And in a later passage referring to the image: Ibid., 506e, 533a. Cf. the line of in-

terpretation in Kahn, *Plato and the Socratic Dialogue*, pp. 329ff. My thinking about the *Republic* has also been shaped by the work of Harry Berger Jr.; see, for example, the essays in *Situated Utterances: Texts, Bodies, and Cultural Representations* (New York: Fordham University Press, 2005).

56   "First, the name": Plato, *Letter VII*, 342a–b.

56   "Only when all of these things": Ibid., 344b.

56   "There is no writing of mine about these matters": Ibid., 341c–d.

57   "At the Panathenaea": Epicrates, quoted in Field, *Plato and His Contemporaries*, pp. 38–39.

57   And this goal Plato did not teach only in theory: As confirmed by Werner Jaeger's reading of Aristotle's altar-elegy dedicated to Eudemus; see Werner Jaeger, *Aristotle*, trans. Richard Robinson (New York: Oxford University Press, 1962), pp. 106–109.

57   Contemporary accounts suggest: Quoted in Friedländer, *Plato*, p. 99.

58   "there is no greater evil one can suffer": Plato, *Phaedo*, 89d.

58   In a fragment that has survived: Aristotle, Fragment from a Dialogue, in Themistius, orationes, 295cd, F 64 R^3, in *Complete Works of Aristotle*, ed. Jonathan Barnes (Princeton: Princeton University Press, 1984), 2:2418.

59   Although scholars cannot agree on precise dates: Following the argument of W.K.C. Guthrie, *History of Greek Philosophy* (New York: Cambridge University Press, 1975), 4:285.

59   It revolves around the fictional representation: For details about what else is known about these historical characters, see the prosopography of Plato, Nails, *People of Plato*.

59   "In this city": Plato, *Gorgias*, 521c.

59   Gorgias has just finished: Ibid., 447c; cf. W.K.C. Guthrie, *The Sophists* (Cambridge: Cambridge University Press, 1971), pp. 41–44.

59   A conversation unfolds: Plato, *Gorgias*, 458c.

60   "who he is": Ibid., 447d.

60   "I think it is better for my lyre to be out of tune": Ibid., 482b–c.

60   "I think that I am one of the few Athenians": Ibid., 521d.

60   "He gave everyone the impression": [Olympiodoros], *Life of Plato*, 61.

61   If Plato's students "could not govern a city": Hadot, *What Is Ancient Philosophy?*, p. 60.

61   "On this occasion, as he was going up to the Acropolis": Diogenes Laertius, *Lives*, III, 24.

62   In some cases, Plato's disciples: Plato, *Letter VI*, 322d–e. Cf. Plutarch, *Adversus Colotem*, 1126c–d.

62   In the case of Macedonia: Following the account in Friedländer, *Plato*, pp. 102–103. A more skeptical account of the politics of Plato's Academy is P. A. Brunt, "Plato's Academy and Politics," in *Studies in Greek History and Thought* (New York: Oxford

University Press, 1993), pp. 282–342.

62   "hardly any Athenian ever saw him laugh": Plutarch, *Lives*, "Phocion," 4.

62   Though the demos in the Assembly: Following the account in Peter Green, *Alexander to Actium* (Berkeley: University of California Press, 1990), pp. 40–44.

63   At the behest of Dionysius: Plutarch, *Lives*, "Dion," 17, 49; cf. the interpretation in Grote, *History of Greece*, 10:339n2.

63   "he had spent a long time in the Academy": Plutarch, *Lives*, "Dion," 47.

63   His behavior annoyed his rivals: See Plato, *Letter VII*, 327b.

63   "What better opportunity can we expect" etc.: Ibid., 327e–328a.

64   But he also imagines that a true philosopher: See Plato, *Republic*, 520a, for the need to compel the philosophers to care for others.

64   "compelled me, in a way": Plato, *Letter VII*, 350c.

64   "lest I appear to myself as a pure theorist": Ibid., 328b.

64   "If in [Dionysius's] empire": Ibid., 335d.

64   For a while, the palace entourage: Plutarch, *Lives*, "Dion," 13.

65   "hoping that [Dionysius] might somehow": Plato, *Letter VII*, 330b.

65   There are four letters addressed to Dionysius the Younger: Passages quoted from Plato, *Letter I*, 309c; *Letter II*, 312c; *Letter III*, 318e; *Letter XIII*, 361c–362a.

65   "It is a law of nature": Plato, *Letter II*, 310e–311c.

66   "persistently urged me not to disobey": Plato, *Letter VII*, 338b.

66   "Besides, I thought": Ibid., 339e.

67   "I told Dionysius": Ibid., 347b–c.

67   "Before all Sicily": Ibid., 348a.

67   it was a very visible summit meeting: See Plato, *Letter VII*, 350b; and Diogenes Laertius, *Lives*, III, 25.

68   "He fancied himself competent": Grote, *History of Greece*, 10:407.

68   "they did not listen to me": Plato, *Letter VII*, 350d–e.

68   "Philosophers in fact are inexperienced": Plato, *Gorgias*, 484d.

69   "ideal starting point": Plato, *Laws*, IV, 710e.

69   In the *Laws*, Plato warns: Ibid., V, 731e–732a.

70   "I must tell the truth": Plato, *Letter VII*, 339a.

70   "had a dream of himself as a swan": *Prolegomena to Platonic Philosophy*, I, p. 4.

70   Plato's body was laid to rest: See Diogenes Laertius, *Lives*, III, 41.

70   "his wish always was to leave a memorial": Ibid., 40.

71   might finally end "troubles": Plato, *Republic*, 473d.

71   "infer the divinity of his nature": *Prolegomena to Platonic Philosophy*, I, pp. 12–14.

DIOGENES

75   "looking for a man": Diogenes Laertius, *Lives*, VI, 41.

75   "the example of the trainers of choruses": Ibid., 35.

75   His father, Hicesias: Ibid., 76.

76   But Eubulides, a contemporary of Aristotle: Ibid., 20.

76   In the twentieth century, scholars were able: See Donald R. Dudley, *A History of Cynicism* (London: 1937), pp. 21, 54–55, and Luis E. Navia, *Classical Cynicism* (Westport, CT: Greenwood, 1996), pp. 88–89.

76   Some modern historians: See C. T. Seltman, "Diogenes of Sinope, Son of the Banker Hikesias," in J. H. Mattingly and E.S.G. Robinson, eds., *Transactions of the International Numismatic Conference of 1936* (London, 1938).

76   "Deface the currency": Diogenes Laertius, *Lives*, VI, 21. The Greek phrase *para-charattein to nomisma* can also be translated as "falsify the money" or "alter the coinage."

77   "He really defaced the currency": Ibid., 71 (using the translation of A. A. Long for the first part of the sentence).

77   "citizen of the world": Ibid., 63.

77   "Virtue," Antisthenes declared: Ibid., 11.

77   "the ability to converse with myself": Ibid., 6.

77   As Plutarch recounts the episode: Plutarch, *Moralia*, 77e–78a. Cf. Diogenes Laertius, *Lives*, VI, 22.

78   "Fool that I am": Seneca, *Epistulae*, 90, 14.

78   *kuon* in Greek: A usage first attested to in Aristotle, *Rhetoric*, 1411a24.

78   "I fawn on those who give me anything": Diogenes Laertius, *Lives*, VI, 60.

78   One author attributed thirteen dialogues to him: Ibid., 20, 80; Dio Chrysostom, *Discourses*, X, 30, and see Derek Krueger, "The Bawdy and Society," in R. Bracht Branham and Marie-Odile Goulet-Cazé, eds., *The Cynics* (Berkeley: University of California Press, 1996), p. 226.

79   According to Philodemus: See the excerpts from Philodemus translated into French in Tiziano Dorandi, "La *Politeia* de Diogène de Sinope et quelques remarques sur sa pensée politique," in Marie-Odile Goulet-Cazé and Richard Goulet, eds., *Le Cynisme ancien et ses prolongements* (Paris: Presses Universitaires de France, 1993), pp. 59–61.

79   "For it was his custom": Dio Chrysostom, *Discourses*, VIII, 6.

79   "all who should follow his treatment": Ibid., 8.

80   "It was his habit to do everything in public": Diogenes Laertius, *Lives*, VI, xx.

80   "throwing all the bones to him": Ibid., 46.

80   "ceased speaking and, squatting on the ground": Dio Chrysostom, *Discourses*, VIII, 36.

80   "warned him not to spit": Diogenes Laertius, *Lives*, VI, 32.

80   "When he was taken prisoner": Philo, *Quod Omnis Probus Liber Sit*, 121–22.

81   " 'ruling over men' ": Ibid., 123.

81   "in all that pertains to yourself": Epictetus, *Discourses*, III, xxii, 13; see also III, xxii, 18.

81   conversations with Alexander the Great: See Diogenes Laertius, *Lives*, VI, 69.

81   "many statesmen and philosophers came to [Alexander]": Plutarch, *Lives*, "Alexander," xiv.

82   "When he saw so many people approaching": Ibid.

82   "You may say what you like": Ibid.

82   "This shows shrewd percipience": Peter Green, *Alexander of Macedon* (Berkeley: University of California Press, 1991), p. 123.

82   "Alexander [once] came to visit him": Dimitri Gutas, "Sayings by Diogenes Preserved in Arabic," in Goulet-Cazé and Goulet, *Le Cynisme ancien*, 39.1, p. 486.

82   "That which prevents you from coming to us": Ibid., 40.1, p. 486.

83   "Plato had defined Man as an animal": Diogenes Laertius, *Lives*, VI, 40.

83   " 'Table and cup I see,' said Diogenes": Ibid., 53.

83   "Had you paid court to Dionysius": Ibid., 58.

83   "Aren't you ashamed, Socrates": Plato, *Gorgias*, 487b–e.

84   "Seeing a young man behaving effeminately": Diogenes Laertius, *Lives*, VI, 65.

84   "for it is the enemy of considerate behavior": Cicero, *De Officiis*, I, 148.

85   "I am inclined to think": Augustine, *City of God*, XIV, 20.

85   Once, when a boy shattered his clay tub: Diogenes Laertius, *Lives*, VI, 43.

86   According to still another account, he simply held his breath: Ibid., 76–78.

86   "Even bronze grows old with time": Quoted in Navia, *Classical Cynicism*, p. 81.

86   In the fourth of his speeches: Dio Chrysostom, *Discourses*, IV, on Kingship, perhaps delivered before the emperor Trajan on his birthday, September 18, A.D. 103.

ARISTOTLE

89   "the Master of those who know," etc.: Quoting Dante, Averroës, and Aquinas, respectively.

89   "an ideal of human excellence": Jonathan Barnes, *Aristotle: A Very Short Introduction* (New York: Oxford University Press, 2000), p. 139.

89   "untroubled by passion": William Turner, "Aristotle," an article affirming medieval Christian opinion in the *Catholic Encyclopedia*, first published in English in 1914.

90   "The man was born": Martin Heidegger, *Grundbegriffe der aristotelischen Philosophie* (Frankfurt: Klostermann, 2002), p. 5.

90   "like eating dried hay": Quoted in Jonathan Barnes, "Life and Work," in *Cambridge Companion to Aristotle* (New York: Cambridge University Press, 1995), pp. 15, 12.

90   modern scholars have been able to trace: See Ingemar Düring, *Aristotle in the*

Ancient Biographical Tradition (Gothenburg, Sweden: Institute of Classical Studies, 1957), an anthology of the relevant fragments with commentary.

91   some sources report that he was subsequently raised: *Vita Marciana*, 3, ibid., pp. 96–97.

91   "debauchee and a glutton": Diogenes Laertius, *Lives,* X, 4, recording the views of Epicurus.

91   Others said that the pursuit of political power: Philodemus, *De Rhetorica, Vol. rhet.* II, p. 50, Sudhaus, col. XLVIII, 36; in Düring, *Aristotle*, pp. 299–300, 303.

91   Still other early sources claim: See, e.g., the Arab biography by Ibn Abi Usaibia, in Düring, *Aristotle*, p. 215.

91   But a dramatically different tale is told: See, e.g., *Vita Syriaca*, ibid., p. 185.

92   a chronological impossibility: The hypothesis that the chronology in Hermippus suggests that Aristotle probably studied with Isocrates was first advanced by the nineteenth-century German historian of philosophy Eduard Zeller in *History of Greek Philosophy* (London, 1881).

92   The school of Isocrates: Isocrates, *Antidosis*, 277. The locus classicus for his use of the word *philosophy* is Isocrates, *Panegyricus*, 47–51. The debate between Plato and Isocrates over the meaning of *philosophy* is discussed in Nightingale, *Genres in Dialogue*, pp. 13–59.

92   one of the first and finest large private libraries: Strabo, *Geographia*, XIII, 1, 54.

92   Socrates as a kind of mathematical recluse: As Werner Jaeger puts it in *Aristotle*, p. 15. Though modern scholars disagree about the precise dating of different Platonic dialogues, there is little dispute that the *Thaetatus* belongs to a group written near the end of his life.

92   Although Aristotle may have been inspired: Jaeger's argument for the supposed youthful idealism of Aristotle, ibid., pp. 21–22, has not persuaded many later scholars.

93   he was critical of the Pythagorean assumption: Aristotle, *Metaphysics*, 992a32.

93   Plato nicknamed Aristotle "*nous*": See *Vita Marciana*, 7, in Düring, *Aristotle*, p. 98, a passage discussed by Düring on p. 109.

93   "To the philosopher alone": Iamblichus, *Protreticus*, 54.10–56 Pistelli; in Barnes, *Complete Works of Aristotle*, 2:2410. Cf. Philodemus, who reports that Aristotle justified his interest in politics in part by arguing, like Plato, that "politics will make great progress in a city which is well governed." See Philodemus, *De Rhetorica, Vol. rhet.* II, p. 50, Sudhaus, col. XLVIII, 36; in Düring, *Aristotle*, pp. 299–300, 303.

93   rhetoric, which he evaluated more positively: See Aristotle's later treatise on *Rhetoric*, in which he cites Isocrates more than any other ancient authority on rhetoric; earlier lectures may have been more critical.

94   He wanted to appropriate everything: Paraphrasing Karl Jaspers, speaking of the

philosophers who were in his words "creative orderers" or "great systemizers"; see *The Great Philosophers*, trans. Edith Ehrlich and Leonard H. Ehrlich (New York: Harcourt, 1993), 3:188.

94   the capital virtue he called *phronesis*: I am using the work of Terence Irwin, who helpfully explains the range of possible English meanings of *phronesis* in the extensive glossary to his translation of Aristotle, *Nichomachean Ethics* (Indianapolis: Hackett, 1999), p. 345.

94   Upon the death of Eubulus: The most detailed and interesting modern summary of the evidence that I know of is Jaeger, *Aristotle*, pp. 111–17. It should be compared with the extant fragments describing Hermias; see Düring, *Aristotle*, pp. 272–83.

95   a letter that Plato supposedly addressed to Hermias: Plato, *Letter VI*, 322c.

95   "self-defense against the base and wicked": Ibid., 322d.

95   "into a single bond of friendship": Ibid., 323a–c.

95   "made friends of Coriscus and Erastus and Aristotle": Didymus, *In Demosth. Comm.*, ed. H. Diels and W. Schubart, *Berliner Klassikertexte*, I, 1904, pp. 17ff, in Düring, *Aristotle*, pp. 272–77; following Jaeger's translation in *Aristotle*, pp. 114–15n.

96   Philip was merciless in victory: The chief relevant passages in ancient literature are the *Olynthiac Orations* of Demosthenes, and Xenophon, *Hell*. v. 2.

96   "a concubine of Hermias": Diogenes Laertius, *Lives*, V, 4.

96   But other sources explain: Ibid., 3.

96   To judge from the number of fauna: See Marjorie Grene, *A Portrait of Aristotle* (Chicago: University of Chicago Press, 1963), p. 32.

97   "That [Aristotle] undertook the work": Jaeger, *Aristotle*, p. 121.

97   "Now, Philip could see": Plutarch, "Alexander," 7. Plutarch's probable sources are exhaustively evaluated in Düring, *Aristotle*, pp. 284–99.

97   "Alexander not only received from Aristotle": Plutarch, "Alexander," 7.

98   "Philip gave Aristotle and Alexander": Ibid.

98   According to the legend, his last wish: Following the summary of the ancient evidence in Jaeger, *Aristotle*, p. 117.

98   "Virtue, greatly striven for by mankind": Diogenes Laertius, *Lives*, V, 7, following the translation in Barnes, *Complete Works of Aristotle*, 2:2463.

98   "He regarded and referred to the *Iliad*": Plutarch, "Alexander," 8.

98   Alexander thus "admired Aristotle": Ibid.

99   according to some ancient sources, he supervised the rebuilding: See Düring, *Aristotle*, pp. 290–94.

99   Aristotle "was so valued by Philip": *Vita Marciana*, 73–80, in Barnes, *Complete Works of Aristotle*, 2:2459–60.

100   Alexander and his soldiers marched promptly to Thebes: Plutarch, "Alexander," 11.

100 "vanity and prodigious ingratitude": Pierre Bayle, "Aristotle," *Dictionnaire historique et critique* (Amsterdam, 1740), 1:324–25. Bayle's entry shows the durability of the ancient biographical traditions.

100 "where he would walk up and down philosophizing": Diogenes Laertius, *Lives*, V, 5.

101 It was an institution open to the public: See Lynch, *Aristotle's School*, esp. pp. 68–96.

101 Aristotle began to number important men among his pupils: See Jaeger, *Aristotle*, p. 125.

101 Pliny the Elder: Pliny the Elder, *Natural History*, VIII, 16, 14.

101 Xenocrates refused gifts to the Academy: See George Grote, *Aristotle* (London, 1872), 1:14.

102 "All things have by nature something divine": Aristotle, *Nichomachean Ethics*, VII, 13, 1153b32.

102 "God and nature create": Aristotle, *On the Heavens*, I, 4, 271a33.

102 Aristotle lectured at night: Aulus Gellius, *Noctes Atticae*, XX, 5.

102 "wisdom and not merely philosophy": Leo Strauss to Alexandre Kojève, May 28, 1957, in Strauss, *On Tyranny*, expanded ed., ed. Victor Gourevitch and Michael S. Roth (New York: Free Press, 1991), p. 277.

103 Aristotle was honored with an official inscription: See Düring, *Aristotle*, pp. 339–40, and the discussion in Barnes, "Life and Work," in *Cambridge Companion to Aristotle*, p. 6.

103 An ancient bust of Aristotle: "Acropolis Museum Dig Unearths Hoard," *New York Times*, January 4, 2007, p. E2.

103 "he was conspicuous by his attire": Diogenes Laertius, *Lives*, V, 1.

103 "when Diogenes offered him dried figs": Ibid., 18.

103 "so orderly, dignified, and self-sufficient": Plutarch, "Alexander," 53.

104 Plutarch recounts how he criticized his nephew's lack of prudence: Ibid., 54.

104 "Callisthenes died a vastly overweight, louse-ridden man": Ibid., 56.

105 "Aristotle put Antipater up to the deed": Ibid., 77.

105 He was of course suspected of treason: Origen, *Contra Celsum*, I, 380, Migne, II, p. 781 B, cited in Düring, *Aristotle*, p. 343, who evaluates all the ancient sources on p. 344.

105 The problem with his panegyric to Hermias: Following the conjecture of Grote, *Aristotle*, 1:18–19.

105 "As for the honor which was voted me at Delphi": Aelian, *Varia Historia*, XV 1 = F666R³, in Barnes, *Complete Works of Aristotle*, 2:2461.

106 "I will not allow the Athenians to wrong philosophy twice": *Vita Marciana*, 184–91 = F667R³, ibid.

106 early Christian writers spread the rumor: Psuedo-Justin Martyr, as recounted in

Joseph Williams Blakesley, *A Life of Aristotle* (London, 1839), p. 95.

106 In his will: Diogenes Laertius, *Lives*, V, 11–16.

106 "Aristotle reveals himself in this testament": D. S. Hutchinson, "Ethics," in Barnes, *Cambridge Companion to Aristotle*, p. 196.

106 "Don't fear god": See Brad Inwood and L. P. Gerson, eds. and trans., *The Epicurus Reader: Selected Writings and Testimonia* (Indianapolis: Hackett, 1994), p. vii, quoting Philodemus of Gadara.

106 Epicurus lashed out: The subsequent quotes in this paragraph come from Philodemus, *De Rhetorica*, Vol. rhet. II, p. 50, Sudhaus, col. XLVIII, 36; discussed in Düring, *Aristotle*, pp. 302–11.

107 "To Hermias the eunuch": Diogenes Laertius, *Lives*, V, 11.

107 "roughly speaking, perhaps": Aristotle, *Topics*, III, 118a14–15.

108 "any choice or possession of the natural goods": Aristotle, *Eudemian Ethics*, VIII, 1249b16–21.

108 "Man is by nature an animal intended to live in a *polis*": Aristotle, *Politics*, I, 2, 1253a3–4 (as translated by Ernest Barker [New York: Oxford University Press, 1958]).

108 the best practicable form of polis: Aristotle, *Politics*, IV, 1294a30–1294b41.

108 "Hence we ought to examine what has been said": Aristotle, *Nichomachean Ethics*, X, 8, 1179a21–24.

109 But at least one modern scholar: Jaeger, *Aristotle*, p. 321.

109 At the time, his most powerful ally: See Grote, *Aristotle*, 1:14–17, 37.

109 "the absolutely objective way": Jaeger, *Aristotle*, p. 321.

110 "Suppose there were men who had always lived underground": Cicero, quoting Aristotle, in *De Natura Deorum*, II, xxxvii, 95.

111 When Aristotle in the *Posterior Analytics*: Aristotle, *Posterior Analytics*, 71b9–13.

111 the acquisition of such knowledge: Following a distinction drawn by Alasdair MacIntyre between the Augustinian and Thomist traditions in philosophy, in *Three Rival Versions of Moral Enquiry* (Notre Dame: University of Notre Dame Press, 1990), p. 103.

111 "All men by nature desire to know": Aristotle, *Metaphysics*, A, 980a21.

111 "In everything natural there is something marvelous": Aristotle, *Parts of Animals*, 645a23.

111 "difficult to know whether one knows or not": Aristotle, *Posterior Analytics*, 76a26.

111 "As with most ancient personalities": Jaeger, *Aristotle*, p. 321.

SENECA

115 his foremost modern biographer: see Miriam Griffin, *Seneca: A Philosopher in*

Politics (New York: Oxford University Press, 1992). The most recent argument for Seneca's central importance as a philosopher *thinking* in Latin is Brad Inwood, *Reading Seneca* (New York: Oxford University Press, 2005). Cicero by contrast tends to gloss Greek terminology in Latin, in prose that lacks the sinewy bluntness of Seneca's.

116 a legend arose that Seneca had: Jerome, *De Viris Illustribus*, 12.

116 "the conscience of an empire": Pierre Grimal, *Sénèque, ou la conscience de l'Empire* (Paris: Belles Lettres, 1978). Though more guarded, Miriam Griffin leaves a comparable impression in *Seneca*.

116 "By what wisdom": Tacitus, *Annals*, 13, 42.4.

116 "though he censured the extravagance of others": Dio Cassius, *Roman History*, 61, 10, 3.

117 a reader must keep in mind: Cf. Grimal, *Sénèque*, pp. 105–106.

117 one of the primary aims of the *Moral Letters*: See Seneca, *Epistulae Morales*, CXVIII, 2–3.

117 "Never have I trusted Fortune": Seneca, *Dialogi*, XII, *De Consolatione ad Helviam*, v, 4.

118 "These men argue so well": Plutarch, *Lives*, "Cato the Elder," 22; cf. Miriam Griffin, "Philosophers, Politics, and Politicians," in Miriam Griffin and Jonathan Barnes, eds., *Philosophia Togata: Essays on Philosophy and Roman Society* (New York: Oxford University Press, 1989), pp. 2–5.

118 "pattern for imitation in perfect consistency with his teaching": Diogenes Laertius, *Lives*, "Zeno," VII, 10–11.

118 Stoicism evolved into a comprehensive system: For more in English, see J. M. Rist, *Stoic Philosophy* (Cambridge: Cambridge University Press, 1969); F. H. Sandbach, *The Stoics* (New York: Norton, 1975); Andrew Erskine, *The Hellenistic Stoa* (Ithaca: Cornell University Press, 1990); A. A. Long, *Stoic Studies* (Berkeley: University of California Press, 1996); Malcolm Schofield, *The Stoic Idea of the City* (Chicago: University of Chicago Press, 1999); and Brad Inwood, ed., *The Cambridge Companion to the Stoics* (New York: Cambridge University Press, 2003).

119 "a systematic plan of life": A. A. Long, *Epictetus* (New York: Oxford University Press, 2002), p. 20.

120 in the absence of a living scholarch: See David Sedley, "Plato's *Auctoritas* and the Rebirth of the Commentary Tradition," in Jonathan Barnes and Miriam Griffin, eds., *Philosophia Togata II: Plato and Aristotle at Rome* (New York: Oxford University Press, 1997), pp. 110–29.

120 a lively debate over the relative merits: See Griffin, *Seneca*, p. 315.

120 the "peculiar misery of the Roman people": Edward Gibbon, *The Decline and Fall of the Roman Empire*, 1:3.

120 "Fortune will totter back and forth": Seneca, *Thyestes*, 33–36 (in the translation of

Caryl Churchill [London: Nick Hern Books, 1993]).

121 the Stoic Attalus: See E. Vernon Arnold, *Roman Stoicism* (Cambridge: Cambridge University Press, 1911), esp. pp. 111–12.

121 "When I used to hear Attalus denouncing sin": Seneca, *Epistulae Morales*, CVIII, 13–15.

121 "My God, what strength and spirit" and "Sextius had this habit": Seneca, *Dialogi*, V, *De Ira*, III, xxxvi, 1–2.

121 "the man communicated a disposition": Seneca, *Epistuale Morales*, C, 3.

121 a philosopher in the "true and ancient" sense: Seneca, *Dialogi*, X, *De Brevitate Vitae*, x, 1.

122 "Philosophy is both contemplative and active": Seneca, *Epistuale Morales*, XCV, 10, 1; cf. Grimal, *Sénèque*, p. 12: "By combining the life of a Roman aristocrat with the inner odyssey of the heart, Seneca was not disloyal to philosophy, and certainly not to the tradition of Roman philosophy."

122 After hearing an especially eloquent speech: See Dio Cassius, *Annals of Rome*, LIX, 19; and Suetonius, *Gaius*, 53.

122 "His body was ugly": Giannozzo Manetti, *Vita Senecae*, 28. For an English translation of this *Vita*, see Manetti, *Biographical Writings*, trans. and ed. Stefano U. Baldassarri and Rolf Bagemihl (Cambridge, MA: Harvard University Press, 2003), 234–87.

122 it "was but a moment ago": Seneca, *Epistulae Morales*, XLIX, 2.

123 Julia Lavilla was rumored to have slept: Dio Cassius, *Annals of Rome*, LX, 8; and Suetonius, *Gaius*, 24.

123 a thinly veiled plea for a pardon: See Grimal, *Sénèque*, pp. 97–98.

123 In his *Annals*, Tacitus gives three reasons: Tacitus, *Annals*, 12.8.2.

124 "hid the works of the early rhetoricians": Suetonius, *Nero*, 52.

124 modern accounts of his philosophy: See, e.g., Griffin, *Seneca*, pp. 24–25n.

125 a chaotic world of infinite cruelty: See R. J. Tarrant, "Greek and Roman in Seneca's Tragedies," *Harvard Studies in Classical Philology* 97 (1995): 215–30; cf. William M. Calder III, "Seneca: Tragedian of Imperial Rome," *Classical Journal* 72, no. 1 (1976): 3.

125 The young Nero was an aspiring singer: Suetonius, *Nero*, 11.

125 "Finally, Rome had a thinker": Paul Veyne, *Seneca: The Life of a Stoic*, trans. David Sullivan (New York: Routledge, 2003), p. 9.

126 an officially appointed *amicus principis*: For the institution of the *amicus principis*, see J. A. Crook, *Consilium Principis* (Cambridge: Cambridge University Press, 1955), pp. 21–30.

126 "more often experienced free speaking": Tacitus, *Annals*, 15, 61, 1.

126 Nero impassively witnessed: Ibid., 13, 16, 3.

126 "to begin a reign with the murder of a potential rival": Veyne, *Seneca*, p. 19.

126 And a few months later: Griffin and Grimal both argue independently, and convincingly, that *De Clementia* must have been written *after* the murder of Britannicus.

127 "testify to the honorableness": Tacitus, *Annals*, 13, 11, 2.

127 "mirrors were invented": Seneca, *Naturales Quaestiones*, I, 17, 4.

127 "chosen to serve on earth as vicar of the gods": Seneca, *De Clementia*, I, 1, 1–4.

127 "It is the rarest praise": Ibid., 1, 5.

127 "In a position of unlimited power": Ibid., 11, 2.

127 "the general trend toward slaughter": Tacitus, *Annals*, 13, 2, 1.

128 "five good years" of Nero: The attribution to Trajan of Nero's "quinquennio" appears in two fourth-century works, Sextus Aurelius Victor's *Liber de Caesaribus* (5, 1–4) and *Epitome de Caesaribus* (5, 1–5).

128 "For while denouncing tyranny": Dio Cassius, *Roman History*, 61, 10.

128 In response to Sullius's attack: Grimal and Griffin (more guardedly) agree that the essay is probably a response, in part, to Sullius.

128 "increasing his mighty wealth": Tacitus, *Annals*, 14, 52.

128 amassing one of the greatest fortunes of his age: Pliny, *Natural History*, 14, 50–52; cf. Griffin, *Seneca*, pp. 287–89.

128 "I am not wise": Seneca, *De Vita Beata*, 17, 3.

128 "is not said of myself": Ibid., 17, 4.

128 "taunt Plato": Ibid., 27, 5.

129 the author, "who, looking from a height": Ibid., 28, 1.

129 "in the middle of the day": Tacitus, *Annals*, 14, 2, 1.

129 "sought from a female some defense": Ibid., 14, 2, 1.

129 "to kill her": Ibid., 14, 3, 1.

129 There was a long silence: Ibid., 14, 7, 3.

130 "Who could be found so dull": Ibid., 14, 11, 2.

130 a parody of the moral principles: See Griffin, *Seneca*, p. 171.

130 contend with mounting complaints: See Tacitus, *Annals*, 14, 52, 2–4.

130 "You have surrounded me with immeasurable favor": Ibid., 14, 53, 5; cf. Veyne, *Seneca*, p. 12, on wealth as a "kind of duty."

130 "Every surplus creates resentment": Tacitus, *Annals*, 14, 54, 1, 2–3.

131 "More has been held by men who are in no way equal": Ibid., 14, 55, 4–5.

131 "It will be neither your moderation": Ibid., 14, 56, 2.

131 "pleaded for retirement": Ibid., 15, 45, 3.

131 accept Seneca's offer of money: Dio Cassius, *Roman History*, 62, 25, 3.

131 a kind of inner exile: See Veyne, *Seneca*, p. 25.

132 Younger than Seneca by several years: See Griffin, *Seneca*, p. 91.

132 represented his last will and philosophical testament: See Seneca, *Epistulae Morales*, XXI, 5.

132 The remainder of the letters: See the useful summary in Griffin, *Seneca*, pp. 347–49.

132 The moral progress ascribed to Lucilius: Ibid., p. 417, expressing the conviction that the letters are fictional—a view contested by Grimal, but otherwise now widely accepted.

133 "I am ashamed of mankind": Seneca, *Epistulae Morales*, LXXVI, 4.

133 a "sick man": Ibid., XXVII, 1.

133 "His last years": Veyne, *Seneca*, p. 157.

133 "Nature weds us to no vice": Seneca, *Epistulae Morales*, XCIV, 56.

134 "Hasten to find me": Ibid., XXXV, 4.

134 "Let this be the kernel of my idea": Ibid., LXXV, 4.

134 "I will watch myself continually": Ibid., LXXXIII, 2.

134 "It is a great thing to play the role of man": Ibid., CXX, 22.

134 the histories of autobiography and self-examination: See Georg Misch, *A History of Autobiography in Antiquity*, trans. E. W. Dickes (Cambridge, MA: Harvard University Press, 1951), 2:404–35; A. A. Long, "Representation and the Self in Stoicism," in Stephen Everson, ed., *Companions to Ancient Thought 2: Psychology* (New York: Cambridge University Press, 1991), pp. 102–20; and Catherine Edwards, "Self-Scrutiny and Self-Transformation in Seneca's Letters," *Greece & Rome*, 2nd ser., 44, no. 1 (April 1997): 23–38.

134 "The task of testing oneself": Michel Foucault, *The Care of the Self*, trans. Robert Hurley (New York: Random House, 1986), p. 68. The passage is referring not just to Seneca but to Roman Stoicism generally, from Seneca to Epictetus and Marcus Aurelius.

135 It is Latin that allows him to link *voluntas*: See Charles H. Kahn, "Discovering the Will: From Aristotle to Augustine," in John M. Dillon and A. A. Long, eds., *The Question of "Eclecticism": Studies in Later Greek Philosophy* (Berkeley: University of California Press, 1988), pp. 234–59; a dissenting view, which minimizes the novelty of Seneca's notion of the will, is presented in Inwood, *Reading Seneca*, pp. 132–56.

135 "Conduct cannot be right": Seneca, *Epistulae Morales*, XCV, 57.

135 "So the wise man will develop virtue": Ibid., LXXXV, 40.

136 "Listen to me": Ibid., XXVII, 1.

136 letters that lay out his manifold shortcomings: See Michel Foucault, "Self Writing," in Foucault, *Ethics*, ed. Paul Rabinow (New York: New Press, 1997), pp. 207–22.

136 "If you like, live": Seneca, *Epistulae Morales*, LXX, 16.

136 "dying well": Ibid., LXX, 6, 14.

137 "It is a mistake": Ibid., LXXIII, 1.

137 an open letter to the emperor: See Veyne, *Seneca*, pp. 160–63, who argues that the *Letters* are "an oppositional work."

137 Nero had first tried to poison Seneca: Tacitus, *Annals*, 15, 45, 3.
137 Nero's paranoia, already pronounced: See Miriam T. Griffin, *Nero: The End of a Dynasty* (New Haven: Yale University Press, 1985), pp. 166–70.
137 "no signs of panic": Tacitus, *Annals*, 15, 61, 2.
137 Seneca "turned to his friends": Ibid., 15, 62, 1–2.
138 "'In such a brave outcome as this'": Ibid., 15, 63, 2.
138 The philosopher was frail: Ibid., 15, 63, 3.
138 "by which those condemned by the Athenians' public court": Ibid., 15, 64, 3; cf. the account in Dio Cassius, *Roman History*, 62, 25.
138 "asphyxiated by the steam": Tacitus, *Annals*, 15, 64, 4.
138 In the years that followed, the practice of philosophy: See Miriam T. Griffin, "Philosophy, Politics, and Politicians," in Griffin and Barnes, *Philosophia Togata*, pp. 19–22.
139 "Both were men most zealous": Manetti, *Vita Senecae*, 46.

AUGUSTINE

142 "At once, with the last words": Augustine, *Confessions*, VIII, xii, 29.
144 "There is more than one road to wisdom": Augustine, *Soliloquies*, I, xiii, 23: an assertion explicitly disavowed years later in his *Retractiones*, I, iv, 3.
144 "a lust for experimenting and knowing": Augustine, *Confessions*, X, xxxv, 55.
144 Augustine thought "in questions": Jaspers, *The Great Philosophers*, 1:185.
145 the surviving documentation: See Peter Brown, *Augustine of Hippo* (Berkeley: University of California Press, 2000); and James J. O'Donnell, *Augustine* (New York: Harper, 2005); a great short biography is Garry Wills, *Saint Augustine* (New York: Viking, 1999).
145 "When I was still a boy": Augustine, *Confessions*, I, xi, 17.
146 "weighed the precise meaning of every word": Augustine, *De Beata Vita*, iv, 31.
146 "Suddenly, all empty hope for my career": Augustine, *Confessions*, III, iv, 7.
146 Mani was a Gnostic visionary: See Kurt Rudolph, *Gnosis*, trans. Robert McLachlan Wilson (San Francisco: Harper, 1983), pp. 329–31.
147 "Honor to the Perfect Man": C.R.C. Allberry, *A Manichaean Psalm-Book*, vol. II, part II (Stuttgart: Kohlhammer, 1938), pp. 42, 20–25.
148 "I noticed, repeatedly, in the sermons": Augustine, *De Beata Vita*, i, 4.
148 This circle at first involved only old friends: See Augustine, *Confessions*, VI, vii, 11.
149 "for I was so submerged and blinded": Ibid., VI, xvi, 26.
149 "sins multiplied": Ibid., VI, xv, 25.
149 Mallius Theodorus, a committed Neoplatonist: See Pierre Courcelle, *Late Latin Writers and Their Greek Sources*, trans. Harry E. Wedeck (Cambridge, MA: Harvard University Press, 1969), p. 138.

149 Ambrose, for one, sternly discouraged: See Brown, *Augustine of Hippo*, p. 486.

149 Augustine finally embarked on a serious study: See Pierre Courcelle, *Recherches sur les Confessions de Saint Augustin* (Paris: Boccard, 1968), which led to a reevaluation of the importance of Plotinus to Augustine. In his English translation of the *Confessions* (New York: Oxford University Press, 1991), Henry Chadwick carefully annotates all the blind references to Plotinus in the text. Cf. the commentary by James J. O'Donnell, *Augustine: Confessions* (New York: Oxford University Press, 1992), 2:413–18, which is more skeptical about the importance of Plotinus.

150 "We thought that the flame": Augustine, *Contra Academicos*, 2, 2, 5.

150 "Plotinus," the *vita* starts: Porphyry, *Vita Plotini*, 1.

150 "Persian methods": Ibid., 3.

150 "Plotinus possessed by birth": Ibid., 10.

151 "It is for those Beings to come to me": Ibid., 10, 11.

151 "filled with God": Plotinus, *Enneads*, VI, 9, 11.

151 "Go back inside yourself and look": Ibid., I, 6, 9, 7–24, using the English translation of Michael Chase of Pierre Hadot, *Plotinus or the Simplicity of Vision* (Chicago: University of Chicago Press, 1993), p. 21.

152 "By the Platonic books," Augustine, *Confessions*, VII, x, 16, using the wonderfully readable English translation by Henry Chadwick. Cf. the account in *De Beata Vita*, 4, 35, composed soon after his mystic experience. In quoting from the *Confessions*, I have deliberately omitted a crucial early clause in this long passage ("I entered into my innermost citadel *and was given power to do so because you had become my helper*"), because I think it acknowledges the necessity of grace in retrospect, presumably in order to exonerate Augustine of the sin of pride. This long passage is replete with allusions to and paraphrases of the *Enneads* of Plotinus; see the annotations in Chadwick, and the comments in O'Donnell, *Augustine: Confessions*, 2:436. I take this passage in the *Confessions* to be an account of bringing about the presence of God visibly, using the introspective spiritual exercises of Plotinus—i.e., a theurgy (and here I disagree with O'Donnell, 2:415).

152 "Whatever things exist are good": Augustine, *Confessions*, VII, xii, 18.

152 "a perversity of will": Ibid., VII, xvi, 22.

152 "My God, I was caught up to you": Ibid., VII, xvii, 23.

152 "a desire for that of which I had the aroma": Ibid.

153 "looked back on the religion implanted in us": Augustine, *Contra Academicos*, 2, 2, 5.

153 He read again Paul's letters: See Augustine, *Confessions*, VIII, i, 1–ii, 3; cf. Wills, *Saint Augustine*, pp. 44–45, and Brown, *Augustine of Hippo*, p. 97.

153 "Platonopolis": Porphyry, *Vita Plotini*, 12.

153 In the late summer of 386: On the context for the philosophical community at Cassiciacum, see Dennis E. Trout, "Augustine at Cassiciacum: *Otium Honestum* and

the Social Dimensions of Christianity," *Vigiliae Christianae* 42 (1988): 132–46.

154 "This philosophy is not of this world": Augustine, *Contra Academicos*, 3, 19, 42.

154 an ideal of "friendship": Ibid., 3, 6, 13; cf. Cicero, *On Friendship*, 6, 20.

154 written down by a stenographer: See Augustine, *De Beata Vita*, 2, 15.

154 by dint of a "rational choice": Ibid., 1, 1.

154 "monstrous pride": Augustine, *Confessions*, VII, ix, 13.

155 "For a long time": Augustine, *Soliloquies*, I, 1, 3.

155 "I want to know God and the soul": Ibid., II, 14, 25–26; cf. the reference to Plato reborn in Plotinus in Augustine, *Contra Academicos*, 3, 18, 43. Where I imply that there is an allusion to Plotinus, other scholars find a reference either to Mallius Theodorus or to Ambrose: see O'Donnell, *Augustine: Confessions*, 2:341–43.

155 "believe your reasoning": Augustine, *Soliloquies*, II, 19, 33.

155 "Believe in God": Ibid., I, 15, 30.

156 a hagiographic life of the famous desert anchorite: See Athanasius, *The Life of St. Antony*, trans. Robert T. Meyer (Westminster, MD: Newman Press, 1950).

156 "No small part of the work of late antique hagiography": Peter Brown, *Authority and the Sacred* (New York: Cambridge University Press, 1995), p. 68.

156 Augustine symbolically reverses Adam's exile: See Wills, *Saint Augustine*, p. 39.

157 "meditated taking flight": Augustine, *Confessions*, X, xliii, 70.

157 "He did not sell all he had": O'Donnell, *Augustine*, p. 61.

157 After a short period in Ostia: See Brown, *Augustine of Hippo*, p. 126.

158 "the voice of Christ": Nebridius to Augustine, 389, *Epistulae*, VI.

158 "In the inward man dwells truth": Augustine, *De Vera Religione*, xxix, 72, using the translation of Catherine Conybeare.

158 He embodied the Word of God: John 1:14.

158 "Catholics were by now aware" to "he was weeping copiously": Possidius, *Sancta Augustini Vita Scripta*, iv.

159 "accusation of oneself": Augustine, *Sermons*, 67, 2, quoted in Brown, *Augustine of Hippo*, p. 169.

159 "Sometimes you cause me to enter": Augustine, *Confessions*, X, xl, 65.

159 "if they wish," all people who trust: Augustine, *On Genesis: A Refutation of the Manichees*, I, 3, 6.

160 "prepared by God": Augustine, *Retractiones*, I, 10; II, 27.

160 "The storms of incoherent events": Augustine, *Confessions*, XI, xxix, 39.

160 "I cannot judge rightly": Ibid., X, xxxvii, 60, using the English translation of Garry Wills.

161 "What then am I, my God?": Ibid., X, xvii, 26.

161 "By thinking we, as it were, gather together": Ibid., X, xi, 18, using the English translation of Henry Chadwick.

161 "his clothes and food, and bedclothes": Possidius, *Sancta Augustini Vita Scripta*, xxii.

162 He guarded his chastity: See ibid., xxvi.

162 "emotions that affected him intimately": Brown, *Augustine of Hippo*, p. 200.

162 show heretics "by reasoned argument": Possidius, *Sancta Augustini Vita Scripta*, ix.

162 forced back into the cave of common humanity: Cf. Augustine, *Contra Academicos*, 3, 17, 37.

162 "things I could not see": Augustine, *Confessions*, VI, v, 7; cf. Augustine, *Contra Academicos*, 3, 20, 43.

162 perplexed "as to the way": Augustine to Paulinus, 408, *Epistulae*, XCV, 5, 6.

163 "Seeing that God, by a hidden, though just, disposition": Augustine, *Epistles*, CCIV (translated in Brown, *Augustine of Hippo*, p. 336).

163 "rules for behavior and the conduct of a holy life": Pelagius, *ad Demetriadem*, 2 (quoted in Brown, *Augustine of Hippo*, p. 342).

164 "That is why the Scripture says": Augustine, *City of God*, XIX, 4, glossing Habakkuk 2:4 and Romans 1:17.

164 "For no one is known to another": Augustine to Proba, 412, *Epistulae*, CXXX, ii, 4, quoting 1 Corinthians 4:5.

164 "If Rome can perish": Jerome, quoted in Brown, *Augustine of Hippo*, p. 288.

165 "With God, the crimes": Augustine to Lord Volusianus, 412, *Epistulae*, CXXXVII, v, 20.

165 preaching that the Lord's "wrath: Augustine, *Frang.* 2, 8 (quoted in Brown, *Augustine of Hippo*, p. 246).

165 "Fallen man had come to need restraint": Brown, *Augustine of Hippo*, p. 234.

165 ridicules the Neoplatonist Porphyry: Augustine, *City of God*, X, 32.

165 "harmony of the Scriptures": Ibid., XVIII, 41; but cf. XXII, 22, where Augustine, after conceding that philosophy may have consoled a few pagans, speaks of Christianity as "true philosophy."

165 "impressive reasoning of the wise": Ibid., XXII, 4, going on to quote Psalms 94:11.

166 "As far as man's nature is concerned": Augustine, *Retractiones*, 1, 1, 2.

166 "by God's will and permission": Possidius, *Sancta Augustini Vita Scripta*, xxviii.

166 "My prayer to God": Ibid., xxix.

166 "cities overthrown and destroyed": Ibid., xxviii.

166 "the maxim of a certain wise man": Ibid., going on to paraphrase without attribution Plotinus, *Enneads*, I, iv, 7.

167 he would look up, "gazing at them": Ibid., xxxi.

167 "he made no will": Ibid.

167 "No one can read what he wrote on theology": Ibid.

168 "It was the tragic destiny of Christianity": Wilhelm Dilthey, *Introduction to the*

Human Sciences, trans. Ramon J. Betanzos (Detroit: Wayne State University Press, 1988), II, sec. 3, 2: 233.

168 in the Catholic West: In the Muslim world, by contrast, the philosophical life epitomized by Socrates and Plato continued to influence religious thinkers such as Shihab al-Din Suhrawardi, a twelfth-century Sufi mystic and the author of *The Philosophical Illuminations*.

MONTAIGNE

170 "There is no man so good": Montaigne, *Essays*, III, 9, p. 990 (757). Page references are to the French edition of Villey and (in parentheses) the English translation of Frame: Montaigne, *Les Essais*, ed. Pierre Villey and V.-L. Saulnier, 3 vols. (Paris: Presses Universitaires de France, 1965), and Montaigne, *Essays*, in *The Complete Works*, trans. Donald M. Frame (Stanford: Stanford University Press, 1957). The Everyman edition of Frame, *Complete Works*, published in 2003, has different pagination.

171 "They want to get out of themselves": Montaigne, *Essays*, III, 13, p. 1115 (856).

172 "there is no beast in the world": Montaigne, *Essays*, II, 19, p. 671 (509), paraphrasing the emperor Julian. In context, Montaigne is writing about "freedom of conscience" and about the violence of some schismatics in ancient and modern Christianity.

172 the earliest of the *Essays* are modeled: On Montaigne's use of Plutarch, Machiavelli, and Erasmus, the best source is Hugo Friedrich, *Montaigne*, trans. Dawn Eng (Berkeley: University of California Press, 1991), esp. pp. 184–85, 197–99, 307–309. For the popularity and different editions of the *Adages*, see William Barker, ed., *The Adages of Erasmus* (Toronto: University of Toronto Press, 2001).

172 "I am myself the matter of my book": Montaigne, *Essays*, "To the Reader," p. 3 (2).

172 "My actions," he writes: Ibid., II, 6, p. 379 (274). Cf. Xenophon, *Memorabilia*, IV, iv, 10.

173 the outlines of his life, both public and private: See, for example, Donald M. Frame, *Montaigne: A Biography* (New York: Harcourt, 1965), which I have relied on for biographical details, supplemented by Roger Trinquet, *La jeunesse de Montaigne: Ses origines familiales, son enfance et ses études* (Paris: Nizet, 1973). See also Madeleine Lazard, *Michel de Montaigne* (Paris: Fayard, 1992) and Claude-Gilbert Dubois, *Montaigne et Henri IV* (Biarritz: J&D Editions, 1996).

174 Thus began a civil war between Catholics and Huguenots: See Mack P. Holt, *The French Wars of Religion, 1562–1629* (New York: Cambridge University Press, 1995).

174 it is arguable that Montaigne: The conclusions of Cecil Roth, "The Jewish Ancestry of Michel de Montaigne," *Personalities and Events in Jewish History* (Philadelphia: Jewish Publication Society, 1953), pp. 212–25, are carefully qualified in

Trinquet, *La jeunesse de Montaigne*, pp. 117–59.

174 "custom and length of time": Montaigne, *Essays*, I, 14, p. 54 (36).

174 learned the language "without artificial means": Ibid., I, 26, p. 173 (128).

174 "we must wage war with ourselves": Erasmus, *Enchiridion militis Christiani* (The Handbook of a Christian Knight), 3: "The crown of wisdom is that you know yourself," in *The Essential Erasmus*, trans. John P. Dolan (New York: New American Library, 1964), p. 40. In this widely read text, first published in 1503, Erasmus urges readers to combine classical philosophical forms of self-examination with a close reading of the Bible, in order to create a new, more inward and reflective form of Christian spirituality.

175 Montaigne next studied law: It has been argued that this legal training helps to explain some distinctive features of Montaigne's style of writing: See André Tournon, *Montaigne: La glose et l'essai* (Paris: Champion, 2000).

175 "I have a distaste for mastery": Montaigne, *Essays*, III, p. 917 (700). Cf. Frame, *Montaigne: A Biography*, p. 64: "He would rather be importunate and indiscreet than a dissimulating flatterer."

175 "Now laws remain in credit": Montaigne, *Essays*, III, 13, p. 1072 (821).

176 La Boétie was a true Renaissance man: See Paul Bonnefon, introduction to Étienne de La Boétie, *Oeuvres Complètes* (Bordeaux, 1892); and Murray Rothbard, introduction to Étienne de La Boétie, *The Discourse of Voluntary Servitude*, trans. Harry Kurz (New York: Free Life Editions, 1975).

176 "self-imposed immaturity": Kant, "What Is Enlightenment?" (1783).

176 "Particularly in the matter of natural gifts": Montaigne, *Essays*, I, 28, pp. 184 (135); 188 (139).

177 philosophy in Montaigne's day: See Cesare Vasoli, "The Renaissance Concept of Philosophy," in Charles B. Schmitt, ed., *The Cambridge History of Renaissance Philosophy* (New York: Cambridge University Press, 1988), pp. 57–74.

177 trying to emulate Socrates: See the epigraph to Erasmus, *Enchiridion Militis Christiani*: "Let this book lead to a theological life rather than theological disputation."

177 a "confusing morass of court factions": Holt, *French Wars of Religion*, p. 1.

178 La Boétie accompanied troops: See Harry Kurz, "Montaigne and La Boétie in the Chapter on Friendship," *PMLA* 65, no. 4 (June 1950): 494.

178 In a letter to his father: Montaigne to his father [1563?] on the death of La Boétie, Letter 2 (published in 1570).

179 "In the year of Christ 1571": Cited in Villey, Montaigne, *Essays*, I, p. xxxiv.

179 "It was a melancholy humor": Montaigne, *Essays*, II, 8, p. 385 (278).

180 "the tenderest, sweetest, and closest companion": Cited in Frame, *Montaigne*, p. 80.

180 "My trade and my art is living": Montaigne, *Essays*, II, 6, p. 379 (274).

180 "to know himself and to die well": Ibid., I, 26, p. 159 (117).

180 "His mind was molded in the pattern": Ibid., I, 28, p. 194 (144).

180 "lofty, virtuous, and full of very certain resolution": Montaigne to his father on the death of La Boétie, Letter 2.

180 Christian humanist: For an astute extended look at Montaigne's differences with Christian Neoplatonism and Augustine, see Friedrich, *Montaigne*, pp. 214–19.

181 to bear arms in his king's army: See Lazard, *Michel de Montaigne*, pp. 217–25.

182 Montaigne's conviction, as reported by de Thou: Jacques-Auguste de Thou, *Memoirs*, quoted in Frame, *Montaigne*, pp. 140–41.

182 sensational stories about the villains: See Robert M. Kingdon, *Myths About the St. Bartholomew's Day Massacres, 1572–1576* (Cambridge, MA: Harvard University Press, 1988).

183 Montaigne changed his plan: See Roger Trinquet, "Montaigne et la divulgation du *Contr'Un*," *Bulletin de la Société des Amis de Montaigne*, 3rd series, no. 29 (January–March 1964): 9–10.

183 "so that the memory of the author may not be damaged": Montaigne, *Essays*, I, 28, p. 194 (144).

183 a master of oblique criticism: On Montaigne's implicit criticism of the Parlement of Bordeaux, see George Hoffmann, *Montaigne's Career* (New York: Clarendon Press, 1998), p. 136.

183 Modern scholars agree: See Frame, *Montaigne*, p. 171.

184 It is true, as modern scholars have pointed out: See Friedrich, *Montaigne*, pp. 97–98.

184 "In order to 'defend' Sebond's thesis": Richard H. Popkin, *The History of Scepticism from Erasmus to Descartes* (New York: Humanities Press, 1964), p. 46. Cf. the outlines offered in Pierre Villey's edition of the *Essais*, p. 433; the outline in Frame, *Montaigne*, pp. 172–73; and the structural account in Jean Starobinski, *Montaigne in Motion*, trans. Arthur Goldhammer (Chicago: University of Chicago Press, 1985), pp. 131–32.

184 "and that no one can achieve any certainty": Popkin, *History of Scepticism*, p. 46.

185 "Our mind is an erratic, dangerous, and heedless tool": Montaigne, *Essays*, II, 12, p. 559 (419).

186 "I have put all my efforts into forming my life": Ibid., II, 37, p. 784 (596).

186 Montaigne's business associate: See Hoffmann, *Montaigne's Career*, esp. pp. 63–83.

187 "dedicated . . . to the private convenience": Montaigne, *Essays*, "Au lecteur," p. 3 (2).

187 "Montaigne responds to the contemporary crisis": David Quint, *Montaigne and the Quality of Mercy* (Princeton: Princeton University Press, 1998), p. ix.

187 "Whom shall we believe": Montaigne, *Essays*, II, 18, p. 666 (505).

187 "We owe ourselves in part to society": Ibid., II, 18, p. 665 (504).

188 "all the little thoughts": Ibid.

188 "I do not portray being": Ibid., III, 2, p. 805 (611).

188 "There is no occupation so pleasant as the military": Ibid., III, 13, p. 1096 (841).

189 "in the loudest and most magisterial voice": Montaigne, *Travel Journal*, "Italy: Rome" (November 20, 1580–April 19, 1581), in *The Complete Works*, Everyman edition (New York: Knopf, 2003), p. 1156.

189 "redress what I should see was in bad taste": Ibid., p. 1166.

189 Montaigne visited a synagogue: Ibid., pp. 1152–53.

189 "as they were simply an account": La Croix du Maine, *Bibliothèque françoise*, 1584, quoted in Frame, *Montaigne*, pp. 208, 371n.

189 "enlarged by a third book": From the title page to the fifth edition, quoted ibid., p. 250.

190 "a man free in spirit": de Thou, quoted ibid., p. 229.

190 a discreet advocate of clemency and of mercy: These aspects of Montaigne's work are brilliantly illuminated in Quint, *Montaigne and the Quality of Mercy*, and also Geralde Nakam, *Les Essais de Montaigne, miroir et procès de leur temps* (Paris: H. Champion, 2001).

191 "saw his role essentially as that of a negotiator": Max Horkheimer, "Montaigne and the Function of Skepticism" (1938), in Horkheimer, *Between Philosophy and Social Science*, trans. G. Frederick Hunter, Matthew S. Kramer, and John Torpey (Cambridge, MA: MIT Press, 1993), p. 269.

191 nice things about the notorious Alcibiades: Montaigne, *Essays*, I, 26, p. 167 (124), and II, 36, pp. 753, 757 (570, 573). The passages on Alcibiades date from all periods of the book's composition, both early and late.

192 "throughout my life, in any public activity": Plato, *Apology*, 33a.

192 "We are all patchwork": Montaigne, *Essays*, II, 1, p. 337 (244).

192 "love virtue too much": Ibid., I, 30, p. 197 (146).

192 "fairest souls": Ibid., III, 3, p. 818 (621).

192 "Be not wiser than you should": Romans 12:3, cited ibid., I, 30, p. 197 (146).

192 "I do not know if the ardor that is born of spite": Ibid., II, 12, pp. 566–67 (426).

192 "The best and soundest side": Ibid., II, 19, p. 668 (506).

192 he believes no such thing: See, e.g., ibid., II, 12, p. 565 (425), on the pliability of reason.

193 "I was belabored from every quarter": Ibid., III, 12, p. 1044 (798).

193 "I am no philosopher": Ibid., III, 9, p. 950 (725).

193 "A new figure": Ibid., II, 12, p. 546 (409), from a passage added to the 1588 edition of the book. A recent reading of Montaigne that shows why this claim is worth taking seriously is Ann Hartle, *Michel de Montaigne: Accidental Philosopher* (New York: Cambridge University Press, 2003). Cf. André Comte-Sponville, *"Je ne suis pas philosophe": Montaigne et la philosophie* (Paris: H. Champion, 1993).

193 "It is a thorny undertaking": Montaigne, *Essays*, II, 6, p. 378 (273).

194 "the abyss of human consciousness": Augustine, *Confessions*, X, i, 1.

194 "I have not, like Socrates": Montaigne, *Essays*, III, 12, p. 1059 (811).

195 *"If we could view that expanse of countries"*: Ibid., III, 6, p. 907 (692). In the French *Essais*, the passage is in Latin, and in italics and between quotation marks. Without attribution, Montaigne here rewrites a passage from a dialogue by Cicero, *De Natura Deorum*, I, xx. In context, the speaker in Cicero's dialogue, an avowed Epicurean, is ridiculing Stoic notions of God as a living, rational being presiding over a providentially ordered cosmos.

195 And in his *Essays*, Montaigne proves it: See Montaigne, *Essays*, I, 5, p. 25 (16), and I, 44, p. 272 (199).

195 "each man bears the entire form": Ibid., III, 2, p. 805 (611). See also ibid., III, 1, p. 795 (603).

196 To the end of his life, he remained an intermediary: See Frame, *Montaigne*, pp. 269–76.

196 "When the priest came to the elevation of the *Corpus Domini*": Étienne Pasquier, quoted ibid., p. 305.

196 "the true pattern": Pierre de Brach, quoted ibid.

197 "another Seneca in our language": Étienne Pasquier, "À M. de Pelgé, conseiller du roi et maître en sa chambre des comptes de Paris," in Pasquier, *Oeuvres choisies*, ed. Léon Feugère (Geneva: Slatkine, 1968), p. 394.

DESCARTES

200 "What can cause more harm": See Richard Watson, *Cogito, Ergo Sum: The Life of René Descartes* (Boston: Godine, 2002), p. 281ff.

201 "the very idea of a law of nature": Daniel Garber, "Voetius and Other Voids," *Times Literary Supplement*, September 8, 2006, p. 8.

201 a hero of unfettered intellect: See, e.g., G.W.F. Hegel, *Lectures on the History of Philosophy*, trans. E. S. Haldane (London, 1896), 3:224–25.

202 "The Lord has made three marvels": Descartes, *Cogitationes Privatae*, AT X, 218; *PW*, I, p. 5.

202 "all those to whom God has given": Descartes to Mersenne, April 15, 1630, AT I, 144; *PW* III, p. 22.

202 "Death weighs on him who is known to all": Descartes to Chanut, November 1, 1646, AT IV, 537; *PW* III, p. 300, quoting Seneca, *Thyestes*, 401–403.

202 "the mathematical truths which you call eternal": Descartes to Mersenne, April 15, 1630, AT I, 145; *PW* III, pp. 22–23.

202 "to the largest extent possible": Bernard Williams, "Philosophy as a Humanistic Discipline," in Williams, *Philosophy as a Humanistic Discipline* (Princeton: Princeton University Press, 2006), p. 184, glossing a central claim of his book *Descartes: The Project of Pure Enquiry*, 2d ed. (New York: Routledge, 2005).

202 "a general science that explains all": Descartes, *Rules for the Direction of the*

Mind, Rule Four, AT X, 378; *PW* I, p. 19.

203 René was born: Here and elsewhere, biographical details are drawn from the original source, Adrien Baillet, *La Vie de Monsieur Des-Cartes* (Paris, 1691), who had access to many papers that have since been lost, and from three recent works in English: Steven Gaukroger, *Descartes: An Intellectual Biography* (New York: Oxford University Press, 1995), very good on the historical and cultural context; Desmond M. Clarke, *Descartes: A Biography* (New York: Cambridge University Press, 2006), strong on the science, weaker on the philosophy; and Richard Watson, *Cogito, Ergo Sum: The Life of René Descartes* (Boston: Godine 2002), the liveliest, and most pungent, on the character of Descartes.

204 "smell the smoke": from the Fifth Exercise of the First Week, as specified in *The Spiritual Exercises of St. Ignatius*. See also the reconstruction of the spiritual aspects of "Descartes au collège" in Sophie Jama, *La Nuit de songes de René Descartes* (Paris: Aubier, 1998).

204 "Sonnet on the death of the king Henry the Great": See Stephen Toulmin, *Cosmopolis: The Hidden Agenda of Modernity* (New York: Free Press, 1990). Toulmin reprints and analyzes the sonnet on pp. 56–62, 215.

204 the eighteen-year-old math whiz became a cardsharp: Baillet, *La Vie de Monsieur Des-Cartes*, 1:36.

205 his own private *het collegium mechanicum*: See Margaret C. Jacob, *Scientific Culture and the Making of the Industrial West* (New York: Oxford University Press, 1997), pp. 40–41, and the reviews of Klaas van Berkel, *Isaac Beeckman (1588–1637) en de mechanisering van het wereldbeeld* by Lettie S. Multhauf, in *Technology and Culture* 25, no. 2 (April 1984): 334–35, and by W. D. Hackman in *Isis* 76, no. 2 (June 1985): 273–74.

206 "It was you alone": Descartes to Beeckman, April 23, 1619, AT X, 163; *PW* III, p. 4.

206 the Rosicrucians mixed mathematical research: See Frances Yates, *The Rosicrucian Enlightenment* (New York: Routledge, 1972).

206 "The great ferment of alchemists": Watson, *Cogito, Ergo Sum*, p. 107.

207 though rarely given a central role in modern accounts: Among recent biographers, only Gaukroger takes the dreams seriously—only to suggest that they show that Descartes had suffered a nervous breakdown.

207 Three different sources document the event: The most authoritative assessment of these documents is John R. Cole, *The Olympian Dreams & Youthful Rebellion of René Descartes* (Urbana: University of Illinois Press, 1992). His interpretation is usefully supplemented by Alice Browne, "Descartes's Dreams," *Journal of the Warburg and Courtauld Institutes* 40 (1977): 256–73; Jama, *La Nuit de songes de René Descartes*; and Anthony Grafton, "Traditions of Conversion: Descartes and His Demon," *Occasional Papers of the Doreen B. Townsend Center for the Humanities*, no. 22 (2000).

207 "I stayed all day shut up alone": Descartes, *Discourse on the Method*, Part Two, AT VI, 11; *PW* I, p. 116.
207 "nothing can be imagined which is too strange": Ibid., AT VI, 16; *PW* I, p. 118.
207 "considered the customs of other men": Ibid., Part One, AT VI, 10; *PW* I, p. 115.
207 "study also myself": Ibid., p. 116.
207 "And so I thought": Ibid., Part Two, AT VI, 12–13; *PW* I, p. 117.
208 "all at one go": Ibid., AT VI, 13–14; *PW* I, p. 117.
208 "like a man who walks alone": Ibid., AT VI, 16; *PW* I, p. 119.
208 "provisional moral code": Ibid., Part Three, AT VI, 22–27; *PW* I, pp. 122–24.
208 "nothing was left": Baillet, *La Vie de Monsieur Des-Cartes*, 1:81.
209 He awoke feeling a "real pain": Ibid., 1:82.
209 When he "opened his eyes": Ibid.
209 "What way in life shall I follow?": Ibid., 1:83.
209 "all the Sciences gathered together": Ibid., 1:83–84.
209 "Spirit of God": Ibid., 1:84–85.
210 Descartes would defy his father: See Cole's interpretation in *Olympian Dreams*, which on this point I find convincing.
210 "'God separated the light from the darkness'" and "So far, I have been a spectator": Descartes, *Early Writings*, AT X, 213; *PW* I, p. 2.
210 "the good angels hold cheap all the knowledge": Augustine, *City of God*, IX, 22; cf. XIX, 4, on the special vulnerability to demonic possession of those pagan philosophers who claimed to be able to attain the Supreme Good by themselves, without God's grace.
210 "it is characteristic of the evil one": Ignatius, *The Spiritual Exercises*, Rules for the Discernment, Second Week, 4.
211 "witch-craze": H. R. Trevor-Roper, "The European Witch-Craze of the Sixteenth and Seventeenth Centuries," in *The Crisis of the Seventeenth Century: Religion, the Reformation and Social Change* (New York: Harper, 1968).
211 "some malicious demon": Descartes, *Meditations*, AT VII, 22; *PW* II, p. 15.
211 He starts with "intuition": Descartes, *Rules for the Direction of the Mind*, Rule Twelve, AT X, 425–27; *PW* I, pp. 48–49.
211 a leading advocate for the education of women: See Baillet, *La Vie de Monsieur Des-Cartes*, 2:433–34.
212 he witnessed the surrender of the Huguenot redoubt: Ibid., 1:155–60.
213 Mersenne also advocated a strong doctrine of matter: See Gaukroger, *Descartes*, pp. 146–52.
213 as "an obligation of conscience": Baillet, *La Vie de Monsieur Des-Cartes*, 1:166.
213 These were fraught years: See Jacob, *Scientific Culture*, p. 38; and Gaukroger, *Descartes*, p. 136.
214 "more than a worthwhile experiment in philosophical method": Toulmin, *Cos-*

mopolis, p. 80.

214 "I have been able to lead a life as solitary": Descartes, *Discourse on the Method*, IV, AT VI, 31; *PW* I, p. 126.

214 "The good life Descartes maintained": Watson, *Cogito, Ergo Sum*, p. 151.

214 "Rather than explaining any one phenomenon": Descartes to Mersenne, November 13, 1629, AT I, 70; *PW* III, pp. 7–8.

215 "found a way of proving metaphysical truths": Descartes to Mersenne, April 15, 1630, AT I, 144; *PW* III, p. 22.

215 "nothing but a statue or machine": Descartes, *Treatise on Man*, AT XI, 120; *PW* I, p. 99.

215 "caught up in the heavens": Descartes to Mersenne, May 10, 1632, AT I, 250; *PW* III, pp. 37–38.

215 "I had intended to send you *Le Monde*" to "such an integral part of my treatise": Descartes to Mersenne, end of November 1633, AT I, 270–72; *PW* III, pp. 40–41.

216 "I desire to live in peace": Descartes to Mersenne, April 1634, AT I, 286; *PW* III, p. 43.

216 "The mistake that he had made one time in his life": Baillet, *La Vie de Monsieur Des-Cartes*, 2:502.

216 "those who get them after my death": Descartes, *Discourse on the Method*, VI, AT VI, 66; *PW* I, p. 145.

217 In 1628, he had promised some friends: See Gaukroger, *Descartes*, p. 181.

217 "history or, if you prefer, a fable": Descartes, *Discourse on the Method*, I, AT VI, 4; *PW* I, p. 112.

217 "I always try to lean towards diffidence": Ibid., I, AT VI, 3–4; *PW* I, p. 112.

217 "undertake studies within myself": Ibid., I, AT VI, 5, 10; *PW* I, p. 113.

217 "long chains of very simple and easy reasonings": Ibid., II, AT VI, 19; *PW* I, p. 120.

218 in his original autobiographical narrative: Ibid., III, AT VI, 28; *PW* I, p. 125.

218 "*I think, therefore I am*": Ibid., IV, AT VI, 32; *PW* I, p. 127. Cf. Augustine, *De libero arbitrio voluntatis*, II, 3, 20–21, and Augustine, *City of God*, XI, 24.

218 "is not a piece of reasoning": Paul Valéry, from a 1910 notebook commenting on Descartes, in Paul Valéry, *Masters and Friends*, trans. Martin Turnell, vol. 9, *The Collected Works of Paul Valéry* (Princeton: Princeton University Press, 1968), p. 309.

218 "at least as certain as any geometrical proof": Descartes, *Discourse on the Method*, IV, AT VI, 33, 36; *PW* I, pp. 127, 129.

218 "questions that are being debated": Ibid., V, AT VI, 40; *PW* I, p. 131.

218 "through this philosophy we could know": Ibid., VI, AT VI, 62; *PW* I, pp. 142–43.

219 "The Delphic motto, 'Know Thyself!'": Edmund Husserl, *Cartesian Meditations*, trans. Dorion Cairns (The Hague: M. Nijhoff, 1960), p. 157.

219 "Do not go out": Augustine, *De vera religione*, xxxix, 72. For Augustine's influ-

ence on Descartes more generally, see Stephen Menn, *Descartes and Augustine* (New York: Cambridge University Press, 1998).

219 "general notions in physics": Descartes, *Discourse on the Method*, V, AT VI, 61; *PW* I, p. 142.

219 "became the most famous text": Jacob, *Scientific Culture*, p. 43.

220 so transparently unconvincing: The most elaborate form of this critique was made by the Calvinist Voetius, see Watson, *Cogito, Ergo Sum*, pp. 224–30.

220 propositions that a good Catholic like himself will also accept: Descartes, *Meditations*, Dedicatory letter to the Sorbonne, AT VII, 2; *PW* II, p. 3.

220 "not God, who is supremely good": Ibid., I, AT VII, 22; *PW* II, p. 15.

221 "the true God": Ibid., IV, AT VII, 53; *PW* II, p. 37.

221 "they possess all the properties": Ibid., VI, AT VII, 79–80; *PW* II, p. 55.

221 the "startling possibility": Popkin, *History of Scepticism*, p. 185. Cf. [Bourdin] in Descartes, *Meditations*, Seventh Set of Objections with Replies, AT VII, 470–71; *PW* II, pp. 316–17.

222 he "should not devote so much attention": Conversation with Burman, April 16, 1648, AT V, 165; *PW* III, p. 346.

222 "Come with me": See Watson, *Cogito, Ergo Sum*, p. 257.

222 an automaton of his own design: See Gaukroger, *Descartes*, p. 1.

223 "there are a thousand errors for one truth": Elizabeth to Descartes, November 30, 1645, AT IV, 337.

223 "We should pay little attention": Descartes to Elizabeth, January 1646, AT IV 355; *PW* III, p. 283.

224 "in all affairs where there are different sides": Ibid., AT IV, 352; *PW* III, p. 281.

225 "before Descartes, one could not be impure": Michel Foucault, "On the Genealogy of Ethics," in *Ethics*, p. 279.

226 "Anyone who seriously intends to become a philosopher": Husserl, *Cartesian Meditations*, pp. 2, 156, based on a 1929 series of lectures that can be read both as a brief introduction of Husserl's own phenomenological method and as an implicit critique of Heidegger's dismissive treatment of Descartes in *Being and Time*.

226 a catastrophic occlusion: Martin Heidegger, *Sein und Zeit* (Tübingen, 1927), p. 24.

ROUSSEAU

228 "His piercing gaze": Quoted in Bernard Gagnebin, ed., *Album Rousseau* (Paris, Gallimard, 1976), p. 215.

229 "If anything ever resembled a sudden inspiration": Rousseau, *Confessions*, Book VIII, *OC* I, p. 351.

229 "At the moment of that reading": Rousseau to M. de Malesherbes, January 12,

1762, *OC* I, p. 1135.

229 "Suddenly I felt my mind dazzled": Ibid., *OC* I, pp. 1135–36.

230 "I gave up gilt and white gloves": Rousseau, *Confessions*, Book VIII, *OC* I, p. 363.

230 "a moral dwarf on stilts": Mme. d'Épinay in a letter to Grimm, quoted in Maurice Cranston, *The Noble Savage: Jean-Jacques Rousseau 1754–1762* (Chicago: University of Chicago Press, 1991), p. 72.

230 "preferred to be a man of paradoxes": Rousseau, *Émile*, Book II, *OC* IV, p. 323.

230 Rousseau was born in Geneva: For biographical details in what follows, I rely on the most authoritative life in English, Maurice Cranston: *Jean-Jacques* (New York: Norton, 1983), *The Noble Savage*, and *The Solitary Self* (Chicago: University of Chicago Press, 1997); and also the most recent comprehensive life in French, Raymond Trousson, *Jean-Jacques Rousseau* (Paris: Jules Tallandier, 2003). Also useful is Leo Damrosch, *Jean-Jacques Rousseau: Restless Genius* (Boston: Houghton Mifflin, 2005). All these biographies draw on the invaluable *Correspondance complète de Jean Jacques Rousseau*, ed. R. A. Leigh. An unrivaled psychological interpretation of Rousseau's life and work is offered in Jean Starobinski, *Jean-Jacques Rousseau: La transparence et l'obstacle* (Paris: Gallimard, 1971). I have also drawn from my own previous work on Rousseau: James Miller, *Rousseau: Dreamer of Democracy* (New Haven: Yale University Press, 1984), and "'The Abyss of Philosophy': Rousseau's Concept of Freedom," *Modern Intellectual History* 3, no. 1 (April 2006): 95–103.

231 "love of his fatherland": Rousseau, *Confessions*, Book I, *OC* I, p. 8.

231 "felt before thinking": Ibid., p. 9.

232 "those qualities of sweetness": Robert Wokler, *Rousseau: A Very Short Introduction* (New York: Oxford University Press, 1995), p. 4.

232 a variety of other young artists: See Mark Hulliung's chapter on "philosophical history" and the *Encyclopedia* in *The Autocritique of Enlightenment* (Cambridge, MA: Harvard University Press, 1994), pp. 38–75.

233 "I made up my mind cheerfully": Rousseau, *Confessions*, Book VII, *OC* I, p. 344.

234 "innocent industry": Rousseau, "Épître à M. Bordes," *OC* II, pp. 1131–32.

234 "Suspicions, offenses, fears": Rousseau, *Discourse on the Sciences and the Arts*, First Part, *OC* III, p. 8.

234 "How sweet it would be": Ibid., p. 7.

235 "subtle Diogenes": Immanuel Kant, *Lectures on Ethics*, trans. Peter Heath (New York: Cambridge University Press, 1997), p. 45; and Kant, *Gesammelte Schriften* (Berlin, 1900–), 27:248.

235 Rousseau responded with a lengthy letter: See Rousseau to Mme. Francueil, April 20, 1751, *CC* II, pp. 142–46.

236 "to think this great matter out at my leisure": Rousseau, *Confessions*, Book VIII, *OC* I, p. 388.

237 set "aside all the facts": Rousseau, *Discourse on the Origin and Foundations of Inequality Among Men* [hereafter *Inequality*], prelude to Part I, *OC* III, p. 132.

237 "meditating on the first and most simple operations": Rousseau, *Inequality*, Preface, *OC* III, p. 125.

237 "Where could the painter and apologist of nature": Rousseau, *Rousseau, Judge of Jean-Jacques*, Third Dialogue, *OC* I, p. 936.

237 "during this period of his effervescence": Ibid., Second Dialogue, *OC* I, p. 871.

238 "It is not so much understanding": *Inequality*, *OC* III, p. 141.

238 "the word freedom is void of sense": Diderot, *Landois*, June 29, 1756, quoted in Hulliung, *Autocritique of Enlightenment*, p. 190.

239 "Every motion not produced by another": Rousseau, *Émile*, Book IV, *OC* IV, pp. 576, 586. Cf. Kant, *Critique of Pure Reason*, A533/B561 (where the "transcendental idea of freedom" refers to "the power of beginning a state *spontaneously*," without needing to be preceded by any other cause), and Hobbes, *Leviathan*, part 2, chapter XXI ("because every act of man's will, and every desire, and inclination proceedeth from some cause, and from that cause, in a continual chain"; all acts said to "proceed from *liberty*" also "proceed from *necessity*"). Some important eighteenth-century monists, including Toland and La Mettrie, disputed Rousseau's claim that spontaneity could not be an attribute of matter.

239 "not simply a sensitive and passive being": Rousseau, *Émile*, Book IV, *OC* IV, p. 573.

239 "There is in man a power of self-determination": Kant, *Critique of Pure Reason*, A534/B562.

239 "metaphysical side": *Inequality*, First Part, *OC* III, p. 141.

239 "*We do not know*": Rousseau, *Émile*, Book IV, *OC* IV, p. 568.

241 "And whatever the outcome of these brief and frequent revolutions": *Inequality*, Second Part, *OC* III, p. 191.

241 "The principle of freedom dawned on the world": Hegel, *Lectures on the History of Philosophy*, vol. III, pt. III, sec. 1, ch. 2, §2, 3C.

242 "Tell us, celebrated Arouet": Rousseau, *Discourse on the Sciences and the Arts*, Second Part, *OC* III, p. 21.

242 "I have received, Sir, your new book": Voltaire to Rousseau, August 30, 1755, *CC* IV, p. 158.

242 "If I had pursued my first vocation": Rousseau to Voltaire, September 10, 1755, *OC* III, p. 227.

242 "intolerant unbelievers": Rousseau to Voltaire, August 18, 1756, *OC* IV, p. 1073.

242 "judged kings and republics": Voltaire, "Rescript of the Emperor of China on the Occasion of the Plan for Perpetual Peace," in Voltaire, *Mélanges* (Paris: Gallimard, 1961), p. 413.

243 "There are some circumstances": Rousseau, *Émile*, Book V, *OC* IV, pp. 858–59.

244 "a genuinely new spectacle": Rousseau, *La Nouvelle Hélöise*, Second Preface, *OC*

II, p. 14.

244 "I made a golden age at my whim": Rousseau to Malesherbes, January 26, 1762, *OC* I, p. 1140.

244 "are not French, not sophisticates": Rousseau, *La Nouvelle Héloïse*, Second Preface, *OC* II, p. 6.

244 "add the urbanity of Athens": Jean le Rond d'Alembert, "Geneva," in Diderot and d'Alembert, eds., *Encyclopédie ou Dictionnaire raisonné des sciences, des arts et des métiers* (Paris, 1751–72).

244 to write "against my own interest": Rousseau, *Letter to d'Alembert on the Theater*, *OC* V, p. 120n.

245 "this arch-madman": Voltaire to d'Alembert, March 19, 1761, quoted in Damrosch, *Jean-Jacques Rousseau*, pp. 301–302.

245 "One must suffocate": Abbé Cahagne to Rousseau, February 27, 1761, *CC* VIII, p. 148.

245 "Your divine works": Quoted in Robert Darnton, "Readers Respond to Rousseau," in *The Great Cat Massacre* (New York: Basic Books, 1984), p. 247.

245 "two lovers who live in a small town": Rousseau, *La Nouvelle Héloïse*, Second Preface, *OC* II, p. 21.

246 "I myself was the Hero of this novel": Rousseau, *Confessions*, Book XI, *OC* I, p. 547.

246 "Of the diverse works that I had in hand": Ibid., Book IX, *OC* I, p. 404.

246 "wants only what he can do": Rousseau, *Émile*, Book II, *OC* IV, p. 309.

247 "Being that wills": Ibid., Book IV, *OC* IV, p. 581. That the vicar's views are Rousseau's own is confirmed by texts such as Rousseau's "Letter to Beaumont," in which Rousseau defends his good faith against the charges laid by the archbishop of Paris.

247 "I [can] sense Him in me": Rousseau, *Émile*, Book IV, *OC* IV, p. 581.

247 "Everything is good as it leaves the hands": Ibid., p. 245.

247 "a beast cannot deviate from the rule": Rousseau, *Discourse*, p. 113; *OC* III, p. 141. Cf. Augustine, *De libero arbitrio voluntatis*, III, 167: "If the will were in accord with its nature, it would surely maintain that nature, not harm it; and therefore, it would not be wicked. From this we gather the root of evil is this: not being in accord with nature."

247 the "first depravity" of men: Rousseau, *Émile*, Book IV, *OC* IV, p. 604.

247 "God has conferred upon men liberty": Pelagius, as cited in Augustine, *De natura et gratia, contra Pelagium*, LXIV.

247 "To prevent man from being wicked": Rousseau, *Émile*, Book IV, *OC* IV, p. 587.

247 "I am not free to want what is bad for me": Ibid., p. 586.

247 "all our first inclinations are legitimate": Ibid., p. 604.

247 "I have always the power of will": Ibid., p. 586.

249 a problem of human "negligence": Augustine, *De natura et gratia, contra Pela-*

gium, XIII. The affinities between Pelagius and Rousseau are usefully traced in Joshua Karant, "A Peculiar Faith" (Ph.D. diss., Political Science Department, University of Maryland, 2004), esp. pp. 102–13.

249 "the Fall, and any possible redemption": Susan Neiman, *Evil in Modern Thought* (Princeton: Princeton University Press, 2002), p. 43. Neiman gives a good account of Rousseau's theological views and their influence on Kant.

249 "Since man could fall by will": Augustine, *Retractationum libri duo*, 6.

249 "extreme freedom is the deity of the author": Jean-Robert Tronchin, "Conclusion of the Public Prosecutor," delivered in Geneva on June 19, 1762, *CC* XI, pp. 298–99.

249 "The fundamental principle of all morality": Rousseau, *Letter to Beaumont*, *OC* IV, pp. 935–36.

250 "the democratic constitution is certainly the masterpiece": Rousseau, *Letters Written from the Mountain*, *OC* III, pp. 837–38.

250 "Punish him with the full severity of the laws": Voltaire to François Tronchin, December 25, 1764, quoted in Damrosch, *Jean-Jacques Rousseau*, p. 390.

250 "at the door of an orphanage": *The Sentiment of the Citizens*, *CC* XXIII, p. 381.

250 "M. Rousseau is of small stature": Hume to Hugh Blair, December 28, 1765, written just before Hume brought Rousseau to London, in J.Y.T. Greig, ed., *The Letters of David Hume* (Oxford: Clarendon Press, 1932), 1:297–303.

251 "great moderation in all my passions": Hume, "My Own Life," in *Essays, Moral, Political, and Literary*, vol. 1.

252 "No! No! David Hume is no traitor!": Rousseau to Hume, July 10, 1766, *CC* XXX, p. 35.

252 Rousseau's evidence for treachery: *The Miscellany No. 11, by Nathaniel Freebody Esq.*, January 15, 1767, as summarized in Damrosch, *Jean-Jacques Rousseau*, pp. 427–28.

252 "By abandoning my children": Rousseau, *Confessions*, Book V.III, *OC* I, p. 357.

252 "compensation for my sacrifice": Rousseau, *Rêveries*, Ninth Walk, *OC* I, pp. 1087–88.

253 "The only response was a gloomy silence": Jean-Joseph Dusaulx, *De mes rapports avec J. J. Rousseau* (Paris, 1789), pp. 62–65.

253 "if anyone knows some things contrary": Rousseau, *Confessions*, Book XII, *OC* I, p. 656.

253 "He is a man without malice rather than good": Rousseau, *Rousseau, Judge of Jean-Jacques*, Second Dialogue, *OC* I, p. 774.

254 "rather like the one that may result from our conversation": Ibid., p. 836.

254 "A motive for virtue": Rousseau, *Rêveries*, *OC* I, p. 1051.

254 "to dare to profess great virtues": Ibid., pp. 1024, 1039.

254 "to act against my inclination": Ibid., p. 1053.

254 "In my present situation": Ibid., p. 1060.

255 "perfectly free": Ibid., p. 1099.

255 a finding corroborated in 1897: "Voltaire and Rousseau Again," *New York Times*, December 19, 1897, p. 6.

255 "If my husband is not a saint": Reported by the architect Paris in *Récit de la Mort de Rousseau*, quoted in Damrosch, *Jean-Jacques Rousseau*, p. 491.

255 "It is he himself who has talked with me": See Gordon H. McNeil, "The Cult of Rousseau and the French Revolution," *Journal of the History of Ideas* 6, no. 2 (April 1945): 197–212.

256 a cortege bearing his body: See Louis Trenard, "La diffusion du *Contrat social* (1762–1832)," in *Études sur le "Contrat social" de J. J. Rousseau* (Dijon: University of Dijon, 1964), p. 447.

KANT

259 a "little schoolmaster": Johann Georg Hamann to Johann Gottfried Herder, April 14, 1785, in Hamann, *Briefwechsel*, ed. Walther Ziesemer and Arthur Henkel (Wiesbaden: Insel Verlag, 1955–79), 5:418.

259 a small man with a frail body: See the contemporary etching included as a frontispiece in J.H.W. Stuckenberg, *The Life of Immanuel Kant* (London, 1882).

259 Year in and year out, he lectured: On Kant's career as a lecturer, see the introduction to Immanuel Kant, *Lectures on Metaphysics*, trans. and ed. Karl Ameriks and Steve Naragon (New York: Cambridge University Press, 1997), p. xx.

260 "appears as a city to be built": Michel Foucault, *Introduction à l'anthropologie de Kant*, Ier tome (typescript in Bibliothèque de la Sorbonne; filed in 1961), p. 17.

260 "it is difficult to write the history of the life of Immanuel Kant": Heine, *On the History of Religion and Philosophy in Germany*, trans. Howard Pollack-Milgate (New York: Cambridge University Press, 2007), p. 79.

260 "how his individuality blends ever more closely": Ernst Cassirer, *Kant's Life and Thought*, trans. James Haden (New Haven: Yale University Press, 1981), p. 6.

260 "If we take the ancient Greek philosophers": Kant, *Vorlesungen über die Philosophische Enzyklopädie*, AK 29:8–9. The early volumes are also available at www.korpora.org/Kant/verzeichnisse-gesamt.html. These lectures are briefly discussed in Hadot, *What Is Ancient Philosophy?*, pp. 266–67. The notes are probably from the Philosophical Encyclopedia course given in the winter semester of 1777–78: see Steve Naragon, "Kant in the Classroom," http://users.manchester.edu/Facstaff/SSNaragon/Kant/Lectures/lecturesIntro.htm.

260 "God is with him": See Manfred Kuehn, *Kant: A Biography* (New York: Cambridge University Press, 2001), p. 26. The primary sources for Kant's biography are his correspondence and the short biographical memoirs by three friends—

L. E. Borowski, R. B. Jachmann, and C. H. Wasianski—first published in 1804, soon after Kant's death. Kuehn's book, repetitive and marred by wooden prose, is the standard modern biography. Generally reliable (though mistaken about Rousseau's philosophy and its impact on Kant), it incorporates much recent historical scholarship. In what follows, most biographical details come from it. I have supplemented Kuehn with Stuckenberg, *The Life of Immanuel Kant*, a splendidly readable nineteenth-century narrative filled with long quotes from primary sources; Cassirer, *Kant's Life and Thought*, a neo-Kantian hagiography; Karl Vorländer, *Immanuel Kant: Der Mann und das Werk* (Hamburg: Meiner, 1977, [1964]), until Kuehn, the most comprehensive modern source; and Arsenij Gulyga, *Immanuel Kant: His Life and Thought*, trans. Marijan Despalatovic (Boston: Birkhauser, 1987). Originally published in Russia, this is a pungent and lively short account. Where these authors disagree about a fact, I present the version in Kuehn unless otherwise noted.

261 "One may say about Pietism what one will": Kuehn, *Kant*, p. 40, quoting F. T. Rink, a student and associate of Kant's from 1786 on.

261 "enthusiasm and insanity": Kant, *Anthropology from a Pragmatic Point of View*, Book I, 4, AK 7:132; ET, p. 15.

261 He shuddered when he recalled: See Kuehn, *Kant*, p. 45, quoting Kant's friend Hippel.

263 In this *Natural History*: Following the summary in Stuckenberg, *The Life of Immanuel Kant*, pp. 61–62.

264 "better to be a fool": Kuehn, *Kant*, p. 115, quoting Borowski.

265 "He calculated income and expenses": Ibid., p. 117, quoting Heilsberg.

265 "Real radicalism is absent": Cassirer, *Kant's Life and Thought*, p. 53.

265 "Every human being makes his own plan": Kant, "Thoughts on the Occasion of Mr. Johann Friedrich von Funk's Untimely Death," AK 2:41, quoted in Kuehn, *Kant*, p. 126.

266 an "absolute unity of the inner principle of conduct": Kant, *Anthropology from a Pragmatic Point of View*, AK 7:295; ET, p. 206.

266 "a rare man of strict righteousness": Kuehn, *Kant*, p. 154, quoting Jachmann.

266 resolutely followed "maxims": See Kant, *Anthropology from a Pragmatic Point of View*, AK 7:293–94; ET, p. 205.

267 "gave him friendly greetings": Heine, *On the History of Religion*, p. 79.

267 a "constant striving": Kuehn, *Kant*, p. 222, quoting Borowski; cf. p. 273.

267 "I myself have a natural disposition": Kant, *Conflict of the Faculties*, III, "The Principle of the Regimen," 1, AK 7:104. For Kant's hypochondria, see the brilliant discussion in Susan Meld Shell, *The Embodiment of Reason* (Chicago: University of Chicago Press, 1996), pp. 264–305.

268 "distracting occupations": Kant, *Anthropology from a Pragmatic Point of View*,

I, 50, AK 7:212; ET, p. 109; cf. I, 3, AK 7:131; ET, p. 14: "Abstraction . . . gives evidence of a freedom of the faculty of thought and sovereignty of the mind in having the condition of one's sense impressions under one's control."

268 "the power of the mind to master its morbid feelings": Kant, *Conflict of the Faculties*, III, AK 7:97.

268 In later years, Kant credited his longevity: Kant, AK 23:463, from a preliminary draft of the section on hypochondria in *Conflict of the Faculties*.

268 "I have mastered its influence": Kant, *Conflict of the Faculties*, III, "The Principle of the Regimen," AK 7:104.

268 "Character," he claimed: Kant, *Anthropology from a Pragmatic Point of View*, II, A, AK 7:293–94; ET, pp. 205–206.

268 "I am by inclination an inquirer": Kant, *Remarks Concerning "Observations on the Feeling of the Beautiful and the Sublime,"* AK 20:44.

269 "I must read Rousseau": Ibid., AK 20:30.

269 "there is a perfect world": Ibid., AK 20:16.

269 how "properly to fulfill the place": Ibid., AK 20:45.

269 "Everything goes by us in a flux": Ibid., AK 20:46.

269 "natural first principles become dubious": Ibid., AK 20:48.

269 "The movements of matter": Ibid., AK 20:93.

269 "one can describe Kant's entire philosophy": Dieter Henrich, *Aesthetic Judgment and the Moral Image of the World: Studies in Kant* (Stanford: Stanford University Press, 1992), p. 10. Cf. Cassirer, *Kant's Life and Thought*, pp. 86–90, and Richard Velkley, *Freedom and the End of Reason* (Chicago: University of Chicago Press, 1989), which marshals the evidence for Rousseau's formative influence on Kant's "critical turn."

270 "the gentle but sensitive tranquility" of the philosopher: Kant to Johann Gottfried Herder, May 9, 1768, AK 10:73–74.

270 "All change frightens me": Kant to Marcus Herz, early April 1778, AK 10:231.

271 The "*perfectio noumenon*": Passages quoted in summary in Kuehn, *Kant*, pp. 190–92.

271 "What are the *principia prima*": *Handschriftlicher Nachlass: Moralphilosophie, Rechtsphilosophie und Religionsphilosophie*, AK 19:116–17, 103.

271 "the *dependence* of moral feeling": Kuehn, *Kant*, p. 202.

271 "The ostensible obscurity of certain passages": Moses Mendelssohn to Kant, December 25, 1770, AK 10:133; ET, p. 74.

272 "the grey, dry style of a paper bag": Heine, *On the History of Religion*, p. 80.

272 "The method of my discourse": Quoted in Cassirer, *Kant's Life and Thought*, p. 140.

272 "I attended his lectures right away": Baczko, quoted in Kuehn, *Kant*, p. 211.

272 "almost no private acquaintance with my auditors": Kant to Marcus Herz, Octo-

ber 20, 1778, AK 10:232.

272   "I do not understand myself": Kant to Jacob Sigismund Beck, July 1, 1794, AK 11:515.

272   "to spin out to greater length": Kant to Marcus Herz, early April 1778, AK 10:231.

273   "This famous philosopher": Bernoulli, quoted in Kuehn, *Kant*, p. 218.

273   "There will probably be few readers": Hamann, letter to Kant's publisher, April 8, 1781, quoted in Stuckenberg, *The Life of Immanuel Kant*, p. 261.

273   "Sancho Panza's transcendental philosophy": Hamann, letter to Herder, September 15, 1781, quoted ibid., p. 463n114.

273   "a monument to the nobility and subtlety": 1782 review in the *Gothaische gelehrte Anzeigen*, quoted in Kuehn, *Kant*, p. 254.

274   "thoughts without content": Kant, *Critique of Pure Reason*, A51/B75.

274   "Human reason": Ibid., Avii.

274   "stands only for the absolute spontaneity": Ibid., A448/B476, A534/B562.

274   "a constitution allowing *the greatest possible human freedom*": Ibid., A316–17/B373–74.

275   "a science of the highest maxim": Kant, *Groundwork of the Metaphysics of Morals*, I, AK 4:403–404. Kant, *The Metaphysics of Morals*, Part I, Introduction, III, AK 6:226. See, also Kant, *Logic*, Introduction, III, AK 9:25 (English translation by Robert S. Hartman and Wolfgang Schwarz [New York: Bobbs Merrill, 1974], pp. 28–29).

275   "The saying, *Perfect yourself*": Kant, *Handschriftlicher Nachlass*; AK 19:298.

275   "highest possible perfection": Georg Ludwig Collins, From the Lectures of Professor Kant, Königsberg, Winter semester 1784–85, On the Final Destiny of Mankind, AK 27:471.

275   "a rich mine with various ores": Stuckenberg, *The Life of Immanuel Kant*, p. 273.

276   "artist of reason": A person unfavorably compared to the ancient Greek philosophers in Kant, *Vorlesungen über die Philosophische Enzyklopädie*, AK 29:8–9.

276   "You can tell how diligently the students here are studying": Christian Gottfried Schutz to Kant, February 1786, AK 10:430–31.

277   One correspondent told Kant: See Stuckenberg, *The Life of Immanuel Kant*, p. 370.

277   "God said, Let there be light": Quoted ibid., p. 374.

277   "autonomy of the will": Kant, *Groundwork of the Metaphysics of Morals*, AK 4:440.

277   his "supreme principle of morality" puts philosophy: Ibid., AK 4:425.

277   "carnal enjoyment" outside of marriage: Kant, *Metaphysics of Morals*, Part I, Appendix, 3, AK 6:359.

278   "only the descent into the hell": Ibid., Part II, Section II, §14, AK 6:441.

278   "an evil will actually present": Ibid.

278   man "abuses his freedom": Kant, "Ideas for a Universal History from a Cosmo-

politan Point of View," AK 8:23.

278 "impossible, for from such crooked timber": Ibid.

278 "single, all-embracing systems": Isaiah Berlin, "Two Concepts of Liberty," in *Four Essays on Liberty* (New York: Oxford University Press, 1969), p. 170.

279 "concepts to which real objects belong": Kant, *Critique of Practical Reason*, Book II, Chapter II, vii, AK 5:134.

279 "Tragedy is followed by farce": Heine, *On the History of Religion*, in Heine, *Sämtliche Schriften* (Munich: Hanser Verlag, 1971), 3:604.

279 "I learned to honor human beings": Kant, *Remarks Concerning "Observations on the Feeling of the Beautiful and the Sublime,"* AK 20:44.

279 "In regard to the essential ends of human nature": Kant, *Critique of Pure Reason*, A831/B859.

280 "intellectual contentment": See Kant, *Critique of Practical Reason*, Book II, Chapter II, AK 5:117–18.

280 "a man who believes": Kant to Johann Casper Lavater, April 28, 1775, AK 10:175–76.

280 *Sapere aude!*: Kant, "What Is Enlightenment?" (1784), AK 8:35.

280 "self-imposed immaturity": Ibid.

280 "Argue as much as you will": Ibid., AK 8:41.

280 "enlighten an *age*": Kant, "What Does It Mean to Orient Oneself in Thinking?" (1786), AK 8:146.

281 "His head was adorned with a finely powdered wig": Kuehn, *Kant*, p. 318, quoting Reusch.

281 "He lived and moved in it": Ibid., pp. 341–42, quoting Malter.

281 he would suggest they avoid the subject: See ibid., p. 343.

281 "any resistance to the supreme legislative power": Kant, "On the common saying: That may be correct in theory, but it is of no use in practice," AK 8:299. Wilhelm Rehberg's *Examination of the French Revolution*, published in Prussia earlier in 1793, alleges that metaphysics was a cause of the revolution, and Kant's preliminary notes for the essay indicate that he had the charge in view: see the introduction to the "common saying" essay in Kant, *Practical Philosophy*, trans. and ed. Mary J. Gregor (New York: Cambridge University Press, 1996), pp. 275–76.

281 In a private notebook: Kant, *Handschriftlicher Nachlass*, AK 19:595–96.

282 *"Apart from a good life-conduct"*: Kant, *Religion Within the Boundaries of Mere Reason*, AK 6:170–71.

282 "king in Königsberg": The phrase used by Fredrich Lupin, who visited Kant in 1794.

282 "our most high person has long observed": Friedrich Wilhelm II to Kant, October 1, 1794, AK 11:525.

282 "As Your Majesty's loyal subject": Kant to Friedrich Wilhelm II, October 12, 1794,

AK 11:530.

282 "Although there are many things that I think": Kant to Moses Mendelssohn, April 6, 1766, AK 10:69.

283 "an enlightened statesman": Kant, *Conflict of the Faculties*, AK 7:11.

283 "Kant does not read his writings any longer": Kuehn, *Kant*, p. 391, quoting Pörschke.

283 "Going to sleep became a fixed, elaborate ritual": Ben-Ami Scharfstein, *The Philosophers: Their Lives and the Nature of Their Thought* (New York: Oxford University Press, 1980), p. 221; Scharfstein's section on Kant is especially incisive.

283 "If a man were to say and write all he thinks": Stuckenberg, *The Life of Immanuel Kant*, p. 466n133, quoting Hippel.

283 "Almost every night he imagined himself surrounded": A. C. Wasianski, *Immanuel Kant: Sein Leben in Darstellungen von Zeitgenossen* (Berlin, 1912), pp. 278–79.

284 In one section, Kant claimed: See Kant, *Opus postumum*, AK 21:222.

284 "*Es est gut*": Kuehn, *Kant*, p. 422, quoting Wasianski.

284 Precise measurement confirmed: Carl Kupffer and Fritz Bessel-Hagen, *Der Schädel Immanuel Kant's*, in *Archiv fur Anthropologie* 13 (1881): 359–410. See also Michael Hagner, "Skulls, Brains, and Memorial Culture: On Cerebral Biographies of Scientists in the Nineteenth Century," *Science in Context* 16 (2003): 195–218.

284 it has become the custom for bridal parties: See Carlin Romano, "Special K: Kant, Königsberg, and Kaliningrad," *Chronicle of Higher Education*, May 16, 2003; and Erika Wolf, "Kant's Brides: A Readymade Photographic Chronotope," in *Art-Guide: Königsberg-Kaliningrad Now*, http://art-guide.ncca-kaliningrad.ru/?by=p &aglang=eng&au=027wolf.

285 "Two things fill the mind": Kant, *Critique of Practical Reason*, Part Two, Conclusion, AK 5:161.

EMERSON

289 "*philosophical chiliasm*": Kant, *Religion Within the Boundaries of Mere Reason*, AK 4:34.

289 "Natural Supernaturalism": See Thomas Carlyle, *Sartor Resartus: The Life and Opinions of Herr Teufelsdröckh in Three Books* (first published 1833–34), ed. Rodger L. Tarr and Mark Engel (Berkeley: University of California Press, 2000), p. 187. The phrase reappears as the title of a superb study of romantic literature, M. H. Abrams, *Natural Supernaturalism* (New York: Norton, 1971).

290 "the philosopher of democracy": John Dewey, "Emerson—The Philosopher of Democracy," *International Journal of Ethics* 13 (July 1903): 412, on the occasion

of the centenary of Emerson's birth.

290 "He delineates himself so perfectly": Oliver Wendell Holmes, *Ralph Waldo Emerson* (Boston, 1885), Introduction.

291 he had "in his veins the blood of several lines of 'painful preachers'": James Elliot Cabot, *A Memoir of Ralph Waldo Emerson* (Boston, 1887), 1:7. Cabot's two-volume life originally appeared as volumes 13 and 14 of *The Complete Works of Ralph Waldo Emerson* (Boston, 1883–93). In what follows, I draw on Cabot, as well as three more recent biographies: Ralph L. Rusk, *The Life of Ralph Waldo Emerson* (New York: Scribner, 1949); Joel Porte, *Representative Man: Ralph Waldo Emerson in His Time* (New York: Oxford University Press, 1979); and—in a class by itself—Robert D. Richardson Jr., *Emerson: The Mind on Fire* (Berkeley: University of California Press, 1995), a masterpiece of modern biography.

291 Like his forebears: Cabot, *Memoir of Ralph Waldo Emerson*, 1:24.

291 Mary Moody was a visionary and a mystic: Richardson, *Emerson*, pp. 23–25.

291 "I love to be a vessel of cumbersomeness": Rusk, *Life of Ralph Waldo Emerson*, p. 25, quoting Mary Moody Emerson; Cabot, *Memoir of Ralph Waldo Emerson*, 1:31, quoting Mary Moody Emerson.

292 He was elected to a student club: See Cabot, *Memoir of Ralph Waldo Emerson*, 1:66; and Rusk, *Life of Ralph Waldo Emerson*, p. 73.

292 A major turning point: See Richardson, *Emerson*, pp. 11ff.

292 The writing of diaries: See Phyllis Cole, *Mary Moody Emerson and the Origins of Transcendentalism* (New York: Oxford University Press, 1998).

292 his journals allowed Emerson: *EJ*, p. 1.

292 "disjointed dreams, audacities": Emerson to Carlyle, in Joseph Slater, ed., *The Correspondence of Emerson and Carlyle* (New York: Columbia University Press, 1964), p. 272, quoted in Richardson, *Emerson*, p. 320.

292 "Man Thinking": Emerson, "The American Scholar," *EL*, p. 54.

293 "Socrates' daimon": See Rusk, *Life of Ralph Waldo Emerson*, p. 78. In later years, Emerson lectured on "demonology."

293 "the most extraordinary book ever written": Ibid., p. 79.

293 spending the rest of his life as a "schoolmaster": Emerson Journals, May 7, 1822, *JMN* 1:130; *EJ*: 12.

293 David Hume, whose skepticism: Richardson, *Emerson*, pp. 44–45.

293 "Mistrust no more your ability": Emerson Journals, March 23, 1823, *JMN* 2:113, 112; *EJ*: 27.

293 "Why may not I act & speak & write": Ibid., December 21, 1823, *JMN* 2:189–90; *EJ*: 38.

294 "a strong imagination": Ibid., April 18, 1824, *JMN* 2:239; *EJ*: 45–47.

294 "a certain awe": Ibid., January 17, 1829, *JMN* 3:149–50; *EJ*: 68.

294 "I am embarrassed by doubts": Ibid., January 16, 1828, *JMN* 3:102; *EJ*: 66.

295 "so imbued with his manner of thinking": Mary Moody Emerson quoted in Rich-

ardson, *Emerson*, p. 63.

295   "the idea of the divine unity": Ibid., p. 66.

295   the tenets of "self-culture": William Ellery Channing, "Self Culture," an "Address Introductory to the Franklin Lectures, delivered at Boston, September, 1838," www.americanunitarian.org/selfculture.htm.

295   "It seemed to me as if I had myself written the book": Emerson, *Representative Men*, "Montaigne; or, the Skeptic," *EL*: 697.

295   electrified by Coleridge's *Aids to Reflection*: See Douglas Hedley, *Coleridge, Philosophy and Religion: Aids to Reflection and the Mirror of the Spirit* (New York: Cambridge University Press, 2000), p. 17.

295   "His eye," Emerson later remarked: Emerson, "Modern Aspects of Letters," from lecture course "English Literature," delivered January 1836, in Stephen E. Whicher and Robert E. Spiller, eds., *The Early Lectures of Ralph Waldo Emerson* (Cambridge, MA: Harvard University Press, 1959–72), 1:378.

296   "*that image of God*": James Marsh, introduction to Samuel Taylor Coleridge, *Aids to Reflection* (Boston, 1829), p. 42.

296   the soul's "fluxions and mobility": Emerson, *Representative Men*, "Montaigne; or, the Skeptic," *EL*: 696.

296   "like day after twilight": Emerson Journals, June 2, 1830, *JMN* 3:186.

296   "In listening more intently to our soul": "Self Trust," in Teresa Toulouse and Andrew Delbanco, *The Complete Sermons of Ralph Waldo Emerson* (Columbia: University of Missouri Press, 1989–92), 2:266–67.

296   "the complete wreck of earthly good": Emerson to Mary Moody Emerson, February 8, 1831, *SL*, pp. 111–12.

296   "The days pass over me": poem in *JMN* 3:227.

296   "God cannot be intellectually discerned": Emerson Journals, July 21, 1831, *JMN* 3:274; *EJ*: 79.

297   "In my study my faith is perfect": Ibid., December 28, 1831, *JMN*, 3:314.

297   "It is the best part of the man": Ibid., January 10, 1832, *JMN* 3:318; *EJ*: 81.

297   "I regard it as the irresistible effect": Quoted in Richardson, *Emerson*, p. 124.

297   "The good of going into the mountains": Emerson Journals, July 14, 1832, *JMN* 4:29.

297   Emerson speculates that "religion": Ibid., July 6, 1832, *JMN* 4:27; *EJ*: 83.

298   "I would think, I would feel": Ibid., July 14, 1832, *JMN* 4:28; *EJ*: 83.

298   a "modern Plutarch": Ibid., August 12, 1832, *JMN* 4:35; on Fox, see *JMN* 4:31.

298   "every great man": Ibid., September 17, 1832, *JMN* 4:43.

298   "We want lives": Ibid., October 28, 1832, *JMN* 4:54.

298   "and then will our true heaven be entered": Ibid., November 29, 1832, *JMN*, 4:66.

298   dismiss him from the "pastoral charge": Emerson to the Proprietors of the Second Church, September 11, 1832, *SL*: 114.

298   "I would be free, I cannot be": Emerson Journals, October 9 [?], 1832, *JMN* 4:47;

EJ: 86.

298 "The true philosophy is the only prophet": Ibid., October 9 and 13, 1832, *JMN* 4:47, 48.

298 "Here stand I, I cannot otherwise": Ibid., October 27, 1832, *JMN* 4:53; *EJ*: 87.

299 "At each step, or level,": Stanley Cavell, "Finding as Founding," in Cavell, *Emerson's Transcendental Études* (Stanford: Stanford University Press, 2003), p. 139.

299 he set sail for Europe: See Rusk, *Life of Ralph Waldo Emerson*, p. 195.

299 "What is it that is to convince the faithful": Emerson Journals, [September 3, 1833?], *JMN* 4:84, an uncompleted entry, a quarter of a page is left blank after the word *I*.

300 "pledged if health & opportunity be granted me": Ibid., July 11, 1833, *JMN* 4:77.

300 "A lecture is a new literature": Ibid., July 5, 1839, *JMN* 7:224–25; *EJ*: 221.

300 More talks quickly followed: See Whicher and Spiller, Introduction to *Early Lectures of Ralph Waldo Emerson*, 1:xx–xii.

301 the so-called lyceum movement: See Carl Bode, *The American Lyceum* (New York: Oxford University Press, 1956), and Donald M. Scott, "The Popular Lecture and the Creation of a Public in Mid-Nineteenth-Century America," *Journal of American History* 66, no. 4 (March 1980): 791–809.

301 besides giving 64 lectures in England and Scotland: William Charvat, *Emerson's American Lecture Engagements: A Chronological List* (New York: New York Public Library, 1961), p. 7, and Townsend Scudder III, "A Chronological List of Emerson's Lectures on His British Lecture Tour of 1847–1848," *PMLA* 51, no. 1 (March 1936): 243–48.

301 "speaking in a voice not much exalted": George Gilfillan, describing "Eloquence," a lecture Emerson delivered in 1848, *Dundee Advertiser*, March 16, 1874, quoted in Townsend Scudder III, "Emerson's British Lecture Tour, 1847–1848, Part II," *American Literature* 7, no. 2 (May 1935): 170.

301 In order to reach a popular audience: See A. M. Baumgartner, "'The Lyceum Is My Pulpit': Homiletics in Emerson's Early Lectures," *American Literature* 34, no. 4 (January 1963): 477–86.

301 "I will say at Public Lectures & the like": Emerson Journals, November 15, 1834, *JMN* 4:335; *EJ*: 128.

302 "The smell of a field": Emerson, "The Naturalist," delivered in May 1834, in Whicher and Spiller, *Early Lectures of Ralph Waldo Emerson*, 1:74.

302 "The intellect is stimulated": Emerson, *The Conduct of Life*, "Illusions," *EL*: 1123.

302 "not to utter any speech, poem, or book": Emerson Journals, November 15, 1834, *JMN* 4:335; *EJ*: 128.

302 "You are impressed by the inexhaustible gigantic riches": Emerson, "The Uses of Natural History," delivered on November 5, 1833, in Whicher and Spiller, *Early Lectures of Ralph Waldo Emerson*, 1:10.

303 a passage from Plotinus: See *The Collected Works of Ralph Waldo Emerson*, vol. I:

Nature, Addresses, and Lectures, ed. Robert E. Spiller and Alfred R. Ferguson (Cambridge, MA: Harvard University Press, 1971), p. 7 and corresponding note.

303 "Man is a kind of very minute heaven": Emerson, *Representative Men*, "Sweden-borg; or, the Mystic," *EL*: 672.

303 "I am born a poet": Emerson to Lydia Jackson, February 1, 1835, *SL*: 142–43.

304 "I am nothing; I see all": Emerson, *Nature*, chap. 1, *EL*: 10.

304 "The reader feels as in a disturbed dream": Francis Bowen, "Transcendentalism," *Christian Examiner* 21 (1837): 371–85.

304 "the voice of the Supreme Being to the Individual": Emerson Journal, August 21, 1837, *JMN* 5:371; *EJ*: 167.

305 "an event without any former parallel": James Russell Lowell, "Thoreau's Letters," *North American Review* 101 (October 1865): 600, quoted in Kenneth S. Sacks, *Understanding Emerson: "The American Scholar" and His Struggle for Self-Reliance* (Princeton: Princeton University Press, 2003), p. 18.

305 "One Man": Emerson, "The American Scholar," *EL*: 53–54.

305 "converted into thought as mulberry leaf": Ibid., *EL*: 60–61.

305 "decent, indolent, complaisant": Ibid., *EL*: 70–71.

305 "This grand Oration": Holmes, *Ralph Waldo Emerson*, p. 115.

306 "misty, dreamy, unintelligible": John Pierce, quoted in Sacks, *Understanding Emerson*, p. 17.

306 "Men have come to speak of the revelation": Emerson, "The Divinity School Address," *EL*: 83, 89.

306 with "neither good divinity nor good sense": *Christian Examiner* 25 (1838): 266. *The Biblical Repertory and Princeton Review* (a Presbyterian journal), quoted in Rusk, *Life of Ralph Waldo Emerson*, p. 271.

306 "to induce men to think for themselves": Orestes Brownson, Review of R. W. Emerson's "Divinity School Address," *Boston Quarterly Review*, October 1838, pp. 500–14.

307 "He is perfectly quiet amidst the storm": Cabot, *Memoir of Ralph Waldo Emerson*, 1:337.

307 "It is a poor-spirited age": Emerson Journals, October 19, 1838, *JMN* 7:110–11; *EJ*: 202.

307 "the doctrine of the perpetual revelation": Ibid., *JMN* 7:111; *EJ*: 202.

307 "The attendance was large": Cabot, *Memoir of Ralph Waldo Emerson*, 2:383–84.

307 "The true preacher": Emerson, "The Divinity School Address," *EL*: 85.

308 "Accept the hint of shame": Emerson, "Literary Ethics," lecture delivered in July 1838, *EL*: 105–106.

309 "The way, the thought, the good": Emerson, "Self-Reliance," *EL*: 271.

309 "the way, and the truth, and the life": John 14:6. See also Alan Hodder, "'After a

High Negative Way': Emerson's 'Self-Reliance' and the Rhetoric of Conversion,"
Harvard Theological Review 84, no. 4 (October 1991): 423–46.

309 "I dreamed that I floated at will": Emerson Journals, October 25, 1840, *JMN* 7:525.

309 "If I am the Devil's child": Emerson, *Essays*, "Self-Reliance," *EL*: 262.

310 "a foolish consistency": Ibid., *EL*: 265.

310 "made to themselves a circle of readers": Margaret Fuller, "Emerson's *Essays*,"
New-York Tribune, December 7, 1844.

310 American "Teacher of Wisdom": Francis Espinasse, article on Emerson in *Manchester Examiner*, October 20, 1847, quoted in Scudder, "Emerson's British Lecture Tour, 1847–1848, Part I," *American Literature* 7, no. 1 (March 1935): 19.

310 audiences throughout North America flocked: See Mary Kupiec Cayton, "The Making of an American Prophet: Emerson, His Audiences, and the Rise of the Culture Industry in Nineteenth-Century America," *American Historical Review* 92, no. 3 (June 1987): 597–620.

311 "The lecture," reported the *Cincinnati Daily Enquirer*: *Cincinnati Daily Enquirer*, January 28, 1857, quoted in C. David Mead, *Yankee Eloquence in the Middle West* (East Lansing: Michigan State University Press, 1951), pp. 42–43. Compare the descriptions of Emerson's speaking style collected in Scudder, "Emerson's British Lecture Tour, 1847–1848, Part II," pp. 167–69.

312 "a puppet show of Eleusinian Mysteries": Quoted in Rusk, *Life of Ralph Waldo Emerson*, p. 309.

312 "would be like carrying soda-water": *Cincinnati Daily Enquirer*, January 28, 1857, quoted in Mead, *Yankee Eloquence*, p. 43.

312 "will make the gallows as glorious as the cross": See Emerson, *Collected Works*, Riverside ed., 11:249–63; and Rusk, *Life of Ralph Waldo Emerson*, p. 402.

313 Like Kant, Emerson was fated: Rusk, *Life of Ralph Waldo Emerson*, pp. 499, 503.

313 "He kept (when awake) repeating in his sonorous voice": Cabot, *Memoir of Ralph Waldo Emerson*, p. 683.

NIETZSCHE

316 An idealized replica: See Michael Hertl, *Der Mythos Friedrich Nietzsche and seine Totenmasken* (Würzburg, Königshausen: Neumann, 2007).

316 "Around every profound spirit": Nietzsche, *Beyond Good and Evil*, 40, *KSA* 5, p. 58.

317 "I have many stylistic possibilities": Nietzsche, "Why I Write Such Good Books," 4, *Ecce Homo*, *KSA* 6, p. 304.

317 "Tell me what you need": Kurt Tucholsky, "Fräulein Nietzsche," in *Gesammelte Werke* (Hamburg: Rowohlt, 1975), 10:14.

317 "Why am I alive?": Nietzsche, *Untimely Meditations*, "Schopenhauer as Educa-

tor," 4, *KSA* 1, p. 374.

318 He was born in Prussia in 1844: In what follows, I rely on a variety of primary
sources for Nietzsche's biography: the collected correspondence of Nietzsche,
Sämtliche Briefe, Kritische Studienausgabe, ed. Giorgio Colli and Mazzino Montinari; a good selection of letters appears in English in *Selected Letters of Friedrich
Nietzsche*, trans. and ed. Christopher Middleton (Chicago: University of Chicago
Press, 1969); the autobiographical remarks of Nietzsche himself, from his adolescent years, in Karl Schlechta, ed., *Friedrich Nietzsche Werke in 3 Bänden* (Munich, 1956); the retrospective remarks that appear in his 1886 prefaces to the new
editions of his previous books; and the autobiographical account that appears in
Ecce Homo, published posthumously but completed in 1888, shortly before his
final mental breakdown. Also helpful is the anecdotal evidence in various memoirs written by Nietzsche's acquaintances and friends, in Sander L. Gilman, ed.,
Conversations with Nietzsche: A Life in the Words of His Contemporaries, trans.
David J. Parent (New York: Oxford University Press, 1987). The standard modern
biography is Curt Paul Janz, *Friedrich Nietzsche, Biographie* (Munich: Hanser,
1979), a comprehensive and judicious three-volume work. The best basic biography in English is Ronald Hayman, *Nietzsche: A Critical Life* (New York: Oxford
University Press, 1980). Also useful is the *Chronik zu Nietzsches Leben* that appears in volume 15 of the standard German reference text of the collected works
of Nietzsche, Colli and Montinari's *Sämtliche Werke*. Still pertinent are the first
biographical interpretations of Nietzsche's lifework: Lou Andreas-Salomé, *Friedrich Nietzsche in seinen Werken* published in 1894, and the lengthy biography that
forms Book I of Karl Jaspers, *Nietzsche: Einführung in das Verstandnis seines
Philosophierens* (Berlin: W. de Gruyter, 1936). Both works have been translated
into English: Salomé, *Nietzsche*, trans. Siegfried Mandel (Urbana: University of
Illinois Press, 2001), and Jaspers, *Nietzsche*, trans. Charles F. Wallraff and Frederick J. Schmitz (Tucson: University of Arizona Press, 1965). Much more controversial is the 1989 work of Joachim Köhler, partially translated into English as
Zarathustra's Secret: The Interior Life of Friedrich Nietzsche, trans. Ronald Taylor
(New Haven: Yale University Press, 2002), a work that has the great virtue of collecting in one place a lot of interesting circumstantial evidence about Nietzsche's
inner demons, especially as regards his sexuality, and the great vice of offering a
crudely reductionist interpretation of this evidence. In giving English versions of
Nietzsche's text, I have relied (with a few revisions of my own) on the translations,
where available, of Walter Kaufmann and R. J. Hollingdale for the works, and of
Christopher Middleton for the letters, which I have generally cited only by date
and correspondent.

318 "destined to spend only a short time": Friedrich Nietzsche, *Ecce Homo*, "Why
I Am So Wise," 1, *KSA*, 6, p. 264.

318 "How can we set about painting a picture": Nietzsche, "Mein Leben [Aus dem Jahre 1863]," in Schlechta, *Friedrich Nietzsche Werke*, 3:815–16.

319 he still sometimes heard his father's voice: See Peter Bergmann, *Nietzsche: "The Last Antipolitical German"* (Bloomington: Indiana University Press, 1987), p. 13.

319 "All my yearnings": "Mein Leben [Aus dem Jahre 1859]," in Schlechta, *Friedrich Nietzsche Werke*, 3:40.

319 "He is a strong stout man": Quoted in Janz, *Nietzsche*, 1:129.

319 "Envy," Nietzsche wrote: "Kann der Neidische je wahrhaft glücklich sein?" September 1863, in Hans Joachim Mette, *Nietzsche Jugendschriften, Historisch-Kritische Gesamtausgabe* (Munich: Musarion Verlag, 1933–34), also www.geocities.com/thenietzschechannel/1863.htm.

319 "I want to know thee": Quoted in Janz, *Nietzsche*, 1:124.

320 "As soon as it becomes possible": Nietzsche, "Fate and History, " trans. George J. Stack, *Philosophy Today* 37, no. 2 (1993): 154–56.

320 "Certainly, faith alone brings salvation": Nietzsche to Elisabeth Nietzsche, June 11, 1865.

321 "What I fear": Nietzsche, "Aus dem Jahre 1868/69," in Schlechta, *Friedrich Nietzsche Werke*, 3:148.

321 "I saw this book": Nietzsche, "Rückblick auf meine zwei Leipziger Jahre," ibid., 3:133.

321 "Willing and striving are its whole essence": Arthur Schopenhauer, *The World as Will and Representation*, trans. E.F.J. Payne (New York: Dover, 1969), vol. 1, 57, p. 312.

322 "for the spirit of this powerful, mysterious genius": Nietzsche, "Rückblick auf meine zwei Leipziger Jahre," in Schlechta, *Friedrich Nietzsche Werke*, 3:133.

322 Heraclitus, whose "extraordinary power": Nietzsche, *Philosophy in the Tragic Age of the Greeks*, trans. Marianne Cowan (Chicago: Regnery, 1962), p. 52.

322 "Perhaps I do not belong at all": Nietzsche to Carl von Gersdorff, April 11, 1869.

322 treated by a doctor for syphilis: See Janz, *Nietzsche*, 1:202.

322 syphilis in the nineteenth century: See Deborah Hayden, *Pox: Genius, Madness, and the Mysteries of Syphilis* (New York: Basic Books, 2003).

323 "I have not felt a moment's depression": Nietzsche to Erwin Rohde, November 3, 1867.

323 the city of Basel was unique: See Lionel Gossman, *Basel in the Age of Burckhardt: A Study in Unseasonable Ideas* (Chicago: University of Chicago Press, 2000).

323 "Only without God": Franz Overbeck, *Christentum und Kultur*, ed. C. A. Bernoulli (Basel, 1919), p. 286, quoted in Gossman, *Basel in the Age of Burckhardt*, p. 423.

324 "a trace of femininity": Ida Overbeck, "Erinnerungen," in Carl Albrecht Bernoulli, *Franz Overbeck und Friedrich Nietzsche: Eine Freundschaft* (Jena, 1908),

1:234, quoted in Gilman, *Conversations with Nietzsche*, pp. 32–33.

324 "adjusts the ills of an honorless": Richard Wagner, "Art and Revolution" (1849), in *Richard Wagner's Prose Works*, trans. W. Ashton Ellis (London, 1895), 1:37.

324 "perfect Art-work": Ibid., 1:53.

325 "he came back full of his god": Luise Elisabeth Bachofen, quoted in Hermann Randa, *Nietzsche, Overbeck und Basel* (Bern, 1937), and in Gilman, *Conversations with Nietzsche*, p. 50.

326 "tragic myth, reborn from music": Nietzsche, *Birth of Tragedy*, 24, KSA, 1, p. 154.

326 "a piece of pseudo-aesthetic, unscholarly religious mystification": Friedrich Ritschl to Wilhelm Vischer, February 2, 1873, quoted in *KSA*, 15, pp. 38–39.

326 "ignorance and lack of love of truth": Ulrich von Wilamowitz-Moellendorff, *Zukunftsphilologie* (Berlin, 1872), p. 32, quoted in Walter Kaufmann in the introduction to his translation of *The Birth of Tragedy* (New York: Vintage, 1967), p. 5.

326 he drafted dozens of different outlines: See Nietzsche to Erwin Rohde, November 21, 1872, and Nietzsche to Rohde, December 7, 1872. The notebook in question is number 19 = P I 20b, Summer 1872–Early 1873, *KSA* 7, pp. 417–520.

326 "the absurd notion . . . that *water*" and "From him proceeds": Nietzsche, *The Pre-Platonic Philosophers*, trans. Greg Whitlock (Urbana: University of Illinois Press, 2001), pp. 144–45. A scholarly edition of the German text of this series of lectures, written for delivery at Basel in the fall of 1872, was first published in 1995, in *Nietzsche: Werke, Kritische Gesamtausgabe*, as part 2, vol. 4, *Vorlesungsaufzeichnungen*, pp. 211–362.

327 "a metaphysical theorem, taken on faith": Nietzsche, *Philosophy in the Tragic Age of the Greeks*, 3, *KSA*, 1, p. 813.

327 "If all goes well": Nietzsche, *Human, All Too Human*, vol. 2: "The Wanderer and His Shadow," 86, *KSA* 2, p. 591.

327 "An era which suffers": Nietzsche, *Philosophy in the Tragic Age of the Greeks*, 2, *KSA* 1, p. 812.

328 "his *life* (which occupies the most important position)": Nietzsche, *Notebook Fragments*, Summer–Fall 1873, 29 [205], *KSA* 7, p. 712; 29 [211], *KSA* 7, p. 714; 29 [204], *KSA* 7, p. 712.

328 a "horrible consequence of Darwinism": Nietzsche, *Notebook Fragments*, Summer 1872—Beginning 1873, 19 [132], *KSA* 7, p. 461.

328 "*The human being became a knowing being*": Ibid., 19 [179], *KSA* 7, p. 475.

328 "He must organize the chaos": Nietzsche, "On the Uses and Disadvantages of History for Life," 10, *Untimely Meditations*, II, *KSA* 1, p. 333.

329 "'Beware,'" writes Nietzsche, quoting Emerson: Nietzsche, "Schopenhauer as Educator," 8, *Untimely Meditations*, III, *KSA* 1, p. 426.

330 "My father died of an inflammation of the brain": Nietzsche to Carl von Gersdorff, January 18, 1876.

330 "was of short rather than medium height": The direct quotes in this and the next
     three paragraphs come from Ludwig von Scheffler, "Wie ich Nietzsche kennen
     lernte," *Neue Freie Presse* (Vienna), August 6 and 7, 1907; translated in Gilman,
     Conversations with Nietzsche, pp. 63–76.

332 "convulsed, torn loose, torn away": Nietzsche, *Human, All Too Human*, vol. 1,
     Preface, 3, *KSA* 2, pp. 16–17.

333 "remorse or pangs of guilt": Ibid., vol. 1, 39, *KSA* 2, p. 64.

333 "He scourges his self-idolatry": Ibid., vol. 1, 142, *KSA* 2, p. 138.

333 "a double-brain": Ibid., vol. 1, 251, *KSA* 2, p. 209.

334 "unnatural perversions, with allusions to pederasty": Nietzsche to Peter Gast,
     1883, *Sämtliche Briefe*, 6:365, quoted in Köhler, *Zarathustra's Secret*, p. 103.

334 "Was this still the same man": von Scheffler, "Wie ich Nietzsche kennen lernte,"
     in Gilman, *Conversations with Nietzsche*, p. 103.

334 "my existence is a fearful burden": Nietzsche to Dr. Eiser, early January 1880,
     quoted in Ronald Hayman, *Nietzsche: A Critical Life* (New York: Oxford Univer-
     sity Press, 1980), p. 219.

335 "Not only is his whole tendency like my own": Nietzsche to Franz Overbeck, post-
     marked July 30, 1881.

335 "Beginning of August 1881 in Sils-Maria": Nietzsche, *Notebook Fragments*,
     Spring–Summer 1881, 11 [141], *KSA* 9, p. 494.

335 "On my horizon, thoughts have arisen": Nietzsche to Peter Gast, August 14, 1881.

336 "To the poet, to the philosopher": The epigraph appears on the title page only of
     the first edition, published in 1882. It comes from Emerson's essay "History," *EL*,
     p. 242.

336 *Incipit tragoedia*: Nietzsche, *The Gay Science*, 342, *KSA* 3, p. 571.

336 "The madman": Ibid., 125, *KSA* 3, pp. 480–82.

337 "uniquely ready for the till now almost undisclosed": Nietzsche to Franz Over-
     beck, probably October 1882.

337 "personal records of their authors": Lou Andreas-Salomé to Nietzsche, probably
     September 16, 1882.

337 "To the extent that cruel people are also masochists": Lou Andreas-Salomé, *In der
     Schule bei Freud*, ed. Ernst Pfeiffer (Zurich: Max Niehans, 1958), pp. 155–56.

338 "Consider me, the two of you": Nietzsche to Lou Andreas-Salomé and Paul Rée,
     probably mid-December 1882.

338 "contains an image of myself": Nietzsche to Franz Overbeck, received on Febru-
     ary 11, 1883, from Rapallo.

338 "Nietzsche was already inhabited by Zarathustra": Overbeck, *Werke und Nachlaß*,
     4:18–19, quoted in Gossman, *Basel in the Age of Burckhardt*, p. 437.

338 "the most splendid chance to prove": Nietzsche to Franz Overbeck, postmarked
     Rapallo, December 25, 1882.

339 "When I was younger": Nietzsche, *Notebook Fragments*, June–July 1885, 38 [13], *KSA* 11, pp. 611–12.

339 "the deep movement of the god-seeker": See Lou Andreas-Salomé, *Lebensruck-blick*, ed. Ernst Pfeiffer (Zurich: Max Nichans, 1951), pp. 98–107, in Gilman, *Conversations with Nietzsche*, p. 118.

339 "This life as you now live it": Nietzsche, *The Gay Science*, 341, *KSA* 3, p. 570.

339 "*Yes* to the world as it is": Nietzsche, *Notebook Fragments*, Fall 1887, 10 [3], *KSA* 12, p. 455.

340 "Has anyone at the end of the nineteenth century": Nietzsche, *Ecce Homo*, "Thus Spoke Zarathustra," 3, *KSA* 6, pp. 339–40.

341 "to compose into one and bring together": Nietzsche, *Thus Spoke Zarathustra*, III, "On Old and New Tablets," 3, *KSA* 4, pp. 248–49.

341 "Precisely this is godliness": Ibid., 4, 7, 11, *KSA* 4, pp. 249, 251, 254.

341 "It is possible for the first time": Nietzsche to Franz Overbeck, March 20, 1884, and April 7, 1884.

341 "the gruesome silence one hears all around one": Nietzsche, *Ecce Homo*, "Thus Spoke Zarathustra," 5, *KSA* 6, p. 342.

341 "immediately began to speak about the unbearableness of his ailment": Resa von Schirnhofer, in Hans Lohberger, "Friedrich Nietzsche und Resa von Schirnhofer," *Zeitschrift fur philosophische Forschung* 22 (1969): 441–45, in Gilman, *Conversations with Nietzsche*, p. 164.

342 "An indescribable atmosphere of peculiarity": Erwin Rohde in a letter to Franz Overbeck, quoted in Rüdiger Safranski, *Nietzsche: A Philosophical Biography*, trans. Shelley Frisch (New York: Norton, 2002), pp. 367–77.

343 In his correspondence: Nietzsche to August Strindberg, December 7, 1888; to Carl Fuchs, December 18, 1888; to Franziska Nietzsche, December 21, 1888; to Franz Overbeck, December 25, 1888; to Meta von Salis, December 29, 1888.

343 "capering around in the nude": Anacleto Verrecchia, *Zarathustras Ende* (Vienna: Hermann Böhlaus, 1986), p. 265, quoted in Köhler, *Zarathustra's Secret*, p. 193.

343 "huddled up reading in the corner of a sofa": Overbeck, quoted in Safranski, *Nietzsche*, p. 371.

344 "I call myself the last philosopher": Nietzsche, *Notebook Fragments*, Summer 1872–Early 1873, 19 [131], *KSA* 7, pp. 460–61.

EPILOGUE

348 "we are necessarily strangers to ourselves": Nietzsche, *Genealogy of Morals*, Preface, 1, *KSA* 5, p. 247.

348 "melancholy humor": Montaigne, *Essays*, II, 8, p. 385 (278).

349 "the question of truth": Foucault, *Care of the Self*, p. 68.

349 "the investigator without knowledge": Montaigne, *Essays*, III, 9, p. 1001 (766).

350 "You want people always to be consistent": Rousseau, *La Nouvelle Hélöise*, Second Preface, *OC* II, p. 27.

350 "philosophy," as Nietzsche complained: Nietzsche, *Philosophy in the Tragic Age of the Greeks*, 2, *KSA* 1, p. 812.

350 "You won't discover your life's meaning": Rick Warren, *What on Earth Am I Here For?* (Grand Rapids: Zondervan, 2004), p. 5.

351 "is like a star-shower": Karl Jaspers, *Man in the Modern Age*, trans. Eden and Cedar Paul (London: G. Routledge, 1933), pp. 193–94.

ACKNOWLEDGMENTS

Much of this book was researched and written in 2006–2007, during a fellow-ship at the Dorothy and Lewis Cullman Center for Writers and Scholars at the New York Public Library. I thank the library and its staff for their generous support, and also the director of the Cullman Center, Jean Strouse, and the fellows that year who became my most important interlocutors: James Shapiro, Maya Jasanoff, David Blight, Jeff Talarigo, Nelson Smith, and Ben Katchor. For crucial conversations early in the project, I thank Alexander Nehamas, Stanley Cavell, Richard Shusterman, and my friend and New School colleague Richard J. Bernstein.

The New School for Social Research gave me time off from my teaching to start writing in the spring of 2003, and extended me support in 2006–2007.

The New York State Summer Writers Institute gave me a forum to read early drafts of the project before colleagues and students there. Special thanks go to Robert and Peg Boyers, the directors of the institute, as well as to fellow scribblers Lee Abbott, Elizabeth Benedict, Frank Bidart, Nicholas Delbanco, Carolyn Forché, Mary Gaitskill, Mary Gordon, and Marc Woodworth.

My friend and former student Timothy Don, who is the art director for *Lapham's Quarterly* and production manager for *The Nation*, helped me find and then organize the images of the philosophers reprinted in the book.

For counsel and encouragement, I relied, as always, on Raphael Sagalyn, of the Sagalyn Literary Agency; he's been a friend for more than two decades, and I can't imagine a keener advocate.

Jonathan Galassi at Farrar, Straus and Giroux instructed me to write a book that he would want to read, which gave me a goal to aim at. Eric Chinski, his colleague at FSG, brought me closer to achieving that goal, thanks to his superb skills as an editor and his deep knowledge of the history of philosophy.

But in the end, my first and last reader was Ruth Klue, and our song was Kurt Weill's "Speak Low." Without her, and the music we share, I don't think I could have survived.

INDEX

Page numbers in *italics* refer to illustrations.

416   INDEX

Phi Beta Kappa, 298, 306
Philip II, King of Macedonia, 56, 75,
    85, 89–94, 102
Philistus, 58–9
Philodemus, 73
Philo of Alexandria, 74–5
"Philosopher, The" (Nietzsche), 320,
    338
philosopher-kings, 52, 54–5, 57–8, 89,
    102, 162, 182, 241; Dionysius the
    Younger as, 57–64, 86, 122;
    Marcus Aurelius as, 132; Roman
    idea of, 114, 115
philosophers, 5–10; Diogenes as model
    of conduct for, 78; Hellenistic,
    47–8; modern, 5–7, 9–10, 31, 254,
    270, 344; as politically inept,
    62–3; as popular heroes, 283–4;
    pre-Socratic, 8; Roman, 114, 115,
    131, 132
philosophers' cloak, 113
Philosophical Letters (Voltaire), 235
philosophical life, 5–10, 48, 69–80, 83,
    100–102, 125, 126, 130, 140, 161,
    186, 220, 302, 304, 341–75;
    authenticity in, 10–11, 345, 349; of
    Callisthenes, 97–8; codes of
    conduct in, 5, 10, 31, 33–4, 44–5,
    101, 112, 114, 189; Epicurean, 101;
    exemplary biography of, 5–6,
    30–1; of Kant, 264, 270, 276;
    modern, 5–10, 341, 342; of
    Montaigne, 170–1, 172–3, 187–90;
    Nietzsche on, 9–10, 320–3, 328,
    333; of Plato, 50, 54, 64–5, 86; of
    Plotinus, 144–5; problem of, 6–7;
    of Rousseau, 224, 228–9, 230,
    231–2, 236, 237–8, 249–50, 254; of
    Stoics, 113; stories traditionally
    told about, 5, 30–1

Philosophical Principles (Descartes),
    218
philosophic schools, 6, 19, 21, 48,
    112–14, 115, 144, 189; Augustine's
    communities as, 142–3, 147–52; of
    Epicurus, 100, 112, 171; of
    Isocrates, 86, 94, 101; of Plotinus,
    144–5, 150–1; see also Aristotle's
    Lyceum; Plato's Academy
philosophy: modern, 5, 9, 220, 283;
    Plato's definition of, 15–16, 29–30,
    39, 41; in Roman public life,
    112–15; science vs., 9, 10, 105,
    344–5; as term, 8
Phocion, 56, 57, 63
Phoenicia, 44, 46
Phormion, 56
phronesis, 88, 98
Pico della Mirandola, Count
    Giovanni, 171, 188, 189
Pietism, 254–5, 256
Piso, Calpurnius, 131
Platen, August Graf von, 324, 325–6
Plato, 6, 8, 10, 19, 20, 21, 25, 27, 28,
    29–35, 37–65, 38, 71, 73, 85, 86–8,
    103, 104–5, 128, 130, 144, 148,
    149, 158, 159, 160, 170, 171, 181,
    185, 189, 229, 234, 284, 286, 289,
    290, 292–3, 314, 335, 341, 343,
    345; Apollo as sire of, 40; birth of,
    38, 39–41, 65; canonical works of,
    52–6, 59–64, 65, 84; cave parable
    of, 50, 58, 152; death of, 64, 65, 88;
    Diogenes the Cynic as viewed by,
    77–8; Dionysius the Younger's
    relationship with, 57–64, 86, 89,
    122; disciples of, 46–8, 56–63;
    exemplary biography tradition
    established by, 30; Forms as
    concept of, 43, 50, 52, 54, 55, 56,

Socratic conversations (*Sokratikoi logos*), 30–5, 52; inconsistent depiction of Socrates in, 31–2; Plato's *Apology*, 17, 32–5
Socratics, 8, 29–35, 47, 48, 64, 71, 142
Soliloquies (Augustine), 148–50, 160
Solon, 16, 39, 59
Sophist (Plato), 44
Sophists, 16, 73, 94, 214
Sophocles, 314
Sophroniscus, 14
soul, 39, 105, 129, 141, 142, 171, 231, 268, 272; Augustine's view of, 149–50; Descartes and, 208, 209, 211, 214, 218; Emerson on, 290, 300, 302; Plato's view of, 49, 50–1, 52, 54–5, 63, 64, 65; Plotinus on, 145–6; Pythagorean belief in, 44, 46; Socrates on, 23–4, 29
Soviet Union, 278
Sparta, 14, 15, 18, 21, 22, 25, 26, 27, 29, 41–43, 44, 57, 201
Speusippus, 88, 94
Spinoza, Baruch, 8, 329
Stagira, 84–5, 90, 91–2, 93, 100, 102
Stoics, 71, 112–16, 144, 158, 171, 181, 186, 198, 217, 237–8, 248, 262, 321; Diogenes the Cynic as forerunner of, 73, 75, 78, 79; good life as defined by, 113; La Boétie as, 174, 180; Seneca as, 110, 111, 112–16, 118, 119, 120, 124, 126, 127, 128, 132, 171, 302; teachings of, 112–23; tranquility as goal of, 113, 119
Strauss, David, 323
Strauss, Leo, 96
Suetonius, 110
Sulla, 64
Sullius Rufus, Publius, 110, 122

Swedenborg, Emanuel, 297
symbolic logic, 220
Symposium (Plato), 18, 22–3, 314
Syracuse, 46–8, 57–64, 86

Tacitus, 109–10, 120, 121, 122, 123, 124, 131–2, 170
Tarentum, 45–6, 47, 60
Tears from La Flèche, 198
Thaetatus (Plato), 44, 86
Thales of Miletus, 16, 320–2, 334
Theatatus, 49
Theocritus of Chios, 101
Theodorus, 44
Theodosius, Emperor of Rome, 139
Theophrastus, 90, 95, 100
Thirty Years War, 206
Thoreau, Henry David, 302
Thrasyllus, 52, 59
Thucydides, 25
Thus Spake Zarathustra (Nietzsche), 332, 333–5
Thyestes (Seneca), 114, 119
Tiberius, Emperor of Rome, 112, 114, 119
Tractatus Logico-Philosophicus (Wittgenstein), 220
Trajan, Emperor of Rome, 80, 121–2, 132
Transcendental Club, 302
Trinity, The (Augustine), 138, 155
True Estimation of the Living Forces (Kant), 256
"Trust Yourself" (Emerson), 288
Twilight of the Idols (Nietzsche), 336

Unitarians, 285, 289, 300, 307
"Uses of Natural History, The" (Emerson), 296–7